Energy Market and Energy Finance

Energy Market and Energy Finance

Topic Editors

Junhua Zhao
Julien Chevallier

MDPI

Basel • Beijing • Wuhan • Barcelona • Belgrade • Novi Sad • Cluj • Manchester

Topic Editors
Junhua Zhao
School of Science and Engineering
The Chinese University of Hong Kong (Shenzhen)
Shenzhen
China

Julien Chevallier
Laboratoire d'Économie Dionysien (LED)
University Paris Saint-Denis
France

Editorial Office
MDPI AG
Grosspeteranlage 5
4052 Basel, Switzerland

This is a reprint of the Topic, published open access by the journals *Commodities* (ISSN 2813-2432), *Economies* (ISSN 2227-7099), *Energies* (ISSN 1996-1073), *Journal of Risk and Financial Management* (ISSN 1911-8074) and *Sustainability* (ISSN 2071-1050), freely accessible at: https://www.mdpi.com/topics/23YK2J82GQ.

For citation purposes, cite each article independently as indicated on the article page online and as indicated below:

Lastname, A.A.; Lastname, B.B. Article Title. *Journal Name* **Year**, *Volume Number*, Page Range.

ISBN 978-3-7258-7418-7 (Hbk)
ISBN 978-3-7258-7419-4 (PDF)
https://doi.org/10.3390/books978-3-7258-7419-4

Contents

About the Editors

Junhua Zhao

Junhua Zhao is a professor at the School of Science and Engineering, The Chinese University of Hong Kong (Shenzhen), Shenzhen, China. His research interests focus on power system analysis, smart grids, electricity and energy markets, energy finance, data analytics, and artificial intelligence applications in energy systems. He is the Executive Director of the CUHKSZ–CSIJRI Joint Centre of Smart Energy Storage, Director of the Energy Market and Energy Finance Laboratory at the Shenzhen Finance Institute, and a researcher at the Shenzhen Institute of Artificial Intelligence and Robotics for Society. His research projects span smart grid operation, low-carbon energy transition, market mechanism design, and the integration of data-driven and AI-based methods into power and energy systems, with several outcomes adopted in real-world electricity market design and energy trading practices in China. He has published more than 300 peer-reviewed journal articles in leading outlets such as *Joule, Patterns,* and *IEEE Transactions,* co-authored two books, and his work has received over 19,000 citations with an H-index above 65. His achievements include election as a Fellow of the Institution of Engineering and Technology, multiple Best Paper Awards, provincial and national science and technology awards, recognition as an Elsevier Highly Cited Scholar of China, and the International Financial Forum Global Green Finance Award.

Julien Chevallier

Julien Chevallier is a Full Professor of Economics at the University Paris VIII Vincennes Saint-Denis and an internal member of the Dionysian Economics Lab (LED), with affiliations that include editorial roles in several academic journals focused on energy, finance, and econometrics. His research interests encompass empirical finance, applied time-series econometrics, commodity and energy markets, and carbon trading schemes, with a particular emphasis on the informational efficiency and risk dynamics of emissions trading systems such as the EU ETS. He holds a Ph.D. in Economics from the University Paris West Nanterre La Défense (2008) and an M.Sc. from the London School of Economics (2005), and has held visiting research positions at Imperial College London, the London School of Economics, Georgetown University, and the World Bank. Professor Chevallier is the author of *Econometric Analysis of Carbon Markets* and co-author of *The Economics of Commodity Markets,* and his work has appeared in leading journals including the *Journal of Empirical Finance, Quantitative Finance,* and the *Journal of Forecasting.* His contributions have been recognized with invitations as a keynote speaker at major conferences and awards for best papers in international symposia. His current projects analyze global CO_2 trading schemes and their implications for market design, price discovery, and the transition to low-carbon economies.

Preface

This Reprint assembles eight peer-reviewed contributions that collectively examine key developments in energy markets and energy finance, with a focus on pricing dynamics, risk management, market design, and investment decision-making under uncertainty. The scope of this Reprint spans oil and commodity markets, electricity and carbon trading systems, energy sector financing, derivatives valuation, and the interaction between energy assets and alternative financial instruments. The purpose of this Reprint is to consolidate recent empirical and methodological advances that address the growing complexity and financialization of energy systems in a period marked by volatility, decarbonization, and regulatory transformation.

The motivation for compiling these studies arises from the increasing need for robust analytical frameworks capable of capturing nonlinear dynamics, cross-market linkages, and structural changes in energy and financial markets. The selected articles employ a diverse set of quantitative approaches, including nonlinear dynamic regression, stochastic and fractional Brownian motion models, option-based risk measures, closed-form approximations for energy derivatives, and data-driven methods incorporating large language models. Several contributions explore forecasting performance and risk preferences in oil and energy markets, while others address the cost of capital in emerging and dollarized economies, the role of market makers in electricity markets, and the coupled evolution of electricity and carbon markets. This Reprint also includes an analysis of portfolio diversification and hedging strategies involving commodities and Bitcoin, highlighting cross-asset interactions relevant to energy-related financial risk management.

This Reprint is intended for academic researchers in energy economics and finance, quantitative analysts, market practitioners, and policymakers seeking rigorous empirical evidence and methodological insights to support market design, investment strategy, and policy formulation. By bringing together these complementary studies, this Reprint aims to foster interdisciplinary dialogue and encourage further research on efficient, resilient, and sustainable energy markets.

Junhua Zhao and Julien Chevallier
Topic Editors

Journal of
Risk and Financial Management

MDPI

Article

Forecasting the Performance of the Energy Sector at the Saudi Stock Exchange Market by Using GBM and GFBM Models

Mohammed Alhagyan

Mathematics Department, College of Humanities and Science, Prince Sattam bin Abdulaziz University, Al-Kharj 11912, Saudi Arabia; m.alhagyan@psau.edu.sa

Abstract: Future index prices are viewed as a critical issue for any trader and investor. In the literature, various models have been developed for forecasting index prices. For example, the geometric Brownian motion (GBM) model is one of the most popular tools. This work examined four types of GBM models in terms of the presence of memory and the kind of volatility estimations. These models include the classical GBM model with memoryless and constant volatility assumptions, the SVGBM model with memoryless and stochastic volatility assumptions, the GFBM model with memory and constant volatility assumptions, and the SVGFBM model with memory and stochastic volatility assumptions. In this study, these models were utilized in an empirical study to forecast the future index price of the energy sector in the Saudi Stock Exchange Market. The assessment was led by utilizing two error standards, the mean square error (MSE) and mean absolute percentage error (MAPE). The results show that the SVGFBM model demonstrates the highest accuracy, resulting in the lowest MSE and MAPE, while the GBM model was the least accurate of all the models under study. These results affirm the benefits of combining memory and stochastic volatility assumptions into the GBM model, which is also supported by the findings of numerous earlier studies. Furthermore, the findings of this study show that GFBM models are more accurate than GBM models, regardless of the type of volatility. Furthermore, under the same type of memory, the models with a stochastic volatility assumption are more accurate than the corresponding models with a constant volatility assumption. In general, all models considered in this work showed a high accuracy, with MAPE $\leq 10\%$. This indicates that these models can be applied in real financial environments. Based on the results of this empirical study, the future of the energy sector in Saudi Arabia is forecast to be predictable and stable, and we urge financial investors and stockholders to trade and invest in this sector.

Keywords: energy sector; GBM; GFBM; stochastic volatility

1. Introduction

The Kingdom of Saudi Arabia is the largest producer and exporter of oil in the world. For this reason, Saudi Arabia recognizes the significance of diversifying its energy mix to maintain long-term economic prosperity. Both domestic and foreign partners in the energy sector play an important role in the Kingdom's transition toward a sustainable and renewable future. Therefore, the energy sector is very important in the Saudi Exchange stock market. The energy sector in Saudi Arabia consists of six companies with a total capital exceeding SAR 7 trillion (USD 1.86 trillion). Hence, there are a large number of investors, traders, and speculators involved in this sector. Therefore, the future performance of this sector is considered a fundamental issue for all types of traders to gain profits and avoid possible losses. For this purpose, a need for a tool that can forecast future prices as precisely as possible arose. There are two approaches to describing and forecasting index prices: discrete time setting and continuous time setting. Since the intuitive setting for market trading is typically continuous, we are motivated to focus on the study of continuous time setting in a financial environment. Scholars have proposed several continuous models as tools that employ historical data to forecast future prices, such as random walk, jump-diffusion, Brownian motion process, and geometric Brownian motion (GBM) models. This work investigates some of the GBM models by incorporating the assumptions of stochastic volatility and memory.

2. Geometric Brownian Motion Models

The econophysics concept of the GBM model explains the nature of stock price randomness and arbitrary fluctuation calculations more accurately (Kumar et al. 2024). Occasionally, the GBM model has been called "the standard model of finance" (Ibe 2013), where it is employed in forecasting the price of a stock over time. The GBM model is the adapted version of the Brownian motion (BM) process.

Definition 1. *A Wiener Process or Brownian motion (BM) is a stochastic process B_t that satisfies the following conditions:*

i. B_t *is a continuous function of time with* $B_0 = 0$.
ii. B_t *has independent increments* ($B_t - B_s$ *and* $B_v - B_u$ *are independent for all* $v > v > t > s$).
iii. $B_t - B_s \sim N(0,\ t - s)$ *for all* $t > s$.

According to the above definition, the BM process is continuous everywhere, but it is not differentiable anywhere. The BM is self-similar (i.e., if any part of the BM time-series trajectory is like the entire trajectory). If the BM touches any specific value, it will return to this value again an infinite number of times.

These properties encouraged Ross (1999) to model stock prices directly depending on the BM. However, this way of modeling has faced reasonable blame because of the nature of the BM, which permits the price to be negative when the stock price is supposed to be a normal random variable. As a treatment of this issue, the GBM model has been presented as an adaptation of the BM.

Model 1. Geometric Brownian Motion (GBM)

The stochastic process X_t is said to follow GBM if it satisfies the following stochastic differential equation (SDE):

$$dX_t = \mu X_t dt + \sigma X_t dB_t \tag{1}$$

where B_t is a BM, and μ and σ are drift and volatility, respectively. The general solution of this SDE is provided by the following equation:

$$X_t = X_0 exp\left\{ \left(\mu - \frac{1}{2}\sigma^2 \right) t + \sigma B_t \right\} \tag{2}$$

where X_0 is an initial value.

The GBM model is a non-negative variation of the BM. Consequently, the GBM model can be employed in many financial applications, such as index prices, exchange rates, option pricing, mortgage insurance, and value at risk. The GBM model is valuable for modeling random price fluctuation over time and investigating a commodity's price performance. Hence, the GBM model is used widely to predict future prices.

The classical GBM model assumes the independence of prices. Meanwhile, many researchers have drawn attention to the existence of memory in the GBM model, for example Han et al. (2020), Rejichi and Aloui (2012), Alhagyan and Yassen (2023), Painter (1998), Alhagyan (2018), Grau-Carles (2000), and Kim et al. (2020).

The results of these studies indicated the necessity of further developing the GBM model by incorporating the properties of memory. The improved model is called the geometric fractional Brownian motion (GFBM) model. The GFBM model is obtained by replacing the classical BM process (no memory) with a developed process called the fractional Brownian motion (FBM) process (with memory).

Definition 2. *The fractional Brownian motion (FBM), $\{B_H(t)\}$, with Hurst parameter $H \in (0,1)$ is a centered Gaussian process whose paths are continuous with probability 1, and its distribution is defined by the following covariance structure:*

$$E[B_H(t)B_H(s)] = \frac{1}{2}(t^{2H} + s^{2H} - |t-s|^{2H})$$

The correlation between the increments of FBM ($B_H(t) - B_H(s)$ and $B_H(v) - B_H(u)$ for all $v > v > t > s$) fluctuates conveniently with self-similarity or Hurst parameter H. The Hurst parameter name refers to Harold Edwin Hurst (1880–1978), who examined the erratic rainfall and drought circumstances along the Nile River over a long period. Three types of memories appeared according to the value of H: a short memory when $0 < H < 0.5$, no memory if $H = 0.5$, and a long memory when $0.5 < H < 1$. Now, by replacing BM in Equation (1) with FBM, we obtained the GFBM model that is presented as follows:

Model 2. Geometric Fractional Brownian Motion (GFBM)

The stochastic process X_t is said to follow GFBM if it satisfies the following SDE:

$$dX_t = \mu X_t dt + \sigma X_t \, dB_{H_1}(t) \tag{3}$$

where $B_{H_1}(t)$ is FBM, and μ and σ are drift and volatility, respectively. The solution is provided by the following equation:

$$X(t) = X_0 exp\left[\left(\mu - \frac{1}{2}\sigma^2 t^{2H_1 - 1}\right)t + \sigma B_{H_1}(t)\right] \tag{4}$$

where X_0 is an arbitrary initial value.

The GFBM model is considered a developed version of the GBM model, so it can be employed in the same financial applications, such as option pricing (Misiran 2010; Misiran et al. 2012; Alhagyan et al. 2016), index prices (Alhagyan and Alduais 2020; Abbas and Alhagyan 2022; Xiao et al. 2015), value at risk (Alhagyan et al. 2021; Wang et al. 2017), exchange rate (Gözgör 2013; Mansour and Ayasrah 2022; Alhagyan 2022), and mortgage insurance (Bardhan et al. 2006; Alhagyan et al. 2021; Chen et al. 2013).

A constant assumption of volatility (σ) was used in the GBM models to simplify calculations. However, this assumption was not supported by some empirical studies, such as those of Stein (1989), Bakshi et al. (2000), and Aït-Sahalia and Lo (1998), which concluded that the assumption of constant volatility does not describe the real-life situation accurately. For this reason, there have been many attempts to address this issue by replacing the constant volatility (σ) in the deterministic function of the stochastic process or volatility process $\sigma(Y_t)$ in GBM models, where Y_t is the solution of other stochastic differential equations (SDEs) that is driven by other stochastic volatility noise. Examples of this research are reported in the efforts of Scott (1987), Hull and White (1987), Alhagyan et al. (2016), Stein and Stein (1991), Heston (1993), Alhagyan and Yassen (2023), Hagan et al. (2002), Alhagyan (2022), Comte and Renault (1998), Chronopoulou and Viens (2012a, 2012b), Wang and Zhang (2014), and Alhagyan (2018).

SV models are considerable in the environment of the financial market because of their ability to capture the effect of time-varying volatility. SV models permit both volatility and the common dependence between variables to fluctuate over time. This implies that SV models have two sources of randomness. Table 1 presents some SDE equations describing the stochastic process Y_t.

Table 1. Models of stochastic processes describing Y_t in SV models.

Name	Model
Lognormal process	$dY_t = \alpha Y_t dt + \beta Y_t dB_{2t}$
Cox–Ingersoll–Ross (CIR) process	$dY_t = \theta(\omega - Y_t)dt + \xi\sqrt{Y_t}dB_{2t}$
Ornstein–Uhlenbeck (OU) process	$dY_t = \alpha(m - Y_t)dt + \beta dB_{2t}$
Not mean reverting process	$dY_t = \alpha Y_t dB_{2t}$
Fractional Ornstein–Uhlenbeck (FOU) process	$dY_t = \alpha(m - Y_t)dt + \beta dB_{H_2}(t)$

In what follows, two models of SV under study are presented.

Model 3. GBM perturbed using FOU (SVGBM)

The stochastic process X_t is said to follow GBM perturbed by SV (FOU) if it satisfies the following SDE:

$$dX_t = \mu X_t dt + \sigma(Y_t) X_t dB_{1t} \tag{5}$$

where μ is a mean of return, Y_t is a stochastic process, B_{1t} is a BM, and $\sigma(Y_t) = Y_t$ is a deterministic function. Let the dynamics of volatility Y_t follow the fractional Ornstein–Uhlenbeck (FOU) process, which is the solution of the following SDE:

$$dY_t = \alpha(m - Y_t)dt + \beta dB_{H_2}(t) \tag{6}$$

where $\alpha,\ \beta$, and m are the mean reverting of volatility, volatility of volatility, and mean of volatility, respectively. $B_{H_2}(t)$ is an FBM which is independent from B_{1t}.

Model 4. GFBM perturbed using FOU (SVGFBM)

The stochastic process X_t is said to follow a GFBM perturbed by SV (FOU) if it satisfies the following SDE:

$$dX_t = \mu\ X_t dt + \sigma(Y_t) X_t dB_{H_1}(t) \tag{7}$$

where μ is the mean of return, Y_t is a stochastic process, $B_{H_1}(t)$ is an FBM with Hurst index H_1, *and* $\sigma(Y_t) = Y_t$ is a deterministic function. Let the dynamics of volatility Y_t be described by the fractional Ornstein–Uhlenbeck (FOU) p rocess, which is the solution of the following SDE:

$$dY_t = \alpha(m - Y_t)dt + \beta dB_{H_2}(t) \tag{8}$$

where $\alpha,\ \beta$, and m are constant parameters that represent the mean reverting of volatility, volatility of volatility, and mean of volatility, respectively. $B_{H_2}(t)$ is an FBM, which is independent from $B_{H_1}(t)$.

3. Forecasting

This study employs the four models mentioned in the previous section to forecast the future index prices of seven companies in the energy sector in Saudi Arabia depending on historical data. In this empirical study, we examine the influence of incorporating both memory and stochastic volatility into the GBM model.

We relied on two measures of error to evaluate and compare the performance of each model under study. These measures are the mean square error (MSE) and mean absolute percentage error ($MAPE$):

$$MSE = \frac{\sum_{i=1}^{n}(Y_i - F_i)^2}{n} \text{ and } MAPE = \frac{\sum_{i=1}^{n}\frac{|Y_i - F_i|}{Y_i}}{n},$$

where F_i and Y_i represent the forecast and actual price at day i, respectively, while n represents the total forecasting days. Lawrence et al. (2009) recapped the judgment on any forecasting method using MAPE in Table 2.

Table 2. MAPE judgment accuracy of forecasting method.

Judgment of Accuracy	MAPE
Highly accurate	$MAPE < 10\%$
Good accuracy	$10\% \leq MAPE < 20\%$
Reasonable	$20\% \leq MAPE < 50\%$
Inaccurate	$MAPE \geq 50\%$

3.1. Description of Historical Data

The historical energy index data are available online at https://www.saudiexchange.sa (accessed on 12 February 2024). The total working days are 43 days, from 1 November 2023 to 31 December 2023. To avoid high fluctuation in data, the return series is considered in logarithm (i.e., $r_n = \ln(S/S_{n-1})$). Figures 1 and 2 show the close prices and their return series.

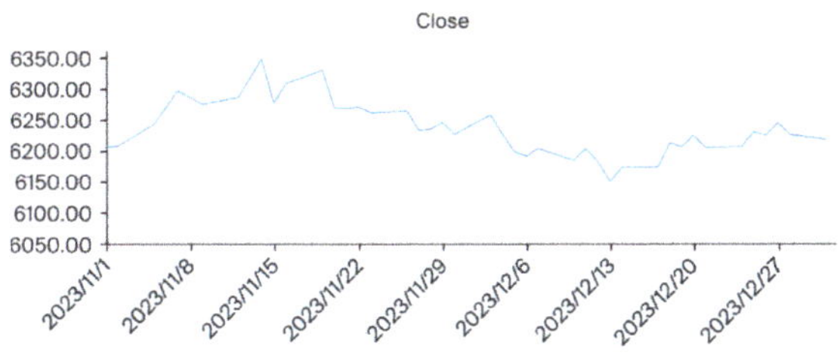

Figure 1. Daily energy index close price.

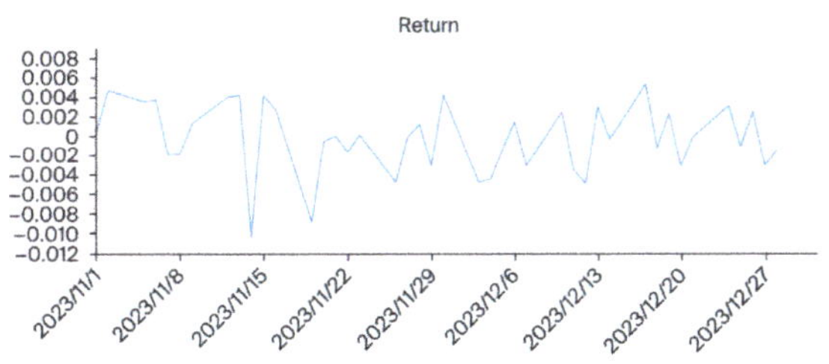

Figure 2. Daily returns of energy index.

3.2. Forecasting and Evaluation

According to the historical data of energy sector indices, all parameters involved in the four models under study were calculated by using Mathematica 10 software and then employed to compute constant volatility and stochastic volatility. Table 3 lists all computed parameters and volatilities.

Table 3. Parameter and volatility values.

Parameter	Value	Parameter	Value
H_1	0.3279	β	0.00002
H_2	0.2520	m	0.00001
μ	0.00004	α	4.62705
Computed Volatility			
σ	0.0036		
$\sigma(Y_t)$	0.0010		

Then, the close price of the next month (January 2024) was forecast based on the values of the parameters in Table 3. The forecasting was computed using the following four models: GBM, GFBM, SVGBM, and SVGFBM. Table 4 shows the accuracy of each model. Meanwhile, Table 5 shows the forecast prices beside the actual prices of the energy indices.

Table 4. The accuracy ranking level of the forecasting model is based on MAPE and MSE values.

Model	MAPE	MSE
SVGFBM	2.753%	44,861
GFBM	2.758%	44,921
SVGBM	2.759%	44,946
GBM	2.887%	48,457

Table 5. Actual and forecast prices.

Date	Actual	GBM	GFBM	SV GBM	SV GFBM
1/1/2024	6231.24	6240.65	6230.96	6228.20	6231.33
1/2/2024	6234.45	6243.74	6231.77	6231.27	6231.74
1/3/2024	6208.98	6244.15	6230.47	6231.68	6231.56
1/4/2024	6231.12	6244.03	6228.52	6231.59	6231.21
1/7/2024	6264.88	6243	6232.38	6230.56	6232.46
1/8/2024	6298.10	6245.29	6232.93	6232.84	6232.8
1/9/2024	6258.55	6247.55	6230.89	6235.09	6232.42
1/10/2024	6194.68	6243.82	6233.67	6235.34	6233.37
1/11/2024	6184.72	6243.25	6233.11	6230.77	6233.4
1/14/2024	6185.47	6244.28	6233.75	6234.82	6233.76
1/15/2024	6104.82	6245.72	6235.91	6233.24	6234.54
1/16/2024	6026.77	6246.9	6233.81	6234.45	6234.14
1/17/2024	5989.73	6246.56	6235.95	6234.11	6234.92
1/18/2024	6014.71	6246.06	6233.42	6236.59	6234.4
1/21/2024	6030.20	6246.09	6235.19	6236.62	6235.07
1/22/2024	5973.57	6248.83	6235.01	6236.35	6233.2
1/23/2024	5978.97	6247.24	6233.49	6236.75	6234.97
1/24/2024	5987.34	6246.39	6236.14	6236.91	6235.89
1/25/2024	5958.15	6246.5	6236.04	6234.04	6233.04
1/28/2024	5932.13	6247.66	6234.01	6235.19	6235.66
1/29/2024	5904.70	6243.1	6237.73	6236.62	6236.87
1/30/2024	5896.26	6247.03	6235.71	6234.57	6235.5
1/31/2024	5766.84	6247.19	6236.92	6234.71	6237.01

In light of the smaller MSE and MAPE values, the results show that the SVGFBM model has the highest accuracy. This was due to the presence of two sources of memory (H_1 and H_2) along with the stochastic volatility assumption. The GBM model placed last because of the existence of one source of randomness in addition to the constant volatility assumption. The outcomes demonstrated that the models under memory assumption (SVGFBM and GFBM models) are more appropriate for forecasting future stock costs than the models without memory (SVGBM and GBM models).

As per Lawrence's table (Table 2), all models achieved MAPE < 10%, which indicates a high forecasting accuracy in these models. Moreover, one can observe that the MSE values of the SVGFBM, GFBM, and SVGBM models are close together in number, while the MSE value of the GBM model is larger. These outcomes are in line with many experimental studies, for instance, Willinger et al. (1999), Rejichi and Aloui (2012), Alhagyan (2022), Painter (1998), Alhagyan and Yassen (2023), and Abbas and Alhagyan (2022).

Figure 3 illustrates the comparison between the actual close prices versus forecast close prices. One can see that the historical prices appearing in Figure 1 are more stable than the actual prices appearing in Figure 3. This stability in the historical time series affected the computations of all parameters, including the forecasting methods under study. Therefore, the forecast prices fluctuate less than the actual prices, which ensures that the forecast prices are closer together.

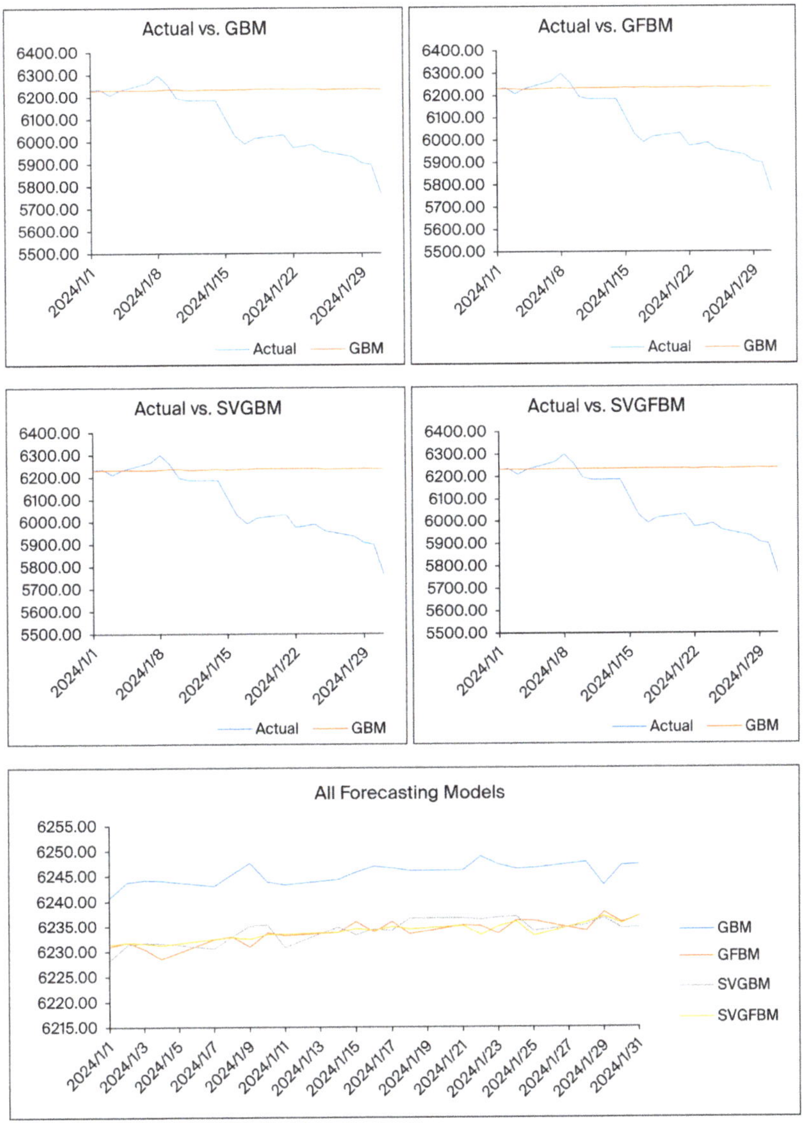

Figure 3. Actual prices vs. forecast prices.

4. Conclusions

Index price reflects financial stability and economic growth. Therefore, forecasting the future performance of index prices is one of the top tasks of stakeholders and investors. For this task, several models have been presented in the literature. The GBM model is one of the most popular and important forecasting models. Furthermore, a number of models have been developed based on the classical GBM model, which depends on the assumption of the existence (or absence) of memory in time-series financial data in addition to the assumption of volatility (constant or stochastic). To discuss the benefits of these assumptions, this work examined four GBM models, including the classical GBM model (absence of memory and constant volatility), the GFBM model (existence of memory and constant volatility), the SVGBM model (absence of memory and stochastic volatility), and the SVGFBM model (memory and stochastic volatility). These models are described in Section 2 of this manuscript. The examination in this study was conducted by applying these models to forecast the energy sector in the Saudi Stock Exchange Market. Two statistical criteria of error were utilized (MSE and MAPE) to evaluate the performance of each model.

The findings of this empirical examination show that the SVGFBM model achieved the smallest MSE and MAPE and, therefore, the best performance. This result was achieved because of the existence of two sources of randomness with memory (dB_{H_1} and dB_{H_2}) and the assumption of stochastic volatility. The GBM model ranked last because of the existence of one source of randomness without memory ($H = 0.5$) and the assumption of constant volatility.

The results demonstrate that GFBM models are more accurate than GBM models for forecasting future stock prices. Furthermore, under the same assumption of memory, the models of stochastic volatility assumption are more accurate than the models of constant volatility assumption. This outcome proved the direct positive benefits of incorporating memory and stochastic volatility together into GBM models.

Moreover, the MSE values for the SVGFBM, GFBM, and SVGBM models were close in number and thus more stable, while those of the GBM model were moderately larger than the others. Generally, according to Lawrence's table of judgment accuracy (Table 2), all the models exhibited a high performance because of the MAPEs < 10%, which indicates that all the models under study can be used as tools for forecasting future index prices of the energy sector in Saudi Arabia.

In general, the empirical results of this study agree with earlier empirical studies, such as those by Abbas and Alhagyan (2022, 2023), Mansour and Ayasrah (2022), Alhagyan and Yassen (2023), Alhagyan (2022), Willinger et al. (1999), Painter (1998), and Rejichi and Aloui (2012). Therefore, under normal circumstances, we encourage investors and traders to invest in Saudi Arabia's energy sector because of its demonstrated predictability and stability.

Funding: This research received no external funding.

Institutional Review Board Statement: Not applicable.

Informed Consent Statement: Not applicable.

Data Availability Statement: The historical energy index data are available online at https://www.saudiexchange.sa (accessed on 12 February 2024).

Acknowledgments: The author extends appreciation to Prince Sattam Bin Abdulaziz University for funding this research work through the project number (IF2/PSAU/2023/01/24999).

Conflicts of Interest: The author declares that there is no known competing financial interests or personal relationships that could have appeared to influence the work reported in this article.

References

Abbas, Anas, and Mohammed Alhagyan. 2022. The effect of incorporating memory and stochastic volatility into geometric Brownian motion in forecasting the performance of Tadawul all share Index (TASI). *Advances and Applications in Statistics* 74: 47–62. [CrossRef]

Abbas, Anas, and Mohammed Alhagyan. 2023. Forecasting exchange rate of SAR/CNY by incorporating memory and stochastic volatility into GBM model. *Advances and Applications in Statistics* 86: 65–78. [CrossRef]

Aït-Sahalia, Yacine, and Andrew W. Lo. 1998. Nonparametric estimation of state–price densities implicit in financial asset prices. *The Journal of Finance* 53: 499–547. [CrossRef]

Alhagyan, Mohammed. 2022. The effects of incorporating memory and stochastic volatility into GBM to forecast exchange rates of Euro. *Alexandria Engineering Journal* 61: 9601–608. [CrossRef]

Alhagyan, Mohammed Kamel. 2018. Modeling Financial Environments Using Geometric Fractional Brownian Motion Model with Long Memory Stochastic Volatility. PhD. thesis, Universiti Utara Malaysia, Sintok, Malaysia.

Alhagyan, Mohammed, and Fuad Alduais. 2020. Forecasting the performance of Tadawul all share index (TASI) using geometric Brownian motion and geometric fractional Brownian motion. *Advances and Applications in Statistics* 62: 55–65. [CrossRef]

Alhagyan, Mohammed, and Mansour F. Yassen. 2023. Incorporating stochastic volatility and long memory into geometric Brownian motion model to forecast performance of Standard and Poor's 500 index. *AIMS Mathematics* 8: 18581–95. [CrossRef]

Alhagyan, Mohammed, Masnita Misiran, and Zurni Omar. 2016. Estimation of geometric fractional Brownian motion perturbed by stochastic volatility model. *Far East Journal of Mathematical Sciences* 99: 221.

Alhagyan, Mohammed, Masnita Misiran, and Zurni Omar. 2021. On effects of stochastic volatility and long memory towards mortgage insurance models: An empirical study. *Advances and Applications in Statistics* 66: 165–74. [CrossRef]

Bakshi, Gurdip, Charles Cao, and Zhiwu Chen. 2000. Pricing and hedging long–term options. *Journal of Econometrics* 94: 277–318. [CrossRef]

Bardhan, Ashok, Raša Karapandža, and Branko Urošević. 2006. Valuing mortgage insurance contracts in emerging market economies. *The Journal of Real Estate Finance and Economics* 32: 9–20. [CrossRef]

Chen, Chao-Chun, Shih-Kuei Liny, and Wen-Shih Chenz. 2013. *Mortgage Insurance Premiums and Business Cycle*. Tunghai University Working Paper. Taiching: Tunghai University.

Chronopoulou, Alexandra, and Frederi G. Viens. 2012a. Estimation and pricing under long–memory stochastic volatility. *Annals of Finance* 8: 379–403. [CrossRef]

Chronopoulou, Alexandra, and Frederi G. Viens. 2012b. Stochastic volatility and option pricing with long–memory in discrete and continuous time. *Quantitative Finance* 12: 635–49. [CrossRef]

Comte, Fabienne, and Eric Renault. 1998. Long memory in continuous-time stochastic volatility models. *Mathematical Finance* 8: 291–323. [CrossRef]

Gözgör, Giray. 2013. The application of stochastic processes in exchange rate forecasting: Benchmark test for the EUR/USD and the USD/TRY. *Economic Computation and Economic Cybernetics Studies and Research* 47: 225–46.

Grau-Carles, Pilar. 2000. Empirical evidence of long–range correlations in stock returns. *Physica A: Statistical Mechanics and Its Applications* 287: 396–404. [CrossRef]

Hagan, Patrick S., Deep Kumar, Andrew Lesniewski, and Diana Woodward. 2002. Managing smile risk. *The Best of Wilmott* 1: 249–96.

Han, Chenyu, Yiming Wang, and Yingying Xu. 2020. Nonlinearity and efficiency dynamics of foreign exchange markets: Evidence from multifractality and volatility of major exchange rates. *Economic Research-Ekonomska Istraživanja* 33: 731–51. [CrossRef]

Heston, Steven L. 1993. A closed-form solution for options with stochastic volatility with applications to bond and currency options. *Review of Financial Studies* 6: 327–43. [CrossRef]

Hull, John, and Alan White. 1987. The pricing of options on assets with stochastic volatilities. *Journal of Finance* 42: 281–300. [CrossRef]

Ibe, Oliver C. 2013. *Markov Processes for Stochastic Modeling*. Amsterdam: Elsevier.

Kim, Kyong-Hui, Nam-Ung Kim, Dong-Chol Ju, and Ju-Hyang Ri. 2020. Efficient hedging currency options in fractional Brownian motion model with jumps. *Physica A: Statistical Mechanics and Its Applications* 539: 122868. [CrossRef]

Kumar, Anay, Isa Jamadar, Radhika Goel, Ram Charan Petluri, and Wei Feng. 2024. Mathematically Forecasting Stock Prices with Geometric Brownian Motion. *The North Carolina Journal of Mathematics and Statistics* 10: 1–14.

Lawrence, Kenneth, Ronald K. Klimberg, and Sheila M. Lawrence. 2009. *Fundamentals of Forecasting Using Excel*. New York: Industrial Press.

Mansour, Mustafa, and Mohammed Ayasrah. 2022. Forecast exchange rates of Euro using geometric Brownian motion model according to four different ways to compute volatility. *Advances and Applications in Statistics* 76: 39–52. [CrossRef]

Misiran, Masnita. 2010. Modeling and Pricing Financial Assets under Long Memory Processes. Doctoral dissertation, Curtin University of Technology, Perth, Australia.

Misiran, Masnita, Zudi Lu, Kok Lay Teo, and Grace Aw. 2012. Estimating dynamic geometric fractional Brownian motion and its application to long–memory option pricing. *Dynamic Systems and Applications* 21: 49–66.

Painter, Scott. 1998. Numerical method for conditional simulation of Levy random fields. *Mathematical Geology* 30: 163–79. [CrossRef]

Rejichi, Imen Zgueb, and Chaker Aloui. 2012. Hurst exponent behavior and assessment of the MENA stock markets efficiency. *Research in International Business and Finance* 26: 353–70. [CrossRef]

Ross, Sheldon M. 1999. *An Introduction to Mathematical Finance: Option and Other Topics*. Cambridge, MA: Cambridge University Press.

Scott, Louis O. 1987. Option pricing when the variance changes randomly: Theory, estimation, and an application. *Journal of Financial and Quantitative Analysis* 22: 419–38. [CrossRef]

Stein, Elias M., and Jeremy C. Stein. 1991. Stock price distributions with stochastic volatility: An analytic approach. *Review of Financial Studies* 4: 727–52. [CrossRef]

Stein, Jeremy C. 1989. Overreactions in the options market. *Journal of Finance* 44: 1011–23. [CrossRef]

Wang, Xiaohui, and Weiguo Zhang. 2014. Parameter estimation for long-memory stochastic volatility at discrete observation. In *Abstract and Applied Analysis*. New York: Hindawi Publishing Corporation.

Wang, Xiaoyu, Dejun Xie, Jingjing Jiang, Xiaoxia Wu, and Jia He. 2017. Value-at-Risk estimation with stochastic interest rate models for option-bond portfolios. *Finance Research Letters* 21: 10–20. [CrossRef]

Willinger, Walter, Murad S. Taqqu, and Vadim Teverovsky. 1999. Stock market prices and long–range dependence. *Finance and Stochastics* 3: 1–13. [CrossRef]

Xiao, Weilin, Weiguo Zhang, and Xili Zhang. 2015. Parameter identification for the discretely observed geometric fractional Brownian motion. *Journal of Statistical Computation and Simulation* 85: 269–83. [CrossRef] *energies*

MDPI

Article

Forecasting Oil Prices with Non-Linear Dynamic Regression Modeling

Pedro Moreno [1,*], Isabel Figuerola-Ferretti [2] and Antonio Muñoz [3]

[1] ICAI School of Engineering, Comillas Pontifical University, 28015 Madrid, Spain
[2] ICADE and Center for Low Carbon Hydrogen Studies, Comillas Pontifical University, 28015 Madrid, Spain; ifiguerola@comillas.edu
[3] Institute for Research in Technology (IIT), ICAI School of Engineering, Comillas Pontifical University, 28015 Madrid, Spain; antonio.munoz@iit.comillas.edu
* Correspondence: pmoreno@comillas.edu

Abstract: The recent energy crisis has renewed interest in forecasting crude oil prices. This paper focuses on identifying the main drivers determining the evolution of crude oil prices and proposes a statistical learning forecasting algorithm based on regression analysis that can be used to generate future oil price scenarios. A combination of a generalized additive model with a linear transfer function with ARIMA noise is used to capture the existence of combinations of non-linear and linear relationships between selected input variables and the crude oil price. The results demonstrate that the physical market balance or fundamental is the most important metric in explaining the evolution of oil prices. The effect of the trading activity and volatility variables are significant under abnormal market conditions. We show that forecast accuracy under the proposed model supersedes benchmark specifications, including the futures prices and analysts' forecasts. Four oil price scenarios are considered for expository purposes.

Keywords: oil prices forecasting; Brent futures; GAM model; transfer function models; scenarios analysis

1. Introduction

Oil markets have exhibited multiple regime changes over the last two decades. This has created renewed interest in modeling and forecasting oil prices. Oil is a crucial factor in the global economy as it is not only a significant component of gross domestic product but also a key driver of inflation and interest rates. Therefore, the accurate forecast of oil prices is critical for central banks, financial analysts, energy corporations, utilities, investors, governments, and international organizations to implement policy responses to achieve an optimal allocation of resources.

The time series evolution of crude oil prices has been impacted by a wide range of variables, including global demand and supply disruptions, macroeconomic factors, geopolitical events, as well as regulation changes designed to foster the transition to a low-carbon economy. The interplay of different factors over the last two decades gave rise to four unanticipated steep oil price shocks, including the 2007–2008 Global Financial Crisis, the 2014 oil price collapse, the COVID pandemic, the June 2021–August 2022 energy crisis, and the war in Ukraine [1–3]. The persistence of underinvestment initiated during the 2014–2016 oil price shock [4] has been enhanced by the energy transition, which is expected to restrict long-term supply and add further shocks to the behavior of energy prices. Indeed, the global push to phase out fossil fuels is gaining new momentum as the COP28 celebrated, in November 2023, advocates for a historical transition from fossil fuels in energy systems to achieve net zero by 2050 (see "Ten key conclusions from COP28: a farewell to fossil fuels", January 2023, the Oxford Institute for Energy Studies) and avoid a climate catastrophe. Such institutional developments suggest that there will be time-changing patterns on the demand side for oil in the medium term (see F.T. article "Peak in fossil fuel demand will happen this decade", by Faith Birol, 12 September 2023).

A significant strand of the literature has developed statistical methods to establish the relationship between fundamentals and generate accurate energy price forecasts. Benchmark contributions include [5–9]. This literature concludes that an appropriate selection of fundamentals can lead to price forecasts that improve the random walk and no-change benchmarks. Vector autoregression (VAR) techniques have been extensively used in this literature, which has also applied the cointegration approach and the vector error correction model (VECM) as a forecasting algorithm for oil [10] and for agricultural commodities [11]. On a parallel dimension, the role of financial variables in predicting commodity prices gained significant momentum with the development of the financialization literature. Ref. [12] highlights the increased exposure to commodity futures of financial institutions and retail investors, empirically demonstrating the emergence of speculative investment flows impacting commodity futures prices [13–15]. Financial variables have also been used in the recent forecasting literature. Ref. [16] compiled a set of indicators to construct a new measure of global economic activity using a multidimensional approach that includes financial indicators.

One of the benchmark sources of crude oil price forecasts is the U.S. Energy Information Administration (EIA), which provides monthly, quarterly, and yearly forecasts for the crude oil price for horizons up to two years. Ref. [6] analyzes the EIA short forecasts, demonstrating that they do not outperform the naïve or no-change forecast. Ref. [17] analyzes the performance of Bloomberg analysts' (1-year) forecast, demonstrating that these underperform the forecast of future prices at the aggregate level.

The work of [8] shows that while some fundamental-based econometric models have outperformed the EIA forecast for some horizons, no methodology is available in the literature performs well at all horizons for which the EIA generates predictions. This issue motivated them to use a combination of six different models considered in the literature, including the no-change forecast, oil futures prices, and VAR models of the global oil market. They concluded that forecast combinations help to improve accuracy and that all models are essential in contributing to forecast accuracy except for the no change. The naïve forecast is vital for comparing the forecast with different horizons as it controls for the maturity and volatility effect [17].

Statistical learning models are essential for accounting for non-linear interactions between input and output variables. This paper introduces the hybrid combination of a generalized additive model (GAM) combined with a linear transfer function time series approach as an oil price forecasting tool.

The existence of non-linear relations between price-driving factors and the price process implies that linear models cannot fully capture the underlying functional relationships. This singularity has motivated the use of machine learning approaches. Particularly noteworthy machine-learning applications in the crude oil forecasting literature include the LASSO regressions in [18]. The authors of that work show that the proposed regression LASSO method significantly improves the forecasting accuracy of prices compared to alternative benchmarks.

The proposed GAM model aims to explain the occurrence of remarkable price changes by capturing the different states and factor dynamics that determine the evolution of the price process. In doing this, it exploits the EIA expert forecast information in two dimensions. First, it uses IEA fundamental forecast data to feed the fundamental variable. Secondly, it uses the quarter Brent price forecast as a benchmark model for assessing predictive accuracy.

By allowing for non-linear relationships, the GAM model adds flexibility to the linear regression framework in analyzing data related to time-changing distributions by considering different price states assigned to the corresponding data of driving factors. GAM models are more interpretable than fully non-linear methods such as bagging, boosting support vector machines, and neural networks (deep learning). These methods are more flexible than the GAM algorithm because they can generate a more comprehensive range of possible shapes to estimate the explained variable. However, they are also less interpretable than linear regressions because predictors and responses are modeled using black-box non-linear functions. The crude oil forecasting literature has acknowledged the importance of considering possible non-linearities in model settings. Ref. [19] proposes a combination forecasting approach that accounts for structural breaks and then applies a time-varying transition probability Markov regime switching (TVIP-MRS) model, showing superior forecasting ability in four statistical tests.

The motivation for using the GAM approach to forecast oil prices is threefold. First, the literature has not identified a decisive outperforming framework for forecasting oil prices. Secondly, many financial time series, such as crude oil prices, contain non-linear characteristics that machine-learning methods can model. Third, within the statistical learning methods, the GAM specification provides the best trade-off between predictive accuracy and interpretability [20].

We aim to contribute in the following areas: First, we address the non-linearities documented in the crude oil price literature pertaining to the aftermath of the Global Financial Crisis. We use calculation and prediction methodologies that move away from the traditionally used linear models [21–23]. Second, we provide a price forecasting algorithm that incorporates the complex interplay of fundamental, financial, and economic factors that determine the evolution of oil prices, maintaining model interpretability. The error measures of simulated prices under the proposed algorithm supersede competing benchmarks, including futures prices. Outperformance with respect to the no-change and the futures price in terms of MAPE reductions is as high as 8% and 7%, respectively. Third, we develop a tool to provide oil price scenarios based on the selected input variables that can be used for the assessment of price risk and optimal decision making. This allows for exploring how much a given forecast would change relative to the baseline prediction under alternative hypotheses about future oil demand and supply conditions. Such a scenario analysis is crucial for end-users of oil price forecasts who are interested in evaluating the risk underlying a given prediction.

Our results have important implications for oil consumers, producers, and investors as accurate forecasts of oil prices lead to an improved allocation of resources. The reported findings are also relevant for regulators that use crude oil prices to set future inflation targets. As underlined by [24], central banks consider the price of oil as one of the instrumental variables in generating macroeconomic projections and determining macroeconomic risk. Accurate forecasting is also important for project investment decision making. Increases in oil price uncertainty complicate the appropriate discount rate for estimations of the net present value [1].

This paper is organized as follows: Section 2 describes the model methodology. Section 3 describes the data used in the forecasting exercise, including summary statistics, feature engineering, the GAM model approach, and preliminary statistical tests. The same also describes the factor selection process. Section 4 presents empirical results, including a sensibility analysis and forecasting results. The proposed forecasting algorithm is applied in Section 5 to generate future price scenarios. We conclude in Section 6.

2. Methodology: Combining the Generalized Additive Model with the Linear Transfer Function

Generalized additive models (GAMs) offer a general framework for extending a standard linear model by allowing non-linear functions of each variable while maintaining additivity. They offer a natural way to extend the multiple regression model to allow for non-linear relationships between each explanatory variable (feature) and the explained variable (response variable). The smooth functions are used as a replacement for the alternative detailed parametric relationship on the covariates. Moreover, this methodology is appropriate for the monthly data required in this study due to the low-frequency availability of oil fundamental data. The GAM methodology supersedes competing machine learning algorithms, such as neural networks, when large volumes of data are unavailable. It is also a preferred method because it allows a straightforward interpretation of results. This method calculates the sensibilities of the forecasted variable with respect to changes in input values, allowing a deeper understanding of underlying relationships than under competing machine learning models.

In essence, a generalized additive model (GAM) is a generalized linear model (GLM) in which the linear predictor is given by a sum of smooth non-linear functions of at least some (or possibly all) covariates [25]). The family of smooth functions is defined as the basis functions. The logarithmic function and a polynomial cubic spline are good examples of this specification class. Each basis function transforms the vector of explanatory variables x in terms of the type of basis considered.

The GAM can be formally expressed as follows:

$$y_t = \beta_0 + \sum_{i=1}^{n} f_i(x_{i,t}) + \varepsilon_t \tag{1}$$

where $i = 1, \ldots, n$, and x_i are the n independent input variables, *fi* is the unknown non-parametric smooth functions of x_i, and ε_t is a i.i.d random error. This structure captures the non-linear relationships while providing a flexible framework for understanding the (linear or non-linear impact) of every variable considered.

We impose restrictions on the number of smooth functions allowed in the framework to prevent problems related to overfitting. For this reason, the specified models are usually fit by penalized likelihood maximization, and each penalty is multiplied by an associated smoothing parameter to control the balance between over- and underfitting. The MGCV implementation of GAM in R is applied. This module characterizes the smooth functions using penalized regression splines with smoothing parameters selected by the restricted maximum likelihood (REML).

In order to make the reported method robust to the existence of residual autocorrelation and dynamic causal effects, we consider a linear transfer function (LTF) with ARIMA noise [26] for the variables transformed by the GAM model.

We assume the series, y_t and $x_{1,t}, \ldots, x_{n,t}$ are stationary variables. The classical multiple linear regression model given by

$$y_t = c + \beta_1 x_{1,t} + \beta_2 x_{2,t} + \ldots + \beta_n x_{n,t} + \varepsilon_t \tag{2}$$

which assumes that the system's noise ε_t is white noise and uncorrelated with the explanatory variables. In order to guarantee uncorrelated residuals and no cross-correlation between the residuals and the regressors, the LTF method with ARIMA noise, introduced by [27], is applied. The dependent variable is modeled as a function of its past values and lagged values of the explanatory variables. The following specification is used for this purpose:

$$y_t = c + \frac{\omega(L)}{\delta(L)} x'_{i,t-b} + v_t \tag{3}$$

$$\omega(L) = \left(\omega_0 - \omega_1 L - \omega_2 L^2 - \ldots - \omega_s L^s\right) \tag{4}$$

$$\delta(L) = \left(1 - \delta_1 L - \delta_2 L^2 - \ldots - \omega_s L^r\right) \tag{5}$$

$$v_t = \frac{(1 - \theta_1 L - \theta_2 L^2 - \ldots - \theta_q L^q)}{(1 - \varphi_1 L - \varphi_2 L^2 - \ldots - \varphi_p L^p)(1 - L)^d} \varepsilon_t \tag{6}$$

where y_t is the dependent output variable at time t, $x_{i,t}$ represents the i-th independent or explanatory input variables, v_t is an autocorrelated ARIMA(p,d,q) noise, r, s, and b are constant integers, ω(L) and δ(L) are lagged polynomials, ε_t is white noise, and $x'_{i,t} = f(x_{i,t})$ are the input variables transformed by the GAM model.

3. Data and Preliminary Results

The primary data used in this analysis have three main sources: The Energy Information Administration (EIA), the Commodity Futures Trading Commission (CFTC), and Bloomberg. We have a sample of monthly observations covering the period from January 1995 to December 2023. A detailed description of the initial variables considered is provided in Table A1. The EIA Short-Term Energy Outlook reports data series related to the fundamental balance in the crude oil market. It publishes monthly data on aggregate crude oil production, supply, and inventories. As shown below, these are used to construct the fundamental variable measure and provide input forecasts based on EIA data. Other fundamental variables that are initially considered but not selected as input variables include OPEC production, spare OPEC production, OECD consumption, OECD total inventory, China consumption, and the stocks–consumption ratio.

The CFTC releases weekly data on investor positions used to construct the financial variable. Data on long and short positions of non-commercial agents and open contracts are obtained for the entire sample period. Other position data that were initially considered but not selected as input data are specified in Table A1. Weekly data are transformed into monthly averages for analysis. Front-month Brent Intercontinental Exchange (ICE) crude oil daily data are downloaded from Bloomberg. This is used to calculate the monthly average price. The log of the monthly Brent price is the target variable within the model. However, model forecasts (provided in logs) are transformed into level Brent spot data to allow a comparison with benchmark forecasting models (the forecasting literature usually is designed to predict the nominal spot price of Brent or WTI prices. See [6]). The nominal Brent spot price returns are used to construct the historical (realized) volatility measure. We use daily quotations of the DXY dollar index to calculate a monthly measure of the dollar variable. We also download daily Brent ICE futures prices for the remaining available maturities (2–12 months) to construct the futures price benchmark as an alternative forecast measure.

3.1. Data Input Selection

The final input variables are selected based on the correlation coefficient between the logarithm of the Brent spot crude oil price and the input variables. Table A2 describes the four selected variables. A detailed correlation analysis of the raw data is provided in Table A3 in the Appendix A. In what follows, we briefly describe the variables selected for the model. The level of these variables is used in the forecasting algorithm.

Note that the variable selection is closely related to specifications similar to those in the crude oil forecasting literature. For example, ref. [19] uses fundamental (demand, supply, and stock), financial market (dollar index, exchange rate of the euro against the U.S. dollar, S&P500 index, speculative factor based on crude oil non-commercial long ratio), and technology indicators. These are the final variables built for the proposed model:

(i) Balance in the physical market (FUN):

We consider the crude oil forecasting literature and define oil-related supply and demand metrics to define the fundamental variable. Ref. [8] include the percentage change in global oil production, the change in global crude oil inventories, and global economic activity, among other factors. Similar ratios as proxies of fundamentals are considered in [28] in their study of the bubble characteristics of non-ferrous metals. They define the consumption–supply ratio (CSR) as a measure of market fundamentals. This is measured as the ratio of metal consumption in the quarter in question to production in the same quarter plus the stock level at the end of the previous quarter. Specifically, we construct the ratio where the numerator is defined as the sum of aggregate OECD crude oil stocks to aggregate crude oil production over a 30-day period. The denominator includes the sum of world oil consumption over the same 30-day period. This fundamental variable (FUN) is specified under Equation (7) and measures the physical market balance. We can see from Table A4 in the Appendix A that it exhibits an inversely proportional relationship with Brent crude oil with a correlation equal to −0.887.

$$Fun = \frac{MAV(6M(Commercial\ OECD\ Stocks)) + 30 \cdot MAV(12M(World\ Supply))}{30 \cdot MAV(12M(World\ Demand))} \quad (7)$$

(ii) Speculation in the crude oil market (FIN):

The variable used to capture the speculative activity and investors' sentiment concerning oil prices is constructed with CFTC data. This requires the definition of the following input ratios. Open interest is the total amount of futures and/or option contracts that remain open overnight (and thus not offset by a transaction, delivery, or exercise). Note that all long open interest aggregates equal short open interest. Secondly, we use "commercial" or "non-commercial" CFTC classifications and define a "net non-commercial ratio" that considers net (long minus short) "non-commercial" positions in the numerator and total open interest in the denominator. The objective is to provide a metric gauging the direction of the market sentiment as "non-commercial" positions are defined as trades not designed for hedging purposes. The second measure is the sum of long and short "non-commercial" positions divided by the total open interest. This aims to provide the magnitude or impact of investors (or speculators) taking oil market positions. The proposed financial variable (denoted as FIN) is defined as the product of two ratios. Note that this metric is related to Working's T-index, which has been used as a futures speculation proxy by [29] in the crude oil price case by [30] for multiple commodity markets and [31] for food commodities. See also [28,32] for the non-ferrous and agricultural market cases, respectively. While the FIN variable correlates with Working's T index, it better fits the proposed forecasting model and is more closely related to the speculation-related measures used in the crude oil forecasting literature [19]. The underlying presumption is that a high (low) level of speculation will encourage higher (lower) prices, as shown by a correlation coefficient between the FIN variable and the crude oil Brent price, which is reported to be 0.51 in Table A4 in the Appendix A. The financial variable is therefore defined as follows:

$$Fin = \frac{Net\ Long\ NonCommercial\ Positions}{Open\ Interest} \cdot \frac{Total\ NonCommercial\ Positions}{Open\ Interest} \quad (8)$$

(iii) Realized Volatility (VOL):

We follow [33] and use a metric of uncertainty related to the crude oil market. Specifically, the realized volatility of Brent front-month futures prices is used. Volatility is often related to market risks and therefore has a negative impact on the price of oil. As reported in Table A4 in the Appendix A, the correlation coefficient of realized volatility with the oil price is equal to −0.21.

(iv) U.S. Dollar (DXY):

The U.S. dollar is the numeraire in most oil contracts quoted in U.S. dollars. We use the DXY index to address the effect of the U.S. dollar on the oil price. As underlined by [34], changes in the exchange rate can be translated into changes in oil consumption for oil-importing countries and non-US-based investors. The dollar index (as well as the euro-dollar exchange rate) is considered by [19] in a recent oil forecasting exercise. Table A4 in the Appendix A shows that the correlation coefficient of the DXY index and the log of the Brent price is −0.52.

3.2. Descriptive Statistics

Table A2 in the Appendix A summarizes the series selected to construct the final variables, including data sources. Table A3 shows the correlations across the log of the Brent price and the main variables selected by the algorithm. The results show that the reported correlations between explanatory variables remain below 0.55, suggesting that the model will not suffer from multicollinearity problems.

Table 1 in the main text reports descriptive statistics of the selected input variables and the output or forecasted variable, which is the log of the Brent spot price labeled as log(Brent). Estimates are based on a sample of monthly data ranging from January 1995 to December 2023 (358 observations). We can see that the Brent spot price level exhibits the highest standard deviation and maximum level.

Table 1. Summary statistics.

Variables	n	Mean	Median	Std	Skew	Kurtosis	Min	Max
Brent	348	58.18	56.81	32.28	0.353	−0.972	10.19	133.81
log(Brent)	348	1.68	1.75	0.28	−0.442	−0.947	1.01	2.13
Fun	348	2.05	2.03	0.09	0.673	−0.336	1.88	2.28
Fin	348	0.03	0.02	0.03	0.476	−0.869	−0.03	0.11
Vol	348	0.32	0.30	0.16	2.788	14.452	0.08	1.54
DXY	348	92.29	92.83	10.69	0.366	−0.428	72.08	119.04

Note: This table reports summary statistics of the Brent spot price, the log of the spot Brent price (log(Brent)), as well as the selected variables used in the forecasting exercise. The table shows mean, median, standard deviation (Std), skew, kurtosis, minimum (Min), and maximum (Max) variable values.

The normality and unit root test results are reported in Table 2. The results of the Jarque-B test and Ljung–Box show that the null hypothesis of normality and white noise errors is rejected for all variables considered. This table also reports results for the augmented Dicky–Fuller (ADF) [35], the Phillips–Peron (P.P.) [36], and Kwiatkowski–Phillips–Schmidt–Shin (KPSS) [37] unit root tests. The reported results show that the unit root hypothesis is accepted for all variables except the volatility variable (Vol). This motivates the use of the LTF model.

Table 2. Normality and unit root test results.

Variables	Jarque-B	Ljung–Box	ADF	PP	KPSS
Brent	21.06 ***	338.26 ***	−2.85	−2.51	1.04 ***
log(Brent)	24.39 ***	340.21 ***	−2.51	−2.22	1.38 ***
Fun	28.42 ***	338.99 ***	−3.48 **	−2.80	0.89 ***
Fin	24.21 ***	322.99 ***	−3.19 *	−3.99 ***	1.04 ***
Vol	3489.10 ***	129.37 ***	−9.15 ***	−9.07 ***	0.13
DXY	10.49 ***	339.84 ***	−1.77	−1.60	1.09 ***

Note: This table provides normality and unit root test results. ***, **, and * denote rejection of the null hypothesis at the 1, 5, and 10 percent levels, respectively.

The Bai and Perron test [38] for detecting multiple structural changes has also been performed for the logarithm of the Brent spot price as well as for the regression with the selected input and explained variables in differences. The results are reported in Tables A5 and A6, respectively. They show that the log of Brent prices exhibits five breakpoints along our sample period (these correspond to September 1999, October 2004, August 2010, and November 2014. Such points are consistent with those detected in for crude oil in the bubble literature [4].). When we run the regression in differences (with log Brent as explained variable and the changes in the fundamental, financial dollar, and volatility as input variables), the reported results do not show evidence of structural breaks. The fact that structural breaks are no longer reported for the regression in differences shows that the input variables have been appropriately selected.

Figure 1 illustrates the complete process of the proposed methodology to forecast oil prices. The starting point is the data obtained from multiple sources, such as EIA or the Commodity Futures Exchange Commission (CFTC). The data are then used to build four variables (FUN, FIN, VOL, and DXY), which are transformed through a GAM model into the final input variables used by the linear transfer function model.

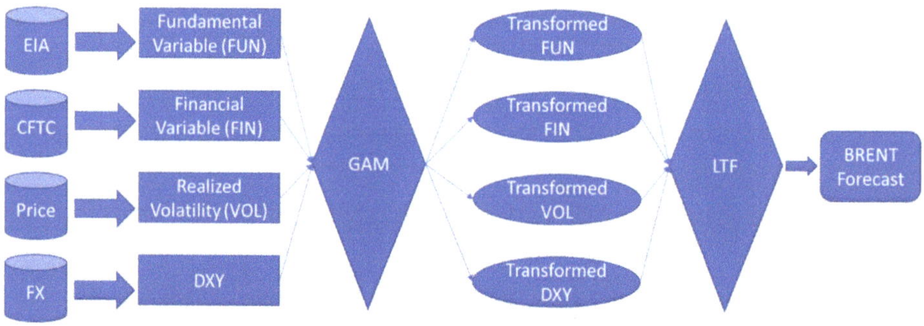

Figure 1. Process of the proposed methodology: This figure exhibits the steps required for GAM method development. Step 1 involves raw data extractions; step 2 requires the creation of featured variables; step 3 performs the transformation through a GAM model into the final variables used by the linear transfer function model in step 4 to create the Brent forecast.

This analysis applies a feature engineering approach to crude oil price forecasting. Feature engineering is the process of using domain knowledge to obtain features (characteristics, properties, and attributes) of the analyzed variables. It involves the extraction and transformation of variables from raw data to a more effective set of inputs so that these can be used for training and prediction to improve the quality of results arising from a machine learning process. This increases model performance as it goes beyond supplying only the raw data to the machine learning process. This study combines a set of transformed variables (using basis functions) to create a parsimonious model specification. The proposed framework allows for an improved understanding of the oil price determinants through four representative variables that allow the development of a simple tool designed for scenario analysis. Feature engineering has been a successful method in machine learning models [39], and in the case of oil price forecasting, it could also be an advantage. The data pre-processing step (first applied under the statistical learning algorithm) adds different variables to create a combined metric representing some market features.

4. Model Identification and Empirical Results

This section describes the building process underlying the two-step method proposed to model the oil price. We first analyze each time series to determine the modeling methodology. The variable to be forecasted is the logarithmic monthly average Brent spot price.

The empirical application covers the January 1995 to June 2023 period and aims to forecast the monthly crude oil Brent price series as the current global crude oil price benchmark. The in-sample period runs up to December 2016. This selection makes the in-sample size comparable to the recent literature; ref. [8] uses an in-sample period ranging from 1997:12 to 2010:6. The model is tested for the 2017–2023 out-of-sample period. Note that this constitutes seven years of monthly data leading to 82 observations. While this out-of-sample window may be considered short compared to other benchmark analyses [8,40], recent research in the literature considering the existence of non-linearities [18] has used shorter out-of-sample periods. Specifically, it evaluates the out-of-sample forecast performance for the 2009:M5 to 2016:M11 period. We therefore follow the recent literature that addresses the sources of non-linearities and use shorter out-of-sample periods in our forecasting exercise. The sources of recent non-linearities include the collapse of the 2014–2016 crude oil price, the 2020 COVID-19 pandemic shock, the ongoing war in Ukraine, and a shift to green energy. Forecasting performance is measured in terms of MAPE values as well as the absolute ratios of MAPE with respect to the no change. The RMSE is also computed in the principal analysis as a means of robustness. The same out-of-sample period is considered for the sensitivity analysis. Possible scenarios are created for the four quarters of 2024.

4.1. Preliminary Analysis

Figure 2 illustrates the partial effects obtained with the GAM model of the transformed fundamental, financial, volatility, and dollar variables on the oil price. For instance, the top left-hand side (LHS) panel of Figure 2 illustrates the fundamental variable on the X-axis and the transformed variable on the Y-axis, indicating the effect of the fundamental on the oil price metric. The dotted lines illustrate 5% confidence intervals. The model results show non-linearities in every variable considered except for the fundamental metric. This is corroborated by "EDF" reported in column 2 of Table 3, representing the effective degrees of freedom, which measure the degree of non-linearities within a given curve. Note that when the reported EDFs are equal to one, as is the case for the fundamental variable, this implies that the curve is linear. The volatility variable depicted in the bottom right-hand side (RHS) panel exhibits the highest level of non-linearity, followed by the dollar in the bottom LHS panel and the financial metric in the top RHS panel.

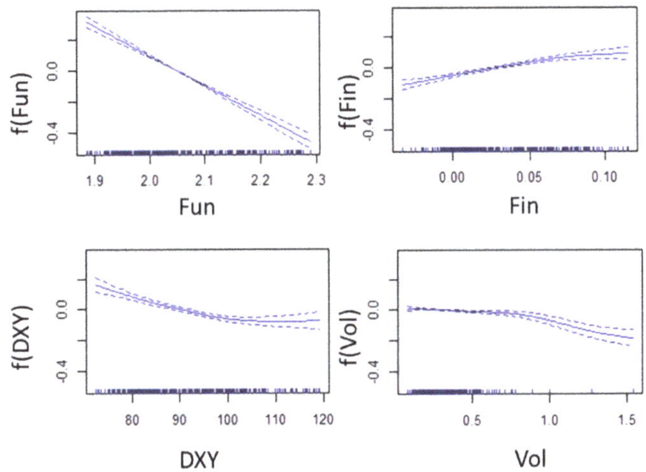

Figure 2. Partial effects illustration under the GAM model: This figure illustrates the non-linear relationship between each of the variables considered and the oil price under the GAM estimation. The row input variables (represented by dots on the horizontal axis) are transformed using the basis functions (denoted by f()). The transformed variables are introduced in the LTF model at a later stage. The effects of the fundamental and financial variables are illustrated under the top left-hand side (LHS) and right-hand side (LHS) panels. The dollar and volatility variables are depicted under the bottom LHS and RHS panels. Moreover, 95% confidence intervals are depicted as dotted lines.

Table 3. Summary of estimated coefficients under a GAM model specification.

Approximate Significance of Smooth Terms:					
Variable:	**Edf**	**Ref Edf**	**F**	***p*-Value**	
Fundamental	1.00	1.00	293.16	$<2 \times 10^{-16}$	***
Financial	3.015	3.985	17.20	7.5×10^{-13}	***
Volatility	4.385	5.471	13.34	1.57×10^{-12}	***
Dollar	3.713	4.900	14.34	2.11×10^{-12}	***
Signif. Codes: 0 '***', 0.001, '.' 0.1"					
R-sq- (adj) = 0.883			Deviance explained = 88.8%		
fREML = −637.32			Scale est. = 0.0035994		
Box–Pierce test = 294.28, df = 1, *p*-value < 2.2×10^{-16}					

Note: This table reports estimates of the GAM model specification. EDF: reflects the degree of non-linearity of a curve. An EDF equal to 1 is equivalent to a linear relationship. *p*-values represent calculated *p*-values from Wald test (significance of each parametric and smooth term of the model). Signif. Codes: 0 '***'.

In what follows, we interpret the plots in Figure 2, illustrating the partial effects for every explanatory variable. Note that the four signs of the function slopes are aligned with the correlation coefficient calculated with the oil prices, reported in Table A4. The top LHS panel in Figure 2 shows that the fundamental variable, which takes a low value under fundamental shortages, exhibits a well-fitted negative linear relationship with the oil Brent price, showing that excess supply market conditions lead to lower oil prices. While the effect of the financial variable on the oil price is almost linear, we can see that the financial variable presents some non-linear features. Specifically, we can see that the slope is slightly smoothed when the market sentiment becomes bullish so that positive investor bets outnumber the negative counterparts. The bottom LHS panel in Figure 2 shows a non-linear inverse relationship between the dollar index and oil benchmark that is significantly smoothed when the index exceeds 105. The negative influence of the dollar value on oil prices has been widely documented in the literature [18,41]. The relationship estimated implies that Brent prices increase under low dollar conditions. A lower dollar leads to higher demand and higher prices as producers try to protect the dollar-adjusted value of their revenues. Oil becomes relatively cheap for foreign investors, and this increases demand. However, the results illustrated in the LHS panel of Figure 2 suggest that the dollar's impact on crude oil prices is lower when the dollar is under stronger conditions. The results depicted in the bottom RHS panel in Figure 2 show the effect of volatility, which is highly significant under high-volatility regimes and negatively affects prices. Episodes of extreme volatility (such as that seen during the 2014 oil price shock) are expected to decrease the oil price, while the volatility effect is reduced under normal market conditions. In fact, we can see that when the volatility is below 40%, it exhibits a reduced impact on oil prices. The existence of volatility-driven regime changes has been considered in the forecasting literature by the authors of [18], who document a "volatility upward regime" via the TVIP-MRS model and forecast the crude oil price.

The preliminary estimation results reported in Table 3 show that the adjusted R2 and the deviance explained demonstrate that the model fits the data correctly. The Box–Pierce test suggests that there is residual autocorrelation. The details can be found in Figure A1 in the Appendix A.

In order to correct this autocorrelation, we include a linear transfer function model with ARIMA noise in the second step. We estimate the LTF specification using an identification, estimation, and diagnosis procedure [42], following a similar approach to constructing the univariate Box–Jenkins ARIMA model [26]. The identification requires fitting a multiple regression model, adding as many lags of the regressors as required, and a low-order autoregressive model for the error term to capture most of the autocorrelation and be able to estimate the impulse response. If regression errors are not stationary, variables are differentiated. The next stage is identifying the transfer function and selecting the appropriate values for b, r, and s. We can identify the orders (b, r, and s) by visually comparing the estimated impulse response function with some standard theoretical functions. Then, the ARMA model for the regression errors must be determined to fit the complete model. Finally, several diagnostic tests are applied to determine the model selection model based on resulting cross-correlation and autocorrelation tests.

The explanatory variables are determined using the previously estimated GAM process. The final model identification suggests an ARIMA (1,1,0) for the residuals. The estimation results are reported in Table 4. We can see that the four independent variables are statistically significant, and the residuals do not exhibit s serial correlation, with Box–Pierce failing to reject that residuals are independently distributed. The partial autocorrelation function (PACF) and auto-correlation function (ACF) confirm the absence of a serial correlation (see Figure A2 in the Appendix A). Note that results reported for the regression in differences under the Bai and Perron test [39] (see Table A6) show that we failed to reject the null hypothesis of no structural breaks. This confirms that the LTF model can be applied to the residuals.

Table 4. Summary of estimated coefficients under final specification.

Approximate Significance of Smooth Terms:					
Variable:	**Estimate**	**Std Error**	**Z Value**	***p*-Value**	
ar	0.268	0.057	4.741	2.12×10^{-16}	***
f(Fundamental)	0.51	0.110	4.654	$<2 \times 10^{-16}$	***
f(Financial)	1.125	0.106	10.622	$<2.11 \times 10^{-12}$	***
f(Volatility)	0.882	0.097	9.088	$<7.5 \times 10^{-12}$	***
f(Dollar)	0.510	0.137	3.710	$<1.57 \times 10^{-12}$	***
Signif. Codes: 0 '***', 0.001, '.' 0.1″					
Box–Pierce test = 0.000040065, df = 1, *p*-value = 0.984					

Note: This table reports estimates of the final model specification with the coefficient of the regression calculated. Signif. Codes: 0 '***'.

The final equation of the complete model is as follows:

$$y_t = \omega_{1,0}x'_{1,t} + \omega_{2,0}x'_{2,t} + \omega_{3,0}x'_{3,t} + \omega_{4,0}x'_{4,t} + \frac{\varepsilon_t}{(1-\varphi L)(1-L)} \tag{9}$$

where $x'_{1,t} = f_1(x_{1,t})$; $x'_{2,t} = f_2(x_{2,t})$; $x'_{3,t} = f_3(x_{3,t})$; and $x'_{4,t} = f_4(x_{4,t})$ are the variables transformed by the GAM model (see Figure 2) and ε_t is the white noise.

Figure 3 depicts the one-month-ahead forecast of the Brent crude oil price under the proposed model versus the observed Brent price as well as the error defined as the difference between the estimated and observed values. A closer look at the figure shows that the goodness of fit is high but clearly deteriorates in times of increased uncertainty, such as during the 2008 crisis, the 2014 crude oil price collapse, or the 2020 COVID crisis.

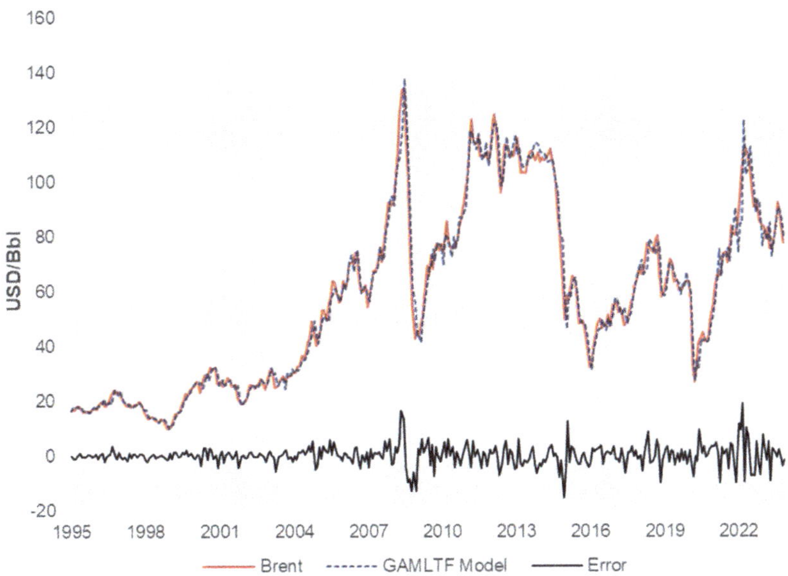

Figure 3. Time series evolution of the Brent spot price level, the forecasted (one-step-ahead) Brent spot price level, and the model error: This figure illustrates the time series evolution of the observed price (Brent) price, the estimated Brent spot price (model), and the forecast error. The GAM model is estimated using the selected input values.

4.2. Sensitivity Analysis

The next step is to provide a sensitivity analysis, developed to show the future evolution of the crude oil price, given a one standard deviation shock to some of the explanatory variables over a six-month horizon, keeping the remaining variables constant. The results are reported in Figure 4.

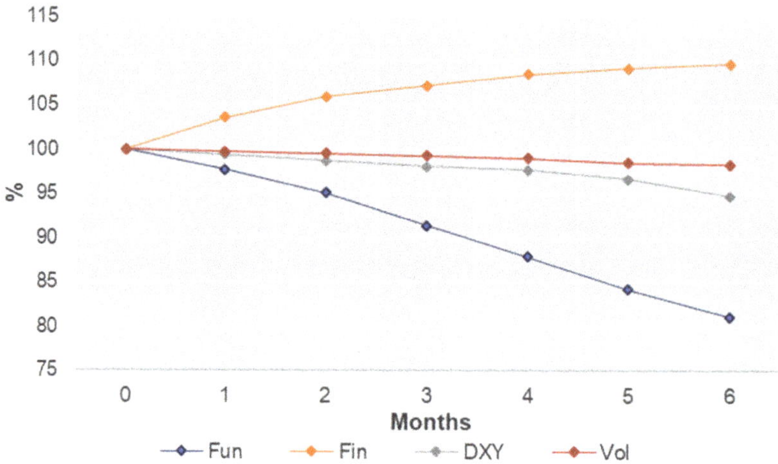

Figure 4. Sensitivity analysis: This figure illustrates the effect of a one standard deviation shock in each explanatory variable on the Brent crude oil price over a 6-month horizon. The January 1995–December 2016 in-sample period is considered for this purpose. The sensitivity analysis is performed for the first two quarters of 2017.

We assume that variables were shocked in December 2016 and evaluated over the next six months.

They show that the variable with the most significant influence on crude oil is the fundamental variable, which decreases the crude oil price by 20% for a given one standard deviation shock. The second most important variable in terms of price impact is the financial variable, which has a positive 10% effect on Brent prices for a given one standard-deviation shock. The same shock applies to the dollar and volatility variables exert a negative impact of 5% and 2%, respectively. Our findings are consistent with the literature supporting supply and demand fundamentals as the main drivers of crude oil prices [7,8,29,43]. The market fundamental variable is the most important factor explaining the time series evolution of crude oil prices, with shocks remaining important after six months. Speculators are informed investors and enter the market to exploit fundamental-related trends [43]. Indeed, Table A4 in the Appendix A shows that the fundamental and financial variables exhibit a significant negative correlation of −0.56, implying that they share common characteristics. When fundamentals are tight, the market has a more significant inflow of speculative activity.

4.3. Forecasting Results

In what follows, we quantify the predictive performance of the proposed model specification. The analysis takes the 2017Q1 to 2023Q4 time frame for the out-of-sample test (21% of data). A forecast for different quarters within a window of 12 months (four quarters) is made at the beginning of every quarter. Data for the last seven years of the sample have been used to compare model performance with four forecasting methods. This implies that there are 25 quarterly forecasting periods. The average monthly forecast for each quarter is considered, and the mean absolute percentage error (MAPE) for each method considered is reported in Table 5. Note that this period represents the recovery from the 2014–2016 price slump and the COVID-induced crude oil price collapse. As discussed in the introduction, crude oil prices have experienced many different price swings over the forecasting period. Therefore, we believe it is essential to provide an appropriate testing framework to account for the observed non-linearities in the data.

Table 5. MAPE error measures for different forecasting methods.

	2017Q1	2017Q2	2017Q3	2017Q4	2018Q1	2018Q2	2018Q3	2018Q4	2019Q1
Constant	6.19%	10.09%	24.62%	20.06%	10.14%	7.30%	10.47%	20.80%	9.96%
Futures	9.84%	10.29%	20.53%	19.21%	9.45%	5.91%	11.75%	23.31%	14.37%
BBG Analysts Median	6.50%	8.77%	12.08%	20.77%	19.48%	8.73%	3.96%	13.30%	9.48%
Department of Energy EIA	5.72%	9.81%	20.50%	22.63%	16.15%	12.05%	4.66%	16.99%	5.68%
GAMLTF Forecasted Inputs	**5.78%**	**9.75%**	**18.72%**	**15.58%**	**14.05%**	**7.10%**	**8.49%**	**21.33%**	**6.41%**
GAMLTF Actual Inputs	**16.11%**	**6.15%**	**8.86%**	**4.80%**	**5.78%**	**11.45%**	**3.86%**	**11.30%**	**7.72%**
LTF Actual Inputs No GAM	17.65%	6.32%	8.13%	9.07%	9.27%	22.79%	3.65%	4.13%	7.09%

	2019Q2	2019Q3	2019Q4	2020Q1	2020Q2	2020Q3	2020Q4	2021Q1	2021Q2
Constant	9.83%	29.17%	34.49%	54.64%	24.77%	22.29%	30.57%	28.53%	15.94%
Futures	10.87%	29.24%	29.81%	48.13%	20.86%	19.84%	26.89%	27.36%	22.64%
BBG Analysts Median	16.04%	39.54%	35.67%	42.36%	10.02%	25.24%	26.14%	33.24%	23.26%
Department of Energy EIA	7.38%	37.00%	32.62%	43.62%	32.28%	16.61%	25.21%	24.85%	20.14%
GAMLTF Forecasted Inputs	**10.39%**	**30.62%**	**42.76%**	**42.15%**	**29.97%**	**23.36%**	**10.80%**	**7.59%**	**13.10%**
GAMLTF Actual Inputs	**5.86%**	**9.83%**	**16.25%**	**12.47%**	**19.46%**	**17.67%**	**12.96%**	**5.95%**	**3.79%**
LTF Actual Inputs No GAM	14.35%	63.13%	93.00%	94.80%	27.15%	27.26%	17.22%	8.85%	13.11%

	2021Q3	2021Q4	2022Q1	2022Q2	2022Q3	2022Q4	2023Q1	TOTAL
Constant	16.66%	21.17%	22.66%	20.27%	36.84%	8.48%	3.10%	19.96%
Futures	19.15%	21.30%	23.45%	6.74%	13.33%	5.29%	4.55%	18.16%
BBG Analysts Median	23.92%	26.33%	22.15%	5.12%	16.60%	14.79%	10.73%	18.97%
Department of Energy EIA	19.95%	20.19%	23.10%	10.64%	13.21%	12.29%	3.86%	18.29%
GAMLTF Forecasted Inputs	**11.98%**	**9.50%**	**13.59%**	**32.05%**	**32.49%**	**8.98%**	**5.86%**	**17.30%**
GAMLTF Actual Inputs	**11.72%**	**14.91%**	**21.22%**	**26.12%**	**20.87%**	**9.29%**	**4.12%**	**11.54%**
LTF Actual Inputs No GAM	8.31%	8.27%	9.96%	43.39%	42.51%	11.08%	5.30%	23.03%

Note: This table reports the forecasting performance in terms of the MAPE measure of the proposed framework for forecasted and actual input data as well as alternative benchmarks, including the LTF framework with no GAM. The in-sample period is 1995–2016, and the out-of-sample or forecasting period is 2017–2023. Forecasting is performed for the next four quarters. The following forecasting methods are considered: No-change: forecasts are the average price of the previous month for the whole forecast period. Futures: forecasts are the average of Brent first-, second-, and third-month contracts for the first quarter, fourth-, fifth-, and sixth-month contracts for the second quarter for the day before beginning the period of forecast. BBG: Bloomberg quarterly surveys are taken as forecasts the day before beginning the period of forecast. EIA: average monthly forecasts to create quarterly forecasts are taken from the last EIA report before beginning the period of forecast. GAMLFT with forecasted inputs: proposed new model fed by forecasted inputs. GAMLFT with actual inputs: proposed new model fed by actual inputs. LFT with actual inputs: linear function transfer model fed by forecasted inputs.

We benchmark the proposed model against the no-change or spot reference price. This uses the last available monthly spot price observation. The no-change forecast is set as the spot price under the previous month of the forecast during the whole forecast period. Next, we consider the forecasting performance of the Intercontinental Exchange (ICE) Brent futures prices. This price aggregates expectations for future price delivery across market participants. The benchmark built based on futures prices takes the average of the first-, second-, and third-month generic future contracts (Brent) for the first quarter forecast and the average of the fourth-, fifth-, and sixth-month contracts for the second quarter forecast. The same method is applied to forecast prices in the subsequent quarters. The benchmark is constructed the day before the forecast period begins, and as previously specified, the data source for the price of the futures prices is Bloomberg.

As an alternative analysts' forecast benchmark, we first use the monthly forecast of the Department of Energy of the U.S. (EIA or DoE) released under the Short-Term Energy Outlook every month. This report calculates monthly Brent price forecasts for maturities ranging between 1 and 12 or up to 24 months. We construct quarterly forecasts by calculating three-month averages using the last report before the start of the forecast period.

The second benchmark source of analysts' forecasts is the prediction provided by the Bloomberg survey with crude oil analyst forecasts (BBG). This offers industry experts' price forecasts for different maturities. The median forecast for each quarter reported in this survey is taken as forecasts the day before the forecast period starts. See [15] for a detailed Bloomberg analysts' forecast survey description.

We report forecasts for the GAMLTF with forecasted EIA fundamental inputs as well as from the actual input data. To measure the contribution of the GAM framework, we report a forecast for the LTF with no GAM. We select the mean absolute percentage error (MAPE) as a metric for evaluating the performance of the forecasting methods, which is defined as follows:

$$MAPE = \frac{1}{n}\sum_{t=1}^{n}\left|\frac{y_t - \widetilde{y}_t}{y_t}\right| \tag{10}$$

The choice of the MAPE metric is motivated by the high oil price variability during the sample period considered. Oil prices range between USD 30 and USD 140, implying that absolute differences in high-price states will be difficult to compare with absolute differences in low-price states. However, the RMSE metric is also included in the main forecasting analysis as a means of robustness.

The forecasting performance of a model with exogenous variables will depend on the forecast accuracy of the future values of the selected regressors. For that reason, we also test under two explanatory variables' predictions. In the real data model, the observed values of the future selected explanatory variables are used for forecasting purposes. In the forecast data model, every explanatory variable is forecasted. In this sense, we use forecasts of the fundamental and U.S. dollar variables from the EIA, available in its Short-term Energy Outlook, providing information for world production, world demand, and OECD inventories. Therefore, we incorporate forward-looking information (based on EIA predictions) into our forecast framework. ARMA models are estimated for the financial and volatility variables.

The results reported in Table 5 show that the performance of each model varies over time. The average MAPE errors indicate that the best model is GAM-LTF with actual inputs followed by the GAM-LTF. However, a close look at the table shows that the no-change and the futures forecasts outperform in periods of high volatility, such as 2020Q3 and 2022Q2. Bloomberg analysts' forecasts perform worse on average than futures prices, consistent with previous results reported in the literature [17]. However, it outperforms all the benchmarks considered during 2017Q3 and 2020Q1. Given that the best results at the average level are achieved when we know the variable data (GAMLTF actual inputs), we propose using the model for scenario analysis as the reported results suggest that it accurately captures the relationships between variables. This analysis is performed in Section 5.

Table A7 in the Appendix A provides the same forecasting results under the MRSE measure. The reported figures are qualitatively similar to those reported in Table 5, suggesting that the relative forecasting ability is not dependent on the forecast performance measure selected for the analysis.

In order to provide a deeper analysis of the results we report, Table 6 provides forecast accuracy in terms of the MAPE metrics for four maturities of the different models analyzed. The average forecast for each quarter is reported. For instance, if the forecast maturity is one quarter, in Q1 of 2016, the forecast for Q2 2016 is performed for each of the models considered and is used to calculate the average forecast for the Q2 forecast period. Similarly, in Q2 of 2016, the forecast for Q3 2016 is performed for each of the models considered for the reported average for the Q3 forecast. The same procedure is followed to calculate the forecast for longer horizons.

Our main findings can be summarized as follows: (i) In line with the previous literature [17], forecast accuracy decreases with maturity. (ii) The best forecasting performance for all horizons considered is reported for the proposed model with actual values of input variables. Furthermore, the second best performance is observed for the proposed model with forecasted input. This confirms that the proposed model can be used as an optimal tool for scenario analysis purposes (details will be provided in Section 5). (iii) The introduction of the GAM specification in the model, considering the non-linearities in the input/output relationships between the explanatory variables and the oil price, is important for improving forecasting results, as can be seen by comparing the last column with columns 5 and 6. The forecast provided by the LTF approach with no GAM is less accurate than that provided under the GAMLTF with actual and forecasted inputs. (iv) The model with forecasted variables (forecast data model) improves the forecasting performance when compared to other benchmarks for all quarters considered.

Table 6. MAPE for different forecasting methods and horizons.

	No-Change	Futures	BBG	Department of Energy EIA	GAMLTF with Forecasted Inputs	GAMLTF with Actual Inputs	LTF with Actual Inputs No GAM
1Q Forecast	8.1%	11.6%	10.2%	9.5%	7.7%	6.0%	8.2%
2Q Forecast	19.8%	21.3%	18.2%	19.5%	17.7%	11.0%	23.1%
3Q Forecast	24.8%	25.0%	22.6%	22.2%	21.1%	12.0%	31.3%
4Q Forecast	30.4%	28.8%	26.9%	27.2%	25.1%	12.5%	39.4%

Note: this table illustrates the model accuracy in terms of the MAPE measure with different forecasting horizons ranging from Q1 to Q4.

Table 7 reports the forecasting performance of the different models in terms of the MAPE metric in relation to the no-change forecast. The prediction horizon ranges from 1Q in the first panel to Q4 in the fourth. In this case, a moving window of six quarters is used to calculate the MAPE metric. The purpose is to quantify the evolution of predictive ability and robustness for the different models considered. Note that this requires changing the in-sample and out-of-sample period for every calculation. For instance, the forecast estimates corresponding to 2019Q4 include 2019Q4, 2020Q1, 2020Q2, 2020Q3, 2020Q4, and 2021Q1. Therefore, the in-sample period covers the January 1995 to December 2019Q3 range. However, the forecast estimate corresponding to 2020Q1 calculates the average prediction for 2020Q1, 2020Q2, 2020Q3, 2020Q4, 2021Q1, and 2021Q2 and uses the 1995Q1-2019Q4 as an in-sample period. As opposed to the results reported in Table 5, we provide forecasting results for every period of the out-of-sample window under each different quarter to analyze the persistence of the relative performance of the different methodologies considered. This is relevant given the high performance of regime-changing events seen during the 2017–2023 window, including the COVID crisis, the war in Ukraine, and the higher-than-expected recovery with high inflation and interest rate rises. Under this reporting format, the ratio takes a value of 1 if a given model performs equally as well as the naïve (no-change model). A close look at Table 5 shows that, as suggested in Figure 1, the forecasting performance of every model varies across time. The calculated results confirm the findings reported in Table 4. The proposed model with actual inputs performs best for almost all subsamples considered. The only exceptions are documented in 2018, a period dominated by the Fed tightening monetary policy. The results also demonstrate that the model with forecasted inputs is, on average, the second best when the horizon ranges from one quarter to two quarters. The model with forecasted inputs does not exhibit a clear outperformance for higher horizons. Since this specification is run based on predicted data, performance depends on the forecast accuracy of the different (EIA forecasted) inputs. We see that the longer the forecast horizon, the lower the forecast accuracy. The reported results confirm the view that the proposed model can be used to consider different (twelve-month maturity) scenarios underlying the selected explanatory variables.

The forecasting ability of futures prices and the Bloomberg analyst survey can be compared with the results reported by [17], which demonstrate that futures prices outperform (at the aggregate level) analyst forecasts when considering forecasts performed on a yearly basis. The current analysis makes it unclear whether future prices will beat Bloomberg analysts' forecasts. This may be explained by the different periods and prediction horizons considered in the forecasting exercise. While [17] considers the average forecast for a given year with Chicago Mercantile Exchange (CME) WTI futures prices for a sample ending in

December 2019, the analysis in this paper uses ICE Brent futures prices and a six-quarter rolling window and includes forecasts ending the last quarter of 2023.

Table 7. Performance evolution versus no-change forecast (a six-quarter window ahead).

1st Quarter Forecast																				
6 Quarter Rolling from	2017Q1	2017Q2	2017Q3	2017Q4	2018Q1	2018Q2	2018Q3	2018Q4	2019Q1	2019Q2	2019Q3	2019Q4	2020Q1	2020Q2	2020Q3	2020Q4	2021Q1	2021Q2	2021Q3	2021Q4
to	2018Q2	2018Q3	2018Q4	2019Q1	2019Q2	2019Q3	2019Q4	2020Q1	2020Q2	2020Q3	2020Q4	2021Q1	2021Q2	2021Q3	2021Q4	2022Q1	2022Q2	2022Q3	2022Q4	2023Q1
Futures	1.28	1.167	1.317	1.447	1.35	1.447	1.568	1.595	1.712	1.589	1.629	1.434	1.135	1.272	0.927	0.937	1.115	0.930	0.892	0.943
BBG	1.511	1.62	1.204	1.283	1.158	1.17	1.029	0.749	0.89	1.152	1.181	1.150	1.346	2.095	1.914	1.371	1.818	1.507	1.550	1.571
DoE	1.281	1.295	1.231	1.316	1.196	1.191	1.145	0.836	1.309	1.386	1.448	1.123	1.134	1.605	0.655	0.645	0.682	0.609	0.630	0.643
GAMLTF Forecasted Inputs	1.024	1.011	0.999	1.013	0.993	0.893	0.774	0.736	0.854	1.138	1.061	0.956	1.224	1.810	1.256	0.848	1.198	1.386	1.127	1.018
GAMLTF Actual Inputs	0.878	0.746	0.651	0.661	0.77	0.745	0.796	0.567	0.649	0.726	0.709	0.707	0.595	0.821	0.658	0.665	0.799	0.763	0.787	0.838
LTF Actual Imputs no GAM	1.423	1.187	0.899	0.931	0.897	0.765	0.474	0.72	0.993	1.139	1.104	1.048	1.255	1.637	1.388	0.919	1.518	1.916	1.951	1.857
2nd Quarter Forecast																				
6 Quarter Rolling from	2017Q1	2017Q2	2017Q3	2017Q4	2018Q1	2018Q2	2018Q3	2018Q4	2019Q1	2019Q2	2019Q3	2019Q4	2020Q1	2020Q2	2020Q3	2020Q4	2021Q1	2021Q2	2021Q3	2021Q4
to	2018Q2	2018Q3	2018Q4	2019Q1	2019Q2	2019Q3	2019Q4	2020Q1	2020Q2	2020Q3	2020Q4	2021Q1	2021Q2	2021Q3	2021Q4	2022Q1	2022Q2	2022Q3	2022Q4	2023Q1
Futures	1.155	1.178	1.143	1.204	1.276	1.316	1.457	1.072	1.03	0.995	0.963	0.968	0.935	0.964	1.011	1.027	0.930	0.769	0.654	0.645
BBG	1.093	0.951	0.816	0.832	0.905	0.89	0.891	0.918	0.864	0.955	0.899	0.889	0.909	1.050	1.243	1.165	1.083	0.864	0.884	0.906
DoE	1.216	1.173	1.051	1.064	1.063	1.048	0.908	0.898	1.005	0.996	0.961	0.914	0.948	1.071	0.917	0.964	0.914	0.762	0.755	0.760
GAMLTF Forecasted Inputs	0.873	0.935	0.939	0.931	1.006	0.966	1.104	0.992	1.016	1.11	0.997	0.883	0.889	0.826	0.649	0.562	0.749	0.915	0.802	0.843
GAMLTF Actual Inputs	0.795	0.583	0.512	0.57	0.616	0.693	0.714	0.449	0.446	0.475	0.521	0.456	0.388	0.535	0.538	0.555	0.649	0.740	0.792	0.869
LTF Actual Imputs no GAM	1.078	0.876	0.663	0.696	0.572	0.631	0.921	1.522	1.629	1.77	1.625	1.413	1.298	0.777	0.617	0.469	0.684	1.030	1.026	1.038
3rd Quarter Forecast																				
6 Quarter Rolling from	2017Q1	2017Q2	2017Q3	2017Q4	2018Q1	2018Q2	2018Q3	2018Q4	2019Q1	2019Q2	2019Q3	2019Q4	2020Q1	2020Q2	2020Q3	2020Q4	2021Q1	2021Q2	2021Q3	2021Q4
to	2018Q2	2018Q3	2018Q4	2019Q1	2019Q2	2019Q3	2019Q4	2020Q1	2020Q2	2020Q3	2020Q4	2021Q1	2021Q2	2021Q3	2021Q4	2022Q1	2022Q2	2022Q3	2022Q4	2023Q1
Futures	1.089	1.026	1.047	1.152	1.214	1.425	1.097	1.05	0.983	0.956	0.943	0.877	0.906	0.958	1.024	1.051	0.949	0.790	0.646	0.578
BBG	0.878	0.757	0.784	0.996	1.118	1.075	1.05	1.044	0.963	0.947	0.9	0.888	0.867	0.962	1.109	1.115	0.980	0.800	0.787	0.742
DoE	1.075	0.995	0.973	0.943	0.824	0.879	0.828	0.861	0.904	0.904	0.898	0.868	0.906	0.972	0.985	1.038	1.002	0.844	0.819	0.750
GAMLTF Forecasted Inputs	0.861	0.876	0.904	0.922	1.012	0.978	1.094	1.009	1.043	1.049	0.928	0.817	0.662	0.620	0.521	0.443	0.645	0.780	0.831	0.909
GAMLTF Actual Inputs	0.616	0.402	0.445	0.597	0.806	0.763	0.503	0.394	0.449	0.494	0.454	0.406	0.376	0.479	0.474	0.462	0.625	0.703	0.828	0.835
LTF Actual Imputs no GAM	0.715	0.435	0.445	0.63	0.858	1.27	1.815	2.027	2.053	1.965	1.73	1.540	1.065	0.672	0.548	0.410	0.654	0.824	0.796	0.958
4th Quarter Forecast																				
6 Quarter Rolling from	2017Q1	2017Q2	2017Q3	2017Q4	2018Q1	2018Q2	2018Q3	2018Q4	2019Q1	2019Q2	2019Q3	2019Q4	2020Q1	2020Q2	2020Q3	2020Q4	2021Q1	2021Q2	2021Q3	2021Q4
to	2018Q2	2018Q3	2018Q4	2019Q1	2019Q2	2019Q3	2019Q4	2020Q1	2020Q2	2020Q3	2020Q4	2021Q1	2021Q2	2021Q3	2021Q4	2022Q1	2022Q2	2022Q3	2022Q4	2023Q1
Futures	0.871	0.885	0.901	0.95	1.197	1.095	1.065	1.012	0.976	0.957	0.875	0.863	0.912	0.970	1.028	1.068	0.954	0.786	0.750	0.665
BBG	0.781	0.728	0.745	0.876	1.034	1.051	1.063	1.051	0.981	0.95	0.889	0.805	0.818	0.881	1.028	1.083	0.925	0.779	0.710	0.641
DoE	0.998	0.889	0.859	0.76	0.687	0.89	0.924	0.955	0.938	0.93	0.92	0.853	0.852	0.894	0.972	1.058	1.003	0.848	0.832	0.749
GAMLTF Forecasted Inputs	0.925	0.832	0.858	0.873	0.954	0.975	1.042	0.985	0.979	0.937	0.835	0.675	0.503	0.514	0.413	0.371	0.576	0.700	0.851	0.929
GAMLTF Actual Inputs	0.578	0.434	0.449	0.488	0.568	0.395	0.312	0.321	0.385	0.394	0.367	0.367	0.418	0.484	0.458	0.503	0.682	0.762	0.861	0.882
LTF Actual Imputs no GAM	0.849	0.714	0.59	0.674	1.236	1.76	1.944	1.963	1.985	1.864	1.679	1.253	0.825	0.615	0.506	0.426	0.610	0.708	0.824	0.916

Note: This table reports the forecasting performance in terms of the ratio of MAPE of the selected method and the no-change method. (Forecasting horizon is a six-quarter average window ahead). The performance for the proposed GAMLTF framework for forecasted and actual input (in bold) data as well as alternative benchmarks, including the LTF framework with no GAM. The in-sample period 1995–2016, out-of-sample or forecasting period 2017–2023. Colour legend: Dark green → best performer, dark red → worst performer.

5. Oil Price Scenario Generation

We have seen in the previous section that the proposed model can explain and forecast very accurately when the observed (and not forecasted) values of the explanatory variables are used in the forecasting process. This tool can help understand the interaction of factors that determine the past oil price evolution and the future paths under different scenarios, quantifying the risk associated with a particular scenario compared to an alternative baseline forecast (selected as the EIA forecast). The proposed model identifies key variables driving upside and downside risks in the oil price forecast. For expository purposes, three scenarios involving hypothetical future oil market conditions are explored, starting in the first quarter of 2024. These main variables and estimated parameters correspond to world production, world demand, OECD stocks, non-commercial long and short positions, open interest, historical volatility, and the U.S. dollar. Figure 5 illustrates the twelve-month forecasts for the four variables in the three scenarios defined from 2024Q1. The illustrative scenarios are focused on the implications of shocks arising from the supply relative to the demand conditions.

Scenario A: Main benchmark scenario with EIA forecast

The main scenario uses the U.S. Department of Energy forecast of the fundamental variable for the next 12 months, performed in December 2023. This includes the concern expressed by the DoE regarding the weakening global economic situation, which leads to lower expectations for global oil demand growth. An increase in demand of 1.3 mb/d is thus considered under this scenario. These views about the economy can potentially offset the upward pressure on prices stemming from lower short-term oil supply due to the OPEC's and Russia's supply cuts in crude oil production. Oil production cuts were first announced in October 2022 for a cut of 2 mb/d and were enhanced in April 2023 to 3.5 mb/d.

Furthermore, in June 2023, the OPEC and Russia decided to extend cuts to December 2024. In July, Saudi Arabia additionally announced voluntary cuts (details can be found at https://

www.reuters.com/business/energy/saudi-arabia-expected-extend-voluntary-oil-cut-september-analysts-say-2023-07-28/ accessed on 15 August 2023). Full compliance (−3.5 mb/d from the level registered in August 2022) is not expected, but the agency forecasted, in December 2023, that production will increase by 0.6 mb/d, representing a slowdown when compared to growth levels reported of 1.6 mb/d in 2023. The fundamental variable is predicted to stay near last year's lows. With the tightening of the physical market, investors will increase their positions. The U.S. dollar stabilizes around 102 as monetary policies are becoming more aligned in the U.S. and Europe. Crude oil price volatility returns to normal conditions, considering the Ukrainian crisis causes no other uncertainty-related spikes.

Scenario B: Physical Market tightening

This represents the case of full compliance with the OPEC's quota supported by increased tensions in the Middle East (particularly in the Red Sea) and a robust economy that sustains oil consumption with a rebound in consumption driven by the airline sector, as forecasted by data from S&P Global. In this case, the fundamental variable will fall to the lowest value registered over our sample period. Under this scenario, investors will be attracted to exploit the upward price trend. The U.S. dollar will be weaker than in the main scenario, and volatility will rebound mildly because of increasing geopolitical pressures. Note that the OPEC plus group has announced an extension of 3 months to their voluntary cuts, making this scenario less likely. See the *Financial Times* article "Opec+ members extend production cuts to boost oil price", 4 March 2024.

Scenario C: Low OPEC compliance and delay on the end of monetary tightening

OPEC compliance is less stringent than the main scenario, implying that production stands at 1 mb/d during 2023Q3–2024Q4. Oil demand growth moderates because of the delay in the monetary tightening. Under this scenario, investors will reduce their oil exposure in their portfolios, volatility will pick up, and the dollar will appreciate slightly.

Our model also allows us to do reverse engineering. This feature implies that we can calculate the values of the underlying variables implied by futures prices. In order to match quoted futures prices observed in December 2023, our framework shows that there should be low compliance with the announced the OPEC cuts in the first half of 2024. The prices are similar to Scenario C.

Forecasts under the different scenarios, including the main and EIA forecasts, are illustrated in Figure 6. First, our main benchmark scenario for the next 12 months is slightly more bullish than that reported by the EIA. Under the supply-stressed scenario (B), oil prices are expected to be higher than USD 100, given the context of deteriorated levels in the physical balance. The increase in geopolitical risk, partly driven by the recent moves by Saudi Arabia and Russia to extend their voluntary supply cuts, drives fears of future inflation and new periods of prolonged periods of low investment in new capacities. This fact is fundamental under the currently announced OPEC's production cuts. While OPEC compliance has always been hesitant, the possibility of future supply cuts remains a primary concern for Western governments already struggling to contain inflation. We could see prices stabilizing around the USD 72/bbl level in the case of low OPEC compliance. The term structure of futures prices is in December 2023 in mild backwardation, with the December 2024 futures price trading at USD 75/bbl. This implies improved fundamentals compared to the term structure seen in November 2023.

Note that the set of scenarios envisaged for the explanatory variables allows the simulation of different geopolitical situations. Given that increased geopolitical tensions influence the price of oil, the proposed tool can be used to consider changes in the explanatory variables (and the corresponding crude oil price forecast) affected by increased geopolitical uncertainty. For instance, we expect that there will be supply disruptions under the surge of an armed conflict. These disruptions will reduce the value of the fundamental variable and therefore lead to a scenario similar to that described in scenario B.

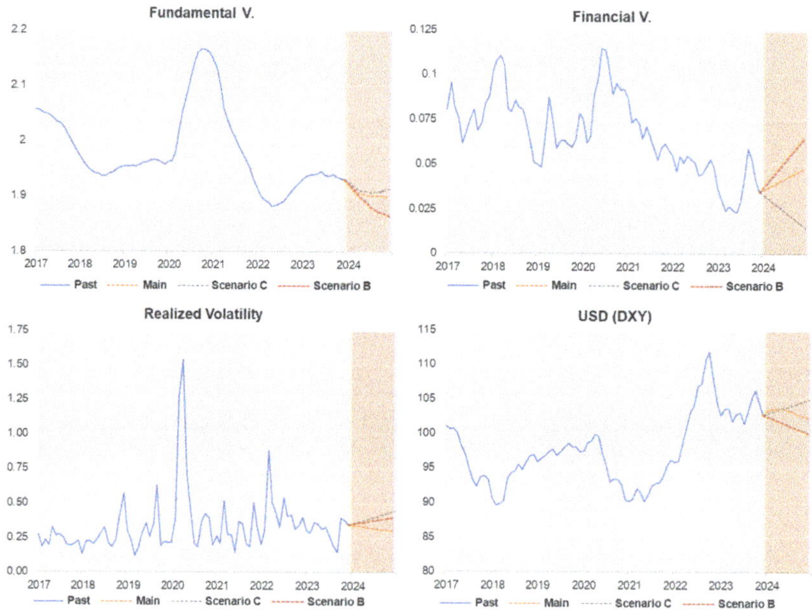

Figure 5. Forecasts of input variables under different scenarios: This figure illustrates the evolution of the input variables used in the different scenarios. The main scenario: Scenario A uses EIA forecast input data. Scenario B analyzes the possibility of physical tightening. Scenario C addresses the case of low OPEC.

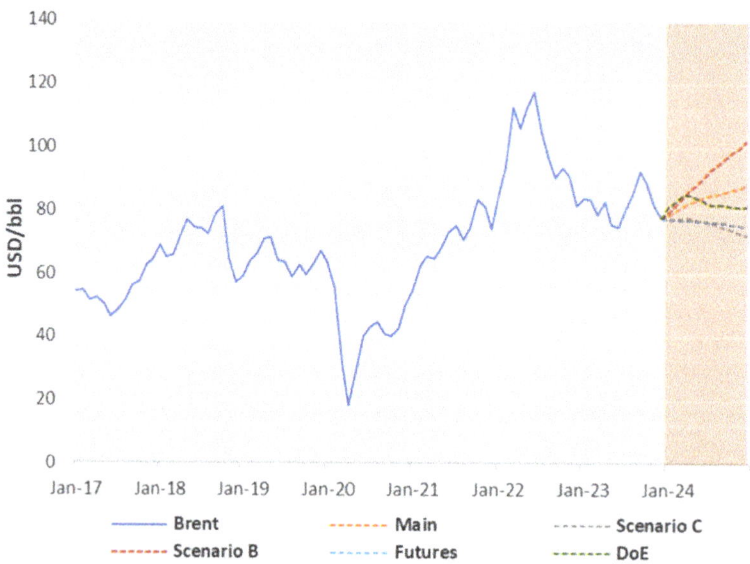

Figure 6. Oil price forecast in different scenarios: The figure illustrates forecasting prices under the different scenarios considered, including the main (using EIA forecast), the EIA forecast (labeled DoE), the forecast implied by futures (labeled Futures), scenario B (tight fundamentals), and scenario C (low OPEC compliance).

6. Conclusions

Recent developments in energy markets have shown that the crude oil market is exposed to time-changing uncertainty. As a result, crude oil prices have been subject to significant fluctuations over the past two decades. This makes oil price prediction a very challenging task. While the forecasting frameworks developed in the literature are wide and varied, there is no consensus about the appropriate methodological framework to apply. This paper combines the classical regression model with machine learning approaches in a hybrid framework, selecting the GAM method across the feature engineering literature jointly with a transfer function with the ARIMA noise approach. Machine learning methods help to incorporate flexible non-linear capability in the modeling process.

Compared to competing machine learning approaches, the advantage of the proposed method is that it captures non-linearities under the analysis of partial effects. This allows input variable interpretation through estimated regression coefficients. The method identifies two main drivers explaining oil prices. The first and most important variable is the fundamental variable, which measures the physical market balance. The second is the financial variable quantifying and capturing crude oil investors' speculative interest. The volatility and the dollar variables contribute to a lower impact on oil price movements. The results show that the non-linear effects are remarkably significant in the dollar and volatility variables. The impact of the dollar index is significant only under weak dollar conditions, while volatility is essential for forecasting purposes under high-volatility states.

We show that the algorithm may be applied using U.S. EIA forecasts of the fundamental and the input variables. The forecasting ability of the proposed framework outperforms benchmark techniques, including the futures prices and analysts' crude oil price predictions provided by Bloomberg and the EIA.

A sensitivity analysis is performed in the second stage, confirming that the variable with the most significant influence on crude oil prices is the fundamental variable. One standard deviation increase in this variable results in an oil price reduction of 20%. The financial variable is the second most important, exerting an impact of 10% for a one standard deviation increase. The impact of the one standard deviation change in the dollar and volatility variables are 5% and 2% price change, respectively.

The proposed model is also highly suitable for scenario analysis. The algorithm demonstrates the ability to quantify the risk associated with a benchmark forecast based on an extensive analysis of how this forecast changes under alternative hypothetical scenarios about future oil demand and oil supply conditions. The main scenario (December 2023) predicts a rebound in oil prices towards USD 88/bbl, delivering higher prices than the EIA. Two additional situations are proposed for 2024, with the market balance variable acting as the main driving force. Under market tightening conditions arising from compliance with the OPEC's and Russia's production cuts, prices are pushed to new highs (above USD 100/bbl). Under a lower OPEC compliance scenario and lower consumption due to higher-than-expected interest rates, we could see a moderation in prices towards USD 72/bbl.

Our results show the relevance of supply and demand fundamentals in the price determination process and confirm that events that disrupt global oil supply are expected to increase oil prices, while events that suppress oil consumption growth will generally decrease oil spot prices (Baumeister and Kilian, 2015) [8]. The proposed hybrid model can be applied to risk management systems of energy corporations and institutions. It can also provide a quantitative assessment of the impact of a range of hypothetical events on the crude oil price. This is crucial in times of multiple sources of uncertainty arising from factors such as geopolitical tensions, interest rate risk, and energy transition-related shocks.

Author Contributions: Conceptualization, P.M., I.F.-F. and A.M.; methodology, P.M. and A.M.; software, P.M.; validation, A.M.; formal analysis, P.M., I.F.-F. and A.M.; investigation, P.M., I.F.-F. and A.M.; data curation, P.M.; writing—original draft preparation, P.M.; writing—review and editing, I.F.-F. and A.M.; supervision, I.F.-F. and A.M. All authors have read and agreed to the published version of the manuscript.

Funding: This research received no external funding.

Data Availability Statement: Data is contained within the articles and sources cited.

Conflicts of Interest: The authors declare no conflict of interest.

Appendix A

Table A1. Raw data description.

Raw Variable	Frequency	History	Source	Model Variable
Brent Log(Brent)	Monthly (average daily data)	from January 1995	Bloomberg	Fundamental Variable
Total World Production OPEC Production Spare OPEC Production Total World Consumption OECD Consumption China Consumption OECD Commercial Inventory OECD Total Inventory Stocks Consumption Ratio	Monthly	from January 1995	U.S. Energy Information Administration	Fundamental Variable
Long non-commercial Futures Short non-commercial Futures Net non-commercial Futures Open Interest Futures Long non-commercial F&O Short non-commercial F&O Net non-commercial F&O Open Interest F&O	Monthly (average weekly data)	from January 1995 from March 1995	Commodity Futures Trading Commission	Financial Variable
DXY USD/EUR	Monthly (average daily data)	from January 1995	Bloomberg	Dollar
Implied Volatility Realized Volatility	Monthly (average daily data)	from January 1995	Bloomberg Price	Volatility

Note: This table describes the data used in the initial stage of algorithm implementation. The second to fourth columns provide variable frequency, data history, and data source. The label "Model variable" in the last column describes the category of the given data series within the fundamental, financial, dollar, and volatility variables, according to dimensions for model input variables.

Table A2. Description of selected input variables.

Model Variable (Equation)	Raw Variable	Frequency	History	Source
Fundamental Variable (7)	Total Crude Oil Supply (World) Total Crude Oil Demand (World) Total Commercial OECD Stocks	Monthly	From January 1995	U.S. Energy Information Administration
Financial Variable (8)	Non-Commercial Long Futures WTI Non-Commercial Short Futures WTI Open Interest Futures WTI	Monthly (average weekly data)	From January 1995	Commodity Futures Trading Commission
Volatility Realized	Price First Brent Contract	Monthly (average daily data)	From January 1995	Price
Dollar	DXY Index	Monthly (average daily data)	From January 1995	Bloomberg

Note: This table describes the selected input data used for GAM model implementation. The third to fifth columns provide variable frequency, data history, and data source. The label "Model variable" in the first column describes the category of the given data series within the fundamental, financial, dollar, and volatility variables according to dimensions for model input variables. The fundamental and financial variable definitions are linked to definitions specified in Equations (7) and (8), respectively.

Table A3. Correlation matrix of primary variables used in the analysis.

	Brent	Log(Brent)	Total World Production	OPEC Production	Spare OPEC Production	Total World Consumption	OECD Consumption	China Consumption	OECD Commercial Inventory	OECD Total Inventory	Stocks Consumption Ratio	Fundamental Variable	Long Non-Commercial Futures	Short Non-Commercial Futures	Net Non-Commercial Futures	Open Interest Futures	Long Non-Commercial F&O	Short Non-Commercial F&O	Net Non-Commercial F&O	Open Interest F&O	Financial Variable Futures	Financial Variable F&O	DXY	USD/EUR	Implied Volatility	Realized Volatility
Brent	1.00	0.96	0.63	0.66	−0.15	0.66	−0.15	0.60	0.00	0.36	−0.79	−0.81	0.51	0.53	0.41	0.61	0.53	0.46	0.48	0.73	0.44	0.36	−0.57	0.55	−0.23	−0.24
Log(Brent)	0.96	1.00	0.74	0.74	−0.16	0.77	−0.10	0.70	0.11	0.49	−0.86	−0.89	0.60	0.64	0.49	0.71	0.62	0.56	0.56	0.81	0.51	0.45	−0.52	0.49	−0.18	−0.21
Total World Production	0.63	0.74	1.00	0.80	−0.17	0.98	−0.22	0.96	0.58	0.79	−0.79	−0.80	0.90	0.73	0.81	0.92	0.90	0.70	0.85	0.87	0.80	0.78	−0.11	0.08	0.00	0.02
OPEC Production	0.66	0.74	0.80	1.00	−0.56	0.78	0.03	0.65	0.35	0.63	−0.71	−0.72	0.64	0.76	0.49	0.70	0.66	0.73	0.56	0.77	0.53	0.48	−0.38	0.35	−0.08	−0.06
Spare OPEC Production	−0.15	−0.16	−0.17	−0.56	1.00	−0.12	−0.41	0.05	0.20	0.07	0.26	0.29	0.05	−0.13	0.11	0.02	0.04	−0.16	0.09	−0.01	0.08	0.09	0.18	−0.16	0.08	−0.01
Total World Consumption	0.66	0.77	0.98	0.78	−0.12	1.00	−0.13	0.95	0.55	0.77	−0.84	−0.80	0.89	0.74	0.79	0.92	0.89	0.70	0.84	0.87	0.78	0.77	−0.14	0.10	−0.06	−0.06
OECD Consumption	−0.15	−0.10	−0.22	0.03	−0.41	−0.13	1.00	−0.38	−0.45	−0.36	−0.16	−0.01	−0.43	−0.14	−0.47	−0.36	−0.42	−0.18	−0.45	−0.29	−0.50	−0.46	0.06	−0.07	−0.06	−0.13
China Consumption	0.60	0.70	0.96	0.65	0.05	0.95	−0.38	1.00	0.64	0.80	−0.72	−0.71	0.93	0.68	0.87	0.95	0.93	0.65	0.91	0.86	0.85	0.85	−0.09	0.07	−0.01	0.00
OECD Commercial Inventory	0.00	0.11	0.58	0.35	0.20	0.55	−0.45	0.64	1.00	0.88	−0.02	−0.05	0.71	0.57	0.65	0.65	0.70	0.61	0.64	0.54	0.65	0.66	0.16	−0.17	0.15	0.14
OECD Total Inventory	0.36	0.49	0.79	0.63	0.07	0.77	−0.36	0.80	0.88	1.00	−0.38	−0.41	0.85	0.81	0.73	0.85	0.85	0.81	0.76	0.81	0.75	0.74	−0.16	0.13	0.07	0.05
Stocks Consumption Ratio	−0.79	−0.86	−0.79	−0.71	0.26	−0.84	−0.16	−0.72	−0.02	−0.38	1.00	0.93	−0.60	−0.56	−0.51	−0.68	−0.61	−0.47	−0.58	−0.71	−0.51	−0.49	0.27	−0.24	0.13	0.14
Fundamental Variable	−0.81	−0.89	−0.80	−0.72	0.29	−0.80	−0.01	−0.71	−0.05	−0.41	0.93	1.00	−0.59	−0.56	−0.50	−0.67	−0.60	−0.48	−0.56	−0.73	−0.50	−0.46	0.28	−0.26	0.02	0.04
Long non-commercial Futures	0.51	0.60	0.90	0.64	0.05	0.89	−0.43	0.93	0.71	0.85	−0.60	−0.59	1.00	0.67	0.96	0.97	1.00	0.66	0.98	0.85	0.94	0.93	−0.13	0.10	−0.10	−0.05
Short non-commercial Futures	0.53	0.64	0.73	0.76	−0.13	0.74	−0.14	0.68	0.57	0.81	−0.56	−0.56	0.67	1.00	0.44	0.73	0.68	0.96	0.52	0.83	0.49	0.47	−0.35	0.32	0.14	0.10
Net non-commercial Futures	0.41	0.49	0.81	0.49	0.11	0.79	−0.47	0.87	0.65	0.73	−0.51	−0.50	0.96	0.44	1.00	0.90	0.95	0.44	0.99	0.72	0.95	0.95	−0.03	0.00	−0.18	−0.10
Open Interest Futures	0.61	0.71	0.92	0.70	0.02	0.92	−0.36	0.95	0.65	0.85	−0.68	−0.67	0.97	0.73	0.90	1.00	0.97	0.70	0.94	0.93	0.86	0.84	−0.21	0.19	−0.09	−0.05
Long non-commercial F&O	0.53	0.62	0.90	0.66	0.04	0.89	−0.42	0.93	0.70	0.85	−0.61	−0.60	1.00	0.68	0.95	0.97	1.00	0.67	0.98	0.86	0.94	0.92	−0.15	0.12	−0.11	−0.06
Short non-commercial F&O	0.46	0.56	0.70	0.73	−0.16	0.70	−0.18	0.65	0.61	0.81	−0.47	−0.48	0.66	0.96	0.44	0.70	0.67	1.00	0.49	0.77	0.51	0.47	−0.30	0.27	0.10	0.09
Net non-commercial F&O	0.48	0.56	0.85	0.56	0.09	0.84	−0.45	0.91	0.64	0.76	−0.58	−0.56	0.98	0.52	0.99	0.94	0.98	0.49	1.00	0.79	0.95	0.95	−0.08	0.06	−0.16	−0.10
Open Interest F&O	0.73	0.81	0.87	0.77	−0.01	0.87	−0.29	0.86	0.54	0.81	−0.71	−0.73	0.85	0.83	0.72	0.93	0.86	0.77	0.79	1.00	0.70	0.65	−0.40	0.38	0.03	0.03
Financial Variable Futures	0.44	0.51	0.80	0.53	0.08	0.78	−0.50	0.85	0.65	0.75	−0.51	−0.50	0.94	0.49	0.95	0.86	0.94	0.51	0.95	0.70	1.00	0.97	−0.10	0.06	−0.18	−0.11
Financial Variable F&O	0.36	0.45	0.78	0.48	0.09	0.77	−0.46	0.85	0.66	0.74	−0.49	−0.46	0.93	0.47	0.95	0.84	0.92	0.47	0.95	0.65	0.97	1.00	−0.03	0.00	−0.18	−0.12
DXY	−0.57	−0.52	−0.11	−0.38	0.18	−0.14	0.06	−0.09	0.16	−0.16	0.27	0.28	−0.13	−0.35	−0.03	−0.21	−0.15	−0.30	−0.08	−0.40	−0.10	−0.03	1.00	−0.98	0.26	0.26
USD/EUR	0.55	0.49	0.08	0.35	−0.16	0.10	−0.07	0.07	−0.17	0.13	−0.24	−0.26	0.10	0.32	0.00	0.19	0.12	0.27	0.06	0.38	0.06	0.00	−0.98	1.00	−0.23	−0.23
Implied Volatility	−0.23	−0.18	0.00	−0.08	0.08	−0.06	−0.06	−0.01	0.15	0.07	0.13	0.02	−0.10	0.14	−0.18	−0.09	−0.11	0.10	−0.16	0.03	−0.18	−0.18	0.26	−0.23	1.00	0.84
Realized Volatility	−0.24	−0.21	0.02	−0.06	−0.01	−0.06	−0.13	0.00	0.14	0.05	0.14	0.04	−0.05	0.10	−0.10	−0.05	−0.06	0.09	−0.10	0.03	−0.11	−0.12	0.26	−0.23	0.84	1.00

Note: This table shows the correlation matrix for every time series initially considered for building the final input (predictive) variables.

Table A4. Correlation matrix of selected predictive variables and the target variable.

	Log(Brent)	**Fundamental Variable**	**Financial Variable**	**Dollar**	**Realized Volatility**
Log(Brent)	-	−0.89	0.51	−0.52	−0.21
Fundamental Variable	−0.89	-	−0.50	0.28	0.04
Financial Variable	0.51	−0.50	-	−0.10	−0.11
Dollar	−0.52	0.28	−0.10	-	0.26
Realized Volatility	−0.21	0.04	−0.11	0.26	-

Note: This table reports correlation coefficients across the variables that have been selected as final input variables. Correlations with the output variable defined as the log of the Brent spot price are also reported.

Table A5. Bai and Perron structural breaks test results for log(Brent).

Sequential F-Statistic Determined Breaks: 5					
Break Test	**F-Statistics**	**Scaled F-Statistic**	**Critical Value ****	**Break Dates:**	**Dates:**
0 vs. 1 *	1080.393	1080.393	8.58	1	09 September
1 vs. 2 *	75.975	75.975	10.13	2	04 October
2 vs. 3 *	55.274	55.274	11.14	3	10 August
3 vs. 4 *	112.946	112.946	11.83	4	14 November
4 vs. 5 *	23.992	23.992	12.25	5	19 April

Note: This table provides the results for structural breaks test. The test report results for the null hypothesis H_0 of no structural break. The alternative hypothesis H_1 test for k structural breaks. There are five structural breaks. * Significant at the 0.05 level, ** Bai–Perron critical values [38] are used.

Table A6. Bai and Perron structural breaks test for equation in differences.

Sequential F-Statistic Determined Breaks: 0			
Break Test	**F-Statistics**	**Scaled F-Statistic**	**Critical Value ****
0 vs. 1	2.321	11.605	18.23

Note: This table provides the results for structural breaks test for an equation that estimates changes in log of Brent as a function of the differences in the fundamental, financial, volatility, and dollar variables. The test report results for the null hypothesis H_0 of no structural break. The alternative hypothesis H_1 tests for k structural breaks. There are no structural breaks. * Significant at the 0.05 level, ** Bai–Perron critical values [38] are used.

Table A7. RMSE error measures for different forecasting methods.

	2017Q1	**2017Q2**	**2017Q3**	**2017Q4**	**2018Q1**	**2018Q2**	**2018Q3**	**2018Q4**	**2019Q1**
Constant	4.144	8.880	18.581	15.593	8.447	6.380	8.179	13.759	6.934
Futures	5.636	7.773	15.878	15.226	8.143	5.323	8.619	15.330	9.668
BBG Analysts Median	3.579	5.715	9.903	15.761	14.872	7.939	3.620	8.961	6.447
Department of Energy EIA	4.122	7.213	16.305	17.359	12.688	9.786	3.722	11.440	5.120
GAMLTF Forecasted Inputs	**5.233**	**7.560**	**14.174**	**12.368**	**10.994**	**6.288**	**6.422**	**14.046**	**4.808**
GAMLTF Actual Inputs	**9.409**	**4.215**	**6.703**	**3.854**	**4.197**	**8.550**	**3.273**	**7.585**	**5.452**
LTF Actual Inputs No GAM	10.088	5.606	6.505	7.905	6.736	16.029	2.616	2.757	4.840
	2019Q2	**2019Q3**	**2019Q4**	**2020Q1**	**2020Q2**	**2020Q3**	**2020Q4**	**2021Q1**	**2021Q2**
Constant	7.253	16.155	16.047	22.900	16.258	17.497	23.071	22.156	16.696
Futures	7.938	15.825	13.880	20.262	12.529	15.967	20.520	21.594	21.916
BBG Analysts Median	11.110	19.716	16.965	17.981	6.908	16.904	19.816	24.502	21.498
Department of Energy EIA	6.009	18.994	15.179	18.653	15.237	12.696	18.851	20.654	20.239
GAMLTF Forecasted Inputs	**7.748**	**17.138**	**20.165**	**17.989**	**16.629**	**14.133**	**8.360**	**6.372**	**11.279**
GAMLTF Actual Inputs	**4.120**	**5.043**	**7.977**	**5.408**	**12.576**	**11.860**	**9.243**	**4.998**	**5.232**
LTF Actual Inputs No GAM	12.689	35.927	44.212	40.622	16.969	18.266	13.300	7.160	10.398

Table A7. *Cont.*

	2021Q3	2021Q4	2022Q1	2022Q2	2022Q3	2022Q4	2023Q1	TOTAL
Constant	22.182	23.929	24.366	20.987	31.913	7.979	3.004	17.040
Futures	25.044	24.891	24.864	7.277	11.495	5.855	3.954	15.323
BBG Analysts Median	27.313	28.984	23.360	10.227	14.378	13.291	9.052	16.031
Department of Energy EIA	26.232	25.283	24.485	10.465	11.659	10.816	3.961	15.400
GAMLTF Forecasted Inputs	**15.823**	**12.759**	**15.853**	**30.541**	**27.898**	**8.644**	**5.754**	**14.341**
GAMLTF Actual Inputs	**16.721**	**17.960**	**22.357**	**25.347**	**18.111**	**8.847**	**3.981**	**11.123**
LTF Actual Inputs No GAM	10.190	9.670	11.454	40.561	37.043	9.519	6.019	20.065

Note: This table reports the forecasting performance in terms of the RMSE measure of the proposed framework for forecasted and actual input data as well as alternative benchmarks, including the LTF framework with no GAM. The in-sample period is 1995–2016, and the out-of-sample or forecasting period is 2017–2023. Forecasts are performed for the next four quarters. The following forecasting methods are considered: No-change: forecasts are the average price of the previous month for the whole forecast period. Futures: forecasts are the average of Brent first-, second-, and third-month contracts for the first quarter, fourth-, fifth-, and sixth-month contracts for the second quarter for the day before beginning the period of forecast. BBG: Bloomberg quarterly surveys are taken as forecasts the day before beginning the period of forecast. EIA: average monthly forecasts to create quarterly forecasts are taken from the last EIA report before beginning the period of forecast. GAMLFT with Forecasted Inputs: proposed new model fed by forecasted inputs. Highlighted in bold. GAMLFT with actual inputs: proposed new model fed by actual inputs. Highlighted in bold. LFT with actual inputs: linear function transfer model fed by forecasted inputs.

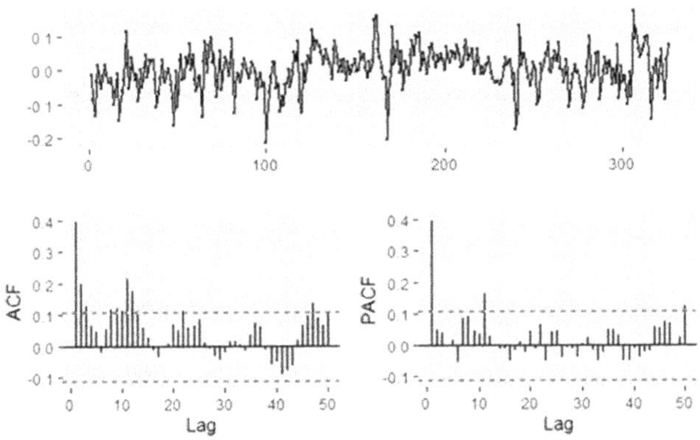

Figure A1. PACF and ACF structure of the error term under a GAM model: This figure shows the PACF and ACF for the initial GAM model error. A clear autocorrelation can be observed in the regression errors since some lags exceed confidence limits.

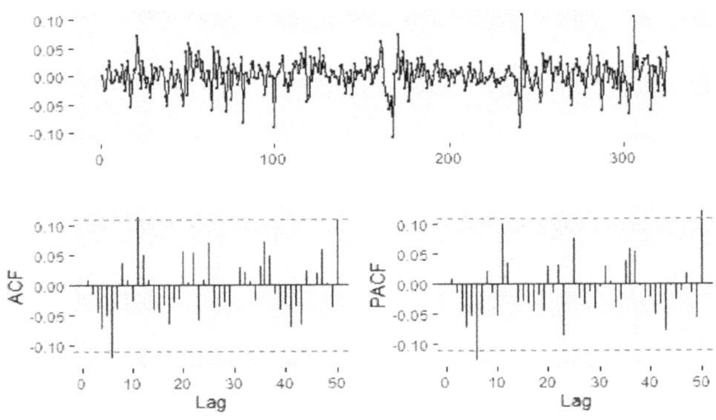

Figure A2. PACF and ACF structures of the error term under GAM with LTF specification: This figure shows the PACF and ACF for the proposed model error. No problem of autocorrelation can be appreciated.

References

1. Weijermars, R.; Sun, Z. Regression analysis of historic oil prices: A basis for future mean reversion prices scenarios. *Glob. Financ. J.* **2018**, *35*, 177–201. [CrossRef]
2. Fabra, N. Reforming European electricity markets: Lessons from the energy crisis. *Energy Econ.* **2023**, *126*, 106963. [CrossRef]
3. Chuliá, H.; Klein, T.; Mendoza, J.A.M.; Uribe, J.M. Vulnerability of European electricity markets: A quantile connectedness approach. *Energy Policy* **2024**, *184*, 113862. [CrossRef]
4. Cervera, I.; Figuerola-Ferretti, I. Credit risk and bubble behavior of credit default swaps in the corporate energy sector. *Int. Rev. Econ. Financ.* **2023**, *89 Pt A*, 702–731. [CrossRef]
5. Alquist, R.; Kilian, L. What Do We Learn from the Price of Crude Oil Futures? *J. Appl. Econom.* **2010**, *25*, 539–573. [CrossRef]
6. Alquist, R.; Kilian, L.; Vigfusson, R.J. Forecasting the Price of Oil. In *Handbook of Economic Forecasting*; Elliott, G., Timmermann, A., Eds.; Elsevier: Amsterdam, The Netherlands, 2013; Volume 2A, pp. 427–507.
7. Baumeister, C.; Kilian, L. Real-Time Analysis of Oil Price Risks using Forecast Scenarios. *IMF Econ. Rev.* **2014**, *62*, 119–145. [CrossRef]
8. Baumeister, C.; Kilian, L. Forecasting the Real Price of Oil in a Changing World: A Forecast Combination Approach. *J. Bus. Econ. Stat.* **2015**, *33*, 338–351. [CrossRef]
9. Ferrari, D.; Ravazzolo, F.; Vespignani, J. Forecasting Energy Commodity Prices: A Large Global Dataset Sparse Approach. CAMA Working Paper No. 90/2019. *Energy Econ.* **2021**, *98*, 105268. [CrossRef]
10. Coppola, A. Forecasting oil price movements: Exploiting the information in the futures market. *J. Futures Mark.* **2008**, *28*, 34–56. [CrossRef]
11. Aliu, F.; Kučera, J.; Hašková, S. Agricultural Commodities in the Context of the Russia-Ukraine War: Evidence from Corn, Wheat, Barley, and Sunflower Oil. *Forecasting* **2023**, *5*, 351–373. [CrossRef]
12. Henderson, B.J.; Person, N.D.; Wang, L. New Evidence on the Financialization of Commodity Markets. *Rev. Financ. Stud.* **2015**, *8*, 1285–1311. [CrossRef]
13. Singleton, K.J. Investor Flows and the 2008 Boom/Bust in Oil Prices. *Manag. Sci.* **2014**, *60*, 300–318. [CrossRef]
14. Hamilton, J.D.; Wu, J.C. Risk premia in crude oil futures prices. *J. Int. Money Financ.* **2014**, *42*, 9–37. [CrossRef]
15. Cheng, I.; Xiong, W. Financialization of Commodity Markets. *Annu. Rev. Financ. Econ.* **2014**, *6*, 419–441. [CrossRef]
16. Baumeister, C.; Korobilis, D.; Lee, T.K. Energy markets and global economic conditions. *Rev. Econ. Stat.* **2022**, *104*, 828–844. [CrossRef]
17. Figuerola-Ferretti, I.; Rodríguez, A.; Schwartz, E. Oil price analysts' forecasts. *J. Futures Mark.* **2021**, *41*, 1351–1374. [CrossRef]
18. Miao, H.; Ramchander, S.; Wang, T.; Yang, D. Influential factors in crude oil price forecasting. *Energy Econ.* **2017**, *68*, 77–88. [CrossRef]
19. Chai, J.; Xing, L.M.; Zhou, X.Y.; Zhang, Z.G.; Li, J.X. Forecasting the WTI crude oil price by a hybrid-refined method. *Energy Econ.* **2018**, *71*, 114–127. [CrossRef]
20. Gareth, J.; Daniela, W.; Trevor, H.; Robert, T. *An Introduction to Statistical Learning: With Applications in R*; Springer Texts in Statistics; Springer: Berlin/Heidelberg, Germany, 2013.
21. Phillips, P.C.B.; Shi, S.-P.; Yu, J. (a) Testing for Multiple Bubbles: Limit Theory of Dating Algorithms. *Int. Econ. Rev.* **2015**, *56*, 1043–1098. [CrossRef]
22. Phillips, P.C.B.; Shi, S.-P.; Yu, J. (b) Supplement to two papers on multiple bubbles. *Int. Econ. Rev.* **2015**, *56*, 1–99.
23. Lammerding, M.; Stephan, P.; Trede, M.; Wilfling, B. Speculative bubbles in recent oil price dynamics: Evidence from a Bayesian Markov-switching state-space approach. *Energy Econ.* **2013**, *36*, 491–502. [CrossRef]
24. Svensson, L. Oil prices and ECB monetary policy. In *Briefing Paper for the Committee on Economic and Monetary Affairs of the European Parliament*; European Parliament: Strasbourg, France, 2005; pp. 1–4.
25. Wood, S.N.; Goude, Y.; Shaw, S. Generalized additive models for large datasets. *J. R. Stat. Soc.* **2015**, *64*, 139–155.
26. Box, G.; Jenkins, G.; Reinsel, G. *Time Series Analysis, Forecasting and Control*, 3rd ed.; Prentice Hall: Englwood Cliffs, NJ, USA, 1994.
27. Liu, L.; Hanssens, D.M. Identification of multiple-input transfer function models. *Commun. Stat. Theory Methods* **1982**, *11*, 297–314. [CrossRef]
28. Figuerola-Ferretti, I.; McCrorie, J.R.; Paraskevopoulos, I. Mild explosivity in recent crude oil prices. *Energy Econ.* **2020**, *87*, 104387. [CrossRef]
29. Figuerola-Ferretti, I.; Gilbert, C.L.; McCrorie, J.R. Testing for mild explosivity and bubbles in LME non-ferrous metals prices. *J. Time Ser. Anal.* **2015**, *36*, 763–782. [CrossRef]
30. Haase, M.; Seiler, Y.; Zimmermann, H. Permanent and transitory price shocks in commodity futures markets and their relation to speculation. *Empir. Econ.* **2019**, *56*, 1359–1382. [CrossRef]
31. Bruno, V.; Büyüksahin, B.; Robe, M.A. The Financialization of Food? *Am. J. Agric. Econ.* **2017**, *99*, 243–264. [CrossRef]
32. Etienne, X.L.; Irwin, S.H.; Garcia, P. Price explosiveness, speculation, and grain futures prices. *Am. J. Agric. Econ.* **2015**, *97*, 65–87. [CrossRef]
33. Calomiris, C.W.; Melek, N.Ç.; Mamaysky, H. *Predicting the Oil Market NBER Working Papers 29379*; National Bureau of Economic Research: Cambridge, MA, USA, 2021.
34. Baumeister, C. *Recent Developments in (Modeling) Energy Market Dynamics, Keynote at the Workshop on "Energy and Climate: Macroeconomic Implications"*; B.I. Norwegian Business School: Oslo, Norway, 2022.

35. Dickey, D.A.; Fuller, W.A. Likelihood ratio statistics for autoregressive time series with a unit root. *Econometrica* **1981**, *49*, 1057–1072. [CrossRef]
36. Phillips, P.C.; Perron, P. Testing for a unit root in time series regression. *Biometrika* **1988**, *75*, 335–346. [CrossRef]
37. Kwiatkowski, D.; Phillips, P.C.; Schmidt, P.; Shin, Y. Testing the null hypothesis of stationarity against the alternative of a unit root: How sure are we that economic time series have a unit root? *J. Econ.* **1992**, *54*, 159–178.
38. Bai, J.; Perron, P. Computation and analysis of multiple structural change models. *J. Appl. Econom.* **2003**, *18*, 1–22. [CrossRef]
39. Duboue, P. *The Art of Feature Engineering: Essentials for Machine Learning*; Cambridge University Press: Cambridge, UK, 2020.
40. Garratt, A.; Vahey, S.P.; Zhang, Y. Real-Time Forecast Combinations for the Oil Price. *J. Appl. Econom.* **2019**, *34*, 1–22. [CrossRef]
41. Beckmann, J.; Czudaj, R.; Arora, V. The Relationship between Oil Prices and Exchange Rates: Revisiting theory and evidence. *Energy Econ.* **2020**, *88*, 104772. [CrossRef]
42. Pankratz, A. *Forecasting with Dynamic Regression Models*; Wiley-Interscience: Hoboken, NJ, USA, 1991.
43. Kaufmann, R.K.; Ullman, B. Oil prices, speculation, and fundamentals: Interpreting causal relations among spot and futures prices. *Energy Econ.* **2009**, *31*, 550–558. [CrossRef]

commodities

MDPI

Article

What Insights Do Short-Maturity (7DTE) Return Predictive Regressions Offer about Risk Preferences in the Oil Market?

Gurdip Bakshi *,†, Xiaohui Gao † and Zhaowei Zhang †

Fox School of Business, Temple University, Philadelphia, PA 19122, USA;
xiaohui.gao.bakshi@temple.edu (X.G.); zhaowei.zhang@temple.edu (Z.Z.)
* Correspondence: gurdip.bakshi@temple.edu
† These authors contributed equally to this work.

Abstract: In this study, we investigate the ability of three higher-order risk-neutral return cumulants to predict short maturity (weekly) returns of oil futures. Our data includes weekly West Texas Crude Oil futures options that expire in 7 days (7DTE). Using a model-free approach, we estimate these risk-neutral return cumulants at the beginning of each options expiration cycle. Our results suggest that the third risk-neutral return cumulant consistently predicts the returns of various oil futures (including WTI, Brent, Dubai, Heating Oil, and RBOB Gasoline). We compare our findings with 14 other predictors and offer a theoretical explanation for the negative coefficient observed for the 7DTE third risk-neutral return cumulant. Our theory connects higher-order risk-neutral return cumulants with the risk premiums of oil futures. Furthermore, our quantitative investment strategy favors the predictability of oil futures returns.

Keywords: weekly (7DTE) options on oil futures; 7DTE risk-neutral return cumulants; oil futures returns; return predictive regressions; jumps

1. Introduction

The ever-changing oil market can be influenced by a range of variables, such as economic data, OPEC's production decisions, geopolitical events, and oil discoveries. To stay ahead, investors closely monitor commodities contracts for oil, particularly the West Texas Intermediate (WTI) crude oil futures and options, which allow them to anticipate these developments and realign their exposures. The recent introduction of weekly options contracts with seven days to expiration (7DTE) for WTI crude oil futures offers new opportunities to manage short maturity price fluctuations.

Our study analyzes the predictability of short maturity returns in these WTI oil futures contracts with options-based information, which are primarily influenced by sudden price changes (jumps) in oil. We demonstrate that our findings are also applicable to futures contracts based on related crude oil products, such as Brent, Dubai, Heating Oil, and RBOB Gasoline.

Empirical measure of 7DTE return asymmetries. Options market-inferred asymmetries of oil futures returns can be a relevant attribute in predicting oil returns, making it a significant area of study for financial economists, investors, and policymakers. In contrast to metrics such as volatility, short maturity return asymmetry provides information about the likely direction of crude oil futures price changes due to its measurement of upside versus downside risk imbalance.

This paper considers the relevance of 7DTE conditional asymmetry of oil futures returns in understanding oil price dynamics and oil futures risk premiums. Using model-free measures of asymmetry, particularly forward-looking asymmetry—the third risk-neutral return cumulant—implied by prices of options, we find that conditional oil asymmetry displays significant variation. This variable contains predictive power for short maturity 7DTE returns of oil futures.

Motivating the role of oil futures return asymmetries and jump risks. There is a scarcity of studies examining the asymmetry of small maturity return distributions in oil markets. Models of oil futures curve and options are often ambivalent about return asymmetries. However, when studying the empirical conditional distributions of small maturity oil futures returns, notable asymmetries emerged, with the sample third risk-neutral return cumulant—inferred from 7DTE options—being stochastic and switches sign.

There are two methods we use to calculate conditional asymmetry, using prices of oil futures and 7DTE options on futures. Realized asymmetry is determined through the actual moments of intraday observed oil futures returns. We utilize returns sampled at five-minute intervals. Conversely, implied asymmetry is based on risk-neutral return cumulants derived from options on oil futures. We concentrate on option-implied third risk-neutral return cumulant for our analysis as it is indicative of subsequent developments, can be updated from the crude oil options market, and is founded in our theory.

Shifts in asymmetry are consistent over periods of time, indicating that the level of downside versus upside risks—as reflected in the relative pricing of 7DTE puts and calls—in the oil futures market is significantly different during these periods. This suggests that investors become more aware about potential market changes and downside versus upside risks to oil prices.

Changes in conditional asymmetry reflect shifts in how oil is perceived and often anticipate changes in supply and demand conditions. This measure contains information for predicting oil price changes. It is a predictor of oil futures returns, even when controlling for other candidate predictors. The COVID-19 pandemic is an example of this predictive power, as implied asymmetry indicated the heightened downside risk to oil and later predicted the rise in oil prices.

Our empirical contribution from 7DTE options and futures returns. Our key finding is that the (model-free) third risk-neutral return cumulant can predict variations in weekly oil futures returns. This finding is new and the third risk-neutral return cumulant survives the inclusion of other considered predictors from oil and equity markets. We provide empirical support based on futures written on WTI, Brent, Dubai, Heating Oil, and RBOB Gasoline.

The combination of the third risk-neutral return cumulant with additional variables, such as realized variance of oil futures returns (calculated from five-minute intraday intervals), leads to an improved ability to predict returns and increases the statistical significance of the predictors. The skewness derived from weekly options on the S&P 500 equity index is another variable that has predictive value, suggesting that both volatility and asymmetric returns in both oil and equity markets play a role in determining subsequent oil futures returns. Additionally, the weekly percentage changes in crude oil stock (available from the U.S. Energy Information Administration) also contributes to predicting short maturity oil futures returns. We also develop a quantitative trading strategy that takes advantage of past options momentum—based on 7DTE third risk-neutral return cumulant—to potentially generate profits in subsequent periods. This strategy is tested in real-world out-of-sample conditions to evaluate its effectiveness.

The remainder of this paper is organized as follows. Section 2 provides a review of the literature, followed, in Section 3, by a presentation of key features of 7DTE options data on WTI oil futures and the S&P 500 index. The question of oil futures return predictability is then examined through various angles (including R^2_{os} statistic and trading strategy) in Section 4. Next, a framework is presented in Section 5 that connects risk-neutral return cumulants to oil futures risk premiums.

2. Forecasting Oil Futures Returns and Relation to the Literature

A common question that has been addressed in various studies is the prediction of oil prices. For instance, [1,2] examine different models and data related to oil prices. Their aim is to determine whether there is predictability in oil price movements and how effective oil futures markets and survey forecasts are in predicting oil prices. Our approach differs in that we focus on using options data to better understand the predictability of weekly (7DTE) futures returns, taking into account the impact of jumps.

Our empirical study is motivated by the insights from a tractable model of oil futures risk premiums without imposing any restrictive assumptions about the stochastic discount factor (SDF) projection. Several recent papers, including [3–7], have examined the impact of different predictors, focusing on both their ability to accurately forecast and their performance on data that was not used for forecasting.

Ref. [7] use an approach commonly seen in empirical studies to investigate the predictability of oil prices. They construct forecast combinations from several individual predictor forecasts and find that these combined forecasts are more accurate than assuming no change in prices. In particular, they observe significant reductions in mean square forecast errors and improved directional accuracy using combination forecasts compared to the no-change forecast. However, when examining forecast accuracy for oil prices, the authors find no significant improvements in forecast errors or directional accuracy. They also note that using these forecasts to inform investment and hedging decisions does not result in superior economic value for investors. This suggests that the statistical and economic significance of oil price forecasts may be affected by how the underlying price series is constructed. In contrast, our study does not involve predicting oil prices but instead centers on forecasting oil futures returns.

This study is distinct from previous research on the impact of oil price shocks on the economy (such as [8,9]. Specifically, we examine short maturity futures return predictive regressions and examine their significance in understanding risk preferences embedded in the properties of risk-neutral return cumulants of oil futures returns.

Our approach involves incorporating information from weekly oil options, while also taking into consideration the impact of jump risks on futures returns and their expected behavior according to risk-neutral cumulants. This differs from other studies (such as [10–15]), which do not take into account the significance of option market variables in predicting oil futures returns.

While [16] examine energy risk premiums, they do not specifically address time-series predictability. Our study connects developments in 7DTE option prices to the predictability of subsequent short maturity oil futures returns.

Ref. [17] investigate the relationship between the skewness of commodity futures returns and expected returns. They find that a strategy focusing on buying futures with highly negative skewness and selling those with highly positive skewness can generate significant excess returns, even after controlling for risk factors. This suggests that the presence of a tradeable skewness factor plays a role in explaining variations in commodity returns, beyond traditional risk premiums. These findings align with investors' preferences for skewness based on cumulative prospect theory, as well as their selective hedging practices.

Ref. [18] conduct a study on the behavior of WTI and Brent crude oil prices, specifically focusing on the debate surrounding the regionalization and globalization of the two oil markets. They utilize a Dynamic Time Warping technique to identify instances of decoupling between the two oil price series. The results of their study suggest that WTI and Brent prices can decouple and recouple based on local market conditions, indicating that the WTI/Brent market is not consistently integrated.

The study undertaken by [19] investigates the influence of various fundamental factors and financial indicators on the realized volatility of WTI. A time-varying parameter vector autoregression model with stochastic volatility is used to analyze weekly data from January 2008 to October 2021. The results revealed that the volatility of WTI oil price is affected by shocks in oil production, oil inventories, the U.S. dollar index, and VIX. On the other hand, it decreases in response to shocks in the U.S. economic activity. Of all the factors, the VIX index has the most significant impact on the volatility of WTI oil price. These findings shed light on the evolving nature and determinants of WTI oil price volatility.

The idea of characterizing risk-neutral moments—as presented by [20,21]—has been applied in a number of recent studies. Examples of such research include [22–24]. Our study places emphasis on distinguishing between downside and upside risks extracted from 7DTE put and call options for WTI crude oil. We show that this distinction has implications for investment management in the 7DTE energy commodities markets.

3. Data on Short Maturity (7DTE) Options and Oil Futures

There has been limited investigation into the information contained in crude oil options with short maturity. To investigate further, let F_t represent the date-t price of the oil futures contract at the beginning of the options expiration cycle. Additionally, $F_{t+\Delta}$ represents the futures price at the expiration date of options at $t + \Delta$, where Δ corresponds to a week (seven days). The (excess) return of a fully collateralized long position in oil futures contract over seven days is $\frac{F_{t+\Delta}}{F_t} - 1$.

WTI crude oil serves as the underlier for the oil futures contract, which is listed on the New York Mercantile Exchange. Price data for WTI crude oil is provided by the Chicago Mercantile Exchange and includes spot prices, futures prices, and options on oil futures. Our dataset combines information on futures and options prices, specifically excluding in-the-money options.

The dataset on oil futures prices, including those for the S&P 500 equity index, is constructed over the weekly options expiration cycles (Friday to Friday). Our data covers the period from 12 August 2016, to 24 February 2023, which includes a total of 341 option expiration cycles. This period encompasses the time-series of model-free risk-neutral return cumulants and captures the COVID-19 crisis period, which poses some challenges due to unprecedented volatility levels, but also presents informative insights on uncertainty and investor preferences. To address these challenges, we analyze empirical models that predict the level of the oil futures returns.

The options available have a maturity of seven days, with an average of 45 puts and 46 calls on WTI futures at the beginning of each option expiration cycle, making it suitable for accurately estimating the higher-order risk-neutral return cumulants. The data on S&P 500 equity index options is from the Chicago Board of Trade. See Table 1 for the summary statistics on the number of put and call options.

Table 1. Number of OTM puts and calls employed in the construction of 7DTE risk-neutral return cumulants.

	Mean	SD	Min.	5th	25th	50th	75th	95th	Max.
WTI crude oil futures: Number of OTM puts	45	29	8	12	19	46	65	95	182
WTI crude oil futures: Number of OTM calls	46	32	11	13	20	44	62	101	203
S&P 500 equity index: Number of OTM puts	98	53	14	36	57	83	136	193	322
S&P 500 equity index: Number of OTM calls	35	24	8	14	19	26	44	87	158

The time frame of our study is confined to 12 August 2016, to 24 February 2023, as we use the weekly (7DTE) options on crude oil futures and the S&P 500 equity index. This period was chosen due to the need for consistent and accurate data at regular intervals, as well as reliable options-derived quantities. Tabulated are the summary statistics on OTM puts and calls at the beginning of the options expiration cycles (on Friday). The options data for WTI crude oil futures are obtained from the Chicago Mercantile Exchange, while the data for matching S&P 500 equity options are obtained from the Chicago Board of Trade. The standard deviation is shown in the column "SD". Our analysis covers a total of 341 weekly option expiration cycles.

Table 2 displays the characteristics of five futures contracts related to oil, namely (i) WTI, (ii) Brent, (iii) Dubai, (iv) Heating Oil, and (v) RBOB Gasoline. In Panel A, we present the summary of returns of a long position in these contracts, while in Panel B, we show the annualized volatility over weekly intervals, computed from intraday returns measured at five-minute intervals. As we analyze the correlation patterns of futures returns in Panels C and D, we observe that the first extracted principal component, which represents the average return factor, explains 78.5% of the common variation and has a positive relationship with the returns of all five oil futures contracts. The second factor, responsible for 10.5% of the common variation, is most influenced by Dubai, while the third principal component, accounting for 4.5% of the variation, is more affected by Brent in a positive direction and by Heating Oil in a negative direction. Figure 1 provides a visual representation of crude oil futures prices at the beginning of oil option expiration cycles.

Table 2. Summary statistics of weekly oil futures returns and volatility of futures returns.

	Mean (%)	SD (%)	Block Bootstrap Lower	Block Bootstrap Upper	NW[p]	Min.	Max.	Acf	Skewness	Kurtosis	$\mathbb{1}_{\{z>0\}}$ (%)
					Panel A: Oil futures returns, $\frac{F_{t+\Delta}}{F_t}-1$ (weekly, %)						
WTI futures	0.24	5.86	⌊−0.32	0.78⌋	0.46	−32.3	24.7	0.11	−0.7	5.9	55
Brent futures	0.30	5.08	⌊−0.18	0.74⌋	0.29	−20.9	23.3	0.00	0.0	2.9	56
Dubai futures	0.31	4.89	⌊−0.26	0.85⌋	0.32	−20.9	35.6	0.11	1.2	13.1	55
Heating Oil futures	0.34	5.31	⌊−0.11	0.80⌋	0.23	−24.1	33.3	−0.01	0.5	6.3	53
RBOB Gasoline futures	0.40	6.13	⌊−0.22	0.97⌋	0.27	−33.0	24.4	0.08	−0.4	5.2	53
Equal weight basket	0.32	4.84	⌊−0.18	0.81⌋	0.28	−22.4	25.1	0.09	0.01	4.1	55
					Panel B: Volatility of oil futures returns (from intraday returns, annualized (%))						
WTI futures	29.0	32.8	⌊24.6	35.0⌋	0.00	9.9	539.2	0.47	11.9	175.4	
Brent futures	27.0	15.4	⌊24.3	30.3⌋	0.00	10.9	163.6	0.73	4.7	31.4	
Dubai futures	27.7	34.3	⌊23.1	33.5⌋	0.00	1.2	349.6	0.36	4.4	28.4	
Heating Oil futures	24.6	13.1	⌊22.0	27.3⌋	0.00	11.7	121.4	0.79	3.3	15.8	
RBOB Gasoline futures	27.6	17.2	⌊24.5	31.5⌋	0.00	13.9	155.8	0.88	4.8	28.4	
	Panel C: Return correlations					Panel D: Correlation between return volatilities					
	WTI	Brent	Dubai	Heating Oil		WTI	Brent	Dubai	Heating Oil		
Brent futures	0.86					0.81					
Dubai futures	0.61	0.58				0.48	0.70				
Heating Oil futures	0.85	0.77	0.62			0.71	0.91	0.70			
RBOB Gasoline futures	0.81	0.81	0.57	0.79		0.76	0.92	0.65	0.87		

The time frame of our study is confined to 12 August 2016, to 24 February 2023, as we use the weekly (7DTE) options on crude oil futures and weekly options on the S&P 500 equity index. All reported returns data is expressed in weekly units. The volatility is annualized and computed from intraday returns, as follows: Weekly (intraday) variance $= \sum_{i=1}^{N}\{z_{t,i}\}^2$, where $z_{t,i} = \log(F_{t,\frac{i}{N}}) - \log(F_{t,\frac{i-1}{N}})$, where N is the number of return observations in a trading week (i.e., $N = 12 \times 6.5 \times 5$). We compute the equal weighted return across the five crude oil futures contracts (i.e., WTI, Brent, Dubai, Heating Oil, and RBOB Gasoline), as $z_{t+\Delta}^{\text{basket, oil}} \equiv \sum_{i=1}^{5}\frac{1}{5}(\frac{F_{t+\Delta}^i}{F_t^i}-1)$. The realized futures returns volatility are based on return observations over five-minute intervals (except for Dubai for which intraday data is unavailable). The source of the matched futures and options data is Chicago Mercantile Exchange. The standard deviation is shown in the column "SD", and Acf is the first-order autocorrelation. Our analysis covers a total of 341 weekly option expiration cycles.

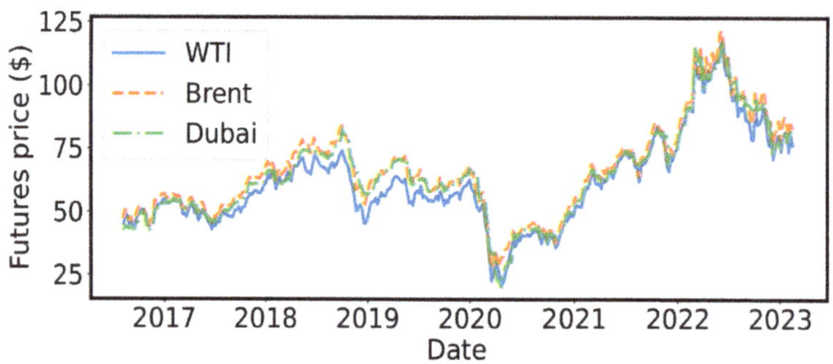

Figure 1. *Cont.*

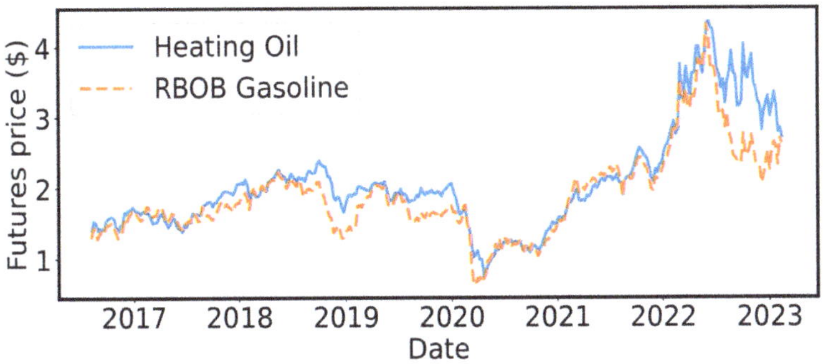

Figure 1. Crude oil prices at the beginning of each option expiration cycle on Friday. We graph the value of oil futures at the start of each weekly options expiration cycle, specifically at the close of trading on Fridays. We have data for 341 cycles, starting from 12 August 2016 and ending on 24 February 2023.

4. Short Maturity (7DTE) Oil Futures Return Predictability

We define the time-varying 7DTE risk-neutral return cumulants as follows:

$$\kappa_{1,t}^{\mathbb{Q},\text{oil}} \equiv \mathbb{E}_t^{\mathbb{Q}}\left(\frac{F_{t+\Delta}}{F_t} - 1\right) = 0, \tag{1}$$

$$\kappa_{2,t}^{\mathbb{Q},\text{oil}} \equiv \mathbb{E}_t^{\mathbb{Q}}\left(\{\frac{F_{t+\Delta}}{F_t} - 1 - \kappa_{1,t}^{\mathbb{Q}}\}^2\right), \tag{2}$$

$$\kappa_{3,t}^{\mathbb{Q},\text{oil}} \equiv \mathbb{E}_t^{\mathbb{Q}}\left(\{\frac{F_{t+\Delta}}{F_t} - 1 - \kappa_{1,t}^{\mathbb{Q}}\}^3\right), \quad \text{and} \tag{3}$$

$$\kappa_{4,t}^{\mathbb{Q},\text{oil}} \equiv \mathbb{E}_t^{\mathbb{Q}}\left(\{\frac{F_{t+\Delta}}{F_t} - 1 - \kappa_{1,t}^{\mathbb{Q}}\}^4\right) - 3\,(\kappa_{2,t}^{\mathbb{Q}})^2, \tag{4}$$

where $\mathbb{E}_t^{\mathbb{Q}}(\cdot)$ denotes conditional expectation under the risk-neutral probability measure $\mathbb{Q}$. Since $\mathbb{E}_t^{\mathbb{Q}}(F_{t+\Delta}) = F_t$ (the martingale condition for futures), the first $\mathbb{Q}$ cumulant is zero. Hence, $\kappa_{1,t}^{\mathbb{Q},\text{oil}}$ contains *no* information about forecasting short maturity oil futures returns $\frac{F_{t+\Delta}}{F_t} - 1$.

In our predictive regressions, we focus on measuring risk-neutral return cumulants empirically by utilizing model-free analogs. These measures do not rely on a specific model and are derived from current prices of oil options with one-week maturity and varying strike prices. This approach is based on the notion that weekly option prices reflect the market's anticipation of return payoffs and, specifically, the jump risks associated with oil, which drive higher-order return cumulants.

Following [20], we have, for $n = 2, 3, 4$, as follows:

$$\mathbb{E}_t^{\mathbb{Q}}\left(\{\frac{F_{t+\Delta}}{F_t} - 1\}^n\right) = \int_{K<F_t} \mathrm{w}[K]\,\mathrm{put}_t[K]\,dK + \int_{K>F_t} \mathrm{w}[K]\,\mathrm{call}_t[K]\,dK, \tag{5}$$

$$\text{with } \mathrm{w}[K] = \frac{R_t^{\text{rf}}(n-1)n\left(\frac{K}{F_t} - 1\right)^{n-2}}{F_t^2}. \tag{6}$$

Here, R_t^{rf} is the gross risk-free return over one week, and $\mathrm{put}_t[K]$ ($\mathrm{call}_t[K]$) are the date-t price of the 7DTE put (call) option, with strike price K, that expires at date $t + \Delta$. These higher-order risk-neutral return cumulants are computed at the beginning of the weekly option expiration cycle.

In economic terms, the second risk-neutral return cumulant represents the conditional return variance when evaluated under the risk-neutral measure, while the third risk-neutral return cumulant reflects conditional return asymmetries. Unlike the S&P 500 index, which demonstrates negative return asymmetries, the oil futures market displays both negative and positive asymmetries. From Table 3, we observe that the 7DTE third risk-neutral return cumulant is negative in 68% of the data points and positive in 32%.

Table 3. Summary statistics of weekly predictors constructed from options and intraday data.

	Mean	SD	Bootstrap Block Lower	Bootstrap Block Upper	NW[p]	Min.	Max.	Acf	Skewness	Kurtosis	$\mathbb{1}_{\{a>0\}}$ (%)
$\kappa_{2,t}^{\mathbb{Q},\text{oil}}$	0.0042	0.0105	$\lfloor$0.0026	0.0065$\rfloor$	0.00	0.0003	0.1328	0.66	8.12	80.3	
$\kappa_{3,t}^{\mathbb{Q},\text{oil}}$	−0.00012	0.00185	$\lfloor$−0.00033	0.00001$\rfloor$	0.24	−0.03211	0.00581	0.17	−15.10	263.6	32
$\kappa_{4,t}^{\mathbb{Q},\text{oil}}$	0.00032	0.00360	$\lfloor$0.00003	0.00083$\rfloor$	0.20	−0.00121	0.06442	0.21	16.92	299.9	
$\text{Skewness}_t^{\mathbb{Q},\text{oil}}$	−0.1773	0.47	$\lfloor$−0.26	−0.09$\rfloor$	0.00	−1.37	1.87	0.62	0.43	1.27	32
$\text{Kurtosis}_t^{\mathbb{Q},\text{oil}}$	6.2	2.4	$\lfloor$5.8	6.5$\rfloor$	0.00	2.8	26.2	0.43	3.56	21.15	
$\text{Variance}_t^{\mathbb{P},\text{oil},5\text{ min}}$	0.0037	0.0306	$\lfloor$0.0013	0.0077$\rfloor$	0.059	0.0002	0.5591	0.12	17.76	322.81	
$\text{Skewness}_t^{\mathbb{P},\text{oil},5\text{ min}}$	−0.1209	1.25	$\lfloor$−0.25	−0.02$\rfloor$	0.08	−9.32	6.63	−0.02	−0.60	12.51	44
$\kappa_{2,t}^{\mathbb{Q},\text{equity}}$	0.00065	0.00116	$\lfloor$0.00047	0.00089$\rfloor$	0.00	0.00006	0.01359	0.78	6.87	61.56	
$\kappa_{3,t}^{\mathbb{Q},\text{equity}}$	−0.000027	0.00010	$\lfloor$−0.00005	−0.00001$\rfloor$	0.00	−0.00107	0.00000	0.71	−8.54	79.77	0
$\kappa_{4,t}^{\mathbb{Q},\text{equity}}$	0.0000024	0.00001	$\lfloor$0.00000	0.00000$\rfloor$	0.02	0.00000	0.00021	0.51	13.20	200.50	
$\text{Skewness}_t^{\mathbb{Q},\text{equity}}$	−1.3	0.5	$\lfloor$−1.3	−1.2$\rfloor$	0.00	−2.7	−0.1	0.61	−0.66	0.22	0
$\text{Kurtosis}_t^{\mathbb{Q},\text{equity}}$	7.4	4.8	$\lfloor$6.6	8.2$\rfloor$	0.00	2.1	48.3	0.51	3.35	18.49	
$\text{Variance}_t^{\mathbb{P},\text{equity},5\text{ min}}$	0.00048	0.00116	$\lfloor$0.00032	0.00071$\rfloor$	0.00	0.00002	0.01443	0.79	8.33	84.51	
$\text{Skewness}_t^{\mathbb{P},\text{equity},5\text{ min}}$	−0.17	0.66	$\lfloor$−0.24	−0.11$\rfloor$	0.00	−4.78	1.71	0.05	−2.41	14.55	40
$\text{EIA}_t^{\text{stock growth}} \times 100$	−0.10	0.56	$\lfloor$−0.18	−0.02$\rfloor$	0.03	−1.72	2.26	0.37	0.61	1.44	41
$\text{EIA}_t^{\text{production growth}} \times 100$	0.11	2.23	$\lfloor$−0.02	0.23$\rfloor$	0.19	−13.98	12.31	−0.20	−0.85	16.02	45
$\text{EIA}_t^{\text{import growth}} \times 100$	−0.10	9.64	$\lfloor$−0.42	0.28$\rfloor$	0.70	−28.38	32.60	−0.53	0.22	0.52	47

The time frame of our study is confined to 12 August 2016, to 24 February 2023, as we use the weekly (7DTE) options on crude oil futures and the S&P 500 equity index. The source of the matched futures and options data is Chicago Mercantile Exchange and Chicago Board of Trade. All data is expressed in weekly units. The 7DTE higher-order cumulants, $\kappa_{n,t}^{\mathbb{Q}}$, are constructed based on both WTI crude oil options and the S&P 500 equity options. The realized variances are based on return observations over five-minute intervals. Our estimates imply an annualized $\mathbb{P}$ ($\mathbb{Q}$) measure oil volatility of 39.2% (28.0%). Acf is the first-order autocorrelation. Our analysis covers a total of 341 weekly option expiration cycles.

The econometric model that we consider is

$$\underbrace{\frac{F_{t+\Delta}}{F_t} - 1}_{\text{weekly oil futures returns}} = \text{constant} + \text{b}^{\text{squared}} \kappa_{2,t}^{\mathbb{Q},\text{oil}} + \text{b}^{\text{cubic}} \kappa_{3,t}^{\mathbb{Q},\text{oil}} + \text{b}^{\text{quartic}} \kappa_{4,t}^{\mathbb{Q},\text{oil}} + \epsilon_{t+\Delta}. \quad (7)$$

We use data from options prices at the beginning of a weekly option expiration period to make predictions about the returns of oil futures. The values and characteristics of these futures prices and return cumulants are influenced by the potential for large oil price fluctuations.

Our predictive exercises are based on linear regressions that use lagged predictor variables to model the (excess) returns of oil futures. The summary statistics and empirical properties for these predictors, which come from both the oil and equity markets, are shown in Table 3. The first-order autocorrelation coefficients—displayed in the "Acf" column—for the predictors are not high. This matters because typically, predictors that have near-unit-root dynamics can lead to inference problems in predictive regressions.

We examine the estimated slope coefficients in predictive regressions and their statistical significance using the p-values of the HAC estimator of Newey and West, with the lag selected automatically. These p-values, designated as NW[p], allow us to determine the level of significance of the predictive coefficients. Additionally, we assess the adequacy of the forecasts by calculating the goodness-of-fit adjusted R^2 ($\overline{R}^2$) value.

The field of commodities has researched methods for forecasting futures returns, but evidence on forecasting 7DTE oil futures returns using 7DTE risk-neutral return cumulants is lacking. This predictive association in Section 5. As a result, our focus is on models in this class that rely on theory. Developing our estimates, our model specifications also include nonstandard models that utilize high-frequency realized returns. These models emphasize the importance of persistence as well as the added predictive power of prior variances and quantities that reflect the perception of jump risks. This can help inform the development of oil models.

Table 4 presents the outcomes of univariate regressions (aligning with multivariate regressions) of the type $\frac{F_{t+\Delta}}{F_t} - 1 = \text{constant} + \mathrm{b} \times \text{Predictor}_t + \epsilon_{t+\Delta}$. Figure 2 plots the time-variation in $\frac{F_{t+\Delta}}{F_t} - 1$ of WTI futures whereas Figure 3 displays the 7DTE $\text{Skewness}_t^{\mathbb{Q},\text{oil}}$. We use seven predictors from the oil market, seven predictors from the equity market, and three predictors from U.S. Energy Information Administration (EIA). We construct the following predictors:

1. $\mathbb{Q}$ skewness from weekly oil options ($\text{Skewness}_t^{\mathbb{Q},\text{oil}}$). This weekly variable is $\frac{\kappa_{3,t}^{\mathbb{Q},\text{oil}}}{\{\kappa_{2,t}^{\mathbb{Q},\text{oil}}\}^{3/2}}$.
2. $\mathbb{Q}$ excess kurtosis from weekly oil options ($\text{Kurtosis}_t^{\mathbb{Q},\text{oil}}$). This weekly variable is $\frac{\kappa_{4,t}^{\mathbb{Q},\text{oil}}}{\{\kappa_{2,t}^{\mathbb{Q},\text{oil}}\}^{2}}$.
3. Realized variance of oil futures returns ($\text{Variance}_t^{\mathbb{P},\text{oil},5\text{ min}}$). This weekly variable is based on oil futures returns sampled at five-minute intervals.
4. Realized skewness from oil futures returns ($\text{Skewness}_t^{\mathbb{P},\text{oil},5\text{ min}}$). This weekly variable is based on oil futures returns sampled at five-minute intervals.
5. $\mathbb{Q}$ second equity return cumulant ($\kappa_{2,t}^{\mathbb{Q},\text{equity}}$). This is based on weekly S&P 500 equity index options prices. We use $\mathbb{E}_t^{\mathbb{Q}}\left(\{\frac{S_{t+\Delta}}{S_t} - R_t^{\text{rf}}\}^n\right) = \int_{K<S_t R_t^{\text{rf}}} \mathrm{w}[K]\,\text{put}_t[K]\,dK + \int_{K>S_t R_t^{\text{rf}}} \mathrm{w}[K]\,\text{call}_t[K]\,dK$, with $\mathrm{w}[K] = \frac{R_t^{\text{rf}}(n-1)n\left(\frac{K}{S_t} - R_t^{\text{rf}}\right)^{n-2}}{S_t^2}$.
6. $\mathbb{Q}$ third equity return cumulant ($\kappa_{3,t}^{\mathbb{Q},\text{equity}}$). This is based on weekly S&P 500 equity index options prices.
7. $\mathbb{Q}$ fourth equity return cumulant ($\kappa_{4,t}^{\mathbb{Q},\text{equity}}$). This is based on weekly S&P 500 equity index options prices.
8. $\mathbb{Q}$ skewness from weekly equity options ($\text{Skewness}_t^{\mathbb{Q},\text{equity}}$). This weekly variable is $\frac{\kappa_{3,t}^{\mathbb{Q},\text{equity}}}{\{\kappa_{2,t}^{\mathbb{Q},\text{equity}}\}^{3/2}}$. We use S&P 500 equity index options prices.
9. $\mathbb{Q}$ excess kurtosis from weekly equity options ($\text{Kurtosis}_t^{\mathbb{Q},\text{equity}}$). This weekly variable is $\frac{\kappa_{4,t}^{\mathbb{Q},\text{equity}}}{\{\kappa_{2,t}^{\mathbb{Q},\text{equity}}\}^{2}}$. We use S&P 500 equity index options prices.
10. Realized variance of equity futures returns ($\text{Variance}_t^{\mathbb{P},\text{equity},5\text{ min}}$). This weekly variable is based on S&P 500 E-mini equity futures returns sampled at five-minute intervals.
11. Realized skewness from equity futures returns ($\text{Skewness}_t^{\mathbb{P},\text{equity},5\text{ min}}$). This weekly variable is based on S&P 500 E-mini equity futures returns sampled at five-minute intervals.
12. Growth rate of crude oil stock ($\text{EIA}_t^{\text{stock growth}}$). This is constructed based on EIA releases of petroleum status reports (https://www.eia.gov/petroleum/supply/weekly/, accessed on 14 May 2024). The underlying quantity is crude oil stock.
13. Growth rate of crude oil production ($\text{EIA}_t^{\text{production growth}}$). The underlying variable is domestic crude oil production (EIA estimates).
14. Growth rate of crude oil imports ($\text{EIA}_t^{\text{import growth}}$). The underlying variable is crude oil imports (EIA estimates).

Table 4. Short-maturity (weekly) predictive regression results for WTI crude oil futures returns.

Predictor (Univariate)	Constant	NW[*p*]	b	NW[*p*]	$\overline{R}^2$ (%)	CORR	Predict (Yes or No)
Panel A: Three 7DTE higher-order risk-neutral return cumulants from oil market							
$\kappa_{2,t}^{\mathbb{Q},\text{oil}}$	0.00	0.45	0.07	0.88	−0.28	0.01	No
$\kappa_{3,t}^{\mathbb{Q},\text{oil}}$	0.00	0.55	−3.57	*0.01*	0.98	−0.11	Yes
$\kappa_{4,t}^{\mathbb{Q},\text{oil}}$	0.00	0.52	0.95	*0.01*	0.05	0.06	Yes
Panel B: Other predictors from oil markets							
$\text{Skewness}_t^{\mathbb{Q},\text{oil}}$	0.00	0.64	−0.01	0.40	−0.11	−0.04	No
$\text{Kurtosis}_t^{\mathbb{Q},\text{oil}}$	−0.01	0.48	0.00	0.21	0.04	0.06	No
$\text{Variance}_t^{\mathbb{P},\text{oil},5\text{ min}}$	0.00	0.56	0.08	0.07	−0.13	0.04	Yes
$\text{Skewness}_t^{\mathbb{P},\text{oil},5\text{ min}}$	0.00	0.57	−0.00	0.33	−0.10	−0.05	No
Panel C: Predictors from equity markets							
$\kappa_{2,t}^{\mathbb{Q},\text{equity}}$	0.01	0.11	−4.75	0.33	0.59	−0.09	No
$\kappa_{3,t}^{\mathbb{Q},\text{equity}}$	0.00	0.11	88.92	0.14	1.88	0.15	No
$\kappa_{4,t}^{\mathbb{Q},\text{equity}}$	0.00	0.32	−295.6	0.30	0.13	−0.07	No
$\text{Skewness}_t^{\mathbb{Q},\text{equity}}$	−0.01	0.16	−0.01	*0.02*	0.40	−0.08	Yes
$\text{Kurtosis}_t^{\mathbb{Q},\text{equity}}$	−0.00	0.58	0.00	0.14	0.14	0.07	No
$\text{Variance}_t^{\mathbb{P},\text{equity},5\text{ min}}$	0.01	0.09	−6.2	0.23	1.22	−0.12	No
$\text{Skewness}_t^{\mathbb{P},\text{equity},5\text{ min}}$	0.00	0.49	0.00	0.81	−0.29	0.01	No
Panel D: Predictors from the Energy Information Administration (EIA)							
$\text{EIA}_t^{\text{stock growth}}$	0.00	0.79	−1.39	*0.03*	1.51	−0.15	Yes
$\text{EIA}_t^{\text{production growth}}$	0.00	0.48	−0.06	0.69	−0.25	−0.02	No
$\text{EIA}_t^{\text{import growth}}$	0.00	0.50	−0.03	0.29	0.01	−0.06	No

The data analyzed involves a predictor based on oil and equity markets to forecast the returns of a fully collateralized long position in weekly futures contract on WTI crude oil. The results are presented in the form of univariate predictive regressions expressed as follows: $\underbrace{\frac{F_{t+\Delta}}{F_t} - 1}_{\text{weekly WTI futures return}} = \text{constant} + \text{b} \times \text{Predictor}_t + \epsilon_{t+\Delta}$, where $\frac{F_{t+\Delta}}{F_t} - 1$ represents the return of the aforementioned position. Reported are the b estimates, as well as two-sided *p*-values for the null hypothesis b $= 0$, denoted by NW[*p*], based on the procedure in Newey and West with the lag automatically selected. The adjusted R^2, denoted by $\overline{R}^2$, is also presented as a measure of goodness-of-fit, expressed as a percentage. The correlation between the predictor and $\frac{F_{t+\Delta}}{F_t} - 1$ is reported as CORR. The predictive regressions are conducted over weekly options expiration cycles, spanning from Friday to Friday. The data is collected from 12 August 2016, to 24 February 2023, covering a total of 341 option expiration cycles.

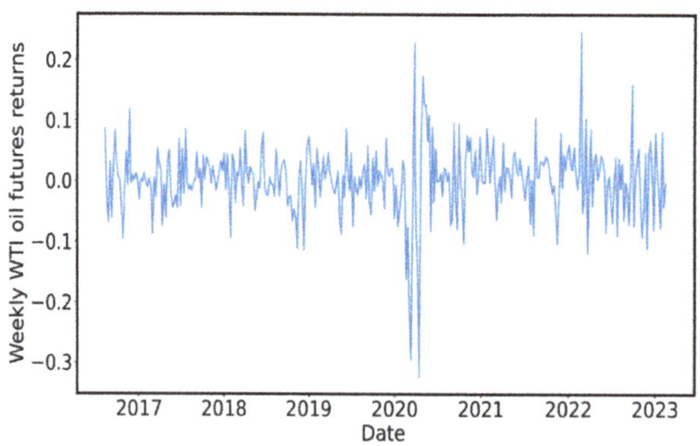

Figure 2. Weekly (Friday to Friday) WTI oil futures returns. We plot the change in the value of oil futures over a weekly options expiration cycle (Friday to Friday), calculated as $\frac{F_{t+\Delta}}{F_t} - 1$. The market for these futures is based on West Texas Intermediate (WTI) crude oil. Our dataset tracks the prices for 341 weekly option expiration cycles, spanning from 12 August 2016, to 24 February 2023.

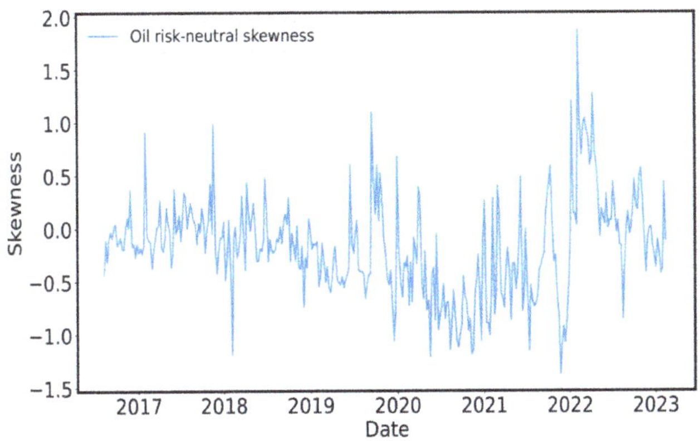

Figure 3. Measure of asymmetry of the risk-neutral return distribution of oil futures. We display the risk-neutral skewness of oil futures over weekly options expiration cycles, with WTI crude oil serving as the underlying asset for the futures. The skewness is calculated for each weekly options expiration cycle from 12 August 2016, to 24 February 2023, which covers a total of 341 cycles. Our formula for skewness is $\text{Skewness}_t^{\mathbb{Q},\text{oil}} = \mathbb{E}_t^{\mathbb{Q}}(\{\frac{F_{t+\Delta}}{F_t} - 1\}^3)/\{\mathbb{E}_t^{\mathbb{Q}}(\{\frac{F_{t+\Delta}}{F_t} - 1\}^2)\}^{3/2}$. Specifically, $\mathbb{E}_t^{\mathbb{Q}}(\{\frac{F_{t+\Delta}}{F_t} - 1\}^n) = \int_{K<F_t} \mathrm{w}[K]\,\text{put}_t[K]\,dK + \int_{K>F_t} \mathrm{w}[K]\,\text{call}_t[K]\,dK$, with $\mathrm{w}[K] = \frac{R_t^{\text{rf}}(n-1)n(\frac{K}{F_t}-1)^{n-2}}{F_t^2}$.

Adhering to our approach, we analyze the influence of various predictive factors such as oil-specific variables and equity market-specific variables on the forecasting performance of our model. We find that the coefficient estimates for the third risk-neutral return cumulant, $\kappa_{3,t}^{\mathbb{Q},\text{oil}}$, and the fourth risk-neutral return cumulant, $\kappa_{4,t}^{\mathbb{Q},\text{oil}}$, are significant with negative and positive values, respectively. The estimate for the second risk-neutral return cumulant, $\kappa_{2,t}^{\mathbb{Q},\text{oil}}$, is close to zero and is not significant. Additionally, many other potential predictors are individually insignificant.

Despite this, the NW[p]-value for the slope coefficient related to the third risk-neutral return cumulant is below the two-sided 5% significance level, indicating significance. Similarly, the predictors $\text{Skewness}_t^{\mathbb{Q},\text{equity}}$ and $\text{EIA}_t^{\text{stock growth}}$ also have NW[p] values below 0.05 and are considered significant predictors. However, at the short maturity weekly forecasting horizon, these univariate predictors explain less than 2% of the variability in crude oil futures returns.

To gain a better understanding of the results in a wider empirical context, we investigate whether the third risk-neutral return cumulant ($\kappa_{3,t}^{\mathbb{Q},\text{oil}}$) maintains its predictive power when other variables are included in bivariate predictive regressions. Specifically, we examine short maturity regressions of the following form:

$$\frac{F_{t+\Delta}}{F_t} - 1 = \text{constant} + \mathrm{b}^{\text{cubic}}\,\kappa_{3,t}^{\mathbb{Q},\text{oil}} + \mathrm{b}^{\text{alter}}\,\text{Predictor}_t + \epsilon_{t+\Delta}. \tag{8}$$

The results in Table 5 show a consistent pattern that $\kappa_{3,t}^{\mathbb{Q},\text{oil}}$ remains a predictor of futures price changes, with $\mathrm{b}^{\text{cubic}}$ negative and statistically significant. This aligns with our theoretical framework presented in Section 5, which suggests that the third risk-neutral return cumulant captures important aspects of asymmetry as well as downside and upside jump risks. We find that $\kappa_{3,t}^{\mathbb{Q},\text{oil}}$ is not highly correlated with other predictors.

Table 5. Evidence from the bivariate predictive regressions (WTI crude oil futures).

Alternative Predictor	Constant	NW[p]	Predictor Is $\underbrace{\kappa_{3,t}^{\mathbb{Q},\text{oil}}}$		$\underbrace{\text{Alternative Predictor}}$		$\overline{R}^2$ (%)	Joint p	R^2_{os} (%)
			b^{cubic}	NW[p]	b^{alter}	NW[p]			
$\kappa_{2,t}^{\mathbb{Q},\text{oil}}$		0.00 0.15	−5.41	0.01	−0.52	0.28	1.23	0.01	0.39
$\kappa_{4,t}^{\mathbb{Q},\text{oil}}$		0.00 0.48	−9.46	0.00	−3.40	*0.01*	1.58	0.00	2.78
$\text{Skewness}_t^{\mathbb{Q},\text{oil}}$	0.00	0.64	−3.43	0.01	0.00	0.65	0.74	0.02	0.52
$\text{Kurtosis}_t^{\mathbb{Q},\text{oil}}$	−0.01	0.46	−3.56	0.01	0.00	0.21	1.02	0.01	1.25
$\text{Variance}_t^{\mathbb{P},\text{oil},5\text{ min}}$	0.00	0.32	−16.1	0.00	−0.82	*0.00*	3.47	0.00	4.10
$\text{Skewness}_t^{\mathbb{P},\text{oil},5\text{ min}}$	0.00	0.64	−3.45	0.01	0.00	0.53	0.79	0.03	1.08
$\kappa_{2,t}^{\mathbb{Q},\text{equity}}$	0.01	0.11	−3.97	0.01	−5.52	0.26	1.88	0.04	0.90
$\kappa_{3,t}^{\mathbb{Q},\text{equity}}$	0.00	0.13	−4.08	0.02	97.1	0.10	3.28	0.04	1.23
$\kappa_{4,t}^{\mathbb{Q},\text{equity}}$	0.00	0.38	−3.84	0.02	−357.9	0.21	1.32	0.04	1.21
$\text{Skewness}_t^{\mathbb{Q},\text{equity}}$	−0.01	0.12	−3.65	0.01	−0.01	*0.02*	1.46	0.00	0.96
$\text{Kurtosis}_t^{\mathbb{Q},\text{equity}}$	−0.00	0.50	−3.63	0.01	0.00	0.12	1.19	0.01	1.00
$\text{Variance}_t^{\mathbb{P},\text{equity},5\text{ min}}$	0.01	0.10	−3.98	0.02	−6.88	0.19	2.53	0.05	1.08
$\text{Skewness}_t^{\mathbb{P},\text{equity},5\text{ min}}$	0.00	0.56	−3.57	0.01	0.00	0.74	0.72	0.03	1.18
$\text{EIA}_t^{\text{stock growth}}$	−0.00	0.90	−3.97	0.00	−0.78	*0.01*	3.37	0.00	0.95
$\text{EIA}_t^{\text{production growth}}$	0.00	0.59	−3.55	0.01	−0.06	0.68	0.75	0.03	1.12
$\text{EIA}_t^{\text{import growth}}$	0.00	0.62	−3.64	0.01	−0.04	0.23	1.08	0.03	1.25

The data analyzed involves a predictor based on oil and equity markets to forecast the returns of a fully collateralized long position in weekly futures contract on WTI crude oil. The results are presented in the form of bivariate predictive regressions expressed as follows: $\underbrace{\frac{F_{t+\Delta}}{F_t} - 1}_{\text{weekly WTI futures return}} = \text{constant} + \text{b}^{\text{cubic}}\,\kappa_{3,t}^{\mathbb{Q},\text{oil}} + \text{b}^{\text{alter}}\,\text{Predictor}_t + \epsilon_{t+\Delta}$, where $\frac{F_{t+\Delta}}{F_t} - 1$ represents the return of the aforementioned position. Reported are the b estimates, as well as two-sided p-values for the null hypothesis $\text{b} = 0$, denoted by NW[p], based on the procedure in Newey and West with the lag automatically selected. The adjusted R^2, denoted by $\overline{R}^2$, is also presented as a measure of goodness-of-fit, expressed as a percentage. The predictive regressions are conducted over weekly options expiration cycles, spanning from Friday to Friday. The out-of-sample performance is reported as $R^2_{\text{os}} = 1 - \frac{\sum_{t=1}^{T}(z_t - \widehat{z}_{t,\text{full}})^2}{\sum_{t=1}^{T}(z_t - \widehat{z}_{t,\text{nested}})^2}$.

Additionally, the NW[p] values for four other variables are below 0.05, making them stand out as predictors: (i) $\kappa_{4,t}^{\mathbb{Q},\text{oil}}$, (ii) $\text{Variance}_t^{\mathbb{P},\text{oil},5\text{ min}}$, (iii) $\text{Skewness}_t^{\mathbb{Q},\text{equity}}$, and (iv) $\text{EIA}_t^{\text{stock growth}}$. The combination of $\kappa_{3,t}^{\mathbb{Q},\text{oil}}$ and $\text{Variance}_t^{\mathbb{P},\text{oil},5\text{ min}}$ has the highest significance and an $\overline{R}^2$ of 3.47%. Comparing these results with other predictors, the slope coefficients (b^{alter}) are not statistically significant and the $\overline{R}^2$ values are lower. However, incorporating S&P 500 equity index based predictors does increase the $\overline{R}^2$ values, suggesting that additional variables from the equity market may be helpful in explaining the variations in oil futures returns.

We further investigate the relationship between oil prices and the third risk-neutral return cumulant by using various approaches to construct the returns of a crude oil basket, including the use of several individual crude oil futures, equal weight basket of five crude oil futures, and regression analysis. Specifically, we construct an equal weight basket of five crude oil futures, including WTI, Brent, Dubai, Heating Oil, and RBOB Gasoline, as follows:

$$z_{t+\Delta}^{\text{basket, oil}} = \sum_{\text{i}=1}^{5} \frac{1}{5}\left(\frac{F_{t+\Delta}^{\text{i}}}{F_t^{\text{i}}} - 1\right). \tag{9}$$

We use this basket, labeled $z_{t+\Delta}^{\text{basket, oil}}$, to smooth out idiosyncratic variations in the five individual oil futures prices. The bivariate regressions in Table 6 shows that the coefficients for 7DTE $\kappa_{3,t}^{\mathbb{Q},\text{oil}}$ are negative, suggesting a significant relationship between $z_{t+\Delta}^{\text{basket, oil}}$ and crude oil options-based $\kappa_{3,t}^{\mathbb{Q},\text{oil}}$. Furthermore, the $\overline{R}^2$ values tend to improve on the bivariate counterparts in Table 5.

Table 6. Evidence from the bivariate predictive regressions (equal weight basket across five oil futures contracts).

Alternative Predictor	Constant	Predictor Is $\kappa_{3,t}^{\mathbb{Q},\text{oil}}$		Alternative Predictor		NW[p]	$\overline{R}^2$ (%)	Joint p	R^2_{os}
		NW[p]	b^{cubic}	NW[p]	b^{alter}				
$\kappa_{2,t}^{\mathbb{Q},\text{oil}}$	0.00	0.15	−4.92	0.01	−0.27	0.52	1.96	0.00	0.51
$\kappa_{4,t}^{\mathbb{Q},\text{oil}}$	0.00	0.33	−6.52	0.00	−1.46	0.21	2.00	0.00	1.56
$\text{Skewness}_t^{\mathbb{Q},\text{oil}}$	0.00	0.40	−3.91	0.00	0.00	0.75	1.79	0.00	0.25
$\text{Kurtosis}_t^{\mathbb{Q},\text{oil}}$	−0.01	0.47	−3.99	0.00	0.00	0.17	2.20	0.00	1.13
$\text{Variance}_t^{\mathbb{P},\text{oil},5\text{ min}}$	0.00	0.25	−11.10	0.00	−0.47	0.00	3.10	0.00	2.21
$\text{Skewness}_t^{\mathbb{P},\text{oil},5\text{ min}}$	0.00	0.44	−3.86	0.00	0.00	0.39	1.94	0.00	0.88
$\kappa_{2,t}^{\mathbb{Q},\text{equity}}$	0.01	0.03	−4.35	0.00	−4.97	0.19	3.23	0.00	0.68
$\kappa_{3,t}^{\mathbb{Q},\text{equity}}$	0.00	0.06	−4.42	0.00	80.79	0.06	4.45	0.00	0.97
$\kappa_{4,t}^{\mathbb{Q},\text{equity}}$	0.00	0.24	−4.20	0.00	−268.28	0.18	2.33	0.00	1.06
$\text{Skewness}_t^{\mathbb{Q},\text{equity}}$	−0.01	0.11	−4.07	0.00	−0.01	0.01	2.81	0.00	0.60
$\text{Kurtosis}_t^{\mathbb{Q},\text{equity}}$	0.00	0.48	−4.06	0.00	0.00	0.09	2.62	0.00	0.95
$\text{Variance}_t^{\mathbb{P},\text{equity},5\text{ min}}$	0.01	0.04	−4.34	0.00	−5.84	0.12	3.77	0.00	0.95
$\text{Skewness}_t^{\mathbb{P},\text{equity},5\text{ min}}$	0.00	0.39	−4.01	0.00	0.00	0.65	1.86	0.00	0.76
$\text{EIA}_t^{\text{stock growth}}$	0.00	0.60	−4.19	0.00	−0.88	0.09	2.85	0.00	0.81
$\text{EIA}_t^{\text{production growth}}$	0.00	0.38	−3.99	0.00	−0.03	0.77	1.80	0.00	0.82
$\text{EIA}_t^{\text{import growth}}$	0.00	0.40	−4.08	0.00	−0.04	0.10	2.49	0.00	1.04

We use regression analysis based on an equal weight basket of five crude oil futures: (i) WTI, (ii) Brent, (iii) Dubai, (iv) Heating Oil, and (v) RBOB Gasoline, as follows: $z_{t+\Delta}^{\text{basket, oil}} = \sum_{i=1}^{5} \frac{1}{5}(\frac{F_{t+\Delta}^i}{F_t^i} - 1)$. The return of the crude oil basket serves to smooth idiosyncratic variations in the oil prices. The data analyzed involves a predictor based on oil and equity markets to forecast the returns of a fully collateralized long position in weekly futures contract on WTI crude oil. The results are presented in the form of bivariate predictive regressions expressed as $\underbrace{\sum_{i=1}^{5} \frac{1}{5}(\frac{F_{t+\Delta}^i}{F_t^i} - 1)}_{\text{equal weight basket}} = \text{constant} + \text{b}^{\text{cubic}} \kappa_{3,t}^{\mathbb{Q},\text{oil}} + \text{b}^{\text{alter}}\,\text{Predictor}_t + \epsilon_{t+\Delta}$, where $\frac{F_{t+\Delta}^i}{F_t^i} - 1$ represents the return of the aforementioned individual futures position. Reported are the b estimates, as well as two-sided p-values for the null hypothesis $\text{b} = 0$, denoted by NW[p], based on the procedure in Newey and West with the lag automatically selected. The adjusted R^2, denoted by $\overline{R}^2$, is also presented as a measure of goodness-of-fit, expressed as a percentage. The out-of-sample performance is reported as $R^2_{\text{os}} = 1 - \frac{\sum_{t=1}^{T}(z_t - \widehat{z}_{t,\text{full}})^2}{\sum_{t=1}^{T}(z_t - \widehat{z}_{t,\text{nested}})^2}$.

Tables 7–10 analyze the impact of individual crude oil futures, respectively, for Brent, Dubai, Heating Oil, and RBOB Gasoline, on predicting weekly oil returns and finds that 7DTE $\kappa_{3,t}^{\mathbb{Q},\text{oil}}$ remains a relevant predictor. All in all, this suggests that the third risk-neutral return cumulant has predictive power for oil futures returns.

Table 7. Evidence from the bivariate predictive regressions (Brent oil futures).

Alternative Predictor	Constant	Predictor Is $\underbrace{\kappa_{3,t}^{\mathbb{Q},\text{oil}}}$		$\underbrace{\text{Alternative Predictor}}$		NW[p]	$\overline{R}^2$ (%)	Joint p
		NW[p]	$\mathsf{b}^{\text{cubic}}$	NW[p]	$\mathsf{b}^{\text{alter}}$			
$\kappa_{2,t}^{\mathbb{Q},\text{oil}}$		0.00 0.11	−3.59	0.08	−0.42	0.18	0.46	0.21
$\kappa_{4,t}^{\mathbb{Q},\text{oil}}$		0.00 0.28	−9.97	0.00	−4.53	0.00	2.11	0.00
$\text{Skewness}_t^{\mathbb{Q},\text{oil}}$	0.00	0.51	−1.90	0.20	−0.01	0.38	0.23	0.22
$\text{Kurtosis}_t^{\mathbb{Q},\text{oil}}$	0.00	0.69	−2.12	0.17	0.00	0.34	0.20	0.28
$\text{Variance}_t^{\mathbb{P},\text{oil},5\text{ min}}$	0.00	0.16	−15.59	0.00	−0.88	0.00	4.30	0.00
$\text{Skewness}_t^{\mathbb{P},\text{oil},5\text{ min}}$	0.00	0.41	−2.02	0.18	0.00	0.44	0.12	0.32
$\kappa_{2,t}^{\mathbb{Q},\text{equity}}$	0.00	0.17	−2.30	0.17	−2.37	0.61	0.31	0.37
$\kappa_{3,t}^{\mathbb{Q},\text{equity}}$	0.00	0.11	−2.40	0.18	52.12	0.34	1.01	0.28
$\kappa_{4,t}^{\mathbb{Q},\text{equity}}$	0.00	0.26	−2.26	0.17	−172.5	0.49	0.21	0.32
$\text{Skewness}_t^{\mathbb{Q},\text{equity}}$	−0.01	0.09	−2.21	0.15	−0.01	0.01	1.00	0.01
$\text{Kurtosis}_t^{\mathbb{Q},\text{equity}}$	0.00	0.54	−2.19	0.15	0.00	0.13	0.59	0.15
$\text{Variance}_t^{\mathbb{P},\text{equity},5\text{ min}}$	0.00	0.09	−2.36	0.17	−3.94	0.37	0.82	0.28
$\text{Skewness}_t^{\mathbb{P},\text{equity},5\text{ min}}$	0.00	0.32	−2.16	0.16	0.00	0.36	0.19	0.26
$\text{EIA}_t^{\text{stock growth}}$	0.00	0.55	−2.30	0.12	−0.75	0.14	0.72	0.12
$\text{EIA}_t^{\text{production growth}}$	0.00	0.36	−2.13	0.17	−0.02	0.87	0.02	0.37
$\text{EIA}_t^{\text{import growth}}$	0.00	0.38	−2.22	0.15	−0.05	0.05	0.87	0.06

The data analyzed involves a predictor based on oil and equity markets to forecast the returns of a fully collateralized long position in weekly futures contract on Brent oil futures. The results are presented in the form of bivariate predictive regressions expressed as follows: $\underbrace{\frac{F_{t+\Delta}}{F_t} - 1}_{\text{Brent}} = \text{constant} + \mathsf{b}^{\text{cubic}}\,\kappa_{3,t}^{\mathbb{Q},\text{oil}} + \mathsf{b}^{\text{alter}}\,\text{Predictor}_t + \epsilon_{t+\Delta}$, where $\frac{F_{t+\Delta}}{F_t} - 1$ represents the return of the aforementioned position. Reported are the b estimates, as well as two-sided p-values for the null hypothesis $\mathsf{b} = 0$, denoted by NW[p], based on the procedure in Newey and West with the lag automatically selected. The adjusted R^2, denoted by $\overline{R}^2$, is also presented as a measure of goodness-of-fit, expressed as a percentage. The predictive regressions are conducted over weekly options expiration cycles, spanning from Friday to Friday.

Table 8. Evidence from the bivariate predictive regressions (Dubai oil futures).

Alternative Predictor	Constant	Predictor Is $\underbrace{\kappa_{3,t}^{\mathbb{Q},\text{oil}}}$		$\underbrace{\text{Alternative Predictor}}$		NW[p]	$\overline{R}^2$ (%)	Joint p
		NW[p]	$\mathsf{b}^{\text{cubic}}$	NW[p]	$\mathsf{b}^{\text{alter}}$			
$\kappa_{2,t}^{\mathbb{Q},\text{oil}}$	0.01	0.04	−10.45	0.00	−0.82	0.12	9.56	0.00
$\kappa_{4,t}^{\mathbb{Q},\text{oil}}$	0.00	0.45	−9.43	0.01	−1.07	0.56	7.81	0.00
$\text{Skewness}_t^{\mathbb{Q},\text{oil}}$	0.00	0.36	−7.74	0.00	0.00	0.48	7.80	0.00
$\text{Kurtosis}_t^{\mathbb{Q},\text{oil}}$	0.00	0.59	−7.57	0.00	0.00	0.24	7.95	0.00
$\text{Variance}_t^{\mathbb{P},\text{oil},5\text{ min}}$	0.00	0.40	−11.48	0.00	−0.26	0.25	8.10	0.00
$\text{Skewness}_t^{\mathbb{P},\text{oil},5\text{ min}}$	0.00	0.58	−7.38	0.00	0.00	0.31	8.06	0.00
$\kappa_{2,t}^{\mathbb{Q},\text{equity}}$	0.01	0.00	−8.35	0.00	−10.46	0.00	13.79	0.00
$\kappa_{3,t}^{\mathbb{Q},\text{equity}}$	0.01	0.05	−8.25	0.00	123.5	0.00	13.69	0.00
$\kappa_{4,t}^{\mathbb{Q},\text{equity}}$	0.00	0.24	−8.04	0.00	−595.8	0.00	10.22	0.00
$\text{Skewness}_t^{\mathbb{Q},\text{equity}}$	−0.01	0.08	−7.68	0.00	−0.01	0.01	9.16	0.00
$\text{Kurtosis}_t^{\mathbb{Q},\text{equity}}$	−0.01	0.28	−7.68	0.00	0.00	0.04	9.05	0.00
$\text{Variance}_t^{\mathbb{P},\text{equity},5\text{ min}}$	0.01	0.02	−8.12	0.00	−8.79	0.00	12.03	0.00

Table 8. *Cont.*

Alternative Predictor	Constant	Predictor Is $\underbrace{\kappa_{3,t}^{\mathbb{Q},oil}}$		Alternative $\underbrace{\text{Predictor}}$		NW[p]	$\overline{R}^2$ (%)	Joint p
		NW[p]	b^{cubic}	NW[p]	b^{alter}			
$\text{Skewness}_t^{\mathbb{P},equity,5\ min}$	0.00	0.68	−7.55	0.00	0.00	0.67	7.86	0.00
$\text{EIA}_t^{stock\ growth}$	0.00	0.71	−7.76	0.00	−0.81	0.25	8.59	0.00
$\text{EIA}_t^{production\ growth}$	0.00	0.51	−7.58	0.00	0.01	0.91	7.71	0.00
$\text{EIA}_t^{import\ growth}$	0.00	0.51	−7.65	0.00	−0.04	0.24	8.24	0.00

The data analyzed involves a predictor based on oil and equity markets to forecast the returns of a fully collateralized long position in weekly futures contract on Dubai oil. The results are presented in the form of bivariate predictive regressions expressed as follows: $\underbrace{\frac{F_{t+\Delta}}{F_t} - 1}_{\text{Dubai}} = \text{constant} + b^{cubic}\,\kappa_{3,t}^{\mathbb{Q},oil} + b^{alter}\,\text{Predictor}_t + \epsilon_{t+\Delta}$, where $\frac{F_{t+\Delta}}{F_t} - 1$ represents the return of the aforementioned position. Reported are the b estimates, as well as two-sided p-values for the null hypothesis b = 0, denoted by NW[p], based on the procedure in Newey and West with the lag automatically selected. The adjusted R^2, denoted by $\overline{R}^2$, is also presented as a measure of goodness-of-fit, expressed as a percentage. The predictive regressions are conducted over weekly options expiration cycles, spanning from Friday to Friday.

Table 9. Evidence from the bivariate predictive regressions (Heating Oil futures).

Alternative Predictor	Constant	Predictor Is $\underbrace{\kappa_{3,t}^{\mathbb{Q},oil}}$		Alternative $\underbrace{\text{Predictor}}$		NW[p]	$\overline{R}^2$ (%)	Joint p
		NW[p]	b^{cubic}	NW[p]	b^{alter}			
$\kappa_{2,t}^{\mathbb{Q},oil}$	0.00	0.20	−3.91	0.01	−0.15	0.63	0.85	0.00
$\kappa_{2,t}^{\mathbb{Q},oil}$	0.00	0.26	−6.41	0.03	−1.76	0.20	1.09	0.00
$\text{Skewness}_t^{\mathbb{Q},oil}$	0.00	0.34	−3.32	0.00	0.00	0.88	0.80	0.00
$\text{Kurtosis}_t^{\mathbb{Q},oil}$	0.00	0.54	−3.36	0.00	0.00	0.21	1.10	0.00
$\text{Variance}_t^{\mathbb{P},oil,5\ min}$	0.00	0.23	−9.51	0.00	−0.40	0.02	1.63	0.00
$\text{Skewness}_t^{\mathbb{P},oil,5\ min}$	0.00	0.38	−3.16	0.00	0.00	0.17	1.13	0.00
$\kappa_{2,t}^{\mathbb{Q},equity}$	0.00	0.08	−3.50	0.00	−2.00	0.46	1.01	0.00
$\kappa_{3,t}^{\mathbb{Q},equity}$	0.00	0.11	−3.56	0.00	38.39	0.21	1.31	0.00
$\kappa_{4,t}^{\mathbb{Q},equity}$	0.00	0.25	−3.34	0.00	24.17	0.87	0.82	0.00
$\text{Skewness}_t^{\mathbb{Q},equity}$	−0.01	0.24	−3.43	0.00	−0.01	0.04	1.52	0.00
$\text{Kurtosis}_t^{\mathbb{Q},equity}$	0.00	0.72	−3.42	0.00	0.00	0.16	1.23	0.00
$\text{Variance}_t^{\mathbb{P},equity,5\ min}$	0.00	0.08	−3.52	0.00	−2.77	0.28	1.18	0.00
$\text{Skewness}_t^{\mathbb{P},equity,5\ min}$	0.00	0.26	−3.38	0.00	0.00	0.58	0.89	0.00
$\text{EIA}_t^{stock\ growth}$	0.00	0.59	−3.64	0.00	−1.24	0.03	2.55	0.00
$\text{EIA}_t^{production\ growth}$	0.00	0.32	−3.36	0.00	−0.03	0.82	0.82	0.00
$\text{EIA}_t^{import\ growth}$	0.00	0.33	−3.45	0.00	−0.04	0.17	1.43	0.00

The data analyzed involves a predictor based on oil and equity markets to forecast the returns of a fully collateralized long position in weekly futures contract on Heating Oil. The results are presented in the form of bivariate predictive regressions expressed as follows: $\underbrace{\frac{F_{t+\Delta}}{F_t} - 1}_{\text{Heating Oil}} = \text{constant} + b^{cubic}\,\kappa_{3,t}^{\mathbb{Q},oil} + b^{alter}\,\text{Predictor}_t + \epsilon_{t+\Delta}$, where $\frac{F_{t+\Delta}}{F_t} - 1$ represents the return of the aforementioned position. Reported are the b estimates, as well as two-sided p-values for the null hypothesis b = 0, denoted by NW[p], based on the procedure in Newey and West with the lag automatically selected. The adjusted R^2, denoted by $\overline{R}^2$, is also presented as a measure of goodness-of-fit, expressed as a percentage. The predictive regressions are conducted over weekly options expiration cycles, spanning from Friday to Friday.

Table 10. Evidence from the bivariate predictive regressions (RBOB Gasoline futures).

Alternative Predictor	Constant	Predictor Is $\kappa_{3,t}^{\mathbb{Q},\text{oil}}$		Alternative Predictor		NW[p]	$\overline{R}^2$ (%)	Joint p
		NW[p]	$\mathsf{b}^{\text{cubic}}$	NW[p]	$\mathsf{b}^{\text{alter}}$			
$\kappa_{2,t}^{\mathbb{Q},\text{oil}}$	0.00	0.68	−1.26	0.63	0.58	0.40	1.03	0.00
$\kappa_{4,t}^{\mathbb{Q},\text{oil}}$	0.00	0.35	2.67	0.47	3.46	0.05	1.26	0.00
$\text{Skewness}_t^{\mathbb{Q},\text{oil}}$	0.00	0.38	−3.17	0.00	0.00	0.62	0.48	0.00
$\text{Kurtosis}_t^{\mathbb{Q},\text{oil}}$	−0.01	0.32	−3.31	0.00	0.00	0.08	1.10	0.00
$\text{Variance}_t^{\mathbb{P},\text{oil},5\text{ min}}$	0.00	0.35	−2.86	0.55	0.03	0.91	0.44	0.00
$\text{Skewness}_t^{\mathbb{P},\text{oil},5\text{ min}}$	0.00	0.37	−3.30	0.00	0.00	0.91	0.43	0.00
$\kappa_{2,t}^{\mathbb{Q},\text{equity}}$	0.01	0.08	−3.65	0.00	−4.48	0.47	1.18	0.00
$\kappa_{3,t}^{\mathbb{Q},\text{equity}}$	0.01	0.05	−3.82	0.00	92.8	0.18	2.66	0.00
$\kappa_{4,t}^{\mathbb{Q},\text{equity}}$	0.00	0.24	−3.50	0.00	−239.4	0.44	0.71	0.00
$\text{Skewness}_t^{\mathbb{Q},\text{equity}}$	−0.01	0.43	−3.38	0.00	−0.01	0.14	0.83	0.00
$\text{Skewness}_t^{\mathbb{Q},\text{equity}}$	0.00	0.57	−3.40	0.00	0.00	0.16	1.08	0.00
$\text{Variance}_t^{\mathbb{P},\text{equity},5\text{ min}}$	0.01	0.04	−3.73	0.00	−6.83	0.27	2.15	0.00
$\text{Skewness}_t^{\mathbb{P},\text{equity},5\text{ min}}$	0.00	0.33	−3.37	0.00	0.00	0.34	0.66	0.00
$\text{EIA}_t^{\text{stock growth}}$	0.00	0.40	−3.35	0.00	−0.13	0.84	0.44	0.00
$\text{EIA}_t^{\text{production growth}}$	0.00	0.34	−3.31	0.00	−0.08	0.57	0.51	0.00
$\text{EIA}_t^{\text{import growth}}$	0.00	0.36	−3.42	0.00	−0.05	0.11	0.98	0.00

The data analyzed involves a predictor based on oil and equity markets to forecast the returns of a fully collateralized long position in weekly futures contract on RBOB Gasoline. The results are presented in the form of bivariate predictive regressions expressed as follows: $\underbrace{\frac{F_{t+\Delta}}{F_t} - 1}_{\text{RBOB Gasoline}} = \text{constant} + \mathsf{b}^{\text{cubic}}\,\kappa_{3,t}^{\mathbb{Q},\text{oil}} + \mathsf{b}^{\text{alter}}\,\text{Predictor}_t + \epsilon_{t+\Delta}$, where $\frac{F_{t+\Delta}}{F_t} - 1$ represents the return of the aforementioned position. Reported are the b estimates, as well as two-sided p-values for the null hypothesis $\mathsf{b} = 0$, denoted by NW[p], based on the procedure in Newey and West with the lag automatically selected. The adjusted R^2, denoted by $\overline{R}^2$, is also presented as a measure of goodness-of-fit, expressed as a percentage. The predictive regressions are conducted over weekly options expiration cycles, spanning from Friday to Friday.

Next, we assess the out-of-sample performance using the [25] statistic, which is calculated as $R^2_{\text{os}} = 1 - \frac{\sum_{t=1}^{T}(z_t - \widehat{z}_{t,\text{full}})^2}{\sum_{t=1}^{T}(z_t - \widehat{z}_{t,\text{nested}})^2}$. We use the portion of the data up until the first weekly cycle of May 2020 (i.e., 194 (out of 341) cycles) as the initial in-sample estimates for coefficients. Our implementation relies on the expanding scheme updated weekly.

- When the nested model is the historical average and $\kappa_{3,t}^{\mathbb{Q},\text{oil}}$ is the full model, the R^2_{os} values are 1.13% and 0.97% for WTI and the oil basket, respectively. These values suggest that using $\kappa_{3,t}^{\mathbb{Q},\text{oil}}$ as a predictor adds to the predictive ability beyond using the historical average.
- When the alternative predictor is the nested model and the bivariate predictor constitutes the full model, the resulting R^2_{os} values reported in Tables 5 and 6 are all positive and range from 0.25% to 4.1%. These R^2_{os} values align with the notion that $\kappa_{3,t}^{\mathbb{Q},\text{oil}}$ has additional predicting power over the considered alternative predictor.

The conclusion to draw is that, in an out-of-sample setting, $\kappa_{3,t}^{\mathbb{Q},\text{oil}}$ is an informative predictor.

Table 11 builds on the empirical results from Tables 5 and 6 and provides further evidence supporting the relevance of 7DTE $\kappa_{3,t}^{\mathbb{Q},\text{oil}}$ as a predictor for oil futures returns. First, to evaluate the statistical significance of our results, we include the effect of all three higher-order risk-neutral return cumulants (as in Equation (7)). Second, we analyze whether there is a significant distinction in oil futures returns between three sample periods: pre-COVID, COVID, and post-COVID. This was done by conducting a regression on weekly oil futures returns using dummy variables to indicate different sample periods, as follows:

$$\overbrace{\frac{F_{t+\Delta}}{F_t}}^{\text{WTI or basket}} - 1 = \text{constant} + \left(\mathsf{b}^{\text{squared, pre-covid}}\,\mathbb{1}_{\text{pre-covid}} + \mathsf{b}^{\text{squared, covid}}\,\mathbb{1}_{\text{covid}} + \mathsf{b}^{\text{squared, post-covid}}\,\mathbb{1}_{\text{post-covid}}\right)\kappa_{2,t}^{\mathbb{Q},\text{oil}} + \left(\mathsf{b}^{\text{cubic, pre-covid}}\,\mathbb{1}_{\text{pre-covid}} + \mathsf{b}^{\text{cubic, covid}}\,\mathbb{1}_{\text{covid}} + \mathsf{b}^{\text{cubic, post-covid}}\,\mathbb{1}_{\text{post-covid}}\right)\kappa_{3,t}^{\mathbb{Q},\text{oil}} + \left(\mathsf{b}^{\text{quartic, pre-covid}}\,\mathbb{1}_{\text{pre-covid}} + \mathsf{b}^{\text{quartic, covid}}\,\mathbb{1}_{\text{covid}} + \mathsf{b}^{\text{quartic, post-covid}}\,\mathbb{1}_{\text{post-covid}}\right)\kappa_{4,t}^{\mathbb{Q},\text{oil}} + \epsilon_{t+\Delta}. \quad (10)$$

The results from the multiple regressions in Table 11 (Panel A) reveal that $\mathsf{b}^{\text{cubic}}$ displays a high level of significance, while the coefficients for the risk-neutral second and fourth return cumulants become insignificant. When $\kappa_{2,t}^{\mathbb{Q},\text{oil}}$, $\kappa_{3,t}^{\mathbb{Q},\text{oil}}$, and $\kappa_{4,t}^{\mathbb{Q},\text{oil}}$ are combined, the overall explanatory power, measured by $\overline{R}^2$, is 1.31%, compared to 3.47% using just $\kappa_{3,t}^{\mathbb{Q},\text{oil}}$ with $\text{variance}_t^{\mathbb{P},\text{oil, 5 min}}$ (see Table 5). This suggests that other variables—related to realized oil futures return variance, the equity market, and EIA data—contribute to explaining the variation in the oil futures returns, compared to using information only from the oil options market.

Table 11. Predictive regression results allowing for COVID-19 dummy variables.

	Panel A: $\frac{F_{t+\Delta}}{F_t} - 1 = \text{constant} + \mathsf{b}^{\text{squared}}\kappa_{2,t}^{\mathbb{Q},\text{oil}} + \mathsf{b}^{\text{cubic}}\kappa_{3,t}^{\mathbb{Q},\text{oil}} + \mathsf{b}^{\text{quartic}}\kappa_{4,t}^{\mathbb{Q},\text{oil}} + \epsilon_{t+\Delta}$								
	constant	NW[p]	$\mathsf{b}^{\text{squared}}$	NW[p]	$\mathsf{b}^{\text{cubic}}$	NW[p]	$\mathsf{b}^{\text{quartic}}$	NW[p]	$\overline{R}^2$ (%)
WTI	0.00	0.33	−0.15	0.87	−9.13	0.01	−2.91	0.42	1.31
Oil basket	0.00	0.20	−0.13	0.84	−6.23	0.01	−1.02	0.65	1.74
			Panel B: Regression with dummy variables						
WTI	constant	NW[p]	$\mathsf{b}^{\text{squared, pre-covid}}$	NW[p]	$\mathsf{b}^{\text{squared, covid}}$	NW[p]	$\mathsf{b}^{\text{squared, post-covid}}$	NW[p]	
	−0.01	0.12	7.31	0.07	−0.21	0.82	6.15	0.01	
			$\mathsf{b}^{\text{cubic, pre-covid}}$	NW[p]	$\mathsf{b}^{\text{cubic, covid}}$	NW[p]	$\mathsf{b}^{\text{cubic, post-covid}}$	NW[p]	
			53.07	0.62	−7.96	0.04	−27.94	0.00	
			$\mathsf{b}^{\text{quartic, pre-covid}}$	NW[p]	$\mathsf{b}^{\text{quartic, covid}}$	NW[p]	$\mathsf{b}^{\text{quartic, post-covid}}$	NW[p]	$\overline{R}^2$ (%)
			−188.34	0.48	−1.96	0.59	−109.46	0.05	2.22
Oil basket	constant	NW[p]	$\mathsf{b}^{\text{squared, pre-covid}}$	NW[p]	$\mathsf{b}^{\text{squared, covid}}$	NW[p]	$\mathsf{b}^{\text{squared, post-covid}}$	NW[p]	
	−0.01	0.30	5.66	0.18	−0.16	0.80	4.51	0.04	
			$\mathsf{b}^{\text{cubic, pre-covid}}$	NW[p]	$\mathsf{b}^{\text{cubic, covid}}$	NW[p]	$\mathsf{b}^{\text{cubic, post-covid}}$	NW[p]	
			83.03	0.39	−4.95	0.05	−24.38	0.01	
			$\mathsf{b}^{\text{quartic, pre-covid}}$	NW[p]	$\mathsf{b}^{\text{quartic, covid}}$	NW[p]	$\mathsf{b}^{\text{quartic, post-covid}}$	NW[p]	$\overline{R}^2$ (%)
			−152.42	0.59	−0.17	0.94	−81.53	0.10	2.33

The dummy variables $\mathbb{1}_{\text{pre-covid}}$, $\mathbb{1}_{\text{covid}}$, and $\mathbb{1}_{\text{post-covid}}$ correspond to the time period before the COVID-19 pandemic (12 August 2016, to January 31, 2020), during the pandemic (7 February 2020, to 5 June 2020), and after the pandemic (12 June 2020, to 23 February 2023). The data analyzed involves predictors based on the oil options market to forecast the returns of a fully collateralized long position in weekly futures contract on WTI crude oil or the basket of oil futures. The results are presented based on the predictive regressions expressed, as follows:

$$\overbrace{\frac{F_{t+\Delta}}{F_t}}^{\text{WTI or basket}} - 1 = \text{constant} + \left(\mathsf{b}^{\text{squared, pre-covid}}\,\mathbb{1}_{\text{pre-covid}} + \mathsf{b}^{\text{squared, covid}}\,\mathbb{1}_{\text{covid}} + \mathsf{b}^{\text{squared, post-covid}}\,\mathbb{1}_{\text{post-covid}}\right)\kappa_{2,t}^{\mathbb{Q},\text{oil}} + \left(\mathsf{b}^{\text{cubic, pre-covid}}\,\mathbb{1}_{\text{pre-covid}} + \mathsf{b}^{\text{cubic, covid}}\,\mathbb{1}_{\text{covid}} + \mathsf{b}^{\text{cubic, post-covid}}\,\mathbb{1}_{\text{post-covid}}\right)\kappa_{3,t}^{\mathbb{Q},\text{oil}} + \left(\mathsf{b}^{\text{quartic, pre-covid}}\,\mathbb{1}_{\text{pre-covid}} + \mathsf{b}^{\text{quartic, covid}}\,\mathbb{1}_{\text{covid}} + \mathsf{b}^{\text{quartic, post-covid}}\,\mathbb{1}_{\text{post-covid}}\right)\kappa_{4,t}^{\mathbb{Q},\text{oil}} + \epsilon_{t+\Delta}.$$

Here $\frac{F_{t+\Delta}}{F_t} - 1$ represents the return of the aforementioned position. Reported are the b estimates, as well as two-sided p-values for the null hypothesis $\mathsf{b} = 0$, denoted by NW[p], based on the procedure in Newey and West with the lag automatically selected. The adjusted R^2, denoted by $\overline{R}^2$, is also presented as a measure of goodness-of-fit, expressed as a percentage. The predictive regressions are conducted over weekly options expiration cycles, spanning from Friday to Friday.

The results, presented in Table 11 (Panel B), show that the returns of oil futures are affected differently by risk-neutral return cumulants. The dummy variables $\mathbb{1}_{\text{pre-covid}}$, $\mathbb{1}_{\text{covid}}$, and $\mathbb{1}_{\text{post-covid}}$ correspond to the time period before the COVID-19 pandemic (12 August 2016, to 31 January 2020), during the pandemic (7 February 2020, to 5 June 2020), and after the pandemic (12 June 2020, to 23 February 2023). We find that $b^{\text{cubic, covid}}$ and $b^{\text{cubic, post-covid}}$ are highly significant, indicating that the changes in the third risk-neutral return cumulant exert an effect on the oil futures returns. The second risk-neutral return cumulant does not show a significant impact on the futures returns.

Overall, we present an approach for predicting futures returns in the oil market using the 7DTE third risk-neutral return cumulant, which is an indicator that varies with economic conditions. This variable is derived from the crude oil options market and, if reliable, can provide insights for predicting oil price movements. However, we must consider that this finding may potentially be a chance discovery and, therefore, it is essential to consider the model's performance on out-of-sample data and trading rule.

Mindful of such possibilities, we implement a trading strategy in which we take a long or short position in the basket of crude oil commodities. The rule that we adhere to is as follows:

$$\text{Trading position}_t = \begin{cases} \text{Long the oil futures basket} & \text{if } \sum_{j=1}^{J} \kappa_{3,t-j\Delta}^{\mathbb{Q},\text{oil}} < 0, \\ \text{Short the oil futures basket} & \text{if } \sum_{j=1}^{J} \kappa_{3,t-j\Delta}^{\mathbb{Q},\text{oil}} > 0. \end{cases} \tag{11}$$

In words, we take a long position in each of the basket components when the prior momentum in third risk-neutral return cumulant is negative (i.e., puts remain more expensive than calls). The return on this signal over the subsequent week is $z_{t+\Delta}^{\text{basket, oil}}$. To the contrary, we take a short position in the basket of oil futures when the prior momentum is positive. The return to this signal is $-z_{t+\Delta}^{\text{basket, oil}}$. It remains to be seen if this empirical model can translate into a viable investment strategy, as it will require consideration of the signal-to-noise ratio and our ability to diversify and rebalance when the signal changes direction.

The results in Table 12 show the mean returns of our strategy, along with the corresponding 90% block bootstrap confidence intervals. While this method shows a positive mean return, it also faces a high level of return variability over the entire sample. However, in the post COVID-19 sample, the strategy produces significantly positive mean returns. For instance, using the prior six week momentum in $\kappa_{3,t}^{\mathbb{Q},\text{oil}}$ results in an average weekly return of 0.77% with a 90% confidence interval of $\lfloor 0.16\% \quad 1.42\% \rfloor$. This strategy yields reliable results with a frequency of 62% and is supported by the reported sizable Sharpe Ratio's. Though the simple structure of the model is appealing, we acknowledge that the predictability of oil prices is influenced by multiple factors beyond just economic cycles related to the 7DTE third risk-neutral return cumulant.

In summary, market expectations of asymmetric behavior in oil futures returns is a consistent predictor of oil returns. This is due to the fact that the third risk-neutral return cumulant, which measures asymmetry and risk imbalances, provides insight into the likely direction of oil changes. In contrast, metrics like volatility offer information only about the magnitude of changes. This paper highlights the significance of conditional asymmetry in explaining oil futures dynamics and risk premiums. By using model-free measures of the third risk-neutral return cumulant, specifically the forward-looking asymmetry derived from option prices, our study reveals that this measure exhibits cyclical variation. Furthermore, this asymmetry measure is a predictor of subsequent oil futures returns and is not subsumed by information obtained from other predictors.

Other papers connect to our analysis, including, for instance, [26–37].

Table 12. Investible trading strategy.

J Weeks	Full Sample 12 August 2016, to 23 February 2023 Weekly Returns (%)				Subsample 12 August 2016, to 5 June 2020 Weekly Returns (%)				Subsample 5 June 2020, to 23 February 2023 Weekly Returns (%)				
	Mean Return	Block Bootstrap	NW[p]	$\mathbb{1}_{z>0}$ (%)	Mean Return	Block Bootstrap	NW[p]	$\mathbb{1}_{z>0}$ (%)	Mean Return	Block Bootstrap	NW[p]	$\mathbb{1}_{z>0}$ (%)	Sharpe Ratio
8	0.13	$\lfloor -0.39 \quad 0.67 \rfloor$	0.68	54	−0.24	$\lfloor -1.13 \quad 0.34 \rfloor$	0.58	48	0.63	$\lfloor 0.04 \quad 1.28 \rfloor$	0.10	63	0.90
7	0.09	$\lfloor -0.42 \quad 0.61 \rfloor$	0.77	53	−0.37	$\lfloor -1.24 \quad 0.18 \rfloor$	0.39	47	0.71	$\lfloor 0.14 \quad 1.34 \rfloor$	0.06	63	1.01
6	0.33	$\lfloor -0.17 \quad 0.85 \rfloor$	0.28	55	0.01	$\lfloor -0.83 \quad 0.54 \rfloor$	0.98	50	0.77	$\lfloor 0.16 \quad 1.42 \rfloor$	0.05	62	1.09
5	0.22	$\lfloor -0.31 \quad 0.75 \rfloor$	0.48	55	−0.01	$\lfloor -0.86 \quad 0.53 \rfloor$	0.97	50	0.54	$\lfloor -0.16 \quad 1.28 \rfloor$	0.17	61	0.76
4	0.04	$\lfloor -0.47 \quad 0.56 \rfloor$	0.89	52	−0.19	$\lfloor -1.03 \quad 0.35 \rfloor$	0.66	47	0.36	$\lfloor -0.29 \quad 1.02 \rfloor$	0.33	60	0.51
3	0.14	$\lfloor -0.38 \quad 0.65 \rfloor$	0.65	53	0.05	$\lfloor -0.78 \quad 0.58 \rfloor$	0.90	51	0.25	$\lfloor -0.40 \quad 0.91 \rfloor$	0.51	56	0.35
2	0.07	$\lfloor -0.44 \quad 0.60 \rfloor$	0.83	54	−0.13	$\lfloor -0.98 \quad 0.43 \rfloor$	0.76	51	0.34	$\lfloor -0.30 \quad 1.01 \rfloor$	0.36	58	0.48
1	0.09	$\lfloor -0.41 \quad 0.64 \rfloor$	0.77	54	−0.13	$\lfloor -0.96 \quad 0.46 \rfloor$	0.76	51	0.40	$\lfloor -0.26 \quad 1.09 \rfloor$	0.29	58	0.57

Our approach follows a quantitative strategy where we take a long position in the five oil futures contracts if the momentum in third risk-neutral return cumulant is negative. Otherwise, we adopt a short position in the five oil commodities. The momentum is calculated over various time intervals. The profits or losses are measured over the next seven days, using an equal weighting method. We present the average weekly return (%), along with the 90% confidence intervals obtained using the block bootstrap technique. Additionally, we report the two-sided p-values, denoted by NW[p], which reflect the hypothesis of a zero mean return, based on the Newey-West procedure with an automatic lag selection. Our strategy is adjusted weekly, in line with options expiration cycles, from Friday to Friday. We collect data from 12 August 2016, to 24 February 2023, capturing a total of 341 options expiration cycles. The entries under the column "Sharpe Ratio" reflect the computed annualized Sharpe Ratio of the strategy.

5. Risk Preferences and the Third Risk-Neutral Return Cumulant

The third risk-neutral return cumulant $\kappa_{3,t}^{\mathbb{Q},\text{oil}}$ is linked to the risk premium of oil futures, and the sign of b^{cubic} in the regressions can provide insights into the characteristics of the risk-neutral oil density and the corresponding futures risk premium. The estimated predictive coefficient, b^{cubic}, has shown a negative pattern in Tables 4–11. A negative (positive) $\kappa_{3,t}^{\mathbb{Q},\text{oil}}$ indicates a left-skewed (right-skewed) futures return distribution, where extreme negative (positive) events are more likely to occur, leading to a higher (lower) oil futures risk premium.

The negative sign of b^{cubic} poses a potential challenge for models explaining the behavior of oil futures returns. This section proposes a framework to reconcile the negative value of b^{cubic} by exploring restrictions on the properties of the SDF of the oil market. Define

$$\text{gross return of oil futures } Z_{t+\Delta} \equiv \frac{F_{t+\Delta}}{F_t} \text{ and net (excess) return } z_{t+\Delta} = \frac{F_{t+\Delta}}{F_t} - 1. \quad (12)$$

Additionally, let $\mathbb{P}$ represent the real-world probability measure and $p[z_{t+\Delta}]$ the density of oil futures returns. Define $\Omega = \{z_{t+\Delta} > -1\}$ and note that $p[z_{t+\Delta}]$ satisfies $1 = \int_\Omega p[z_{t+\Delta}]\, dz_{t+\Delta}$.

5.1. Oil Futures Risk Premiums

Refs. [11,14] have investigated the properties of the SDFs for the crude oil market. However, their studies did not explore the characteristics of 7DTE SDFs. Additionally, the content of weekly oil options and jump behaviors have yet to be fully examined in the existing literature. Furthermore, the potential implications of the negative predictive coefficient on $\kappa_{3,t}^{\mathbb{Q},\text{oil}}$ has not been analyzed.

Our substantive result is a theoretical link between the risk premium of oil futures, namely, $\mathbb{E}_t^{\mathbb{P}}(\frac{F_{t+\Delta}}{F_t} - 1)$, and the higher-order risk-neutral return cumulants. We present a theory that matches the sign of the estimated coefficient b^{cubic} in Equation (7). Furthermore, we show that the constructed 7DTE $\kappa_{3,t}^{\mathbb{Q},\text{oil}}$ can switch direction in the oil market.

We assume that there exists a SDF projection of the oil market, $m[z_{t+\Delta}]$, satisfying

$$m[z_{t+\Delta}] > 0, \quad \mathbb{E}_t^{\mathbb{P}}(m[z_{t+\Delta}]) = \frac{1}{R_t^{\text{rf}}} < \infty, \quad \text{and} \quad \mathbb{E}_t^{\mathbb{P}}(\{m[z_{t+\Delta}]\}^2) < \infty. \tag{13}$$

In line with [38,39], we only need to model $m[z_{t+\Delta}]$ without incorporating state-dependent specifications. We write $\mathbb{Q} \ll \mathbb{P}$ if the measure $\mathbb{Q}$, corresponding to the density $q[z_{t+\Delta}]$, is absolutely continuous with respect to measure $\mathbb{P}$. We assume both $\mathbb{Q} \ll \mathbb{P}$ and $\mathbb{P} \ll \mathbb{Q}$ hold, and, thus, $\mathbb{Q}$ and $\mathbb{P}$ are equivalent.

The n-th order raw conditional return moments of the distribution, under $\mathbb{P}$ and $\mathbb{Q}$, are

$$\mu_{n,t}^{\mathbb{P}} \equiv \int_{\Omega} \{z_{t+\Delta}\}^n \, p[z_{t+\Delta}] \, dz_{t+\Delta} \quad \text{and} \quad \mu_{n,t}^{\mathbb{Q}} \equiv \int_{\Omega} \{z_{t+\Delta}\}^n \, q[z_{t+\Delta}] \, dz_{t+\Delta}, \text{ respectively.} \tag{14}$$

We denote the moment-generating functions under $\mathbb{P}$ and $\mathbb{Q}$, as $\text{mgf}_t^{\mathbb{P}}[\lambda]$ and $\text{mgf}_t^{\mathbb{Q}}[\lambda]$, respectively, for some constant parameter λ. Assume $\text{mgf}_t^{\mathbb{P}}[\lambda] < \infty$ and $\text{mgf}_t^{\mathbb{Q}}[\lambda] < \infty$. For brevity, we omit the oil superscript on both $\kappa_{n,t}^{\mathbb{P},\text{oil}}$ and $\kappa_{n,t}^{\mathbb{Q},\text{oil}}$. To develop expressions that rely on variables constructed from option prices, we assume that $m[z_{t+\Delta}]$ is continuous and infinitely differentiable in $z_{t+\Delta}$; that is, $m[z_{t+\Delta}] \in \mathcal{C}^{\infty}$. We define

$$G[z_{t+\Delta}] \equiv \frac{1}{m[z_{t+\Delta}]}. \tag{15}$$

Pertinent to our formalizations, the properties of $G[z_{t+\Delta}]$ relate to the shape of $m[z_{t+\Delta}]$. The class $G[z_{t+\Delta}] \in \mathcal{C}^{\infty}$ encompasses empirically plausible specifications of $m[z_{t+\Delta}]$. We denote

$$G'[z_{t+\Delta}] \equiv \frac{dG[z_{t+\Delta}]}{dz_{t+\Delta}}, \quad G''[z_{t+\Delta}] \equiv \frac{d^2G[z_{t+\Delta}]}{dz_{t+\Delta}^2}, \quad \text{and} \quad G'''[z_{t+\Delta}] \equiv \frac{d^3G[z_{t+\Delta}]}{dz_{t+\Delta}^3}. \tag{16}$$

Additionally,

$$G[0] = G[z_{t+\Delta}]\Big|_{z_{t+\Delta}=0}, \qquad G'[0] = G'[z_{t+\Delta}]\Big|_{z_{t+\Delta}=0}, \qquad \text{and} \tag{17}$$

$$G''[0] = G''[z_{t+\Delta}]\Big|_{z_{t+\Delta}=0}, \qquad G'''[0] = G'''[z_{t+\Delta}]\Big|_{z_{t+\Delta}=0}. \tag{18}$$

The remaining step is to formulate the expression for the real-world density of oil futures returns in terms of the risk-neutral return density, as follows:

$$p[z_{t+\Delta}] = \frac{G[z_{t+\Delta}] \, q[z_{t+\Delta}]}{\int_{\Omega} G[z_{t+\Delta}] \, q[z_{t+\Delta}] \, dz_{t+\Delta}}. \tag{19}$$

Then, Equation (20) is the oil futures risk premium counterpart of that in [39] for equity market index (proof available from authors):

$$\underbrace{\mathbb{E}_t^{\mathbb{P}}\left(\frac{F_{t+\Delta}}{F_t} - 1\right)}_{\text{oil futures risk premium}} = \frac{G'[0]}{G[0]} \kappa_{2,t}^{\mathbb{Q}} + \frac{1}{2} \frac{G''[0]}{G[0]} \kappa_{3,t}^{\mathbb{Q}} + \frac{1}{6} \frac{G'''[0]}{G[0]} \kappa_{4,t}^{\mathbb{Q}} + \cdots. \tag{20}$$

The expression for $\mathbb{E}_t^{\mathbb{P}}(\frac{F_{t+\Delta}}{F_t} - 1)$ is an infinite series and is determined by its sensitivity to the risk-neutral return cumulants ($\kappa_{n,t}^{\mathbb{Q}}$). This representation is based on the existence and well-definedness of $\frac{G'[0]}{G[0]}$, $\frac{G''[0]}{G[0]}$, and $\frac{G'''[0]}{G[0]}$. Our analysis does not require a parametric assumption about the real-world oil futures return distributions or the risk-neutral oil futures return distributions.

5.2. Sign of $\frac{G''[0]}{G[0]}$ (Theoretical Counterpart to b^{cubic}) in Theoretical Economies

To clarify, our focus is on the $m[z_{t+\Delta}]$ and its reciprocal, the $G[z_{t+\Delta}]$ function, in reproducing the negative value of predictive coefficient b^{cubic} (which coincides with the sign of $\frac{G''[0]}{G[0]}$). In order to ascertain the restrictions needed for this result, our study examines the example economies for the sign of $\frac{G''[0]}{G[0]}$.

Example 1 (Monotonic SDFs). *Suppose that the SDF is monotonic in oil futures returns. That is, for constants* $\mathsf{m}_0 > 0$ *and* ϕ,

$$m[z_{t+\Delta}] \;=\; \mathsf{m}_0 \,\exp(\phi\,(1+z_{t+\Delta})). \tag{21}$$

Here $G[z_{t+\Delta}] = \frac{1}{m[z_{t+\Delta}]} = \frac{1}{\mathsf{m}_0}\exp(-\phi\,(1+z_{t+\Delta}))$. *Hence,* $G'[z_{t+\Delta}] = \frac{-\phi}{\mathsf{m}_0}\exp(-\phi\,(1+z_{t+\Delta}))$, $G''[z_{t+\Delta}] = \frac{\phi^2}{\mathsf{m}_0}\exp(-\phi\,(1+z_{t+\Delta}))$, *and* $G'''[z_{t+\Delta}] = \frac{-\phi^3}{\mathsf{m}_0}\exp(-\phi\,(1+z_{t+\Delta}))$. *In this illustration, it follows that*

$$\frac{G'[0]}{G[0]} = -\phi, \qquad \frac{1}{2}\frac{G''[0]}{G[0]} = \frac{1}{2}\phi^2 > 0, \qquad \text{and} \qquad \frac{1}{6}\frac{G'''[0]}{G[0]} = -\frac{1}{6}\phi^3. \tag{22}$$

Monotonic SDFs ($\phi > 0$ *or* $\phi < 0$) *cannot support the estimated negative* b^{cubic}.

Example 2 (Variance-dependent SDFs). *Suppose that for constants* $\mathsf{m}_0 > 0$ *and* $\eta > 0$,

$$m[z_{t+\Delta}] \;=\; \mathsf{m}_0 \,\exp\Big(\eta\,\{\log(1+z_{t+\Delta})\}^2\Big). \tag{23}$$

The essence of this model is that

$$\frac{G'[0]}{G[0]} = 0, \qquad \frac{1}{2}\frac{G''[0]}{G[0]} = -\,\eta < 0, \qquad \text{and} \qquad \frac{1}{6}\frac{G'''[0]}{G[0]} = \eta > 0. \tag{24}$$

This form of variance-dependent SDF can support the negative b^{cubic}. *Hence, variance-dependent SDFs—that symmetrically weight down and up returns—can be consistent with our findings.*

Example 3 (SDFs that incorporate asymmetry in down and up oil futures return movements). *Suppose that for constants* $\mathsf{m}_0 > 0$ *and* $\eta > 0$,

$$m[z_{t+\Delta}] \;=\; \mathsf{m}_0 \,\exp\left(\frac{\eta}{1+z_{t+\Delta}} \;+\; \frac{\eta}{2}(1+z_{t+\Delta})^2\right). \tag{25}$$

It follows that

$$\frac{G'[0]}{G[0]} = 0, \qquad \frac{1}{2}\frac{G''[0]}{G[0]} = -\frac{3}{2}\eta < 0, \qquad \text{and} \qquad \frac{1}{6}\frac{G'''[0]}{G[0]} = \eta > 0. \tag{26}$$

This form of the SDF gives rise to a negative b^{cubic} *and a positive* $\mathsf{b}^{quartic}$. *Unlike Example 2, this model does not impose equal and opposite signed effects on* b^{cubic} *and* $\mathsf{b}^{quartic}$.

Example 4 (SDFs sensitive to the cubic oil futures return payoff). *Suppose that for constant* $\eta > 0$,

$$m[z_{t+\Delta}] \;=\; \frac{1}{\frac{4}{3}\eta}\exp\left(\frac{\eta}{1+z_{t+\Delta}} \;+\; \frac{\eta}{3}(1+z_{t+\Delta})^3\right). \tag{27}$$

For this model, which implies risk imbalance to the downside versus the upside of returns, it follows that

$$\frac{G'[0]}{G[0]} = 0, \qquad \frac{1}{2}\frac{G''[0]}{G[0]} = -2\,\eta < 0, \qquad \text{and} \qquad \frac{1}{6}\frac{G'''[0]}{G[0]} = \frac{2}{3}\eta > 0. \tag{28}$$

This form of the SDF gives rise to a negative $\mathbb{b}^{\text{cubic}}$ *and a positive* $\mathbb{b}^{\text{quartic}}$*. The SDF* $m[z_{t+\Delta}]$ *is an asymmetric U-shaped function, with greater weights to the downside and is centered at one.*

Example 5 (SDFs exponential quadratic in log futures returns). *Suppose that*

$$m[z_{t+\Delta}] = \exp\Big(-\mathbb{a} \times \log(1 + z_{t+\Delta}) + \mathbb{b} \times \{\log(1 + z_{t+\Delta})\}^2\Big). \tag{29}$$

For constant parameters $\mathbb{a} > 0$ *and* $\mathbb{b} > 0$*, it follows that*

$$\frac{G'[0]}{G[0]} = \mathbb{a}, \ \frac{1}{2}\frac{G''[0]}{G[0]} = \frac{1}{2}\{-\mathbb{a} + \mathbb{a}^2 - 2\,\mathbb{b}\}, \ \frac{1}{6}\frac{G'''[0]}{G[0]} = \frac{1}{6}\{2\mathbb{a} + \mathbb{a}^3 - 3\mathbb{a}(\mathbb{a} + 2\mathbb{b}) + 6\mathbb{b}\}. \tag{30}$$

For $\mathbb{a} = 1.5$ *and* $\mathbb{b} = 9.5$*, this SDF implied* $\mathbb{b}^{\text{cubic}} = -9.12$*,* $\mathbb{b}^{\text{quartic}} = -4.81$*, and* $\mathbb{b}^{\text{squared}} = 1.5$*. The SDF* $m[z_{t+\Delta}]$ *is an asymmetric U-shaped function with greater weighting to the downside of short maturity oil futures returns. This parameterization mimics features of Table 11 (Panel A).*

In summary, the theory proposed suggests that incorporating higher-order return dependence in the SDFs can result in negative predictive coefficients for the third risk-neutral return cumulant. This perspective takes into account the impact of down and up jumps and has not been previously investigated in the analysis of short maturity SDFs.

6. Conclusions

This study reveals that the third risk-neutral return cumulant—inferred from short maturity (weekly expiring (7DTE)) crude oil option prices—is a consistent predictor of short maturity oil futures returns. This finding is supported by evidence across different model specifications, even when other predictors are taken into account. The return predictability is strongest when the 7DTE third risk-neutral return cumulant is combined with measures of (i) realized variance of intraday oil futures returns (based on five-minute returns), (ii) skewness-derived variable from S&P 500 equity options, and (iii) growth rate of crude oil stock. The adjusted R^2 value for weekly horizon oil returns achieves a maximum of 3.47%. We also implement a quantitative trading strategy that reflect the measurement—its prior momentum—of the 7DTE third risk-neutral return cumulant.

These empirical observations from our return predictive regressions support a theoretical framework that includes an SDF projection whose dispersion reflects the effects of varying levels of oil futures return volatility. The estimated negative predictive coefficient for the third risk-neutral return cumulant is also in line with this theory, as it considers the inclusion of squared and cubic return dependence in the SDF projection.

Author Contributions: Conceptualization, G.B., X.G. and Z.Z.; Methodology, G.B.; Formal analysis, G.B., X.G. and Z.Z.; Writing—original draft, G.B., X.G. and Z.Z.; Writing—review & editing, G.B., X.G. and Z.Z. All authors have read and agreed to the published version of the manuscript.

Funding: This research received no external funding.

Institutional Review Board Statement: Not applicable.

Informed Consent Statement: Not applicable.

Data Availability Statement: Available upon request.

Acknowledgments: First Draft: January 2024. We are immensely grateful to two anonymous referees and the Editor for guiding the work done in this paper and for suggesting numerous improvements.

Conflicts of Interest: The authors declare no conflicts of interest.

References

1. Alquist, R.; Kilian, L. What do we learn from the price of crude oil futures? *J. Appl. Econom.* **2010**, *25*, 539–573. [CrossRef]
2. Alquist, R.; Kilian, L.; Vigfusson, R. Forecasting the price of oil. In *Handbook of Economic Forecasting*; Elsevier: Amsterdam, The Netherlands, 2013; Volume 2, pp. 427–507.

3. Miao, H.; Ramchander, S.; Wang, T.; Yang, D. Influential factors in crude oil price forecasting. *Energy Econ.* **2017**, *68*, 77–88. [CrossRef]
4. Funk, C. Forecasting the real price of oil—Time-variation and forecast combination. *Energy Econ.* **2018**, *76*, 288–302. [CrossRef]
5. Cotter, J.; Eyiah-Donkor, E.; Poti, V. *Commodity Futures Return Predictability and Intertemporal Asset Pricing*; Working Paper; University College Dublin: Dublin, Ireland, 2020.
6. Ellwanger, R.; Snudden, S. Forecasts of the real price of oil revisited: Do they beat the random walk? *J. Bank. Financ.* **2023**, *154*, 106962. [CrossRef]
7. Conlon, T.; Cotter, J.; Eyiah-Donkor, E. Forecasting the price of oil: A cautionary note. *J. Commod. Mark.* **2024**, *33*, 100378. [CrossRef]
8. Killian, L. Not all oil price shocks are alike: Disentangling demand and supply shocks in the crude oil market. *Am. Econ. Rev.* **2009**, *99*, 1053–1069. [CrossRef]
9. Baumeister, C.; Hamilton, J. Structural interpretation of vector autoregressions with incomplete identification: Revisiting the role of oil supply and demand shocks. *Am. Econ. Rev.* **2019**, *109*, 1873–1910. [CrossRef]
10. Routledge, B.; Seppi, D.; Spatt, C. Equilibrium forward curves for commodities. *J. Financ.* **2000**, *55*, 1297–1338. [CrossRef]
11. Trolle, A.; Schwartz, E. Unspanned stochastic volatility and the pricing of commodity derivatives. *Rev. Financ. Stud.* **2009**, *22*, 4423–4461. [CrossRef]
12. Chiang, I.; Hughen, K.; Sagi, J. Estimating Oil Risk Factors Using Information from Equity and Derivatives Markets. *J. Financ.* **2015**, *70*, 769–804. [CrossRef]
13. Ready, R. Oil consumption, economic growth, and oil futures: The impact of long-run oil supply uncertainty on asset prices. *J. Monet. Econ.* **2018**, *94*, 1–26. [CrossRef]
14. Christoffersen, P.; Jacobs, K.; Pan, X. The State Price Density Implied by Crude Oil Futures and Option Prices. *Rev. Financ. Stud.* **2022**, *35*, 1064–1103. [CrossRef]
15. Gao, L.; Hitzemann, S.; Shaliastovich, I.; Xu, L. Oil Volatility Risk. *J. Financ. Econ.* **2022**, *144*, 456–494. [CrossRef]
16. Kang, W.; Rouwenhorst, G.; Tang, K. A tale of two premiums: The role of hedgers and speculators in commodity futures markets. *J. Financ.* **2014**, *75*, 377–417. [CrossRef]
17. Fernandez-Perez, A.; Frijns, B.; Fuertes, A.M.; Miffre, J. The skewness of commodity futures returns. *J. Bank. Financ.* **2018**, *86*, 143–158. [CrossRef]
18. Mastroeni, L.; Mazzoccoli, A.; Quaresima, G.; Vellucci, P. Decoupling and recoupling in the crude oil price benchmarks: An investigation of similarity patterns. *Energy Econ.* **2021**, *94*, 105036. [CrossRef]
19. Le, T.H.; Boubaker, S.; Bui, M.T.; Park, D. On the volatility of WTI crude oil prices: A time-varying approach with stochastic volatility. *Energy Econ.* **2023**, *117*, 106474. [CrossRef]
20. Bakshi, G.; Madan, D. Spanning and Derivative-Security Valuation. *J. Financ. Econ.* **2000**, *55*, 205–238. [CrossRef]
21. Bakshi, G.; Kapadia, N.; Madan, D. Stock Return Characteristics, Skew Laws, and the Differential Pricing of Individual Equity Options. *Rev. Financ. Stud.* **2003**, *16*, 101–143. [CrossRef]
22. Prokopczuk, M.; Symeonidis, L.; Simen, C. Variance risk in commodity markets. *J. Bank. Financ.* **2017**, *81*, 136–149. [CrossRef]
23. Ruan, X.; Zhang, J. Risk-neutral moments in the crude oil market. *Energy Econ.* **2018**, *72*, 583–600. [CrossRef]
24. Wong, P. Predicting intraday crude oil returns with higher order risk-neutral moments. *J. Commod. Mark.* **2023**, 100331.. [CrossRef]
25. Campbell, J.; Thompson, S. Predicting Excess Stock Returns Out of Sample: Can Anything Beat the Historical Average? *Rev. Financ. Stud.* **2008**, *21*, 1509–1531. [CrossRef]
26. Fuertes, A.M.; Miffre, J.; Rallis, G. Tactical allocation in commodity futures markets: Combining momentum and term structure signals. *J. Bank. Financ.* **2010**, *34*, 2530–2548. [CrossRef]
27. Casassus, J.; Liu, P.; Tang, K. Economic Linkages, Relative Scarcity, and Commodity Futures Returns. *Rev. Financ. Stud.* **2013**, *26*, 1324–1362. [CrossRef]
28. Ahmed, S.; Tsvetanov, D. The predictive performance of commodity futures risk factors. *J. Bank. Financ.* **2016**, *71*, 20–36. [CrossRef]
29. Gao, X.; Li, B.; Liu, R. The relative pricing of WTI and Brent crude oil futures: Expectations or risk premia? *J. Commod. Mark.* **2023**, *30*, 100274. [CrossRef]
30. Yang, Y.; Zhang, J.; Chen, S. Information effects of monetary policy announcements on oil price. *J. Commod. Mark.* **2023**, *30*, 100268. [CrossRef]
31. Chang, C.L. Extreme events, economic uncertainty and speculation on occurrences of price bubbles in crude oil futures. *Energy Econ.* **2024**, *130*, 107318. [CrossRef]
32. Cui, J.; Maghyereh, A. Unveiling interconnectedness: Exploring higher-order moments among energy, precious metals, industrial metals, and agricultural commodities in the context of geopolitical risks and systemic stress. *J. Commod. Mark.* **2024**, *33*, 100380. [CrossRef]
33. Dai, Z.; Zhang, X.; Liang, C. Efficient predictability of oil price: The role of VIX-based panic index shadow line difference. *Energy Econ.* **2024**, *129*, 107234. [CrossRef]
34. Gronwald, M.; Jin, X. Measuring world oil market integration with a Thick Pen. *Energy Econ.* **2024**, *130*, 107315. [CrossRef]
35. Gupta, R.; Nielsen, J.; Pierdzioch, C. Stock market bubbles and the realized volatility of oil price returns. *Energy Econ.* **2024**, *132*, 107432. [CrossRef]

36. Luo, Q.; Ma, F.; Wang, J.; Wu, Y. Changing determinant driver and oil volatility forecasting: A comprehensive analysis. *Energy Econ.* **2024**, *129*, 107187. [CrossRef]
37. Zhang, L.; Chen, Y.; Bouri, E. Time-varying jump intensity and volatility forecasting of crude oil returns. *Energy Econ.* **2024**, *129*, 107236. [CrossRef]
38. Bakshi, G.; Gao, X.; Xue, J. Recovery with Applications to Forecasting Equity Disaster Probability and Testing the Spanning Hypothesis in the Treasury Market. *J. Financ. Quant. Anal.* **2023**, *58*, 1808–1842. [CrossRef]
39. Bakshi, G.; Crosby, J.; Gao, X.; Zhou, W. *A New Formula for the Expected Excess Return of the Market*; Working Paper; Temple University: Philadelphia, PA, USA, 2024.

commodities

MDPI

Article

Sector Formula for Approximation of Spread Option Value & Greeks and Its Applications

Roza Galeeva [1,*] and Zi Wang [2]

[1] Department of Applied Mathematics and Statistics, Whiting School of Engineering, Johns Hopkins University, Homewood Campus, Baltimore, MD 21218, USA
[2] Questrom School of Business, Boston University, 595 Commonwealth Av., Boston, MA 02215, USA; ziw@bu.edu
* Correspondence: groza@jhu.edu

Abstract: The goal of this paper is to derive closed-form approximation formulas for the spread option value and Greeks by using double integration and investigating the exercise boundary. We have found that the straight-line approximation suggested in previous research does not perform well for curved exercise boundaries. We propose a novel approach: to integrate in a sector and find a closed-form formula expressed in terms of the bivariate normal CDF. We call it the sector formula. Numerical tests show the good accuracy of our sector formula. We demonstrate applications of the formula to the market data of calendar spread options for three major commodities, WTI, Natural Gas, and Corn, listed on the CME site as of May, April, and June 2024.

Keywords: spread option; correlation; integration; commodity; calendar; sector

1. Introduction

The ubiquitous role of spread options in all markets is well known. Examples include foreign exchange markets where spreads involve interest rates in different countries or fixed-income markets with spreads between rates on different maturities or spreads between quality levels; see the overview of the *"zoology"* of spread options in [1].

Spread options are especially important in commodity markets, as many energy assets have spread options embedded in them. For example, the evaluation of power plants can be represented as a spark spread option: the spread between power and fuel prices, as reviewed in [2], for example. Another application involves the evaluation of storage, whose value can be replicated through calendar spread options. This subject is discussed in numerous sources (see a chapter in the recent book [3]). Transmission contracts can be modeled by options on a locational spread, the difference between prices of power or gas at two liquid points. In electricity markets, an interconnector gives the owner the option to transmit electricity between two locations and can be valued as a strip of real options written on the spread between power prices, as considered in [4]. Other examples include the evaluation of refineries through crack spreads, crush spreads in agricultural markets, and many others. Therefore, an accurate evaluation of spread options and their Greeks is utterly important for commodity trading and risk management.

In this paper, we study a classical case of a commodity spread option on two futures, F_1 and F_2, with the payoff

$$\max(F_1(T) - F_2(T) - K, 0) \tag{1}$$

where T is the option expiry, and K is the strike. Using futures simplifies calculations. We also choose futures since the majority of trading in commodities happens in futures markets; applications to commodity markets are our main interest. For the same reason, we only consider the case of positive correlations. We assume the standard setup of the joint normal distribution of futures returns:

$$dF_1(t) = \sqrt{1-\rho^2}\sigma_1 F_1(t)dW_1(t) + \rho\sigma_1 F_2(t)dW_2(t)$$
$$dF_2(t) = \sigma_2 F_2(t)dW_2(t) \tag{2}$$

where $W_1(t)$ and $W_2(t)$ are two independent standard Brownian motions under the risk-neutral measure, σ_1 and σ_2 are the volatilities, and ρ is the correlation between the two Brownian motions. Let $F_1(0) = F_1$ and $F_2(0) = F_2$. The futures' prices at the time of expiry T can be written as

$$F_1(T) = F_1 \exp(-\frac{1}{2}\sigma_1^2 T + \sqrt{1-\rho^2}\sigma_1\sqrt{T}X + \rho\sigma_1\sqrt{T}Y)$$
$$F_2(T) = F_2 \exp(-\frac{1}{2}\sigma_2^2 T + \sigma_2\sqrt{T}Y) \tag{3}$$

where X and Y are two independent standard normal random variables.

The spread call price is the discounted expected payoff under the risk-neutral measure:

$$c(K,T) = e^{-rT}E[(F_1(T) - F_2(T) - K)I_{[F_1(T)-F_2(T)-K\geq 0]}] \tag{4}$$

We call the boundary of the domain

$$F_1(T) - F_2(T) - K \geq 0$$

the *exercise* boundary. A more precise definition will be provided later.

In this paper, we consider only the cases of non-negative strikes, $K \geq 0$. A spread option with a negative strike, $K_1 < 0$, can be transformed into a spread option with a positive strike, $K = -K_1$, as follows: the payoff of a call spread option with a negative strike is equivalent to a put spread option with strike K and a reverse spread:

$$(F_1(T) - F_2(T) - K_1)^+ = (K - (F_2(T) - F_1(T)))^+$$

Using the standard put–call parity and no-arbitrage arguments, we derive the following relationship:

$$c(K_1, T, F_1, F_2) = c(K, T, F_2, F_1) + Ke^{-rT} + (F_1 - F_2)e^{-rT} \tag{5}$$

The inputs to a spread option evaluation include commodity future prices F_1 and F_2, volatilities σ_1 and σ_2, correlation ρ, contractual strike K, and expiration T of the option. For tradable commodity locations, future prices and volatilities are observable from the market; however, a correlation is rarely perceivable. There are different methods to deal with this problem. One method is to employ historical correlations. Another way is to use the *implied correlation*, which is implied by correlation products, spread options in particular. The concept is similar to the implied volatility "implied" by a traded option. The subject of implied correlation is discussed in detail in [5]. The authors developed a general framework employing a Gaussian copula, in which an implied correlation can be rigorously defined for a class of derivative contracts written on two assets.

There is a vast amount of research devoted to the problem of the evaluation of spread options. For the case of a zero strike, $K = 0$ (*exchange* option), the value is given by the well-known Margrabe formula [6]. In the case of a spread between two commodity futures, it is given by the following formula:

$$C_S = e^{-rT}(F_1 N(d_1) - F_2 N(d_2)), d_1 = \frac{\ln\left(\frac{F_1}{F_2}\right) + 1/2\sigma^2 T}{\sigma\sqrt{T}}, d_2 = d_1 - \sigma\sqrt{T} \tag{6}$$

where $\sigma = \sqrt{\sigma_1^2 - 2\rho\sigma_1\sigma_2 + \sigma_2^2}$.

The existing methods to price non-zero-strike spread options involve numerical methods, which include Monte Carlo, tree methods [7], numerical integration [8], and analytical approximations.

Among practitioners, the most popular analytical approximation method for a commodity spread option value is the Kirk formula, ref. [9], due to its simplicity: it is a modified version of the Margrabe formula with adjusted volatility:

$$C(K,T) = e^{-rT}\left(F_1 N(\hat{d}_1) - (F_2+K)N(\hat{d}_2)\right), \hat{d}_1 = \frac{\ln\left(\frac{F_1}{F_2+K}\right) + 1/2\hat{\sigma}^2 T}{\hat{\sigma}\sqrt{T}}, \hat{d}_2 = \hat{d}_1 - \hat{\sigma}\sqrt{T} \tag{7}$$

$$\hat{\sigma} = \sqrt{\sigma_1^2 - 2\rho\sigma_1\hat{\sigma}_2 + (\hat{\sigma}_2)^2}, \hat{\sigma}_2 = \frac{\sigma_2 F_1}{F_2+K}$$

Carmona and Durrleman [10] modeled correlations by a trigonometric function and developed accurate lower bounds for the spread option value by solving a complicated optimization problem.

Bjerksund and Stensland [11] calculated the approximate spread option value by integrating the payoff over the following type of exercise boundary:

$$\{F_1(T) \geq aF_2(T)^b\}$$

$$C_B = e^{-rt}E[(F_1(T) - F_2(T) - K)I_{\{F_1(T)\geq aF_2(T)^b\}}] \tag{8}$$

For any given a, b, they give a general formula for the integral and verify that for $a = F_2 + K$ and $b = \frac{F_2}{F_2+K}$, the above formula gives a good approximation. Their approximated boundary $\{F_1(T) \geq aF_2(T)^b\}$ is a straight line in the (x, y) plane, which implies that the formula works well only if the curvature of the real boundary is small.

Caldana and Fusai [12] extended the lower bound approximation of Bjerksund and Stensland beyond the classical Black–Scholes framework to models such as jump-diffusion models with different jump size distributions, multivariate stochastic volatility models, and mixtures of variance gamma models. Another recent paper [13] on pricing spread options under a non-Gaussian setup exploits the flexibility of the copula function in capturing the dependence between marginals. The authors consider variance gamma, Heston's stochastic volatility, and affine Heston–Nandi GARCH(1,1) models.

Among practitioners, the pricing of the spread option under the assumption of lognormal prices remains the most popular due to its simplicity and ease of implementation. Thus, we chose the classical GBM setup and looked for an approximation formula.

The main contribution of our study to existing research on the problem is as follows: We derived yet another *new* closed-form approximation of the spread option value and Greeks by using double integration and analyzing the exercise boundary. We identified situations in the previous integration formulas that caused large errors. In such cases, we show the superiority of our formula over the previous methods and its good overall accuracy. We demonstrate the application of our sector formula to the market data of calendar spread options for major commodities.

Our approach, in some respects, is similar to the method considered in [14], where the authors propose a quadratic approximation of the exercise boundary. To overcome the difficulty of integration over a domain with a parabolic boundary, they approximate the integration using the assumption that the curvature of the real boundary near the origin is small. As a result, their method is accurate when the assumption holds. The formula is expressed in terms of univariate normal CDF functions whose arguments are defined by the coefficients of the Taylor expansion of the exercise boundary. Ultimately, the ingredients of the formula result from integration over a straight line in the two-dimensional plane.

We tackle the problem in a different way: We carefully analyzed the shape of the exercise boundary, which is defined by the sign of $\sigma_2 - \rho\sigma_1$. We discovered that the straight-line approximation does not perform well for curved exercise boundaries and found explicit conditions of the inputs resulting in a big curvature and, therefore, the situations where [14]'s formula can produce errors. In our proposed approach, we integrate in a *sector*, thoroughly investigate the optimal choice of the sector, and find a closed-form formula expressed in terms of the bivariate normal CDF. This is a new result and can be of interest in itself. The formula is simple and can be easily implemented in Excel.

As in the other papers, we worked out Greeks, such as Delta and sensitivity to correlation (we call it "Rhoza"; see the prehistory of the name in [15]). Since a correlation is often an unknown input, this sensitivity is important for assessing model risk. The sensitivity to correlation is very useful in the calculation of the second-order Greeks of derivatives valued by Monte Carlo, such as gamma and cross-gamma (see [15]). This sensitivity is also discussed in [5], where the authors use the numerical integration formula in a more general setting. Unsurprisingly, the formulas for Greeks are fairly complicated. We identified the main terms that give reasonable estimates of Greeks in most situations.

We compare our results in terms of accuracy and speed with those obtained by three methods, refs. [9,11,14], in different types of scenarios. Our method shows great accuracy in all cases and superiority in scenarios where the curvature near the origin is not small. To compare the results, we randomized the inputs, ran the evaluation, and obtained statistics on the errors and the speed.

To verify the accuracy of closed-form pricing and Greek formulas, as a benchmark, we picked a Monte Carlo simulation method with 10,000,000 paths. We chose the Monte Carlo method because it is a standard industry procedure. To ensure the efficiency and accuracy of MC results, we applied antithetic variables and control variate techniques. Another alternative for a benchmark is to use semi-analytical techniques based on transforming the two-dimensional problem into one-dimensional integration; see [8,14]. Hereinafter, the second benchmark is referred to as "numerical integration". We demonstrate that the two benchmark values are very close and selected the Monte Carlo method for the reasons mentioned above.

To illustrate the details of the sector formula, we give two examples and compare values and Greeks with the MC and numerical integration benchmarks.

We apply our sector formula to the market data of commodity spread options, specifically calendar spread options, for three major commodity futures: WTI, Natural Gas, and Corn. Calendar spread options provide operators of energy assets and professional traders with opportunities to hedge or benefit from moves in commodity futures spreads. These data were listed on the CME site as of 30 April, 7 May, 5 June, and 6 June 2024.

We calculated the implied correlations using the appropriate market inputs, including actively traded calendar spread options. We also applied the numerical integration formula with the same inputs to back up the implied correlations. The results are very close. The advantage of the sector formula is that it does not require any special tools and can be implemented in Excel, including for the approximated Greeks. We also illustrate how the analytical approximation of Rhoza can be utilized to calculate a model valuation adjustment to a CSO value due to the uncertainty in the correlation input. This is a standard practice for arriving at a fair value of the derivative.

The rest of this paper is organized as follows. In Section 2, we discuss the setup and analyze and approximate the exercise boundary. We derive two closed-form approximation formulas for the spread option value based on the straight-line boundary and the sector boundary, the sector formula. We also present closed-form Greeks, Deltas, and Rhoza. In Section 3, we describe the Monte Carlo procedure to arrive at the benchmark value and provide a comparison of the accuracy and speed of our method vs. the three aforementioned methods. In Section 4, we apply the sector formula to the market data of commodity spread options, specifically calendar spread options, taken from the CME site. Section 5 concludes the paper. A few of the details and proofs are provided in the Appendix sections.

2. Analytical Results of Spread Option Evaluation

2.1. Setup and Assumptions

2.1.1. Call Spread Option

Consider the spread call with maturity T and strike K, which has a payoff (1) and the value given by the risk-neutral evaluation (4).

Based on Equation (3), this value can be expressed by the following integral:

$$c(K,T) = e^{-rT} \int\int_{x\geq h(y)} (F_1 e^{-\frac{1}{2}\sigma_1^2 T + \sqrt{1-\rho^2}\sigma_1\sqrt{T}x + \rho\sigma_1\sqrt{T}y} - F_2 e^{-\frac{1}{2}\sigma_2^2 T + \sigma_2\sqrt{T}y} - K)\phi(x)\phi(y)dxdy \quad (9)$$

where the exercise boundary is

$$h(y) = \frac{\ln(F_2 \exp(-\frac{1}{2}\sigma_2^2 T + \sigma_2\sqrt{T}y) + K) - \rho\sigma_1\sqrt{T}y}{\sqrt{1-\rho^2}\sigma_1\sqrt{T}} + \frac{\frac{1}{2}\sigma_1^2 T - \ln F_1}{\sqrt{1-\rho^2}\sigma_1\sqrt{T}} \quad (10)$$

2.1.2. Exercise Boundary

Performing the integration of the payoff over such a boundary is very complicated. Therefore, we can start by investigating the boundary function $h(y)$.

The boundary slope is

$$\frac{\partial h(y)}{\partial y} = \frac{1}{\sqrt{1-\rho^2}\sigma_1\sqrt{T}} \left(\frac{F_2\sigma_2\sqrt{T}e^{-\frac{1}{2}\sigma_2^2 T + \sigma_2\sqrt{T}y}}{F_2 e^{-\frac{1}{2}\sigma_2^2 T + \sigma_2\sqrt{T}y} + K} - \rho\sigma_1\sqrt{T}\right) \quad (11)$$

which converges asymptotically to constant values:

$$\lim_{y\to+\infty} \frac{\partial h(y)}{\partial y} = \frac{\sigma_2 - \rho\sigma_1}{\sqrt{1-\rho^2}\sigma_1}, \qquad \lim_{y\to-\infty} \frac{\partial h(y)}{\partial y} = -\frac{\rho}{\sqrt{1-\rho^2}} \quad (12)$$

Based on these observations, the spread option evaluation can be divided into two cases, depending on the values of σ_1, σ_2, and ρ:

1. In the first case, $\sigma_2 \leq \rho\sigma_1$, and the asymptotic slopes have the same sign.
2. In the second case, $\sigma_2 > \rho\sigma_1$, and the asymptotic slopes have different signs.

We illustrate these two cases in the following Figure 1:

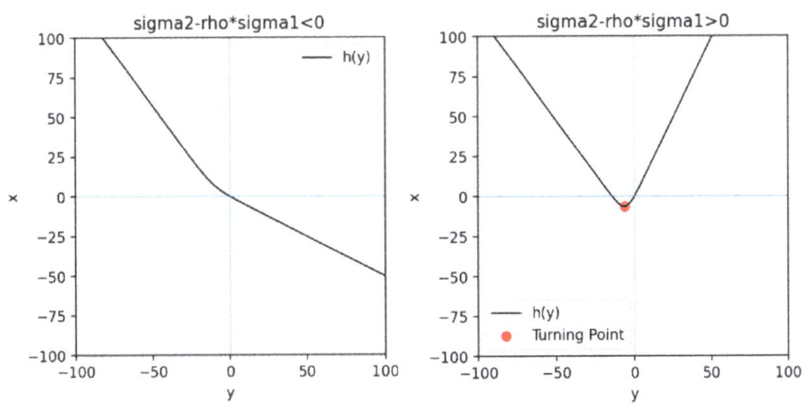

Figure 1. Two types of exercise boundaries.

2.1.3. Boundary Approximation

To approximate the boundary $\{(x,y) : x \geq h(y)\}$, we propose two types of approximations.

1. The first type is a straight-line boundary:
$$A(a,b) = \{(x,y) : x - by \geq a\}$$
2. The second type is a sector boundary:
$$A(a,b,c,d) = \{(x,y) : x - by \geq a, x - dy \geq c\}$$
with $b - d \neq 0$.

The integration of the spread call payoff over the straight-line-type boundary can be calculated as

$$I(a,b) \triangleq e^{-rT} \int\int_{A(a,b)} (F_1 e^{-\frac{1}{2}\sigma_1^2 T + \sqrt{1-\rho^2}\sigma_1\sqrt{T}x + \rho\sigma_1\sqrt{T}y} - F_2 e^{-\frac{1}{2}\sigma_2^2 T + \sigma_2\sqrt{T}y} - K)\phi(x)\phi(y)dxdy \tag{13}$$

Correspondingly, the integration of the call spread payoff over the sector-type boundary can be calculated as

$$J(a,b,c,d) \triangleq e^{-rT} \int\int_{A(a,b,c,d)} (F_1 e^{-\frac{1}{2}\sigma_1^2 T + \sqrt{1-\rho^2}\sigma_1\sqrt{T}x + \rho\sigma_1\sqrt{T}y} - F_2 e^{-\frac{1}{2}\sigma_2^2 T + \sigma_2\sqrt{T}y} - K)\phi(x)\phi(y)dxdy \tag{14}$$

Lemma 1.
$$I(a,b) = e^{-rT}(F_1 N(d_1) - F_2 N(d_2) - KN(d_3)) \tag{15}$$
where
$$d_1 = -\frac{a + (b\rho - \sqrt{1-\rho^2})\sigma_1\sqrt{T}}{\sqrt{1+b^2}}, \quad d_2 = -\frac{a + b\sigma_2\sqrt{T}}{\sqrt{1+b^2}}, \quad d_3 = -\frac{a}{\sqrt{1+b^2}}$$

Proof. See Appendix A. □

Lemma 2.
$$J(a,b,c,d) = e^{-rT}(F_1 M(d_{11}, d_{12}, \tilde{\rho}) - F_2 M(d_{21}, d_{22}, \tilde{\rho}) - KM(d_{31}, d_{32}, \tilde{\rho})) \tag{16}$$
where
$$\tilde{\rho} = \frac{bd + 1}{\sqrt{(1+b^2)(1+d^2)}}$$
$$M(a,b,\tilde{\rho}) = \int\int_{\{x<a,y<b\}} f(x,y,\tilde{\rho})dxdy, \quad f(x,y,\tilde{\rho}) = \frac{1}{2\pi\sqrt{1-\tilde{\rho}^2}} e^{-\frac{x^2+y^2-2\tilde{\rho}xy}{2(1-\tilde{\rho}^2)}}$$
$$d_{11} = -\frac{a + (b\rho - \sqrt{1-\rho^2})\sigma_1\sqrt{T}}{\sqrt{1+b^2}}, \quad d_{21} = -\frac{a + b\sigma_2\sqrt{T}}{\sqrt{1+b^2}}, \quad d_{31} = -\frac{a}{\sqrt{1+b^2}}$$
$$d_{12} = -\frac{c + (d\rho - \sqrt{1-\rho^2})\sigma_1\sqrt{T}}{\sqrt{1+d^2}}, \quad d_{22} = -\frac{c + d\sigma_2\sqrt{T}}{\sqrt{1+d^2}}, \quad d_{32} = -\frac{c}{\sqrt{1+d^2}}$$

Proof. See Appendix B. □

2.2. Domain of Integration in Prices and Returns

The expression $J(a, b, c, d)$ describes the result of the integration of the spread payoff over any sector region in the x-y plane. To clarify its meaning, we can transform x, y into future prices and returns at maturity.

Corollary 1. *For any given (a,b,c,d) with* $b - d \neq 0$*, if* $\rho < 1$*, we have the presentation of the integration* $J(a, b, c, d)$ *as future prices at maturity.*

$$J(a, b, c, d) = e^{-rT} E[(F_1(T) - F_2(T) - K) I_{\{F_{1T} \geq \alpha_1 F_2(T)^{\beta_1}\} \cap \{F_1(T) \geq \alpha_2 F_2(T)^{\beta_2}\}}] \tag{17}$$

where

$$\alpha_1 = \frac{F_1 e^{a\sqrt{1-\rho^2}\sigma_1\sqrt{T} - \frac{1}{2}(\sigma_1^2 - \sigma_2^2\beta_1)T}}{F_2^{\beta_1}}$$

$$\beta_1 = \frac{b\sqrt{1-\rho^2}\sigma_1\sqrt{T} + \rho\sigma_1}{\sigma_2}$$

$$\alpha_2 = \frac{F_1 e^{c\sqrt{1-\rho^2}\sigma_1\sqrt{T} - \frac{1}{2}(\sigma_1^2 - \sigma_2^2\beta_2)T}}{F_2^{\beta_2}}$$

$$\beta_2 = \frac{d\sqrt{1-\rho^2}\sigma_1\sqrt{T} + \rho\sigma_1}{\sigma_2}$$

Proof. See Appendix B. □

Let $R_{1T} = \ln \frac{F_1(T)}{F_1(0)}$ and $R_{2T} = \ln \frac{F_2(T)}{F_2(0)}$ be the returns of the two assets at maturity. Then, we can easily obtain

$$J(a, b, c, d) = e^{-rT} E[(F_1(T) - F_2(T) - K) I_{\{R_{1T} - \beta_1 R_{2T} \geq \ln(\alpha_1 \frac{F_2^{\beta_1}}{F_1})\} \cap \{R_{1T} - \beta_2 R_{2T} \geq \ln(\alpha_2 \frac{F_2^{\beta_2}}{F_1})\}}] \tag{18}$$

This representation shows that the integration region is also a sector shape region in the returns plane, where the sector is defined by $(\alpha_1, \beta_1, \alpha_2, \beta_2)$. The presented domain of integration generalizes the domain suggested in [11].

2.3. Closed-Form Spread Option Formulas

The shape of the exercise boundary depends on the parameters σ_1, σ_2, ρ, and moneyness.

For example, when $\sigma_2 - \rho\sigma_1 \leq 0$, the boundary can be approximated reasonably well by a straight line. This is illustrated by Figure 2, where we plot the exercise boundary for the chosen $F_1, F_2, \sigma_1, \sigma_2$, and T and different choices of correlation ρ and strike K. The ATM strike is defined by $K_{ATM} = F_1 - F_2$.

When $\sigma_2 - \rho\sigma_1 > 0$, there is a turning point on the boundary, where the derivative $h'(y) = 0$. If the strike is small, the turning point is far away from the origin, and the curvature near the origin is small since the boundary $h(y)$ converges to a straight line as $y \to \infty$. However, if K becomes larger, the turning point moves closer to the origin, which leads to a larger curvature near the origin. This is shown in Figure 3.

Other situations that create a bigger curvature are high correlations, differences in σ_1 and σ_2, and longer horizons; more details are provided in Appendix C. In some of the scenarios, previous approximation methods can cause large errors. This will be illustrated by the numerical tests.

We propose two different closed-form approximation formulas based on the straight-line boundary and the sector boundary. For the straight-line-type boundary, we approximate the real boundary by the tangent line of the boundary $h(y)$ at $y = 0$ and obtain our first closed-form approximation formula (see Figures 4 and 5, red lines).

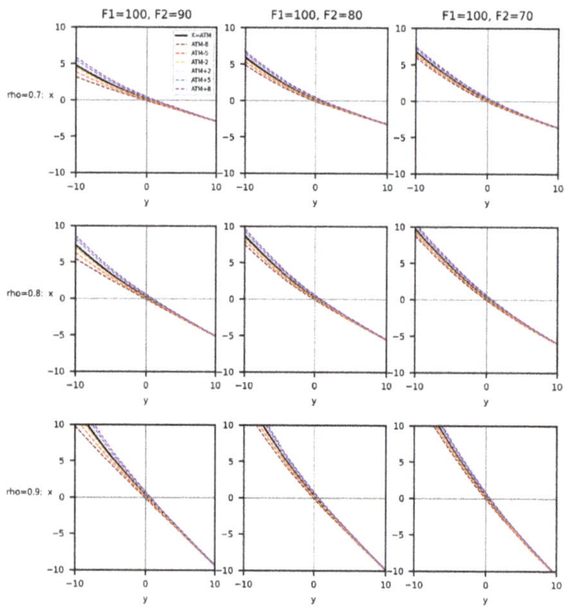

Figure 2. Boundaries in the case of $\sigma_2 - \rho\sigma_1 \leq 0$: $\sigma_1 = 0.4$, $\sigma_2 = 0.2$, $T = 1$.

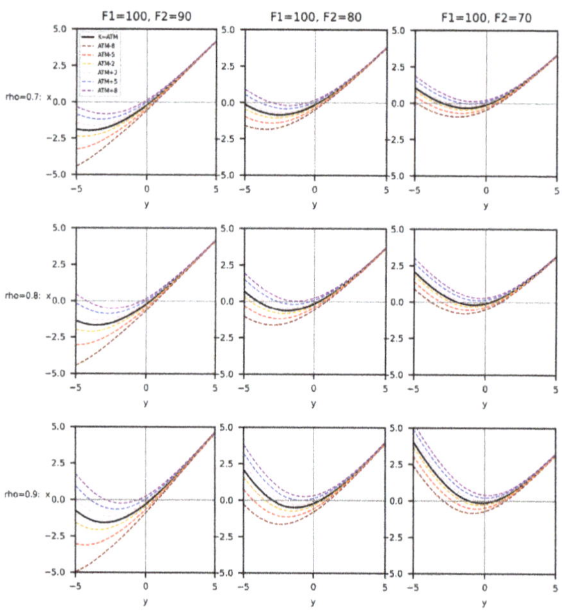

Figure 3. Boundaries in the case of $\sigma_2 - \rho\sigma_1 > 0$: $\sigma_2 = 0.5$, $\sigma_1 = 0.36$, $T = 1$.

Proposition 1. *Let $K \geq 0$ and $|\rho| < 1$. Under the GBM setup and using a straight-line boundary, the approximated spread call value is given by the following formula:*

$$\tilde{c}(F_1, F_2, T, K) = e^{-rT}(F_1 N(d_1) - F_2 N(d_2) - K N(d_3)) \tag{19}$$

where

$$d_1 = -\frac{a + (b\rho - \sqrt{1-\rho^2})\sigma_1\sqrt{T}}{\sqrt{1+b^2}}, \quad d_2 = -\frac{a + b\sigma_2\sqrt{T}}{\sqrt{1+b^2}}, \quad d_3 = -\frac{a}{\sqrt{1+b^2}}$$

$$a = \frac{\ln(F_2\exp(-\frac{1}{2}\sigma_2^2 T) + K) + \frac{1}{2}\sigma_1^2 T - \ln F_1}{\sqrt{1-\rho^2}\sigma_1\sqrt{T}}$$

$$b = \frac{\frac{F_2\exp(-\frac{1}{2}\sigma_2^2 T)\sigma_2}{F_2\exp(-\frac{1}{2}\sigma_2^2 T) + K} - \rho\sigma_1}{\sqrt{1-\rho^2}\sigma_1}$$

Proof. See Appendix C. □

For a U-shape type of boundary, we use the sector determined by two tangent lines near the origin to approximate the real boundary (see Figure 5, blue lines). We develop the second closed-form approximation formula, expressed in terms of the bivariate normal CDF. This is the main result of this paper. We call it the **sector formula** .

Proposition 2. *Let $K \geq 0$ and $|\rho| < 1$. Under the geometric Brownian motion's setup and using a sector boundary, the approximated spread call value is given by the following formula:*

$$\hat{c}(F_1, F_2, T, K) = e^{-rT}(F_1 M(d_{11}, d_{12}, \tilde{\rho}) - F_2 M(d_{21}, d_{22}, \tilde{\rho}) - KM(d_{31}, d_{32}, \tilde{\rho})) \quad (20)$$

where

$$\tilde{\rho} = \frac{bd+1}{\sqrt{(1+b^2)(1+d^2)}}$$

$$M(a, b, \tilde{\rho}) = \int\int_{\{x<a, y<b\}} f(x, y, \tilde{\rho})dxdy, \quad f(x, y, \tilde{\rho}) = \frac{1}{2\pi\sqrt{1-\tilde{\rho}^2}} e^{-\frac{x^2+y^2-2\tilde{\rho}xy}{2(1-\tilde{\rho}^2)}}$$

$$d_{11} = -\frac{a + (b\rho - \sqrt{1-\rho^2})\sigma_1\sqrt{T}}{\sqrt{1+b^2}}, \quad d_{21} = -\frac{a + b\sigma_2\sqrt{T}}{\sqrt{1+b^2}}, \quad d_{31} = -\frac{a}{\sqrt{1+b^2}}$$

$$d_{12} = -\frac{c + (d\rho - \sqrt{1-\rho^2})\sigma_1\sqrt{T}}{\sqrt{1+d^2}}, \quad d_{22} = -\frac{c + d\sigma_2\sqrt{T}}{\sqrt{1+d^2}}, \quad d_{32} = -\frac{c}{\sqrt{1+d^2}}$$

$$a = x_1 - b\cdot y_1, \quad b = h'(y_1), \quad c = x_2 - d\cdot y_2, \quad d = h'(y_2)$$

$$x_1 = h(y_1), \quad y_1 = \frac{-uv + \sqrt{R^2(u^2+1) - v^2}}{u^2+1}$$

$$x_2 = h(y_2), \quad y_2 = \frac{-uv - \sqrt{R^2(u^2+1) - v^2}}{u^2+1}$$

$$u = \frac{\sigma_2 - \rho\sigma_1 - \frac{K\sigma_2}{F_2 e^{-\frac{1}{2}\sigma_2^2 T} + K}}{\sqrt{1-\rho^2}\sigma_1}, \quad v = \frac{\ln\frac{F_2 e^{-\frac{1}{2}\sigma_2^2 T} + K}{F_1} + \frac{1}{2}\sigma_1^2 T}{\sqrt{1-\rho^2}\sigma_1\sqrt{T}}, \quad R = \max(1, \frac{6}{5}|h(0)|)$$

Proof. See Appendix D. □

Both formulas can be used to value spread call pricing. The tangent (red) line formula (Proposition 1) is more suitable for scenarios where the curvature is small near the origin. By contrast, the sector boundary (blue lines) is universal, and it works in all scenarios. This is illustrated in Figures 4 and 5. Using numerical tests, we will show that the sector formula gives better precision. This is not surprising, as by choosing an appropriate sector, we can better approximate the exercise boundary compared with a straight line. We kept the same choices of σ_1, σ_2, and T as before.

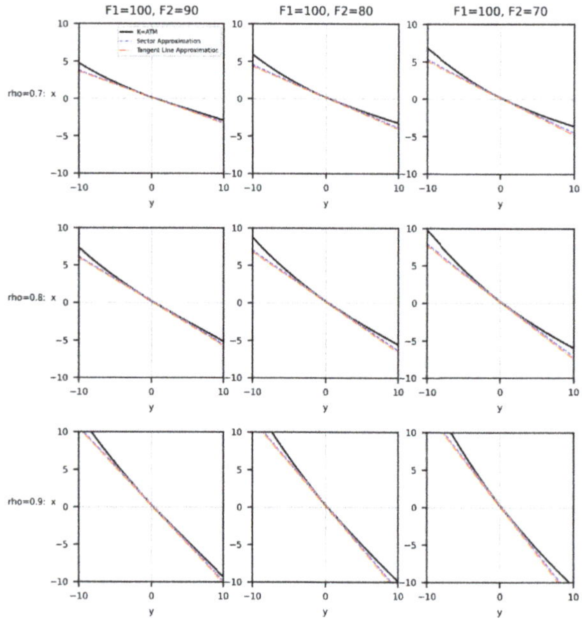

Figure 4. Approximations of the exercise boundary in the case $\sigma_2 - \rho\sigma_1 \leq 0$.

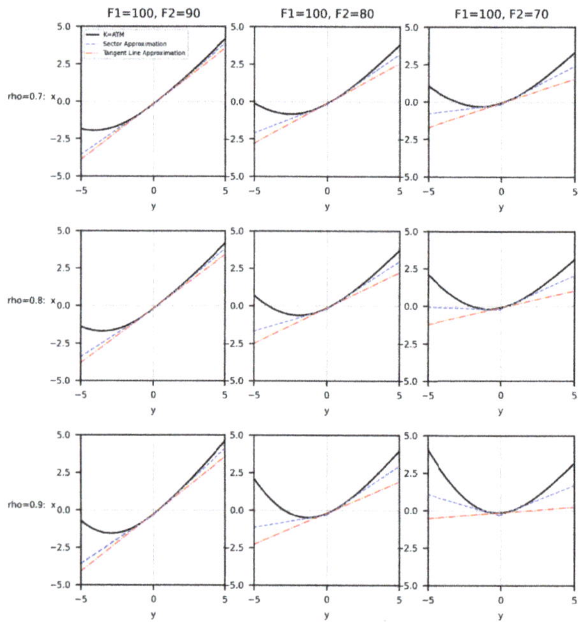

Figure 5. Approximations of the exercise boundary in the case $\sigma_2 - \rho\sigma_1 > 0$.

2.4. Closed-Form Greeks

For the sector formula in Proposition 2, we find closed-form Deltas with respect to F_1 and F_2, as well as a closed-form Rhoza, i.e., the first-order derivative of the call spread option price with respect to correlation ρ. Recall the sector formula:

$$\hat{c}(F_1, F_2, T, K) = e^{-rT}(F_1 M(d_{11}, d_{12}, \tilde{\rho}) - F_2 M(d_{21}, d_{22}, \tilde{\rho}) - K M(d_{31}, d_{32}, \tilde{\rho})) \tag{21}$$

Proposition 3.

$$\frac{\partial \hat{c}(F_1, F_2, T, K)}{\partial F_1} = \Delta_1 + C_1 D_{11} + C_2 D_{12} + C_3 D_{13} + C_4 D_{14} \tag{22}$$

$$\frac{\partial \hat{c}(F_1, F_2, T, K)}{\partial F_2} = \Delta_2 + C_1 D_{21} + C_2 D_{22} + C_3 D_{23} + C_4 D_{24} \tag{23}$$

$$\frac{\partial \hat{c}(F_1, F_2, T, K)}{\partial \rho} = Z + C_1 D_{31} + C_2 D_{32} + C_3 D_{33} + C_4 D_{44} \tag{24}$$

In these expressions, we identify the terms that make the main contributions. For example, for Delta with respect to F_1, it is the term Δ_1 that is multiplied by F_1 (similar to Black Delta $e^{-rT}N(d_1)$); for Delta with respect to F_2, it is the term Δ_2 that is multiplied by F_2. Rhoza's decomposition is less obvious. Specifically,

$$\Delta_1 = e^{-rT} M(d_{11}, d_{12}, \hat{\rho}), \quad \Delta_2 = -e^{-rT} M(d_{21}, d_{22}, \hat{\rho}),$$

$$Z = -e^{-rT}(F_1 M_x(d_{11}, d_{12}, \hat{\rho}) \frac{\sigma_1 \sqrt{T}(b\sqrt{1-\rho^2} + \rho)}{\sqrt{(1+b^2)(1-\rho^2)}} + F_1 M_y(d_{11}, d_{12}, \hat{\rho}) \frac{\sigma_1 \sqrt{T}(d\sqrt{1-\rho^2} + \rho)}{\sqrt{(1+d^2)(1-\rho^2)}}) \tag{25}$$

The derivatives of the binomial normal CDF $M_x(d_{11}, d_{12}, \rho)$,$M_y(d_{11}, d_{12}, \rho)$ can be expressed through the univariate pdf and CDF of the normal distribution:

$$M_x(x, y, \rho) = n(y) N\left(x, \rho y, \sqrt{1-\rho^2}\right)$$

$$M_y(x, y, \rho) = n(y) N\left(y, \rho x, \sqrt{1-\rho^2}\right)$$

where $n(x)$ is the pdf of the standard normal distribution, and $N(a, \mu, \sigma)$ is the normal CDF with mean μ and standard deviation σ evaluated at a.

See Appendix E for further details on the given formulas, such as C_i and D_{ij}.

Unsurprisingly, the above formulas for Greeks are pretty complex. The identified main terms Δ_1, Δ_2, and Z are simple but still pretty accurate approximations of the Greeks $\frac{\partial \hat{c}(K,T)}{\partial F_1}$, $\frac{\partial \hat{c}(K,T)}{\partial F_2}$, and $\frac{\partial \hat{c}(K,T)}{\partial \rho}$ in most situations. This will be verified by our numerical tests.

2.5. Two Examples

We illustrate the details of the sector and line formulas on two examples and compare them with the MC and numerical integration benchmarks. Table 1 demonstrates the comparison of the values. The two benchmarks are very close; the sector formula is more accurate, especially for the second case of higher correlations.

Table 1. Two examples of calculations of spread options by using the line and sector formulas.

Case	F_1	F_2	K	T	σ_1	σ_2	ρ	r	MC	Num Int	Line	Sector
1	100	90	10	1	0.2	0.36	0.7	0	9.2676	9.2677	9.2661	9.2675
2	100	70	30	1	0.3	0.5	0.9	0	6.2108	6.211	6.0072	6.1860

Table 2 gives the ingredients of the line formula (19) for the two examples.

Table 2. Line parameters.

Case	Line	d_1	d_2	d_3	a	b
1	9.2661	0.1430	−0.1182	0.1649	−0.2669	1.2732
2	6.0072	0.2724	0.0515	0.2783	−0.3123	0.5090

Tables 3 and 4 provide the details of the sector formula (20) for the same examples.

Table 3. Sector parameters, part I.

Case	Sector	d_{11}	d_{12}	d_{21}	d_{22}	d_{31}	d_{32}	$\tilde{\rho}$
1	9.2675	0.1465	0.1568	−0.1151	−0.1039	0.1726	0.1753	0.9993
2	6.1860	0.2860	0.5045	0.0358	0.3341	0.3667	0.4251	0.8576

Table 4. Sector parameters, part II.

Case	a	b	c	d	x_1	y_1	x_2	y_2	u	v
1	−0.287	1.330	−0.278	1.229	0.686	0.739	−0.867	−0.477	1.273	−0.267
2	−0.489	0.883	−0.432	0.185	0.378	0.982	−0.567	−0.730	0.509	−0.312

In Table 5, we list the approximate sector Greeks, Deltas, and Rhoza for our examples: D_1, (22), D_2, (23), and Z, (24). We compare them with the Greeks obtained by the finite difference of the numerical integration formula (we used a small bump size of 0.001).

Table 5. Sector Greeks vs. Greeks from numerical integration.

Case	Sector Delta D_1	Sector Delta D_2	Sector Rhoza Z	Delta F_1 num. int	Delta F_2 num. int	Rhoza num. int
1	0.5540	−0.4501	−10.9953	0.5525	−0.4416	−11.001
2	0.5672	−4758	−26.6393	0.5470	−0.4572	−26.6744

In the first case, the sector Deltas and true Deltas are very close, within a 0.3% difference. In the second case, the difference in Deltas is bigger but still reasonable, within 4%. Rhozas are remarkably close in both cases.

3. Numerical Results

3.1. Monte Carlo Simulation

To verify the accuracy of our closed-form pricing and Greek formulas using the sector formula, we selected the Monte Carlo simulation method as a benchmark. To ensure the efficiency and accuracy of the MC results, we applied antithetic variables and control variate techniques. The methodology is described in Appendix F.

We chose ATM options, as these are the most sensitive to inputs.

To verify the accuracy of the MC results, we performed the following steps:

- Randomly generate inputs for five ATM spread call option samples from the following range: $F_1 = 100$, $\frac{K}{F_2} \in (0.05, 0.2)$, $F_1 - F_2 - K = 0$, $T = 1$, $r = 0$, $\sigma_1 = 2$, $\sigma_2 \in (0.2, 0.6)$, $\rho \in (0.7, 0999)$.
- For each ATM sample, repeat the simulation 100 times, and for each simulation, use 10,000,000 paths.
- For a given ATM sample and each sample of 100 simulation sets, calculate the percentage differences between the MC results and the approximation results using the line formula (19) and the sector formula (20). Calculate the percentage errors in the Deltas as well. (We chose percentage errors to remove the dependence of price levels.)

Calculate the benchmark Delta from MC using the central finite difference and the bump size $\epsilon = 0.0001$.

- Calculate the standard deviation of 100 MC results for option values and Deltas and compare them with the average errors over the same 100 simulation sets for option prices and Deltas.

From the results in Tables 6 and 7 (the left three columns in Table 7 correspond to Δ_{F_1} and the right three to Δ_{F_2}), we can observe that the simulation errors are immaterial in comparison with the formula errors. This implies that our simulation method can serve as a reasonable benchmark for our tests.

Table 6. Monte Carlo simulation accuracy, values.

		Price	
No.	**MC Std**	**Line**	**Sector**
1	0.0001	−0.0209	−0.0024
2	0.0000	−0.0079	−0.0006
3	0.0000	−0.0170	−0.0014
4	0.0000	−0.0068	−0.0005
5	0.0000	−0.0004	0.0000

Table 7. Monte Carlo simulation accuracy, Deltas.

		Delta				
No.	**MC Std**	**Line**	**Sector**	**MC Std**	**Line**	**Sector**
1	0.0018	0.0193	0.0061	0.0018	−0.0471	−0.0328
2	0.0022	0.0090	0.0024	0.0008	−0.0188	−0.0117
3	0.0037	0.0158	0.0050	0.0018	−0.0449	−0.0330
4	0.0021	0.0086	0.0024	0.0008	−0.0174	−0.0108
5	0.0005	0.0020	0.0006	0.0004	−0.0026	−0.0012

3.2. *Pricing Accuracy under Different Scenarios*

To test the performance of our sector formula and line formula and compare them with the previous formulas from [9,11,14], we implemented our numerical tests in three different scenarios. In each of the scenarios, we randomly chose the inputs and obtained a distribution of percentage errors vs. the MC benchmark prices. We list the statistics of this distribution below.

3.2.1. Scenario 1: Low Strikes and Correlations

In this scenario, we randomly generated 500 ATM samples with $F_1 = 100$, $T = 1$, $r = 0$, $\sigma_1 \in (0.2, 0.5)$, $\sigma_2 \in (0.2, 0.5)$, $\frac{K}{F_2} \in (0.05, 0.2)$, and $\rho \in (0.6, 0.8)$. The results are given in Table 8.

Table 8. Pricing accuracy of Scenario 1.

	Kirk	**Bjerksund**	**Li**	**Tangent Line**	**Sector**
Mean	0.03%	0.04%	0.00%	0.07%	0.01%
Std	0.04%	0.05%	0.00%	0.08%	0.01%
Max	0.22%	0.26%	0.02%	0.45%	0.05%
Min	0.00%	0.00%	0.00%	0.00%	0.00%
Median	0.02%	0.03%	0.00%	0.04%	0.01%

3.2.2. Scenario 2: Higher Strikes and Correlations and $\sigma_2 - \rho\sigma_1 \leq 0$

In this scenario, we randomly generated 500 ATM samples with $F_1 = 100$, $T = 1$, $r = 0$, $\sigma_1 \in (0.3, 0.4)$, $\frac{\sigma_2}{\rho\sigma_1} \in (0.5, 1)$, $\frac{K}{F_2} \in (0.2, 0.5)$, and $\rho \in (0.8, 0.99)$. See Table 9.

Table 9. Pricing accuracy of Scenario 2.

	Kirk	Bjerksund	Li	Tangent Line	Sector
Mean	0.13%	0.05%	0.00%	0.05%	0.01%
Std	0.11%	0.07%	0.00%	0.07%	0.01%
Max	0.57%	0.64%	0.04%	0.36%	0.05%
Min	0.00%	0.00%	0.00%	0.00%	0.00%
Median	0.09%	0.03%	0.00%	0.02%	0.00%

3.2.3. Scenario 3: Higher Strikes and Correlations and $\sigma_2 - \rho\sigma_1 > 0$

In this scenario, we randomly generated 500 ATM samples with $F_1 = 100$, $T = 1$, $r = 0$, $\sigma_1 \in (0.3, 0.4)$, $\frac{\sigma_2}{\rho\sigma_1} \in (1.5, 2)$, $\frac{K}{F_2} \in (0.2, 0.5)$, and $\rho \in (0.8, 0.99)$. See Table 10.

Table 10. Pricing accuracy of Scenario 3.

	Kirk	Bjerksund	Li	Tangent Line	Sector
Mean	1.83%	1.93%	1.39%	3.68%	0.44%
Std	1.79%	1.77%	4.58%	3.82%	0.47%
Max	18.52%	18.55%	57.53%	37.20%	3.76%
Min	0.08%	0.28%	0.00%	0.36%	0.04%
Median	1.29%	1.38%	0.20%	2.49%	0.29%

From the above numerical results, we can observe that in Scenario 1 and Scenario 2, all five methods are accurate. Among them, the formula in [14] and our sector formula are the most accurate. In Scenario 3, for higher strikes and higher correlations, as expected, all of the errors become larger. Some of the errors are significant. In contrast, the sector formula performs much better, and even in extreme cases, the errors are tolerable.

3.2.4. Pricing Speed

From the 1500 samples in the previous three scenarios, we summarize the calculation speed in Table 11.

Table 11. Pricing speed comparison.

	Kirk	Bjerksund	Li	Tangent Line	Sector
Mean	0.0002	0.0003	0.0003	0.0003	0.0008
Std	0.0000	0.0001	0.0000	0.0001	0.0001
Max	0.0003	0.0004	0.0004	0.0005	0.0013
Min	0.0001	0.0002	0.0002	0.0002	0.0006
Median	0.0002	0.0003	0.0003	0.0004	0.0008

From the above statistics, we see that, for the sector formula, it takes twice as long as other methods to obtain the price of a spread call on average. The reason for this is that, in the sector formula, we use the bivariate normal CDF, which is more complex than the standard normal CDF.

3.3. Greek Accuracy and Speed

3.3.1. Three Methods in Comparison with MC Simulation

In this part, we verify the accuracy of the formulas for Greeks given in Proposition 3. We also check that the main terms give a reasonable approximation in most cases. We use the Monte Carlo Greeks as a benchmark. (Another benchmark for Greeks can be obtained through the numerical integration method by differentiating the integrand with respect to price or correlation and calculating the integral.)

We employ the following three methods:

1. The first method is to use the numerical Greeks calculated by the central finite difference using the formulas in Proposition 3.

$$\frac{\partial \hat{c}(F_1, F_2, T, K)}{\partial F_1}^{(\epsilon)} = \frac{\hat{c}(F_1+\epsilon) - \hat{c}(F_1-\epsilon)}{2\epsilon} \tag{26}$$

$$\frac{\partial \hat{c}(F_1, F_2, T, K)}{\partial F_2}^{(\epsilon)} = \frac{\hat{c}(F_2+\epsilon) - \hat{c}(F_2-\epsilon)}{2\epsilon} \tag{27}$$

$$\frac{\partial \hat{c}(F_1, F_2, T, K)}{\partial \rho}^{(\epsilon)} = \frac{\hat{c}(\rho+\epsilon) - \hat{c}(\rho-\epsilon)}{2\epsilon} \tag{28}$$

2. The second method is to use the formulas given in Proposition 3.
3. The third method is to use only the main terms, i.e., Δ_1, Δ_2, and Z.

3.3.2. Delta Accuracy and Speed

We generated 500 ATM samples with $F_1 = 100$, $\sigma_1 = 0.2$, $T = 1$, and $r = 0$ and randomly chose $K/F_2 \in (0.05, 0.5)$, $\sigma_2 \in (0.2, 0.6)$, and $\rho \in (0.7, 0.99)$. For the numerical Greeks, the bump size is $\epsilon = 0.0001$. As before, the benchmark Delta from MC is calculated using a central finite difference and $\epsilon = 0.0001$. The statistics of the distribution of percentage errors in Greeks for the three methods in comparison with the MC benchmark are listed in Table 12. The errors in Δ_{F_2} are perceptibly bigger than the errors in Δ_{F_1}. The reason for this discrepancy is the errors in our sector formula, mainly caused by F_2-related parts. This leads to a bigger error in the main term, Δ_2, and consequently to a bigger overall error.

Table 12. Delta accuracy.

	Δ_{F_1}			Δ_{F_2}		
	Numerical	**Formula**	**Main Term**	**Numerical**	**Formula**	**Main Term**
Mean	0.42%	0.42%	1.01%	4.45%	4.45%	5.73%
Std	0.45%	0.46%	1.04%	4.98%	4.99%	6.18%
Max	2.39%	2.38%	5.05%	25.01%	25.08%	33.40%
Min	0.00%	0.00%	0.00%	0.11%	0.11%	0.18%
Median	0.25%	0.26%	0.66%	2.57%	2.57%	3.72%

To compare the speed of Delta calculations, we randomly chose 10 samples and compare the statistics in Table 13.

The above results affirm the validity of our Delta formulas in Proposition 3 and also show that the main terms Δ_1 and Δ_2 are reasonable approximations in most situations. It is much faster than the other methods, and its errors are tolerable.

Table 13. Delta speed.

	Numerical	Formula	Main Term
Mean	0.0037	0.0085	0.0006
Std	0.0004	0.0008	0.0001
Max	0.0040	0.0097	0.0007
Min	0.0031	0.0074	0.0005
Median	0.0037	0.0086	0.0006

3.3.3. Rhoza Accuracy and Speed

We generated 500 ATM samples with fixed $F_1 = 100$, $\sigma_1 = 0.2$, $T = 1$, and $r = 0$, randomly choosing $K/F_2 \in (0.05, 0.5)$, $\sigma_2 \in (0.2, 0.6)$, and $\rho \in (0.7, 0.99)$. For the numerical formula, we took $\epsilon = 0.0001$. The errors in Rhoza for the three methods are given in comparison with the MC benchmark. The statistics of the distribution of percentage errors are listed in Table 14.

Table 14. Rhoza accuracy.

	Numerical	Formula	Main Term
Mean	0.10%	0.11%	0.23%
Std	0.13%	0.18%	0.26%
Max	1.60%	2.70%	1.78%
Min	0.00%	0.00%	0.00%
Median	0.05%	0.05%	0.14%

To compare the Delta speed, we chose 10 samples and compare the statistics in Table 15.

Table 15. Rhoza speed.

	Numerical	Formula	Main Term
Mean	0.0014	0.0048	0.0000
Std	0.0002	0.0002	0.0000
Max	0.0017	0.0050	0.0000
Min	0.0011	0.0045	0.0000
Median	0.0014	0.0048	0.0000

The above results validate our Rhoza formula in Proposition 3 and demonstrate that the main term Z gives reasonable accuracy in most practical situations. It is much faster than the other methods, and its errors are tolerable.

4. Applications of the Sector Formula to the Market Data of Commodity Spread Options

Now, we turn our attention to the real commodity data. We apply our sector formula to the market data of commodity spread options taken from the CME site. Specifically, we analyze calendar spread options ("CSOs").

As stated in the CME white paper "Trading Energy Spread Option on Energy Futures", *"Calendar Spread Options (CSOs) are options on the spread between two different futures expirations. The Energy futures term structure represents the time value of Energy market variables, such as storage costs, seasonality, and supply/demand conditions. Calendar Spread Options provide a leveraged means of hedging against, or speculating on, a change in the shape of the futures term structure"*.

Employing our sector formula, market future prices, and volatilities, we calculated the implied correlations, matching the given quotes. We also applied the numerical integration formula with the same inputs to back up implied correlations for verification purposes.

The calendar correlations are vital in the evaluation of commodity assets, such as storage, as well as widespread commodity options, such as swaptions.

We chose to use settlement prices, which are determined by trading activity during a given settlement period and, therefore, represent the fair market value of a commodity or financial derivative. We analyzed the market data of CSOs for three important commodities: WTI, Natural Gas, and Corn. These data change daily. We used website materials and white papers on CSOs published by the CME group.

4.1. WTI CSOs

The Crude Oil futures and options markets are global and are the most liquid and actively traded commodity contracts in the world. The forward term structure of Crude Oil is guided mainly by supply/demand, storage, and production. The shape of the forward curve, backwardation vs. contango, has important implications for inventory management. CSOs provide efficient tools for hedging to minimize the impact of the changes in the shape or trade to express views on oil price movements.

We started with WTI CSOs and used settlement prices from the CME site, https://www.cmegroup.com/markets/energy/crude-oil/light-sweet-crude.settlements.options.html#optionProductId=2952 (CME WTI CSOs, URL accessed on 30 April 2024 and 7 May 2024). The CME Chapter 390 states, "WTI calendar spread option is an option to assume a long position in the first expiring Light Sweet Crude Oil futures contract in the spread and a short position in the second expiring Light Sweet Crude Oil futures contract in the spread". Two futures entering the spread could be consecutive (1-month calendar spread option) or 2, 3, 6, or 12 months apart.

Currently, the only actively traded CSOs that we can find on the CME site are 1-month CSOs, starting with the prompt month and going 12 months forward. The biggest total open interest is observed for the first three months. At the time of writing this section, the prompt month was July 2024, and the total open daily interest for July, August, and September 2024 was around ~95,000–99,000 contracts. It gradually decreased to ~66,000 for December and practically disappeared thereafter. The strikes of the options are listed in increments, typically of USD 0.25, starting with −0.75 up to USD 3.

We use the settlement prices (at the end of the day) of one-month calendar spread options and record the contemporaneous settlement future prices of the contracts on the same day. The implied volatilities are derived ("implied") from the settlements of options on WTI futures (as of the same day); we use ATM options. We chose to employ only actively traded options with a sizable amount of open interest. These are one-month CSOs and strikes close to ATM strikes: $K_{ATM} = F_1 - F_2$. We use Treasury rates for discounts.

In Tables 16 and 17, we list strikes, settlement call CSO prices, and future prices of the underlying contracts and report the calculated implied correlations ("correlation smile") employing our sector formula, and we compare them to the implied correlations obtained with the use of the numerical integration. The results are practically the same.

Table 16. Implied correlations for different strikes K, 24 December/25 January CSO, call quotes as of 30 April 2024, $F_1 = 77.95$, $F_2 = 77.34$, $\sigma_1 = 0.2534$, $\sigma_2 = 0.2537$, and $K_{ATM} = 0.61$.

Case	Strike K	Quote	Implied ρ Sector	Implied ρ num. Integration
1	0.25	0.5	0.9987	0.9987
2	0.75	0.32	0.9977	0.9977
3	1	0.25	0.9974	0.9974
4	1.25	0.2	0.997	0.997
5	1.5	0.15	0.9968	0.9968
6	2	0.1	0.9960	0.9961

Table 17. Implied correlations for different strikes K, 24 July/24 August CSO, call quotes as of 7 May 2024, $F_1 = 78.06$, $F_2 = 77.68$, $\sigma_1 = 0.252$, $\sigma_2 = 0.2456$, and $K_{ATM} = 0.38$.

Case	Strike K	Quote	Implied ρ Sector	Implied ρ num. Integration
1	0.5	0.17	0.9963	0.9963
2	0.75	0.13	0.9943	0.9923
3	1	0.1	0.9923	0.9923
4	1.25	0.08	0.9902	0.9902
5	1.5	0.06	0.9896	0.9896
6	2	0.04	0.9842	0.9842

The ATM correlations from the one-month 24 July/24 August CSO are slightly lower than the correlations from the one-month 24 December/25 January CSO, as they should be, since the first contract is closer for the first CSO; see [16].

4.2. Natural Gas CSOs

The Natural Gas term structure is defined by seasonality. Natural Gas storage is a vital part of the Natural Gas delivery system and helps to balance supply and demand. During the winter season, from November to March, gas consumption peaks as a result of increased heating demand. During the summer season, from April to October, gas demand decreases while production continues, and excess Natural Gas can be stored. Natural Gas storage can be replicated by the option to inject excessive gas during the injection season and sell it during the withdrawal period, factoring in financing and storage costs. CSOs provide physical storage operators and professional traders with opportunities to hedge or benefit from moves in Natural Gas futures spreads.

As with WTI, we use the settlement prices of Natural Gas CSOs, https://www.cmegroup.com/markets/energy/natural-gas/natural-gas.settlements.options.html#optionProductId=2946 (CME NG CSOs, URL accessed on 6 June 2024). We record the contemporaneous settlement future prices of the contracts on the same day and the implied ATM volatilities.

As of 6 June 2024, CME listed the settlement prices for one-month CSOs, with the first contract going from July 2024 through 25 March (missing December), two-month CSOs, and three-month CSOs, with the first contract being in July 2024 or October 2024. Unsurprisingly, the biggest total open daily interest of ~369,000 contracts is observed for the three-month spread for October/January; then, the three-month spread for July/October involved ~45,000 contracts. The pattern of daily interest for one-month CSOs is seasonal, with the biggest total open daily interest for September/October, ~53,000, and then for the prompt month CSOs in July/August. Another actively traded one-month CSO involved spreads from October to November and March to April. Strikes for a one-month CSO are typically given in increments of USD 0.05. The biggest range of strikes can be found for October/January, with strikes starting at -2.5 and going to -0.3.

We transform CSOs with negative strikes (calls) into CSOs with positive strikes (calls) using the relationship in (5). We choose liquid CSOs with sizable open interest, involving important spreads in Natural Gas futures such as October/November, October/January, March/April, and July/October. We list the resulting implied correlations in Table 18.

Table 18. Implied correlations for different strikes K as of 6 June 2024, Natural Gas CSOs.

Months	F_1	F_2	σ_1	σ_2	Strike K	Quote	Implied ρ Sector	Implied ρ num. Integration
July/October	2.757	2.888	0.6844	0.5719	−0.2	0.087	0.9943	0.9943
July/October	2.757	2.888	0.6844	0.5719	−0.15	0.054	0.9914	0.9914
July/October	2.757	2.888	0.6844	0.5719	−0.1	0.031	0.9862	0.9862
July/October	2.757	2.888	0.6844	0.5719	−0.05	0.016	0.9815	0.9815
October/January	2.888	3.901	0.5719	0.5372	−1.25	0.353	0.9428	0.9429
October/January	2.888	3.901	0.5719	0.5372	−1	0.353	0.9450	0.9451
October/January	2.888	3.901	0.5719	0.5372	−0.75	0.192	0.9481	0.9482
October/January	2.888	3.901	0.5719	0.5372	−0.7	0.078	0.9500	0.9500
October/January	2.888	3.901	0.5719	0.5372	−0.6	0.061	0.9555	0.9556
October/November	2.88	3.22	0.5719	0.537	−0.3	0.065	0.9897	0.9897
March/April	3.34	3.107	0.5411	0.4360	1	0.08	0.9350	0.9351

We observe weaker correlations between months in different seasons, such as October and January (see [16]). The resulting correlations based on the two methods are close; for example, for the last CSO, the difference is within 0.02 correlation points (0.0002). We also checked the implied correlation based on the Kirk formula (7) using the last March/April CSO. (The spread for Mar/Apr is called the "widowmaker" because of its potential devastating losses.) The Kirk formula's implied correlation was 0.9445, one correlation point higher than the implied correlation from the sector formula.

4.3. Agricultural CSOs

The standardized trading months for agricultural products, such as Corn, Soybean, and Wheat futures, reflect the seasonal patterns for planting and harvesting the underlying crop. During the planting months, the source of grain that is available for sale or purchase by end users is from crops that were harvested during the previous harvest season, which is considered the "old crop". On the other hand, during the harvest months, the newly harvested crop, called the "new crop", comes to market, and supply is higher. Specifically, Corn is considered an old crop in March, May, July, August, and early September. November, December, and January represent the new crop. As with WTI and Natural Gas, agricultural CSOs represent effective hedging and trading tools.

As of 6 June 2024, CME listed three nearby successive futures calendar spreads: 1-month CSOs, with the first month being July, September, and December; a 12-month December/December CSO; a December/July CSO; and a July/December CSO. The most actively traded CSO for the old/new crop spread is Jul/Dec, with a total open daily interest of ∼15,000 contracts. The next active spread involves December/December, with ∼10,000 contracts, and then consecutive spread in July/August, with a total open daily interest of ∼9000 contracts. The strikes are typically listed in increments of USD 0.01 for consecutive spreads and in increments of USD 0.05 for other spreads.

We considered Corn CSOs that included three nearby successive futures calendar spreads and one old crop/new crop calendar spread, https://www.cmegroup.com/markets/agriculture/grains/corn.settlements.options.html#optionProductId=2702 (CME Corn SCO, URL accessed on 6 May 2024). We chose liquid CSOs with sizable open interest: July/September, a consecutive spread within the same season (old/old crop), and July/December, an old/new crop spread. We list the resulting implied correlations in Table 19.

Table 19. Implied correlations for different strikes K as of 5 June and 10 June 2024, Corn CSOs.

Months	F_1	F_2	σ_1	σ_2	Strike K	Quote	Implied ρ Sector	Implied ρ num. Integration
July/September	4.5175	4.5625	0.2447	0.293	−0.05	0.02375	0.9795	0.9795
July/December	4.3925	4.59	0.2212	0.2387	−0.2	0.03875	0.9094	0.9094
July/December	4.3925	4.59	0.2212	0.2387	−0.15	0.02	0.9014	0.9014
July/December	4.3925	4.59	0.2212	0.2387	−0.1	0.01	0.8884	0.8884
July/December	4.3925	4.59	0.2212	0.2387	−0.05	0.005	0.8725	0.8725
July/December	4.3925	4.59	0.2212	0.2387	0	0.0925	0.8554	0.8554

We spot stronger correlations for contracts in the same crop season, old/old (July/September), and weaker correlations for contracts in different crop seasons, old/new (July/December).

The strength of the correlation skew can be measured by the slope of correlation vs. strike normalized by the spread, $k_s = \frac{K}{F_1 - F_2}$. Choosing an important CSO with the maximum number of strikes (December/January for WTI, October/January for Natural Gas, and July/December for Corn), we detect a strong positive slope for Corn, ∼0.05, and negative slopes for Natural Gas and WTI. The WTI slope is much weaker than the Natural Gas slope: ∼−0.001 vs. ∼−0.017. The positive slope for the Corn correlation skew is the result of the current unusual negative spread between July and December (normally positive). The results are illustrated in Figure 6.

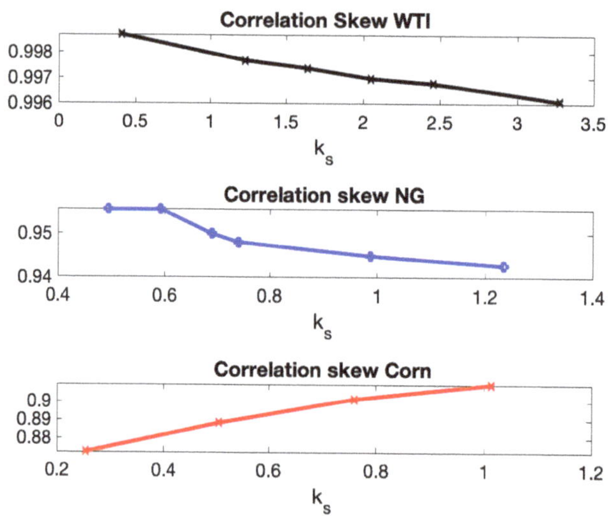

Figure 6. Correlation skew for WTI (December/January), NG (October/January), and Corn (July/December).

4.4. Calculation of Model Valuation Adjustment of CSOs Using the Sector Formula for Greeks

So far, we have demonstrated the use of the sector formula to calculate implied correlations, employing market data for different commodities. Now, we would like to show how sector Greeks, in particular, sensitivity to correlation, i.e., Rhoza, can be utilized to calculate a model valuation adjustment to the value of the spread option due to uncertainty in the correlation input.

If the correlation is assessed through historical data, its estimate $\hat{\rho}$ is a random variable, and the uncertainty in its value leads to uncertainty in the spread option value. The uncertainty in the correlation estimate can be measured either by a standard error or using, for example, a 95% confidence interval, in which the true correlation resides. Since the spread option is a decreasing function of correlation, for a long position to arrive at a *fair* value of the option, one has to use the higher value of the correlation $\hat{\rho} + \Delta\rho$. For small $\Delta\rho$, the fair value can be calculated as follows:

$$V = \hat{V} - MVA$$

where $\hat{V}$ is the value of the spread option calculated for $\hat{\rho}$, and MVA is the model valuation adjustment:

$$MVA \approx \frac{\partial V}{\partial \rho}\Delta\rho$$

The statistical error of the estimator $\hat{\rho}$ of a Pearson correlation coefficient ρ calculated on N bivariate sample pairs (x_i, y_i), $i = 1, \ldots N$ (log-returns), can be found by using the Fisher z transform; see [17]:

$$\hat{z} = \frac{1}{2}\ln\left(\frac{1+\hat{\rho}}{1-\hat{\rho}}\right)$$

If (x, y) has a bivariate normal distribution with correlation ρ, then $\hat{z}$ is approximately normally distributed with the mean

$$\mu = \frac{1}{2}\left(\frac{1+\rho}{1-\rho}\right)$$

and standard deviation $\sigma = \frac{1}{\sqrt{N-3}}$. Consequently, $\Delta\rho$ can be calculated as

$$\Delta\rho = \frac{1}{2}\left(\frac{e^{2z_U}-1}{e^{2z_U}+1} - \frac{e^{2z_L}-1}{e^{2z_L}+1}\right) \tag{29}$$

where

$$z_U = \mu + \beta\sigma, \; z_U = \mu - \beta\sigma$$

are the left and right points of the confidence interval, with $\beta = 1$ for the standard error and $\beta = 1.96$ for the 95% confidence interval.

We illustrate the procedure with an example. Suppose today is 7 June 2024, and we need to price a Natural Gas CSO with an unusual term that is not traded in the market, for example, a 24 September/25 February CSO. All of the inputs are observable in the market, such as future prices, implied volatilities, and discount rates, but not correlation. We choose to use historical data to estimate the correlation using the log-returns of September 2023 and February 2024 NG future prices. Since calendar correlations depend on the time to the first contract (see [16]), we selected a similar time interval for the calculation, 1 June 2023 to 29 August 2023, the expiration date of the September contract (similar to the current situation). The calculation of the correlation between log-returns using the data gives an estimate of the correlation of $\hat{\rho} = 90\%$ with a statistical error $\Delta\rho = 0.0249$ (the relatively large statistical error in this case is caused by the small number of observation points (62)).

Table 20 gives the details of the evaluation and Greeks for the CSO. We list the statistical error of the correlation estimate, the sensitivity Rhoza obtained by the finite difference of the numerical integration formula, and the approximate value of Rhoza given by the main term Z (25).

Table 20. Calculation of model valuation adjustment for NG CSO 24 September/25 February, $F_1 = 2.971$, $F_2 = 3.83$, $\sigma_1 = 0.6048$, $\sigma_2 = 0.5730$, and $K = -0.9$.

$\hat{\rho}$	$\Delta\rho$	Value Sector	Value num. int	Rhoza num. int.	Sector Rhoza Z	MVA
0.9	0.0249	0.2224	0.2225	−0.6678	−0.6661	0.0167

The model valuation adjustment is about 7.5% of the option value. The MVA calculated by using the approximate value Z of Rhoza from the sector formula is practically the same. The advantage is that a sector Rhoza Z does not require revaluations of the CSO by numerical integration or Monte Carlo and can be calculated analytically.

5. Conclusions

The problem of the accurate valuation and calculation of the Greeks of a spread option is very important for practitioners, especially in the field of commodities. Even though there are numerous approximations, including the famous Kirk formula, it is crucial to understand the limitations of approximations and reveal situations where those approximations do not work properly.

In this paper, we present yet another closed-form approximation of the spread option value and Greeks by using double integration and carefully analyzing the exercise boundary. Depending on the sign of $\sigma_2 - \rho\sigma_1$, we identified two major cases with different types of boundaries: in the first case, the asymptotic slopes of the boundary have the same sign, and in the second case, the boundary has a U-shape, with the asymptotic slopes having different signs. The previous research on pricing spread options by integration was based on the assumption of a small curvature of the boundary close to the origin. In such situations, the boundary can be approximated reasonably well by a straight line, and the pricing formulas are expressed in terms of the univariate normal CDF. We identified situations in which the curvature of the boundary close to the origin is not small, and the previous integration formulas produced bigger errors. We derived two general integration formulas for spread option payoff over straight-line- and sector-type boundaries. We found the optimal way to choose a straight line or a particular sector to find the best approximation of the spread option value. The sector formula is expressed in terms of the bivariate normal CDF.

We worked out formulas for Greeks, in particular, Deltas and sensitivity to correlation. We identified the main terms that give reasonable approximations of Greeks in most situations. We compared our results in terms of accuracy and speed with those obtained by three previous methods, including Kirk and two integration formulas in different types of scenarios, using Monte Carlo simulations as a benchmark. Our method shows good accuracy and superiority to the previous methods in some cases.

We demonstrated applications of our sector formula to the market data of calendar spread options for three major commodities: WTI, Natural Gas, and Corn. The data were listed on the CME site as of 30 April, 7 May, 5 June, and 6 June 2024. Specifically, we showed the particular effectiveness of the formula for the calculation of implied correlations and Greeks. We illustrated how the sensitivity to correlation, Rhoza, can be utilized to calculate a model valuation adjustment to a CSO value due to the uncertainty in the correlation input to arrive at a fair value of the derivative.

Author Contributions: Conceptualization, methodology, supervision: R.G. Formal analysis, validation, investigation, original draft preparation: R.G. and Z.W. Visualization: Z.W. and R.G. Software: Z.W. and R.G. Writing, review and editing: R.G. All authors have read and agreed to the published version of the manuscript.

Funding: This research received no external funding.

Institutional Review Board Statement: Not applicable.

Informed Consent Statement: Not applicable.

Data Availability Statement: All data used in the paper (market quotes) is given in the paper.

Acknowledgments: The authors express their gratitude to Alexander Eydeland for insightful discussions. We are also appreciate the editor and referees' constructive feedback, which improved the manuscript.

Conflicts of Interest: The authors declare no conflicts of interest.

Appendix A

Proof of Lemma 1.

$$
\begin{aligned}
I(a,b) &= e^{-rT}\int_{-\infty}^{+\infty}\int_{-\infty}^{+\infty}(F_1(T)-F_2(T)-K)I_{A(a,b)}\phi(x)\phi(y)dxdy \\
&= e^{-rT}\int\int_{A(a,b)}F_1(T)\phi(x)\phi(y)dxdy - e^{-rT}\int\int_{A(a,b)}F_2(T)\phi(x)\phi(y)dxdy \\
&\quad -e^{-rT}K\int\int_{A(a,b)}\phi(x)\phi(y)dxdy
\end{aligned}
$$

For the first part, by taking out $F_2(T)$, we obtain

$$
\begin{aligned}
\hat{p}_1 &= e^{-rT}\int\int_{A(a,b)}F_{1T}\phi(x)\phi(y)dxdy \\
&= e^{-rT}\int\int_{A(a,b)}[F_2e^{-\frac{1}{2}\sigma_2^2T+\sigma_2\sqrt{T}y}g(y)][\frac{F_1}{F_2}e^{-\frac{1}{2}(\sigma_1^2-\sigma_2^2)T+\sqrt{1-\rho^2}\sigma_1\sqrt{T}x+(\rho\sigma_1-\sigma_2)\sqrt{T}y}]\phi(x)dxdy \\
&= \frac{e^{-rT}}{2\pi}\int\int_{A(a,b)}[F_2e^{-\frac{(y-\sigma_2\sqrt{T})^2}{2}}][\frac{F_1}{F_2}e^{-\frac{1}{2}(\sigma_1^2-\sigma_2^2)T+\sqrt{1-\rho^2}\sigma_1\sqrt{T}x+(\rho\sigma_1-\sigma_2)\sqrt{T}y}]e^{-\frac{x^2}{2}}dxdy
\end{aligned}
$$

We make the variable change $\tilde{y} = y - \sigma_2\sqrt{T}$ and then replace the symbol $\tilde{y}$ with y; we have

$$
\begin{aligned}
\hat{p}_1 &= \frac{e^{-rT}}{2\pi}\int\int_{A^*(a,b)}(F_2e^{-\frac{y^2}{2}})[\frac{F_1}{F_2}e^{-\frac{1}{2}(\sigma_1^2-\sigma_2^2)T+\sqrt{1-\rho^2}\sigma_1\sqrt{T}x+(\rho\sigma_1-\sigma_2)\sqrt{T}(y+\sigma_2\sqrt{T})}]e^{-\frac{x^2}{2}}dxdy \\
&= \frac{e^{-rT}F_2}{2\pi}\int\int_{A^*(a,b)}(\frac{F_1}{F_2}e^{\sqrt{1-\rho^2}\sigma_1\sqrt{T}x+(\rho\sigma_1-\sigma_2)\sqrt{T}y-\frac{1}{2}(\sigma_1^2+\sigma_2^2-2\rho\sigma_1\sigma_2)T})e^{-\frac{x^2}{2}}e^{-\frac{y^2}{2}}dxdy \\
&= e^{-rT}F_2\int\int_{A^*(a,b)}\frac{F_1}{F_2}e^{\sqrt{1-\rho^2}\sigma_1\sqrt{T}x+(\rho\sigma_1-\sigma_2)\sqrt{T}y-\frac{1}{2}(\sigma_1^2+\sigma_2^2-2\rho\sigma_1\sigma_2)T}\phi(x)\phi(y)dxdy
\end{aligned}
$$

where

$$
A^*(a,b) = \{(x,y) : x - by \geq a + b\sigma_2\sqrt{T}\}
$$

For the second part, similarly, we take out $F_2(T)$:

$$
\begin{aligned}
\hat{p}_2 &= e^{-rT}\int\int_{A(a,b)}F_2(T)\phi(x)\phi(y)dxdy \\
&= e^{-rT}F_2\int\int_{A(a,b)}[e^{-\frac{1}{2}\sigma_2^2T+\sigma_2\sqrt{T}y}\phi(y)]\phi(x)dxdy \\
&= e^{-rT}F_2\int\int_{A(a,b)}\frac{1}{\sqrt{2\pi}}e^{-\frac{(y-\sigma_2\sqrt{T})^2}{2}}\phi(x)dxdy
\end{aligned}
$$

We make the variable change $\hat{y} = y - \sigma_2\sqrt{T}$ and then replace the symbol $\hat{y}$ with y; we have

$$
\hat{p}_2 = e^{-rT}F_2\int\int_{A^*(a,b)}\phi(x)\phi(y)dxdy
$$

For the third part,

$$\hat{p}_3 = e^{-rT} K \int\int_{A(a,b)} \phi(x)\phi(y)dxdy$$

Let

$$z = \frac{1}{\sqrt{1+b^2}}(x - by)$$

We can also write it as

$$z = \cos(\phi)x + \sin(\phi)y$$

where

$$\phi = \arcsin(\frac{-b}{\sqrt{1+b^2}})$$

Then, we can also define

$$z^* = -\sin(\phi)x + \cos(\phi)y$$

From the variable change,

$$\begin{aligned} z &= \cos(\phi)x + \sin(\phi)y \\ z^* &= -\sin(\phi)x + \cos(\phi)y \end{aligned} \tag{A1}$$

We denote the subset $D(u) \subset R^2$ by

$$D(u) = \{(x,y) : x - by > u\}$$

After the variable change, the corresponding region becomes

$$\{(z,z^*) : z > \frac{u}{\sqrt{1+b^2}}\}$$

To calculate $\hat{p}_3$, we change the variables (x,y) to (z,z^*) in the integration and obtain

$$\begin{aligned} \hat{p}_3 &= e^{-rT} K \int\int_{A(a,b)} \phi(x)\phi(y)dxdy \\ &= e^{-rT} K \int\int_{D(a)} \phi(x)\phi(y)dxdy \\ &= e^{-rT} K \int\int_{\{z>-d_3\}} \phi(z)\phi(z^*)dzdz^* \\ &= e^{-rT} K \int_{-\infty}^{+\infty} \phi(z^*)dz^* \int_{-d_3}^{+\infty} \phi(z)dz \\ &= e^{-rT} K \int_{-d_3}^{+\infty} \phi(z)dz \\ &= e^{-rT} K \int_{-\infty}^{d_3} \phi(z)dz \\ &= e^{-rT} K N(d_3) \end{aligned}$$

where

$$d_3 = -\frac{a}{\sqrt{1+b^2}}$$

To calculate $\hat{p}_2$, similarly, we have

$$\begin{aligned}
\hat{p}_2 &= e^{-rT}F_2 \int\int_{A^*(a,b)} \phi(x)\phi(y)dxdy \\
&= e^{-rT}F_2 \int\int_{D(a+b\sigma_2\sqrt{T})} \phi(x)\phi(y)dxdy \\
&= e^{-rT}F_2 \int\int_{\{z>-d_2\}} \phi(z)\phi(z^*)dzdz^* \\
&= e^{-rT}F_2 \int_{-\infty}^{+\infty} \phi(z^*)dz^* \int_{-d_2}^{+\infty} \phi(z)dz \\
&= e^{-rT}F_2 \int_{-d_2}^{+\infty} \phi(z)dz \\
&= e^{-rT}F_2 \int_{-\infty}^{d_2} \phi(z)dz \\
&= e^{-rT}F_2 N(d_2)
\end{aligned}$$

where

$$d_2 = -\frac{a + b\sigma_2\sqrt{T}}{\sqrt{1+b^2}}$$

For $\hat{p}_1$, we know that

$$\begin{aligned}
\hat{p}_1 &= e^{-rT}F_2 \int\int_{A^*(a,b)} \frac{F_1}{F_2} e^{\sqrt{1-\rho^2}\sigma_1\sqrt{T}x+(\rho\sigma_1-\sigma_2)\sqrt{T}y-\frac{1}{2}(\sigma_1^2+\sigma_2^2-2\rho\sigma_1\sigma_2)T} g(x)g(y)dxdy \\
&= e^{-rT}F_1 \int\int_{A^*(a,b)} \frac{1}{\sqrt{2\pi}} e^{-\frac{(x-\sqrt{1-\rho^2}\sigma_1\sqrt{T})^2}{2}} \frac{1}{\sqrt{2\pi}} e^{-\frac{(y-(\rho\sigma_1-\sigma_2)\sqrt{T})^2}{2}} dxdy \\
&= e^{-rT}F_1 \int\int_{A^{**}(a,b)} \frac{1}{\sqrt{2\pi}} e^{-\frac{\tilde{x}^2}{2}} \frac{1}{\sqrt{2\pi}} e^{-\frac{\tilde{y}^2}{2}} d\tilde{x}d\tilde{y} \\
&= e^{-rT}F_1 \int\int_{A^{**}(a,b)} \phi(\tilde{x})\phi(\tilde{y})d\tilde{x}d\tilde{y}
\end{aligned}$$

where

$$A^{**}(a,b) = \{(x,y) : x - by \geq a + (b\rho - \sqrt{1-\rho^2})\sigma_1\sqrt{T}\}$$

In the above formula, we can replace the symbols $\tilde{x}$ and $\tilde{y}$ with x and y, respectively. Then, we can change the variables (x,y) to (z,z^*):

$$\begin{aligned}
\hat{p}_1 &= e^{-rT}F_1 \int\int_{D(a+(b\rho-\sqrt{1-\rho^2})\sigma_1\sqrt{T})} \phi(x)\phi(y)dxdy \\
&= e^{-rT}F_1 \int\int_{\{z>-d_1\}} \phi(z)\phi(z^*)dzdz^* \\
&= e^{-rT}F_1 \int_{-\infty}^{+\infty} \phi(z^*)dz^* \int_{-d_1}^{+\infty} \phi(z)dz \\
&= e^{-rT}F_1 \int_{-d_1}^{+\infty} \phi(z)dz \\
&= e^{-rT}F_1 \int_{-\infty}^{d_1} \phi(z)dz \\
&= e^{-rT}F_1 N(d_1)
\end{aligned}$$

where

$$d_1 = -\frac{a + (b\rho - \sqrt{1-\rho^2})\sigma_1\sqrt{T}}{\sqrt{1+b^2}}$$

$$I(a,b) = e^{-rT}(F_1N(d_1) - F_2N(d_2) - KN(d_3))$$

□

Appendix B

Proof of Lemma 2. We have

$$\begin{aligned} I(a,b,c,d) &= e^{-rT}\int_{-\infty}^{+\infty}\int_{-\infty}^{+\infty}(F_1(T) - F_2(T) - K)I_{A(a,b,c,d)}\phi(x)\phi(y)dxdy \\ &= e^{-rT}\int\int_{A(a,b,c,d)} F_1(T)\phi(x)\phi(y)dxdy - e^{-rT}\int\int_{A(a,b,c,d)} F_2(T)\phi(x)\phi(y)dxdy \\ &-e^{-rT}K\int\int_{A(a,b,c,d)}\phi(x)\phi(y)dxdy \end{aligned}$$

For the third part, we have

$$\hat{p}_3 = e^{-rT}K\int\int_{A(a,b,c,d)}\phi(x)\phi(y)dxdy$$

For the second part, we have

$$\begin{aligned} \hat{p}_2 &= e^{-rT}\int\int_{A(a,b,c,d)} F_2(T)\phi(x)\phi(y)dxdy \\ &= e^{-rT}F_2\int\int_{A(a,b,c,d)}[e^{-\frac{1}{2}\sigma_2^2T+\sigma_2\sqrt{T}y}\phi(y)]\phi(x)dxdy \\ &= e^{-rT}F_2\int\int_{A(a,b,c,d)}\frac{1}{\sqrt{2\pi}}e^{-\frac{(y-\sigma_2\sqrt{T})^2}{2}}\phi(x)dxdy \end{aligned}$$

We make the variable change $\hat{y} = y - \sigma_2\sqrt{T}, \hat{x} = x$, and then

$$\hat{p}_2 = e^{-rT}F_2\int\int_{\hat{A}(a,b,c,d)}\phi(\hat{x})\phi(\hat{y})d\hat{x}d\hat{y}$$

where

$$\hat{A}(a,b,c,d) = \{(\hat{x},\hat{y}) : \hat{x} - b\hat{y} \geq a + b\sigma_2\sqrt{T}, \hat{x} - d\hat{y} \geq c + d\sigma_2\sqrt{T}\}$$

For the first part, we obtain

$$\begin{aligned} \hat{p}_1 &= e^{-rT}\int\int_{A(a,b,c,d)} F_1(T)\phi(x)\phi(y)dxdy \\ &= e^{-rT}\int\int_{A(a,b,c,d)} F_1\exp(-\frac{1}{2}\sigma_1^2T + \sqrt{1-\rho^2}\sigma_1\sqrt{T}x + \rho\sigma_1\sqrt{T}y)\phi(x)\phi(y)dxdy \\ &= e^{-rT}\int\int_{A(a,b,c,d)}\frac{1}{2\pi}F_1e^{-\frac{1}{2}(x^2-2\sqrt{1-\rho^2}\sigma_1\sqrt{T}x+(1-\rho^2)\sigma_1^2T)-\frac{1}{2}(y^2-2\rho\sigma_1\sqrt{T}y+\rho^2\sigma_1^2T)}dxdy \\ &= e^{-rT}\int\int_{A(a,b,c,d)}\frac{1}{2\pi}F_1e^{-\frac{1}{2}(x-\sqrt{1-\rho^2}\sigma_1\sqrt{T})^2-\frac{1}{2}(y-\rho\sigma_1\sqrt{T})^2} \end{aligned}$$

We make the variable change $\tilde{x} = x - \sqrt{1-\rho^2}\sigma_1\sqrt{T}$, and $\tilde{y} = y - \rho\sigma_1\sqrt{T}$; we have

$$\hat{p}_1 = e^{-rT}F_1\int\int_{\tilde{A}(a,b,c,d)}\phi(\tilde{x})\phi(\tilde{y})d\tilde{x}d\tilde{y}$$

where

$$\tilde{A}(a,b,c,d) = \{(\tilde{x},\tilde{y}) : \tilde{x} - b\tilde{y} \geq a + (b\rho - \sqrt{1-\rho^2})\sigma_1\sqrt{T}, \tilde{x} - d\tilde{y} \geq c + (d\rho - \sqrt{1-\rho^2})\sigma_1\sqrt{T}\}$$

Let

$$z = \frac{1}{\sqrt{1+b^2}}(x - by)$$

$$z^* = \frac{1}{\sqrt{1+d^2}}(x - dy)$$

We can also write it as

$$z = \cos(\phi)x + \sin(\phi)y$$

$$z^* = \cos(\theta)x + \sin(\theta)y$$

where

$$\phi = \arcsin(\frac{-b}{\sqrt{1+b^2}})$$

$$\theta = \arcsin(\frac{-d}{\sqrt{1+d^2}})$$

We denote the subset $D(u,v) \subset R^2$ by

$$D(u,v) = \{(x,y) : x - by \geq u, x - dy \geq v\}$$

After the variable change, the corresponding region becomes

$$\{(z,z^*) : z \geq \frac{u}{\sqrt{1+b^2}}, z^* \geq \frac{v}{\sqrt{1+d^2}}\}$$

We define

$$M(a,b,\rho) = \int\int_{\{x<a,y<b\}} f(x,y,\rho)dxdy$$

To calculate $\hat{p}_3$, we make the variable change:

$$z = \cos(\phi)x + \sin(\phi)y$$

$$z^* = \cos(\theta)x + \sin(\theta)y$$

Then,

$$\begin{aligned}
\hat{p}_3 &= e^{-rT}K\int\int_{A(a,b,c,d)} \phi(x)\phi(y)dxdy \\
&= e^{-rT}K\int\int_{D(a,c)} \phi(x)\phi(y)dxdy \\
&= e^{-rT}K\int\int_{\{z>-d_{31},z^*>-d_{32}\}} f(z,z^*,\tilde{\rho})dzdz^* \\
&= e^{-rT}K\int\int_{\{z<d_{31},z^*<d_{32}\}} f(z,z^*,\tilde{\rho})dzdz^* \\
&= e^{-rT}KM(d_{31},d_{32},\tilde{\rho})
\end{aligned}$$

where

$$d_{31} = -\frac{a}{\sqrt{1+b^2}}$$

$$d_{32} = -\frac{c}{\sqrt{1+d^2}}$$

To calculate $\hat{p}_2$, we make the variable change:

$$z = \cos(\phi)\hat{x} + \sin(\phi)\hat{y}$$

$$z^* = \cos(\theta)\hat{x} + \sin(\theta)\hat{y}$$

Then,

$$\begin{aligned}
\hat{p}_2 &= e^{-rT}F_2 \int\int_{\hat{A}(a,b,c,d)} \phi(\hat{x})\phi(\hat{y})d\hat{x}d\hat{y} \\
&= e^{-rT}F_2 \int\int_{D(a+b\sigma_2\sqrt{T},c-\sigma_2\sqrt{T})} \phi(\hat{x})\phi(\hat{y})d\hat{x}d\hat{y} \\
&= e^{-rT}F_2 \int\int_{\{z>-d_{21},z^*>-d_{22}\}} f(z,z^*,\tilde{\rho})dzdz^* \\
&= e^{-rT}F_2 \int\int_{\{z<d_{21},z^*<d_{22}\}} f(z,z^*,\tilde{\rho})dzdz^* \\
&= e^{-rT}F_2 M(d_{21},d_{22},\tilde{\rho})
\end{aligned}$$

where

$$d_{21} = -\frac{a + b\sigma_2\sqrt{T}}{\sqrt{1+b^2}}$$

$$d_{22} = -\frac{c + d\sigma_2\sqrt{T}}{\sqrt{1+d^2}}$$

To calculate $\hat{p}_1$, we make the variable change:

$$z = \cos(\phi)\tilde{x} + \sin(\phi)\tilde{y}$$

$$z^* = \cos(\theta)\tilde{x} + \sin(\theta)\tilde{y}$$

Then,

$$\begin{aligned}
\hat{p}_1 &= e^{-rT}F_1 \int\int_{\tilde{A}(a,b,c,d)} \phi(\tilde{x})\phi(\tilde{y})d\tilde{x}d\tilde{y} \\
&= e^{-rT}F_1 \int\int_{D(a+(b\rho-\sqrt{1-\rho^2})\sigma_1\sqrt{T},c-(d\sqrt{1-\rho^2}+\rho)\sigma_1\sqrt{T})} \phi(\tilde{x})\phi(\tilde{y})d\tilde{x}d\tilde{y} \\
&= e^{-rT}F_1 \int\int_{\{z>-d_{11},z^*>-d_{12}\}} f(z,z^*,\tilde{\rho})dzdz^* \\
&= e^{-rT}F_1 \int\int_{\{z<d_{11},z^*<d_{12}\}} f(z,z^*,\tilde{\rho})dzdz^* \\
&= e^{-rT}F_1 M(d_{11},d_{12},\tilde{\rho})
\end{aligned}$$

where

$$d_{11} = -\frac{a + (b\rho - \sqrt{1-\rho^2})\sigma_1\sqrt{T}}{\sqrt{1+b^2}}$$

$$d_{12} = -\frac{c + (d\rho - \sqrt{1-\rho^2})\sigma_1\sqrt{T}}{\sqrt{1+d^2}}$$

Therefore, we have the following general formula:

$$\hat{p}(a,b,c,d) = e^{-rT}(F_1 M(d_{11},d_{12},\tilde{\rho}) - F_2 M(d_{21},d_{22},\tilde{\rho}) - KM(d_{31},d_{32},\tilde{\rho}))$$

where

$$M(a,b,\rho) = \int\int_{\{x<a,y<b\}} f(x,y,\rho)dxdy$$

$$\tilde{\rho} = \frac{bd+1}{\sqrt{(1+b^2)(1+d^2)}}$$

$$d_{11} = -\frac{a+(b\rho-\sqrt{1-\rho^2})\sigma_1\sqrt{T}}{\sqrt{1+b^2}}$$

$$d_{12} = -\frac{c+(d\rho-\sqrt{1-\rho^2})\sigma_1\sqrt{T}}{\sqrt{1+d^2}}$$

$$d_{21} = -\frac{a+b\sigma_2\sqrt{T}}{\sqrt{1+b^2}}$$

$$d_{22} = -\frac{c+d\sigma_2\sqrt{T}}{\sqrt{1+d^2}}$$

$$d_{31} = -\frac{a}{\sqrt{1+b^2}}$$

$$d_{32} = -\frac{c}{\sqrt{1+d^2}}$$

□

Appendix C

Conditions for "Big" Curvature

Based on our numerical test, we can give some conditions for "big" curvatures:

$$\frac{K}{F_2} > 0.29, \frac{\sigma_2}{\sigma_1} > 1.5, \sigma_1\sqrt{T} > 0.3, \rho > 0.97$$

When the above four conditions are met at the same time, the curvature will be quite big.

Proof of Proposition 1. From the real boundary, in the neighborhood of $y = 0$, we can observe that

$$\lim_{y\to 0} h(y) = \frac{\ln(F_2\exp(-\frac{1}{2}\sigma_2^2T)+K)+\frac{1}{2}\sigma_1^2T-\ln F_1}{\sqrt{1-\rho^2}\sigma_1\sqrt{T}}$$

$$\lim_{y\to 0}\frac{dh(y)}{dy} = \frac{\frac{F_2\exp(-\frac{1}{2}\sigma_2^2T)\sigma_2\sqrt{T}}{F_2\exp(-\frac{1}{2}\sigma_2^2T)+K}-\rho\sigma_1\sqrt{T}}{\sqrt{1-\rho^2}\sigma_1\sqrt{T}}$$

and then the tangent line $x = by + a$ is determined by

$$a = \frac{\ln(F_2\exp(-\frac{1}{2}\sigma_2^2T)+K)+\frac{1}{2}\sigma_1^2T-\ln F_1}{\sqrt{1-\rho^2}\sigma_1\sqrt{T}}$$

$$b = \frac{\frac{F_2\exp(-\frac{1}{2}\sigma_2^2T)\sigma_2}{F_2\exp(-\frac{1}{2}\sigma_2^2T)+K}-\rho\sigma_1}{\sqrt{1-\rho^2}\sigma_1}$$

□

Appendix D

Proof of Proposition 2. The real boundary of the spread option integral is

$$h(y) = \frac{\ln(F_2 \exp(-\frac{1}{2}\sigma_2^2 T + \sigma_2\sqrt{T}y) + K) - \rho\sigma_1\sqrt{T}y}{\sqrt{1-\rho^2}\sigma_1\sqrt{T}} + \frac{\frac{1}{2}\sigma_1^2 T - \ln F_1}{\sqrt{1-\rho^2}\sigma_1\sqrt{T}}$$

Then,

$$h(0) = \frac{\ln\frac{(F_2\exp(-\frac{1}{2}\sigma_2^2 T)+K)}{F_1} + \frac{1}{2}\sigma_1^2 T}{\sqrt{1-\rho^2}\sigma_1\sqrt{T}}$$

Let $R = \max(1, \frac{6}{5}h(0))$. The first-order Taylor expansion of the boundary is

$$l(y) = \frac{[\ln(F_2 e^{-\frac{1}{2}\sigma_2^2 T} + K) + \sigma_2\sqrt{T}(1 - \frac{K}{F_2 e^{-\frac{1}{2}\sigma_2^2 T}+K})y] - \rho\sigma_1\sqrt{T}y}{\sqrt{1-\rho^2}\sigma_1\sqrt{T}} + \frac{\frac{1}{2}\sigma_1^2 T - \ln F_1}{\sqrt{1-\rho^2}\sigma_1\sqrt{T}}$$

Then, we can solve the two crossing points with the following equation:

$$l(y)^2 + y^2 = R^2$$

Then, we can obtain

$$y_1 = \frac{-uv + \sqrt{R^2(u^2+1) - v^2}}{u^2+1}$$

$$y_2 = \frac{-uv - \sqrt{R^2(u^2+1) - v^2}}{u^2+1}$$

where

$$u = \frac{\sigma_2 - \rho\sigma_1 - \frac{K\sigma_2}{F_2 e^{-\frac{1}{2}\sigma_2^2 T}+K}}{\sqrt{1-\rho^2}\sigma_1}$$

$$v = \frac{\ln\frac{F_2 e^{-\frac{1}{2}\sigma_2^2 T}+K}{F_1} + \frac{1}{2}\sigma_1^2 T}{\sqrt{1-\rho^2}\sigma_1\sqrt{T}}$$

Then,

$$x_1 = h(y_1)$$
$$x_2 = h(y_2)$$

Now, we can obtain (a, b, c, d) with the following formulas:

$$b = h'(y_1)$$

$$a = x_1 - b * y_1$$
$$d = h'(y_2)$$
$$c = x_2 - d * y_2$$

□

Appendix E

Delta and Rhoza Formula Coefficients of Proposition 3

$$
\begin{aligned}
C_1 &= -e^{-rT}\frac{F_1M_x(d_{11},d_{12},\hat{\rho}) - F_2M_x(d_{21},d_{22},\hat{\rho}) - KM_x(d_{31},d_{32},\hat{\rho})}{(1+b^2)^{\frac{1}{2}}} \\
C_2 &= -e^{-rT}\frac{F_1M_y(d_{11},d_{12},\hat{\rho}) - F_2M_y(d_{21},d_{22},\hat{\rho}) - KM_y(d_{31},d_{32},\hat{\rho})}{(1+d^2)^{\frac{1}{2}}} \\
C_3 &= e^{-rT}[\frac{ab(F_1M_x(d_{11},d_{12},\hat{\rho}) - F_2M_x(d_{21},d_{22},\hat{\rho}) - KM_x(d_{31},d_{32},\hat{\rho}))}{(1+b^2)^{\frac{3}{2}}} \\
&\quad -\frac{(b\sqrt{1-\rho^2}+\rho)\sigma_1\sqrt{T}F_1M_x(d_{11},d_{12},\hat{\rho}) - \sigma_2\sqrt{T}F_2M_x(d_{21},d_{22},\hat{\rho})}{(1+b^2)^{\frac{3}{2}}} \\
&\quad +\frac{(d-b)(F_1M_\rho(d_{11},d_{12},\hat{\rho}) - F_2M_\rho(d_{21},d_{22},\hat{\rho}) - KM_\rho(d_{31},d_{32},\hat{\rho}))}{(1+b^2)^{\frac{3}{2}}(1+d^2)^{\frac{1}{2}}}] \\
C_4 &= e^{-rT}[\frac{cd(F_1M_y(d_{11},d_{12},\hat{\rho}) - F_2M_y(d_{21},d_{22},\hat{\rho}) - KM_y(d_{31},d_{32},\hat{\rho}))}{(1+d^2)^{\frac{3}{2}}} \\
&\quad -\frac{(d\sqrt{1-\rho^2}+\rho)\sigma_1\sqrt{T}F_1M_y(d_{11},d_{12},\hat{\rho}) - \sigma_2\sqrt{T}F_2M_y(d_{21},d_{22},\hat{\rho})}{(1+d^2)^{\frac{3}{2}}} \\
&\quad +\frac{(b-d)(F_1M_\rho(d_{11},d_{12},\hat{\rho}) - F_2M_\rho(d_{21},d_{22},\hat{\rho}) - KM_\rho(d_{31},d_{32},\hat{\rho}))}{(1+d^2)^{\frac{3}{2}}(1+b^2)^{\frac{1}{2}}} \\
D_{11} &= (h'(y_1)-b)(\frac{\partial y_1}{\partial u}\frac{\partial u}{\partial F_1} + \frac{\partial y_1}{\partial v}\frac{\partial v}{\partial F_1} + \frac{\partial y_1}{\partial R}\frac{\partial R}{\partial F_1}) + \frac{\partial h(y_1)}{\partial F_1} - D_{13}y_1 \\
D_{12} &= (h'(y_2)-d)(\frac{\partial y_2}{\partial u}\frac{\partial u}{\partial F_1} + \frac{\partial y_2}{\partial v}\frac{\partial v}{\partial F_1} + \frac{\partial y_2}{\partial R}\frac{\partial R}{\partial F_1}) + \frac{\partial h(y_2)}{\partial F_1} - D_{14}y_2 \\
D_{13} &= h''(y_1)(\frac{\partial y_1}{\partial u}\frac{\partial u}{\partial F_1} + \frac{\partial y_1}{\partial v}\frac{\partial v}{\partial F_1} + \frac{\partial y_1}{\partial R}\frac{\partial R}{\partial F_1}),\ D_{14} = h''(y_2)(\frac{\partial y_2}{\partial u}\frac{\partial u}{\partial F_1} + \frac{\partial y_2}{\partial v}\frac{\partial v}{\partial F_1} + \frac{\partial y_2}{\partial R}\frac{\partial R}{\partial F_1}) \\
D_{21} &= (h'(y_1)-b)(\frac{\partial y_1}{\partial u}\frac{\partial u}{\partial F_2} + \frac{\partial y_1}{\partial v}\frac{\partial v}{\partial F_2} + \frac{\partial y_1}{\partial R}\frac{\partial R}{\partial F_2}) + \frac{\partial h(y_1)}{\partial F_2} - D_{23}y_1 \\
D_{22} &= (h'(y_2)-d)(\frac{\partial y_2}{\partial u}\frac{\partial u}{\partial F_2} + \frac{\partial y_2}{\partial v}\frac{\partial v}{\partial F_2} + \frac{\partial y_2}{\partial R}\frac{\partial R}{\partial F_2}) + \frac{\partial h(y_2)}{\partial F_2} - D_{24}y_2 \\
D_{23} &= h''(y_1)(\frac{\partial y_1}{\partial u}\frac{\partial u}{\partial F_2} + \frac{\partial y_1}{\partial v}\frac{\partial v}{\partial F_2} + \frac{\partial y_1}{\partial R}\frac{\partial R}{\partial F_2}) + \frac{\partial h'(y_1)}{\partial F_2} \\
D_{24} &= h''(y_2)(\frac{\partial y_2}{\partial u}\frac{\partial u}{\partial F_2} + \frac{\partial y_2}{\partial v}\frac{\partial v}{\partial F_2} + \frac{\partial y_2}{\partial R}\frac{\partial R}{\partial F_2}) + \frac{\partial h'(y_2)}{\partial F_2} \\
D_{31} &= (h'(y_1)-b)(\frac{\partial y_1}{\partial u}\frac{\partial u}{\partial \rho} + \frac{\partial y_1}{\partial v}\frac{\partial v}{\partial \rho} + \frac{\partial y_1}{\partial R}\frac{\partial R}{\partial \rho}) + \frac{\partial h(y_1)}{\partial \rho} - D_{33}y_1 \\
D_{32} &= (h'(y_2)-d)(\frac{\partial y_2}{\partial u}\frac{\partial u}{\partial \rho} + \frac{\partial y_2}{\partial v}\frac{\partial v}{\partial \rho} + \frac{\partial y_2}{\partial R}\frac{\partial R}{\partial \rho}) + \frac{\partial h(y_2)}{\partial \rho} - D_{34}y_2 \\
D_{33} &= h''(y_1)(\frac{\partial y_1}{\partial u}\frac{\partial u}{\partial \rho} + \frac{\partial y_1}{\partial v}\frac{\partial v}{\partial \rho} + \frac{\partial y_1}{\partial R}\frac{\partial R}{\partial \rho}) + \frac{\partial h'(y_1)}{\partial \rho} \\
D_{34} &= h''(y_2)(\frac{\partial y_2}{\partial u}\frac{\partial u}{\partial \rho} + \frac{\partial y_2}{\partial v}\frac{\partial v}{\partial \rho} + \frac{\partial y_2}{\partial R}\frac{\partial R}{\partial \rho}) + \frac{\partial h'(y_2)}{\partial \rho}
\end{aligned}
$$

$$M_x(d_1,d_2,\rho)=\frac{\partial M(d_1,d_2,\rho)}{\partial d_1}, M_y(d_1,d_2,\rho)=\frac{\partial M(d_1,d_2,\rho)}{\partial d_2}, M_\rho(d_1,d_2,\rho)=\frac{\partial M(d_1,d_2,\rho)}{\partial rho}$$

$$\frac{\partial h(y)}{\partial F_1}=-\frac{1}{\sqrt{1-\rho^2}\sigma_1\sqrt{T}F_1}, \frac{\partial h(y)}{\partial F_2}=\frac{\exp(-\frac{1}{2}\sigma_2^2T+\sigma_2\sqrt{T}y)}{\sqrt{1-\rho^2}\sigma_1\sqrt{T}(F_2\exp(-\frac{1}{2}\sigma_2^2T+\sigma_2\sqrt{T}y)+K)}$$

$$\frac{\partial h(y)}{\partial\rho}=\frac{\rho}{\sqrt{(1-\rho^2)^3}}\frac{\ln(F_2\exp(-\frac{1}{2}\sigma_2^2T+\sigma_2\sqrt{T}y)+K)-\ln F_1+\frac{1}{2}\sigma_1^2T}{\sigma_1\sqrt{T}}-\frac{y}{\sqrt{(1-\rho^2)^3}}$$

$$\frac{\partial h'(y)}{\partial F_1}=0, \frac{\partial h'(y)}{\partial F_2}=\frac{1}{\sqrt{1-\rho^2}\sigma_1\sqrt{T}}\frac{\sigma_2\sqrt{T}e^{-\frac{1}{2}\sigma_2^2T+\sigma_2\sqrt{T}y}K}{(F_2e^{-\frac{1}{2}\sigma_2^2T+\sigma_2\sqrt{T}y}+K)^2}$$

$$\frac{\partial h'(y)}{\partial\rho}=\frac{\rho}{\sqrt{(1-\rho^2)^3}}\frac{F_2\sigma_2e^{-\frac{1}{2}\sigma_2^2T+\sigma_2\sqrt{T}y}}{\sigma_1(F_2e^{-\frac{1}{2}\sigma_2^2T+\sigma_2\sqrt{T}y}+K)}-\frac{1}{\sqrt{(1-\rho^2)^3}}$$

$$h''(y)=\frac{KF_2\sigma_2^2Te^{-\frac{1}{2}\sigma_2^2T+\sigma_2\sqrt{T}y}}{\sqrt{1-\rho^2}\sigma_1\sqrt{T}(F_2e^{-\frac{1}{2}\sigma_2^2T+\sigma_2\sqrt{T}y}+K)^2}$$

$$\frac{\partial u}{\partial F_1}=0, \frac{\partial u}{\partial F_2}=\frac{K\sigma_2}{\sqrt{1-\rho^2}\sigma_1}\frac{e^{-\frac{1}{2}\sigma_2^2T}}{(F_2e^{-\frac{1}{2}\sigma_2^2T}+K)^2},$$

$$\frac{\partial u}{\partial\rho}=\frac{\rho}{\sqrt{(1-\rho^2)^3}}(\sigma_2-\rho\sigma_1-\frac{K\sigma_2}{F_2e^{-\frac{1}{2}\sigma_2^2T}+K})-\frac{\sigma_1}{\sqrt{(1-\rho^2)^3}}$$

$$\frac{\partial v}{\partial F_1}=-\frac{1}{\sqrt{1-\rho^2}\sigma_1\sqrt{T}F_1}, \frac{\partial v}{\partial F_2}=\frac{e^{-\frac{1}{2}\sigma_2^2T}}{\sqrt{1-\rho^2}\sigma_1\sqrt{T}(F_2e^{-\frac{1}{2}\sigma_2^2T}+K)}$$

$$\frac{\partial v}{\partial\rho}=\frac{\rho}{\sqrt{(1-\rho^2)^3}}\frac{\ln\frac{F_2e^{-\frac{1}{2}\sigma_2^2T}+K}{F_1}+\frac{1}{2}\sigma_1^2T}{\sigma_1\sqrt{T}}$$

$$\frac{\partial y_1}{\partial u}=\frac{u^2v-v+\frac{2uv^2-R^2u^2(u^2+1)}{\sqrt{R^2(u^2+1)-v^2}}}{(u^2+1)^2}, \frac{\partial y_1}{\partial v}=-\frac{u}{u^2+1}-\frac{v}{(u^2+1)\sqrt{R^2(u^2+1)-v^2}}$$

$$\frac{\partial y_2}{\partial u}=\frac{u^2v-v-\frac{2uv^2-R^2u^2(u^2+1)}{\sqrt{R^2(u^2+1)-v^2}}}{(u^2+1)^2}, \frac{\partial y_2}{\partial v}=-\frac{u}{u^2+1}+\frac{v}{(u^2+1)\sqrt{R^2(u^2+1)-v^2}}$$

$$\frac{\partial y_1}{\partial R}=\frac{R}{\sqrt{R^2(u^2+1)-v^2}}, \frac{\partial y_2}{\partial R}=-\frac{R}{\sqrt{R^2(u^2+1)-v^2}}$$

Appendix F

Appendix F.1. Monte Carlo Simulation

The original Monte Carlo simulation is based on the following equations:

$$\begin{aligned} c &= e^{-rT}E[(F_{1T}-F_{2T}-K)^+] \\ F_1(T) &= F_1\exp(-\frac{1}{2}\sigma_1^2T+\sqrt{1-\rho^2}\sigma_1\sqrt{T}X+\rho\sigma_1\sqrt{T}Y) \\ F_2(T) &= F_2\exp(-\frac{1}{2}\sigma_2^2T+\sigma_2\sqrt{T}Y) \end{aligned}$$

We generate $N = 1{,}000{,}000$ pairs of independent standard normal variables of X and Y.

Appendix F.2. Sample Cleaning

Then, we clean them by shifting and scaling to make the samples of X and Y have a mean of 0 and std of 1, respectively.

Appendix F.3. Antithetic Variables

Then, we double the trials by taking $-X$ and $-Y$ for each trial to reduce the variance.

Appendix F.4. Control Variates

After that, we also use the control variate technique. We define

$$U = e^{-rT}(F_{1T} - F_{2T} - K)^{+}$$

$$V = e^{-rT}(F_{1T} - F_{2T} - K)I_{\{x-by \geq a\}}$$

We rewrite the equation as

$$\begin{aligned} e^{-rT}E[(F_{1T} - F_{2T} - K)^{+}] &= E[U] \\ &= E[U + c(V - EV)] \\ &= E[U + c(V - \tilde{c}(K,T))] \end{aligned}$$

where $\tilde{c}(K,T)$ is the approximated price given in theorem 1, and $c = -\frac{Cov(U,V)}{Var(V)}$.

Since $Cov(U,V)$ and $Var(V)$ are unknown, we use the simulation above to calculate the sample variance and covariance to calculate c.

Appendix F.5. Greek Simulation

To simulate Deltas with respect to F_1, F_2, and Rhoza, we first calculate the numerical Deltas on each path and then obtain the simulation results by calculating the average of all paths.

References

1. Carmona, R.; Durrleman, V. Pricing and hedging spread options. *Siam Rev.* **2003**, *45*, 627–685. [CrossRef]
2. Luciano, E. *Spark Spread Options When Commodity Prices Are Represented as Time-Changed Processes, Risk Management in Commodity Markets: From Shipping to Agricultural and Energy*; John Wiley & Sons: Hoboken, NJ, USA, 2008; Volume 1.
3. Bouchouev, I. *Spread Options and Virtual Storage, in Virtual Barrels*; Springer Texts in Business and Economics; Springer: Berlin/Heidelberg, Germany, 2023; Volume 1.
4. Cartea, A.; Pedraz, C. How much should we pay for interconnecting electricity markets? A real options approach. *Energy Econ.* **2012**, *4*, 14–30. [CrossRef]
5. Coqueret, G.; Tavin, B. A note on implied correlation for bivariate contracts. *Econ. Bull.* **2020**, *40*, 1388-1396.
6. Margrabe, W. The value of an option to exchange one asset for another. *J. Financ.* **1978**, *33*, 177–186. [CrossRef]
7. Eydeland, A.; Mahoney, D. *The Grid Model for Derivative Pricing*; Technical Report; R.G. Mirant: Atlanta, GA, USA, 2001 .
8. Pearson, N.D. An Efficient Approach for Pricing Spread Options. 1995. Available online: https://ssrn.com/abstract=7010 (accessed on May 2024).
9. Kirk, E.; Aron, J. Correlation in the energy markets. *Manag. Energy Price Risk* **1995**, *1*, 71–78.
10. Carmona, R.; Durrleman, V. *Pricing and Hedging Spread Options in a Log-Normal Model (Technical Report: Department of Operations Research and Financial Engineering)*; Princeton University: Princeton, NJ, USA, 2003.
11. Bjerksund, P.; Stensland, G. Closed form spread option valuation. *Quant. Financ.* **2014**, *14*, 1785–1794. [CrossRef]
12. Caldana R.; Fusai, G. A general closed-form spread option pricing formula. *J. Bank. Financ.* **2012**, *37*, 4893–4906. [CrossRef]
13. Berton, E.; Mercuri, L. An efficient unified approach for spread option pricing in a copula market model. *Ann. Oper. Res.* **2023**, *336*, 307–329. [CrossRef]
14. Li, M.; Deng, S.J.; Zhoc, J. Closed-form approximations for spread option prices and greeks. *J. Deriv.* **2008**, *15*, 58–80. [CrossRef]
15. Galeeva R. Deriving Better Second-Order Derivatives. *J. Deriv.* **2020**, *30*, 32–48. [CrossRef]
16. Galeeva, R.; Haversang, T. Parameterized Calendar Correlations: Decoding Oil and Beyond. *J. Deriv.* **2020**, *27*, 7–25. [CrossRef]
17. Fisher, R. On the probable error of a correlation deduced from a small sample. *Metron* **1921**, *1*, 3–31.

energies

MDPI

Article

The Impact of a Market Maker in an Electricity Market

Sebastián Arias [1,*], Adriana M. Santa-Alvarado [1] and Harold Salazar [2]

1 Faculty of Business Science, Universidad Tecnológica de Pereira, Pereira 660003, Colombia; adriana.santa@utp.edu.co
2 Faculty of Engineering, Universidad Tecnológica de Pereira, Pereira 660003, Colombia; hsi@utp.edu.co
* Correspondence: jsarias@utp.edu.co

Abstract: Electricity retailers in an electricity market use over-the-counter (OTC) contracts, or bilateral, and spot market purchases to meet the energy demands of their users. In some markets, OTC contracts face issues with price discrimination and accessibility. This study reveals some inefficiencies of OTC contracts in Colombia that expose regulated users—approximately 70% of the national demand—to market risk. This risk is aggravated by the current tariff design. To mitigate these inefficiencies, this article proposes the incorporation of a market maker that will improve the liquidity of existing energy futures in the country. These futures are mechanisms that the retailers could implement to hedge their demand and reduce the adverse effects of market risk. The characteristics of the market maker and a quantitative analysis of its impact are developed in this paper. While the characterization of the problem with its solution is developed with Colombian data, the conceptual framework could be extended to other countries that are concerned about how energy users are being affected by increases in tariffs due to high exposure to spot market price volatility.

Keywords: market maker; inefficiencies of the OTC market; market risk; electricity market; energy futures

1. Introduction

The liberalization of the electricity sector was motivated by the benefits that competition brings, including an efficient allocation of production resources and investments from the private sector. Nevertheless, the presence of dominant agents, flaws in the regulatory framework, and demand inelasticity, among other factors, lead to the emergence of inefficiencies that are not typical of competitive markets. These inefficiencies distort the price, and with them, generate misleading signals for market agents to make decisions. For said reasons, any measure that improves the conditions of healthy competition in an electricity market is necessary.

The Colombian wholesale energy market is not invulnerable to market inefficiencies, and as an aggravating factor, regulated demand assumes the inefficiencies of the energy purchases made by the electricity retailers. The regulated demand corresponds to 70% of the country's demand, and they are consumers that, in the last 6 months, had an average power demand of 0.1 MW, or 55 MWh of energy each month. This corresponds primarily to residential, commercial, and small industrial users. While these users have the option to switch their retailer, the practical barriers of technological requirements and associated costs often impede such changes. In practical terms, the regulated demand is captive to the retailer. The aggravating factor lies in the fact that the majority of energy users in Colombia are assuming, through tariffs, the inefficiencies of the electricity retailer in managing their energy purchasing portfolio along with certain risks—primarily market-related. These market-related risks are detailed in Section 3 of this article.

This article shows and discusses the inefficiencies of the Colombian electricity market and how these are assumed by regulated users. For this purpose, an analysis is conducted of how the tariff structure established by the country's regulators, the Energy and Gas Regulatory Commission (CREG by its acronym in Spanish), determines the way in which the costs of energy purchases along with market risk, among other things, are transferred to regulated users. Additionally, some market variables are analyzed that show the current difficulties that retailers face in managing their energy purchasing portfolio, which exacerbates the problem for regulated users.

To overcome these inefficiencies, this article proposes a new agent that fulfills the role of the market maker. This new agent serves as a facilitator in managing the risks of the retailers' energy purchasing portfolio, thereby transferring efficient costs of the tariff to the end-user. And, though the electricity market requires a series of adjustments that have been addressed in other studies [1], this article analyzes the functions and the impact of a market maker, as these aspects have not been studied in depth in previous works, to the best of our knowledge. While the impact of market makers is widely known in developed financial and energy markets, this proposal focuses on an electricity market that has not yet reached an important level of maturity in terms of the number of participants (energy supply) or active demand participation.

This study complements existing literature regarding risk management by incorporating market-maker mechanisms based on factual elements applied to a particular market, a situation not detailed in academic articles. Additionally, as an extra contribution, since Colombia is the first country in Latin America to have an electricity futures market, this proposal serves as a reference for countries with similar contexts and environments as Latin American countries, a situation that, to the best of our knowledge, is not detailed in the academic literature.

Specifically, this work contributes by (i) demonstrating the negative effects on electricity-regulated users in Colombia due to the lack of liquidity in the futures market, which forms the backdrop of the problem, and (ii) developing a conceptual model for the market maker that is tailored to Colombia's current institutional framework to facilitate its integration and thus minimize the regulatory effort required for its implementation. This is crucial as market makers that do not align with the specifics of the existing institutional framework may not achieve the intended effects, (iii) numerically demonstrating the positive impact of incorporating the market maker, and (iv) proposing regulatory measures to support the market maker, aiming to enhance its overall impact.

This article is organized as follows: Section 2 revises existing literature related to the inefficiencies of the energy markets, hedging mechanisms, and the effects of market makers. Section 3 analyzes the tariff structure in Colombia and how it transfers inefficiencies to the end-user. It also illustrates the inefficiencies the current Colombian market faces. Section 4 presents and discusses a new proposal to incorporate a new agent that dynamizes the standardized anonymous market as well as its principal product—energy futures. This new agent will inject liquidity into the energy futures, providing an instrument that allows for effective, active management of different types of risks that the electricity retailers face. A quantitative analysis of the market maker's impact is also presented in Section 4. Finally, the conclusions of this work are found in Section 5.

2. A Review of Hedging Mechanisms for Market Risk and the Impact of Market Makers

The liberalization of the electricity sector brought challenges to creating an efficient market due to the presence of vertically integrated agents, demand inelasticity, energy price volatility, the presence of financial risk, and market power, among other factors. These factors have had a negative effect on market performance. For instance, in [2], it is shown that the restructuring of the wholesale energy market in California resulted in market power abuse, causing energy price increases above competitive levels. In [3], it is pointed out that the lack of regulation for generation companies to declare their costs leads to the introduction of asymmetry in information and market power. In [4], it is argued that the lack of competition, the congestion of the transmission network, and the declaration of unavailability push up electrical energy prices. For said reasons in [5–7], it is recommended to adopt measures to improve the efficiency of the electricity market. Among these measures, it is recommended to promote competition to invigorate the market and to oversee producers' behavior to identify and rectify undesirable practices. Likewise, it is recommended to increase investments in electricity networks and implement regulatory changes when required, with the goal of adequately responding to the changing dynamics of the market and ensuring a competitive and efficient environment.

Conversely, the short-term market exposed agents to market risk due to the high volatility of energy costs, which can lead to economic loss [8]. This volatility is because of many factors, such as electrical energy coming from different technologies, transmission network congestion, errors made in demand projection [9], market design [10], and the stochasticity of renewable energy resources [11–13]. Because of the negative impacts of market risk, ref. [14] suggests that diversifying the generation matrix, improving demand response, and improving regulations will reduce exposure to market volatility.

Traditionally, OTC contracts have been used in energy markets as a means to mitigate market and volume risk [15]. Additionally, they allow for operational and financial planning of companies by managing long-term prices [16]. One of the advantages of these kinds of contracts is that they adjust to the needs of the agents as well as are used to promote investments in the generation and diversification of the energy matrix [17]. Ref. [18] studies the interaction between bilateral contracting and the spot market, concluding that the spot market variance decreases with OTC contracting.

While bilateral contracting is a protection against market risk, it is also true that through it, inefficiencies can occur that affect short-term market prices. Ref. [19] shows how bilateral contracts can be used to manipulate the market when there is an agent with a dominant position. Ref. [16] creates a stochastic model to evaluate bilateral contracts and quantify the risk premium that emerges in this type of negotiation. Ref. [17] quantifies the credit risk and its respective spread in Brazil. Ref. [20] creates an indicator to measure credit risk considering government policies that affect retailers and the market share they serve.

Derivatives markets have emerged as an alternative to OTC contracting, specifically in electricity futures. This is because of the anonymity between purchasing and selling agents, which leads to an efficient price formation, avoiding the inefficiencies of direct negotiation that occur with the OTC [21]. In [22], it is notable that derivatives allow signaling that promotes competition and participation of new agents and investors.

A reliable spot market, one that allows for the precise, quick settlement of positions, must exist for a futures market to develop [23]. Additionally, the commodity price should be volatile to attract speculators to inject liquidity. Nevertheless, energy futures are subject to specific considerations that are different than the majority of commodities. In [24], the lack of storage is shown to prevent arbitrage from pushing the spot price and futures price to converge, causing basis risk. This type of risk can increase as the date of expiration approaches.

The efficiency of futures as a hedging mechanism has been addressed by several authors. Ref. [25] estimates the hedging ratio to minimize the volatility of a portfolio composed of energy purchases in the spot and futures markets. They conclude that short-term futures hedging reduces the volatility of the portfolio. Ref. [26] concludes that electricity futures reduce market risk more effectively than cross-hedging. That is, they are an effective tool for financial risk management in electricity markets. Ref. [27] study the impact of two types of futures contracts (base load and peak load) as hedging tools for retailers. The authors conclude that both contracts allow hedging against market risk. Conversely, ref. [28] illustrates that energy futures, under certain circumstances, show limited coverage. This is principally explained by the low covariance between the spot and futures price.

Market makers are specialized agents whose purpose is to improve the market in terms of liquidity, transparency, price discovery, volatility mitigation, and reducing the spread between bid and ask prices [29]. Additionally, these market makers mitigate the risk associated with information asymmetry [30]. The previous characteristics promote the participation of new agents, competition, and the development of new financial products that can be used for speculation or hedging [31].

The impact of market makers in commodity financial markets, as well as their interactions with other agents, has been explored in academic literature. For instance, in [29], empirical evidence is presented about how market makers increase liquidity and diminish volatility in an emerging market like the Shanghai stock exchange (STAR Market). Alternatively, ref. [32] studies the relationship that market makers have with firms that are geographically close. This proximity allows for better access to formal and informal news, and with that, a better understanding of the local economy, providing more context and, in turn, more efficient price formation. Additionally, in [33], it is studied how the entrance of market makers in places dominated by intermediaries drives a more efficient market structure. Nevertheless, it is important to recognize that, though market makers intend to maximize their utility, this approach can introduce inefficiencies that affect price stability, as is illustrated in [34].

In electricity markets, the effect of the market makers has been addressed by [35], in which the authors show that market makers enabled balancing buying and selling volumes. In [36], it is shown that an increase in the number of market makers decreases the liquidity premium of energy futures. Finally, ref. [37] proposes a decentralized market model through an autonomous market maker for prosumers in isolated geographical areas, guaranteeing the liquidity and formation of a fair price, which demonstrates the innovative and transformative potential of market makers in the electricity sector. While market makers aim to improve the efficiency of the markets, from liquidity to transparency, the effectiveness and the impact of these agents can vary due to a number of factors, including a flawed market design, the regulatory environment, the institutional framework, and the very implementation of the market maker itself [38].

3. Market Risk and the Inefficiencies of the Hedging Mechanisms

In this section, it is evident how market risk currently transfers to regulated users (residential, commercial, and small-industry users) through tariffs and how the principal hedging instrument that is available for an electricity retailer (OTC contracts) presents inefficiencies to mitigate market risk. Though the transfer of market risk to the regulated user is not a problem in and of itself, as the consumer of any kind of good or service assumes the costs of service provision through tariffs, the difficulty lies in the inefficiencies of hedging instruments in fulfilling their objectives and the fact that different obstacles (technological and economic) exist, making it difficult to change the provider for these types of users in Colombia. Also, the inefficiencies of standardized contracting, which could be the other hedging instrument but today lacks liquidity, are evident.

3.1. Market Risk Transfer Via Tariffs

The regulated demand in Colombia is subject to a tariff regime established by the Energy and Gas Regulatory Commission (CREG, in Spanish). The CREG defines service provision costs assumed for this type of user. Specifically, the tariff formula, illustrated in Equation (1) and established in [39], explicitly shows the causality of each one of the costs of the distinct activities. With this, the unitary cost (*CU*, in Spanish) of energy is defined. This tariff is volumetric, though the regulation allows other schemes like demand charges, time of use, etc. However, these other schemes are not widespread in the country. The variables from left to right represent the cost of generation ($G_{m,i,j}$), cost of transmission and distribution (T_m and $D_{m,n}$), cost of retailing ($Cv_{m,i,j}$), cost of losses ($PR_{n,m,i,j}$), and, finally, the cost of restrictions ($R_{m,i}$) that originate as a consequence of limited transport capacity and the fact that in the country, the price formation is at a single node. The subscripts denote the voltage level n for which the *CU* is calculated, month m in which the components of the unitary cost are settled, and the subscripts i and j denote the electricity retailer and the market it served, respectively.

$$CU_{n,m,i,j} = G_{m,i,j} + T_m + D_{m,n} + Cv_{m,i,j} + PR_{n,m,i,j} + R_{m,i} \tag{1}$$

The mechanisms used by retailers to acquire energy and transfer these costs to regulated users are recognized in the G component of the CU. Those of importance for the purpose of this study are illustrated in Equation (2a–d) [40], in which the subscripts that are not required in the context of this article are omitted (see Appendix A for detailed descriptions of the $G_{m,i,j}$).

$$G = \omega_1 Qc(\alpha Pc + (1-\alpha)Mc\,) + \ldots \tag{2a}$$

$$\omega_2 QcPSA + \ldots \tag{2b}$$

$$\sum_{l=3}^{n} \omega_l QcP_l + \ldots \tag{2c}$$

$$(1-Qc)Pb + others \tag{2d}$$

Bilateral contracting has traditionally dominated electrical energy negotiations in Colombia, and most transactions are made through this mechanism. Energy purchases through bilaterial agreements are renumerated as described in (2a), in which the percentage of energy covered by the retailer through these contracts is recognized and denoted by the product $\omega_1 Qc$. Equation (2a) weights the average price of acquired bilateral contracts by the retailer to meet the regulated demand, denoted as Pc, and the average price of all contracts in the market, denoted as Mc. The weighting is determined by the factor α.

In (2b), energy purchases acquired in auctions for long-term contracts for non-conventional renewable energy resources (principally wind and solar) are renumerated, which are used to promote these types of generation sources. The product, $\omega_2 Qc$, determines the percentage of energy acquired for these kinds of contracts that are recognized by the price of auction, denoted as PSA. In (2c), the purchases made through standardized contracting mechanisms, among them electricity futures, are transferred, and the sum total recognizes all the products traded in this market. The logic of (2c) is similar to the aforementioned components in that the percentage of energy acquired by a particular product, $\omega_l Qc$, is recognized at the price of the product, P_l.

Finally, Equation (2d) transfers the percentage of energy not covered by contracting mechanisms and acquired in the spot market, indicated by $(1 - Qc)$, and recognized at the spot market price, Pb. Note that this last term exposes the regulated user to market risk, a situation that can be exacerbated when the supplier has low coverage levels because it brings the expression within the parenthesis closer to one. Also, note that market risk exposure is promoted by the weighting factor α in (2a), in that this value does not allow for a complete transfer of the full contract value.

3.2. *Inefficiencies in Hedging Mechanisms*

3.2.1. A Volatile Asset—The Spot Market Price

The price of electrical energy in the short-term market is highly volatile and explained, in Colombia, by the price of fuel for thermal resources, network transportation limitations, and mostly by the "El Niño" phenomenon, which significantly reduces rainfall and, consequently, reservoir levels in a country that is highly dependent on hydraulic resources. Figure 1a illustrates this situation, in which the average daily spot price in the market in cents per kWh (in dollars) is shown (all monetary values in this paper are in US dollars, using an exchange rate of 3866 USD/COP, which corresponds to the average exchange rate of April 2024). The highest registered price coincides with the El Niño phenomenon, which occurred between 2014 and 2016. Likewise, notable increases are observed in 2010 and 2020. Note how these price changes are transferred to regulated demand, as explained in Equation (2d). While the market counts on a scarcity price that corresponds to the maximum value the demand can pay for electricity in the country, this is not a hedging instrument that provides protection from market spikes.

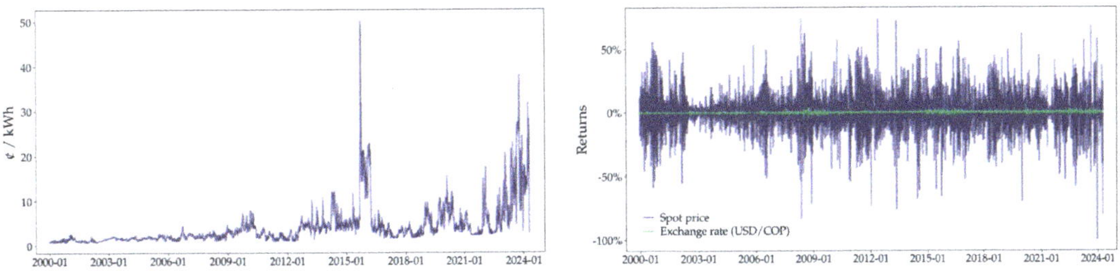

(**a**) (**b**)

Figure 1. (**a**) Average daily spot price. (**b**) Comparison between the volatility of the exchange rate (USD/COP) and the spot price.

Figure 1b evidences the volatility of the price of energy in Figure 1a with an asset that is considered highly volatile in Colombia, the exchange rate between the US Dollar (USD) and the Colombian Peso. Figure 1b is determined as a logarithm of the ratio between the price of the asset (the exchange rates or energy) at two different points in time. Figure 1b shows that the price of energy is much more volatile when it is compared with an asset that is considered high-risk in the country. Moreover, as is illustrated in Section 3.1, this volatility is assumed by regulated users because the tariff structure allows the transfer of this market risk to the user. This volatility poses a risk to the system, particularly in situations of illiquidity and low coverage, such as those currently faced by retailers because of the tariff option (a temporary measure that enabled the freezing of tariff increases during the pandemic, and with that, the accumulation of liabilities that are currently recognized in the tariff). In such cases, a systematic risk event can emerge, endangering the electricity supply in the country.

3.2.2. Inefficiency of OTC Contracts

One mechanism widely used in the wholesale electricity market (MEM by its acronym in Spanish) is bilateral, or OTC, contracts as a hedging instrument to counteract the volatility discussed in the previous section. These negotiations are made through a centralized system of public calls to provide transparency to the negotiation process. Nevertheless, this type of contracting displays discriminatory behavior, like the ones shown in Figure 2a, in which the average price of contracts directed to regulated users is consistently higher than that of non-regulated users. Reasons for this behavior have been a matter of discussion by the regulating agent without reaching any consensus [40]. Figure 2b, the average market price of contracts, is compared with the price at which these contracts were acquired by five retailers. It is evident that some retailers negotiate OTC contracts at a higher-than-average price.

The price differences between retailers can be related to the risk perception that generating agents have towards certain retailers, possibly because of management problems, the delayed payment of their obligations, or non-compliance events in the past. These factors could increase the perceived risk of generators when negotiating bilateral contracts, which can translate to a greater risk premium. Although charging a risk premium that reflects the credit risk characteristics of retailers is a common practice, the inefficiency noted is that regulated users bear this premium without having the necessary tools to manage it effectively. In the worst-case scenario, the inability to secure contracts forces retailers to expose their users, particularly those regulated, to the spot market prices. Additionally, the price difference can be reflected by the lack of contracts. This is confirmed by the fact that in the last three years, on average, 40% of the public calls made through a centralized system of purchases (SICEP by its acronym in Spanish) have been declared unsuccessful. This means that a significant amount of energy has not been able to be covered through OTC contracts.

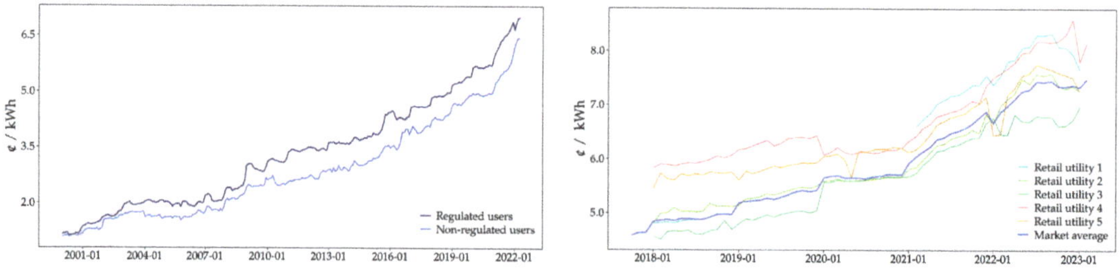

(**a**) (**b**)

Figure 2. (**a**) Current average price of contracts directed at regulated and non-regulated demand. (**b**) Average price of contracts for five retailers.

Finally, in the context of bilateral contracting, there is negotiation asymmetry between the electricity retailers and energy producers, which originates from the nature of their roles. This is because the latter have the option not to enter into contracts according to their expectations of the market price, leaving the retailer exposed.

3.2.3. Inefficiency of Standardized Contracts

The Colombian standardized anonymous market (MAE for its acronym in Spanish) is the first of its kind in Latin America. The principal instrument traded in the MAE is energy futures, which, like the bilateral contracts, allow the marketer to minimize exposure to the spot market. Futures involve an agreement on the future price for electrical energy to mitigate market risk. This price remains fixed until the maturity of the futures and will not be indexed to economic indicators such as inflation, as is the case for bilateral contracting.

Nevertheless, this market is characterized by its illiquidity and the lack of participation of agents in both the electricity and financial sectors. Figure 3 shows the number of times a contract has been traded (left axis) and the percentage of energy covered (right axis), with the maturity indicated on the horizontal axis. For instance, the height of the bar on July 2024 on the left axis indicates that a futures contract has been traded six times and expires in July 2024. This contract covers less than 0.5% of the energy for regulated users, as shown on the right axis. A low volume of transactions and low energy coverage are observed, making it difficult to develop this market.

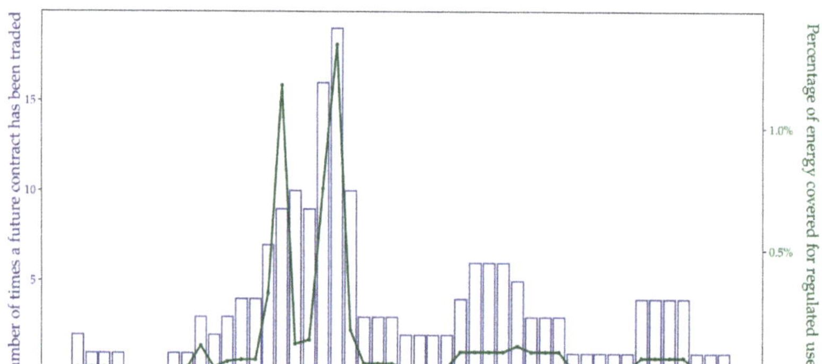

Figure 3. Number of futures contracts traded in the MAE (left axis) and the percentage of energy covered (right axis).

Conversely, Figure 4 shows the average monthly price of electrical energy in the spot market and the most liquid futures reference. Both series exhibit a similar pattern, which is expected behavior in these instruments; nevertheless, the problem emerges with the basis risk, which is spread between the spot and the futures prices, caused by illiquidity. This basis risk is one of the causes that impedes the development of this market because the expectations of the futures price are not coherent with those of the spot price. In fact, both series should converge—in a liquid market—to the same value at maturity.

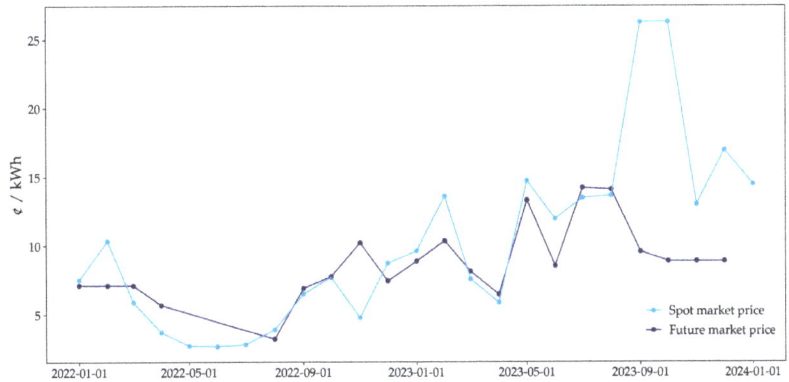

Figure 4. Spread between the average price in the spot market and the most-liquid reference in the futures market.

4. Design and Impact of a Market Maker

A liquid standardized market facilitates the transparent formation of the futures price and their trading because of product characteristics, like the size of the contract, settlement type, underlying asset, and maturity, among other aspects. Likewise, a liquid market generates enough information to understand the behavior of the underlying asset price and its volatility over time, which allows for better financial risk, market risk, and counterparty risk management. In Section 4.1, the conceptual framework of a market maker is developed for the standardized anonymous market in Colombia (MAE by its acronym in Spanish) adapted to the current Colombian electricity market design. The goal is to increase liquidity in electricity futures and, thereby, counteract the situations described in Section 3. Section 4.2 demonstrates that futures protect regulated users from market risk, while Section 4.3 shows how the market maker enhances efficiency and boosts liquidity.

4.1. A Market Maker Coupled with the Current Design of the Colombian Market

Due to the positive impacts a liquid standardized market would have on the Colombian energy market to mitigate market, credit, and systematic risks, this subsection proposes the implementation of a market maker that is compatible with the current design and governance of the standardized market in Colombia. Introducing new agents into a market demands robust regulatory and institutional capabilities. Therefore, any significant changes, like those proposed in this subsection, must align with the existing institutional framework.

In general terms, market makers are specialized financial agents responsible for purchasing and selling financial assets to foster adequate trading conditions. This capability promotes the matching of buyers and sellers. The quantity and price conditions (bid and ask) sent by the market maker in a trading system reflect the market conditions, promoting transparency and allowing all participants to make informed decisions. By ensuring the presence of bid and ask quotes, transactions are executed more quickly, contributing to price stability and liquidity, which is crucial for the market participants' planning and risk management and favorably influencing their behavior.

To compensate for services rendered, the market maker buys from sellers at lower prices and sells to buyers at higher prices. The difference between these prices is known as the spread and represents their profit. The spread not only recognizes the effort, time, and costs associated with providing quotes and the willingness to trade [31], so, too, does it compensate for the risk associated with maintaining an unbalanced portfolio, price fluctuations, and the risk of holding a position that does not close. This spread also allows for adverse selection risk management, which occurs when negotiating with a better-informed agent.

For these reasons, this paper proposes a market maker for the Colombian MAE, categorized within Tier 2 (brokers, investment funds, and other investors operating with their own liquidity). This market maker is distinct from a dealing desk-type broker as it does not represent clients' buy and sell intentions but instead ensures buy and sell prices for the underlying asset over time. This market maker will issue buy and sell orders to Derivex, the current operator of the country's standardized derivatives market.

The idea of using Derivex is to leverage the proposal with an existing agent in the management of derivatives because it already has the technological and financial infrastructure for managing these products. This new market maker will close positions by buying (or selling) futures contracts at a set price and by selling (or buying) them at a different price to close their position and, with that, materialize the spread. The market maker will take a profit because of their participation, which must be transferred into liquidity in the futures market. Additionally, and considering that the futures market settlement is financial and does not require physical delivery, this new agent does not require electrical generation assets to back up the product. This condition expands the possibilities of participation for parties interested in taking on this new role.

Figure 5 shows how the market maker is integrated into the institutional framework of the electrical energy derivatives market. The blue rectangles represent existing agents, and the arrows represent the flow of information between them. Derivex, as previously indicated, is the derivatives market operator and is the recipient of futures' buy and sell orders sent by stock brokerage companies (SCB by its acronym in Spanish). Note that the participation in this market is not limited to agents in the electrical energy sector (generators or marketers of energy). Any investor can access this product through a stock brokerage firm. The Central Risk and Counterparty Chamber (CCRC by its acronym in Spanish) administers the guarantees to mitigate counterparty risk and potential defaults that may occur, and if these are insufficient, they make margin calls, demanding new collateral from the participants. Likewise, pricing and valuation providers responsible for supplying derivative valuation prices enable agents to make decisions based on the best valuation available.

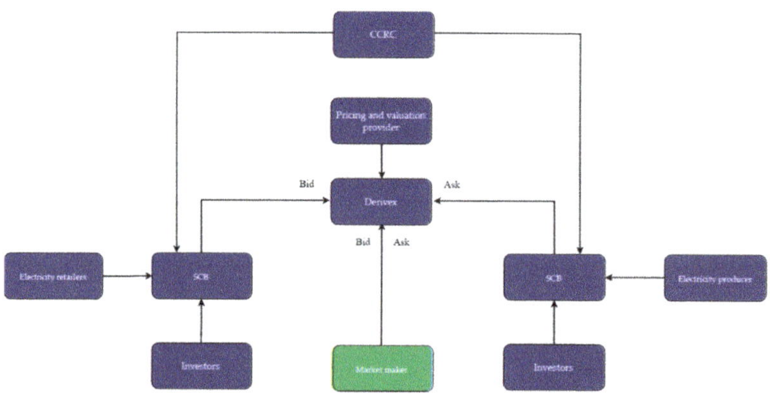

Figure 5. Inclusion of a market maker in the current standardized derivatives energy market.

Figure 5 shows the new market maker, represented in green. This market maker utilizes current information systems provided by Derivex to send buy and sell orders, with the goal of providing liquidity to the market. The essential criteria that this market maker must meet include the following:

1. Continuously and simultaneously quote bid and ask prices, both in the opening and closing auctions of the MAE. The opening auction is crucial for price discovery, as it reveals new information that emerges after the last close. Conversely, the closing auction is important because, in it, futures that can be transferred to regulated users are negotiated.
2. Manage liquidity risk by maintaining positions for long periods of time until finding suitable counterparties or developing alternative hedging strategies with instruments other than those provided by the electricity market. The second option is not available for electricity retailers in Colombia as they are not financial intermediaries. The market maker would have access to several hedging instruments because it is proposed that this new agent be linked to the financial sector.
3. Establish minimum trading volumes in exchange for a preferential contract price. For this, the creation of a negotiation round on Derivex is proposed, in which the market maker can negotiate directly with generators and other institutional participants.
4. Avoid speculative actions in the market, as this could lead to inefficiencies when acting like active investors [34].
5. Allow the market maker to invest in corelated markets, like those of gas and carbon, to manage risk in an unbalanced portfolio. Likewise, comply with and demonstrate a minimum counterparty risk rating.
6. Have solid financial solvency that ensures the ability to execute operations within the market. This financial solvency is essential not only to comply with contractual obligations from market activities but also to maintain the trust of other market participants and regulatory entities. The capacity to withstand market fluctuations without compromising its operations is crucial, ensuring stable and continuous provisions of liquidity to the market. This also implies that the market maker must comply with and demonstrate the minimum technical equity requirement established by a competent authority.
7. Demonstrate effort as a market maker by increasing market liquidity through the continuous quoting of bid and ask prices.
8. Periodically prepare reports about the standardized Colombian futures energy market, its evolution, and prospects.

This market maker, a participant willing to buy and sell the asset at any time, facilitates the trading of contracts and encourages the participation of other market players. Conversely, implementing regulatory measures that are, to date, non-existent is necessary for the market maker to operate efficiently. The most notable regulatory measures include the following: (i) the establishment of regulatory incentives for minimum coverage levels, such as involving the retailer in the savings generated by hedging through futures; (ii) revise and adjust required guarantee levels for the participation in the MAE because excessively demanding requirements could dissuade the participation of agents and, thereby, increase systematic risk; (iii) establish the maximum spread that the market maker can offer; and (iv) develop new financial products in the local market aimed at effectively managing risk associated with an unbalanced portfolio. These products, such as options, contracts for differences, and swaps, must be designed specifically to equip the market maker with the necessary tools for comprehensive risk coverage, (v) incentivize the participation of speculators in the energy futures market so that investors perceive potential value in these instruments and, thereby, increase the market liquidity and efficiency, and (vi) change management actions by conducting awareness and training sessions on the derivatives market for participants.

It is important to note that setting a minimum coverage level would lead to more contracts being closed, thereby increasing transaction volumes, both with and without the market maker's presence. However, if the regulatory coverage requirement solely affects the contract price, this price might not efficiently reflect the contract's true value.

Regulatory demands would shape participants' expectations more than pure supply and demand dynamics. In contrast, a market maker seeks to enhance liquidity by increasing buying and selling activity, which reflects participants' expectations about the traded asset's price. This dynamic tends to reduce price variations due to higher liquidity in buy and sell prices. As proposed in the article, both measures—the establishment of minimum coverage levels with incentives and the implementation of a market maker—are complementary and necessary. While the first measure ensures a base volume of transactions, the second improves market efficiency and transparency, ensuring that prices better reflect real supply and demand conditions and participants' expectations.

Lastly, a regulatory measure currently in effect in the Colombian market aims to implement the reduction in the electricity purchase threshold for retailers that are vertically integrated with generators. Ensuring a reduction in this value allows a portion of this energy to be traded through the MAE. Of equal importance is the recommendation to implement professional certifications in the industry that accredit the technical and professional capabilities of the people associated with the market maker. This can be with a competency validation suitability exam, elevating financial and market standards specific to the Colombian electricity market.

4.2. Impact of Market Maker on Market Risk

The numerical analysis of this subsection is constructed with multiple scenarios using the Bootstrap method, which is widely used in the literature for non-parametric studies. This is because there is little data to determine a distribution for the spot market price or for the futures price in Colombia. Figure 6 shows the average monthly prices observed in the spot market from January 2008 to June 2024, where prices during the El Niño phenomenon are highlighted in red. This phenomenon, characterized by low hydrology conditions, leads to price increases due to reduced hydropower supply (approximately 60% of the energy supply is hydro-dependent).

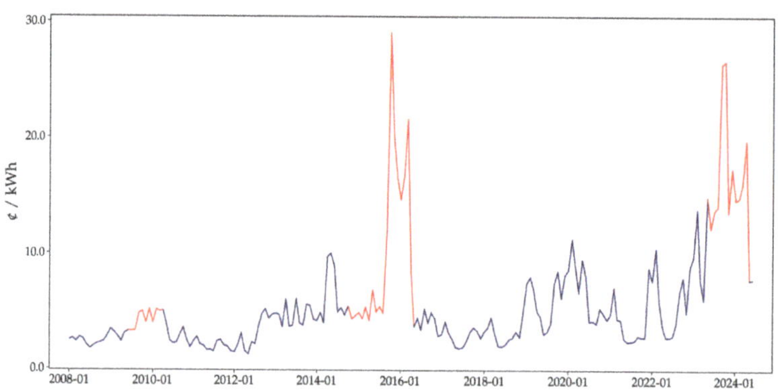

Figure 6. Average monthly spot prices highlighting (in red) the El Niño phenomenon.

Figure 7 shows the prices from Figure 6, separated by each month in which they materialized. For example, the top left box of Figure 7 corresponds to all January prices from Figure 6, the box to its right to February prices, and so on. This separation is performed for sampling purposes.

Figure 8 presents the results of 10,000 simulations of possible scenarios of average monthly spot prices resulting from sampling the values in Figure 7. Each possible scenario—a gray line—is constructed by sampling a January value from the top left box of Figure 7 adjusted to January 2022 using the Producer Price Index (PPI). Then, the February value is sampled and adjusted with its February 2022 PPI value, and so on, until the construction of a possible scenario within the window between January 2022 and January 2024 is complete. This window is selected because, from January 2022, it is possible to transfer purchases made through futures to regulated users, and the Colombian energy derivatives trading platform publishes futures price information from that period. The blue line in Figure 8 represents the realization of futures prices between 2022 and 2024.

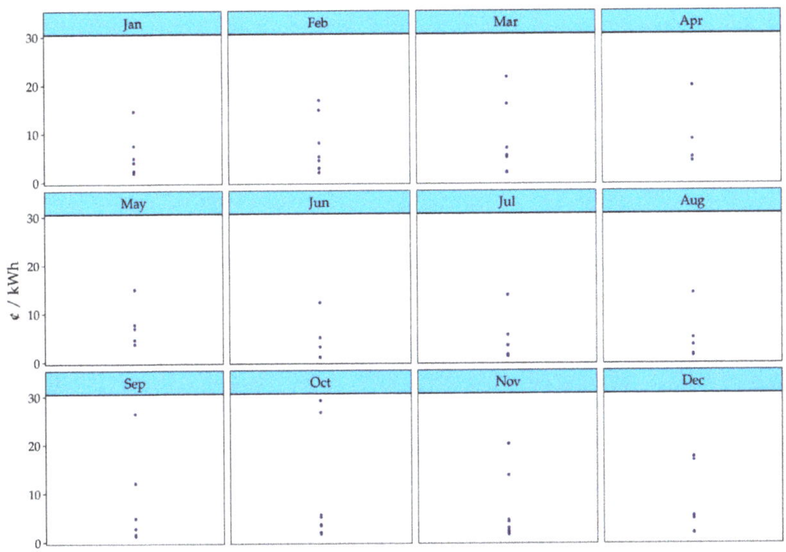

Figure 7. Average monthly spot prices.

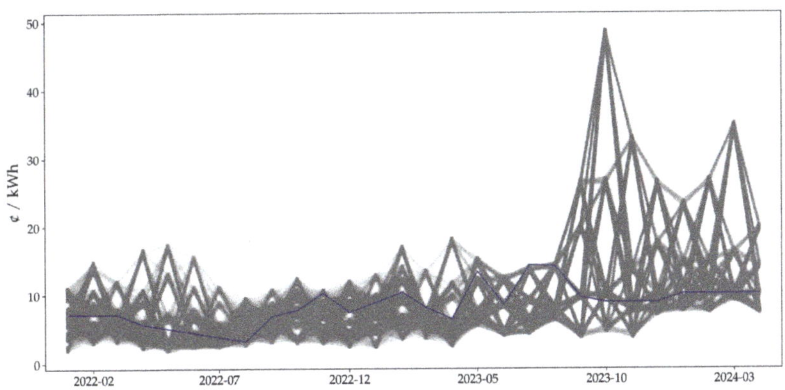

Figure 8. Historical spot price simulation (gray lines) compared to futures price (blue line).

In Figure 8, futures can hedge against market risk, particularly between January and July 2022 and between September 2023 and April 2024, because during these two periods, the simulation scenarios consistently show high prices. However, futures can sometimes be consistently above the average spot price. This is expected behavior for these instruments since hedging involves transferring risk to a counterparty who will not assume it without a premium; however, this strategy is preferable to exposure to extreme events.

With the possible simulation scenarios from Figure 8, it is possible to evaluate the impact on costs transferred to regulated users from spot market purchases and futures, assuming the latter instruments have liquidity promoted by the market maker. The following three analysis strategies for an energy marketer are employed:

- Strategy 1: Buy 5% of the energy in the spot market and 95% in futures.

- Strategy 2: Buy 50% of the energy in the spot market and 50% in futures.
- Strategy 3: Buy 95% of the energy in the spot market and 5% in futures.

The cost transferred to regulated users through these strategies is calculated with component G, detailed in Section 3.1, specifically through expressions (2c) and (2d). Figure 9 shows the density plots of the three employed strategies. In an extreme scenario, a 95% exposure to the spot market leads to users bearing a cost of nearly one hundred million dollars (the point on the far right). Cost dispersion decreases as coverage through futures increases. This dispersion represents the market risk assumed by regulated users, and according to the results, it is mitigated with the hedges that need to be promoted through a liquid futures market, which must be promoted by the market maker proposed in the article.

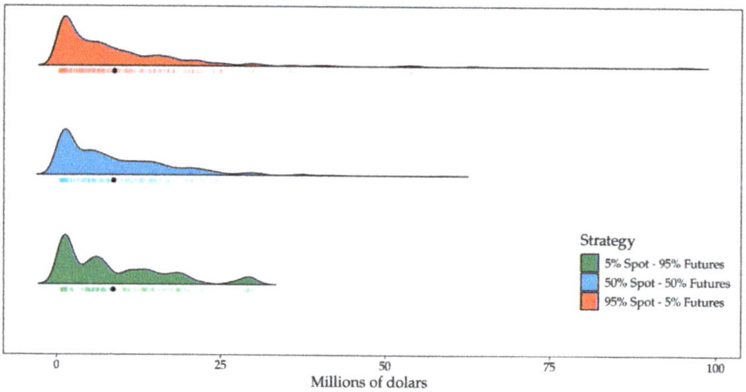

Figure 9. Volatility of cost transferred to regulated users.

In Figure 9, the black dot on each density plot represents the average value of the costs transferred to regulated users for each strategy. These averages are detailed in Table 1. The 95% futures coverage transfers, on average, have a lower value for regulated users. Although these averages are similar for the three strategies, it is important to highlight that covering the regulated demand against extreme events does not increase costs in expected value for regulated users.

Table 1. Average costs transferred per strategy.

Strategy	Average Transferred (USD Million)
Spot 5%—Futures 95%	8.62
Spot 50%—Futures 50%	8.66
Spot 50%—Futures 50%	8.70

Finally, a stress test demonstrates the benefit in terms of economic savings under extreme conditions. This test is constructed with the observed maximum and minimum spot prices; the highest and lowest spot prices from Figure 6 are taken and compared with the observed futures prices. This is shown in Figure 10, where it is noted that futures are a better alternative since, in the analyzed time window, they present a smaller difference with minimum values than with maximum values.

Calculating the average price differences between the maximum values and futures yields a value of 13.1 cents per kWh. Performing the same calculation between futures and minimum values, the value is 7.1 cents per kWh. This means that, in an extreme scenario, as indicated by the red line, hedging with futures saves an average of 13.1 cents per kWh. A scenario with minimum values transfers an average of 7.1 cents per kWh more to regulated users. This represents efficiency from a benefit–cost perspective, as user savings are more significant than the costs they might bear.

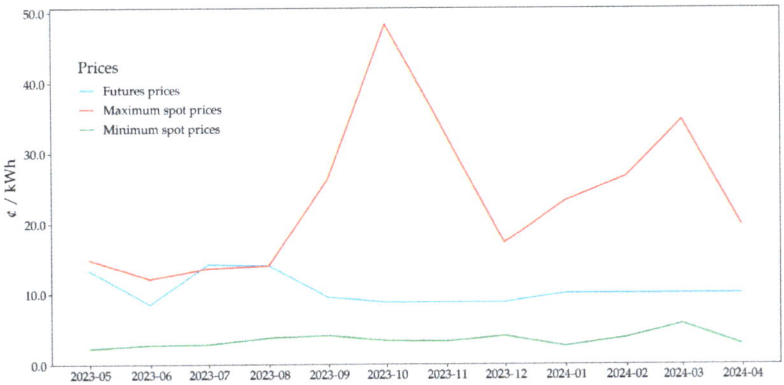

Figure 10. Extreme values of spot prices compared to futures prices.

In summary, the previous analysis clearly demonstrates the significant benefits of implementing futures hedging strategies for regulated users. Although the average costs are similar across the three strategies, it is important to note that hedging against extreme events does not increase the expected value of costs for regulated users. Additionally, a stress test shows that in extreme scenarios, hedging with futures can save an average of 13.1 cents per kWh, whereas minimum value scenarios transfer an additional 7.1 cents per kWh to regulated users. These findings highlight the efficiency and cost-effectiveness of futures hedging.

4.3. Impact of the Market Maker on Liquidity

The impact of the market maker can be approached from different perspectives. This subsection considers a retrospective analysis to establish the coverage effect of regulated demand—the majority of consumers in the country—that a market maker would have. Figure 11 shows the spread from January 2022 to November 2023, with the best bid and ask prices registered on Derivex that did not manage to close. This corresponds to the closest spreads obtained on those trading days without closing. Note that in Figure 11, on a significant number of days, futures contracts did not close. This demonstrates the lack of liquidity currently affecting this derivative, backing the need for a market maker. In fact, of the 626 trading days that correspond to the observation window, 64.22% did not manage to close.

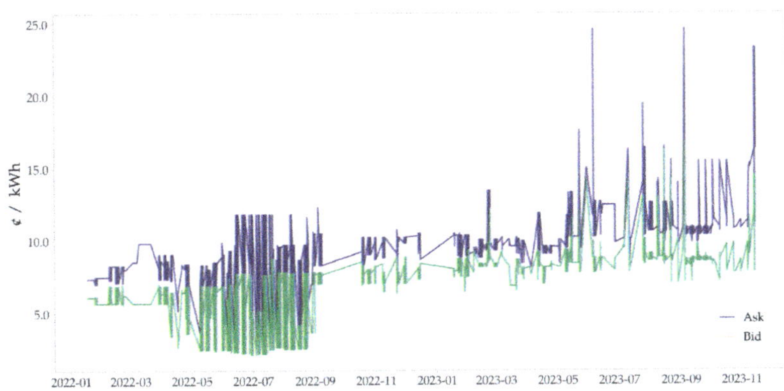

Figure 11. Best bid and ask prices of the future contracts that did not close.

To determine the number of contracts the market maker could close and its impact on liquidity. Data from the standardized market operator Derivex between January 2022 and May 2024 were used for this analysis. These data include variables from the best bid and ask quotes that agents are willing to trade and the price at which futures contracts are traded. For example, the ELMQ23F contract registered a bid of 7.8 cents per kWh and an ask of 9.1 cents per kWh on 25 October 2022. On that same day, the contract traded at 8.3 cents per kWh, indicating that the bid adjusted by 0.5 cents and the ask adjusted by 0.8 cents. Similar observations were made for the entire historical series within the analyzed window.

Figure 12 shows the distributions in cents per dollar of the adjustments made by both ends when trading futures contracts. It is observed that the bid makes larger adjustments than the ask to close the trade. On average, the bid gives up 1.1 cents per kWh, while the ask gives up only 0.52 cents per kWh. The 10th percentile, as a conservative scenario, is 0.16 cents per kWh for the bid and 0.052 cents per kWh for the ask, respectively. This percentile indicates the minimum value that the quotes (bid and ask) have adjusted 90% of the time based on the observed values. If, under the market maker proposed in this paper, these adjustments were maintained, it would increase the number of trades by at least 7% for the study period, resulting in 7% more liquidity. In terms of efficiency, this means that the suggested spread of 0.212 cents per kWh would generate an increase of at least 10% in additional monthly energy coverage for regulated users through the contracts managed by the market maker.

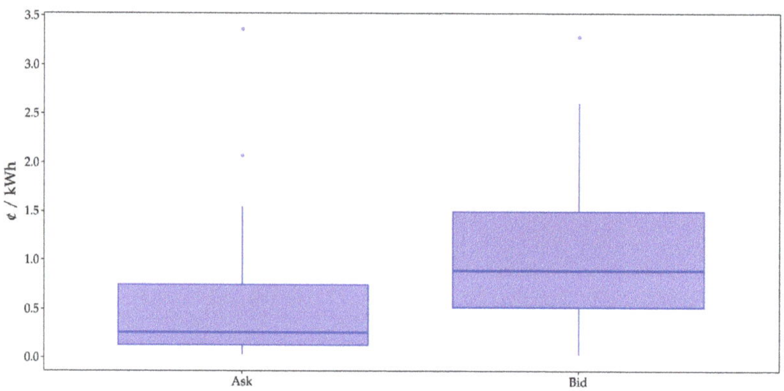

Figure 12. Distributions of the adjustments made by the ask and bid.

5. Conclusions

The need to develop efficient and liquid hedging instruments so that energy retailers do not expose their regulated demand—which faces technological and economic difficulties in changing their retailer—to market risk is a requirement in today's electricity markets. That said, this study evidences some market inefficiencies of OTC (bilateral) contracts and the tariff structure that expose energy retailers in Colombia—and with them their regulated demand—to significant market risk, therefore requiring risk management instruments. As a result, this study establishes the importance of developing a market maker to increase the liquidity of the electricity futures so that the retailers have access to an agile risk management instrument.

The characteristics of the market maker and its incorporation into the current institutional framework of the Colombian electricity market are developed in this study. Likewise, regulatory changes that must be considered so that this new agent fulfills its purpose have been listed. A quantitative analysis supports the benefits of this proposal, as it demonstrates that a percentage of the demand could be covered through futures due to the liquidity provided by the market maker. An average of the impacts of energy purchase costs transferred to the demand by three marketers that, today, face difficulties in OTC contracting also establishes the coverage benefits provided by the market maker. This latter benefit is not a minor issue, as inflationary pressure caused by tariff increases compels regulators to look for measures to counteract these upward effects.

Future research must focus on understanding how market makers can influence the responses and investment strategies of agents from a micro-level perspective. To achieve this, methodologies such as agent-based simulation or game theory should be employed. This will allow for the analysis of the dynamics and interactions between the market maker and the agents, evaluating changes in the investment strategies of individual agents.

Finally, while the classification of the problem (market risk exacerbated by an imperfect OTC market coupled with tariff imperfections) is sustained with Colombian data and the characteristics of a market maker adapted to Colombia's institutional framework, the conceptual framework developed in this study can serve as a reference for entities in other countries, especially those in emerging economies. These countries might have growing concerns about developing market tools to enable derivatives risk management amidst the high volatility of prices in the electric energy sector. The market maker and its impact can serve as a replicable reference in other contexts.

Author Contributions: Conceptualization, S.A., A.M.S.-A., and H.S.; formal analysis, S.A., A.M.S.-A., and H.S.; writing—original draft preparation, S.A.; writing—review and editing, S.A., A.M.S.-A., and H.S.; funding acquisition, S.A., A.M.S.-A., and H.S. All authors have read and agreed to the published version of the manuscript.

Funding: This research was funded by the Ministry of Science and Technology of Colombia, grand number 1110-852-71060-CT 774-2020-PROGRAMA INTEGRA 2023, grand number 909-2021 (tuition expenses for the doctoral program) and the Universidad Tecnológica de Pereira (Colombia), grant number 6-23-4.

Data Availability Statement: All of the data used in this paper are available at the following links: https://sicep.xm.com.co/, https://www.simem.co/, and https://www.derivex.com.co/, all accessed on 3 July 2024.

Conflicts of Interest: The authors declare no conflicts of interest.

Appendix A

This appendix details the G component of the unitary cost.

$$G_{m,i,j} =$$

$$\omega_{1,m-1,i} Qc_{m-1,i} \left(\alpha_{i,j} Pc_{m-1,i} + \left(1 - \alpha_{i,j}\right) Mc_{m-1}\right) + \ldots \tag{A1a}$$

$$\omega_{2,m-1,i} Qc_{m-1,i} PSA_{m-1,i} + CUG_{m-1,i} - EGP_i + \ldots \tag{A1b}$$

$$\sum_{l=3}^{n} \omega_{l,m-1,i} Qc_{m-1,i} P_{l,m-1,i} + \ldots \tag{A1c}$$

$$\left(1 - Qc_{m-1,i} - Qagd_{m-1,i}\right) Pb_{m-1,i} + \ldots \tag{A1d}$$

$$G\_transitorio_{m,i,j} + AJ_{m,i} \tag{A1e}$$

In which:

m	:	Month in which the G component is settled.
i	:	Retailer.
j	:	Commercialization market
$\omega_{1,m-1,i}$	:	Weighting factor for the prices resulting from public calls.
$Qc_{m-1,i}$	:	This is the lower value between one (1) minus $Qagd_{m-1,i}$.
$\alpha_{i,j}$	:	Value of α of the retailer.
$Pc_{m-1,i}$	:	Weighted average cost per unit of energy for purchases made by the marketer resulting from contracts from public calls.
Mc_{m-1}	:	Weighted average cost per unit of energy.

$\omega_{2,m-1,i}$	:	Weighting factor for the prices of long-term contracts.
$PSA_{m-1,i}$	:	Weighted average price associated with long-term contracts adjudicated in auctions managed by the MME.
$CUG_{m-1,i}$	:	Financial cost of contract guarantees adjudicated in the auctions, managed by the Ministry of Mines and Energy (MME).
EGP_i	:	Unit value of the refund to be issued to the user in case the seller defaults on a performance guarantee.
$\omega_{l,m-1,i}$	:	Weighting factor for the prices of the authorized marketing mechanism l.
$P_{l,m-1,i}$	:	Energy cost, expressed in Colombian pesos per kilowatt hour (COP/kWh), of the purchases made by the marketer through mechanism.
$Qagd_{m-1,i}$	:	Defined value in accordance with the provisions outlined in CREG Resolution 174 of 2021.
$Pb_{m-1,i}$	:	Price of energy purchased on the exchange for the marketer.
$G\_transitorio_{m,i,j}$	:	Cost of the energy purchase from AGPE and GD for the retailer.
$AJ_{m,i}$	:	Adjustment factor applied to the maximum cost of the energy purchase.

References

1. Corredor, P.; Helman, U.; Jara, D.; Wolak, F.A. *Mission of Energy Transformation and Modernization of the Electricity Industry: Roadmap for the Energy of the Future*; Inter-American Development Bank-IDB: Bogotá, Colombia, 2020.
2. Borenstein, S.; Bushnell, J.B.; Wolak, F.A. Measuring Market Inefficiencies in California's Restructured Wholesale Electricity Market. *Am. Econ. Rev.* **2002**, *92*, 1376–1405. [CrossRef]
3. Barrientos Marín, J.; Orozco, T.; Velilla, E. Forecasting Electricity Price in Colombia: A Comparison between Neural Network, ARMA Process and Hybrid Models. *Int. J. Energy Econ. Policy* **2018**, *8*, 97–106.
4. Prabhakar Karthikeyan, S.; Jacob Raglend, I.; Kothari, D.P. A Review on Market Power in Deregulated Electricity Market. *Int. J. Electr. Power Energy Syst.* **2013**, *48*, 139–147. [CrossRef]
5. Ahlqvist, V.; Holmberg, P.; Tangerås, T. A Survey Comparing Centralized and Decentralized Electricity Markets. *Energy Strategy Rev.* **2022**, *40*, 100812. [CrossRef]
6. Silva-Rodriguez, L.; Sanjab, A.; Fumagalli, E.; Virag, A.; Gibescu, M. Short Term Wholesale Electricity Market Designs: A Review of Identified Challenges and Promising Solutions. *Renew. Sustain. Energy Rev.* **2022**, *160*, 112228. [CrossRef]
7. Glachant, J.-M.; Joskow, P.L.; Pollitt, M.G. *Handbook on Electricity Markets*; Edward Elgar Publishing: Cheltenham, UK, 2021; Volume 1, ISBN 9781788979955.
8. Liu, M.; Wu, F.F.; Ni, Y. A Survey on Risk Management in Electricity Markets. In Proceedings of the 2006 IEEE Power Engineering Society General Meeting, PES 2006, Montreal, QC, Canada, 18–22 June 2006; pp. 1–6. [CrossRef]
9. Zareipour, H.; Bhattacharya, K.; Cañizares, C.A. Electricity Market Price Volatility: The Case of Ontario. *Energy Policy* **2007**, *35*, 4739–4748. [CrossRef]
10. Mayer, K.; Trück, S. Electricity Markets around the World. *J. Commod. Mark.* **2018**, *9*, 77–100. [CrossRef]
11. Rai, A.; Nunn, O. On the Impact of Increasing Penetration of Variable Renewables on Electricity Spot Price Extremes in Australia. *Econ. Anal. Policy* **2020**, *67*, 67–86. [CrossRef]
12. Mosquera-López, S.; Nursimulu, A. Drivers of Electricity Price Dynamics: Comparative Analysis of Spot and Futures Markets. *Energy Policy* **2019**, *126*, 76–87. [CrossRef]
13. Perez, A.; Garcia-Rendon, J.J. Integration of Non-Conventional Renewable Energy and Spot Price of Electricity: A Counterfactual Analysis for Colombia. *Renew. Energy* **2021**, *167*, 146–161. [CrossRef]
14. Qu, H.; Duan, Q.; Niu, M. Modeling the Volatility of Realized Volatility to Improve Volatility Forecasts in Electricity Markets. *Energy Econ.* **2018**, *74*, 767–776. [CrossRef]
15. Lopes, F.; Rodrigues, T.; Sousa, J. Negotiating Bilateral Contracts in a Multi-Agent Electricity Market: A Case Study. In Proceedings of the International Workshop on Database and Expert Systems Applications, DEXA, Vienna, Austria, 3–7 September 2012; pp. 326–330.
16. Edge, P. An Approximation of Counterparty Credit Risk in Long Term Power Purchase Agreements (PPAs). In Proceedings of the International Conference on the European Energy Market, EEM, Lisbon, Portugal, 19–22 May 2015; IEEE Computer Society: Washington, DC, USA, 2015; Volume 2015.
17. Rocha, K.; Garcia, F.A.A. Credit Risk in the Pool-Implications for Private Capital Investments in Brazilian Power Generation. *Energy Policy* **2006**, *34*, 3827–3835. [CrossRef]
18. Wang, G.; Hung, H.C. Impact of Bilateral Contracts on the Price Volatility in the Electricity Market. In Proceedings of the IEEM2010—IEEE International Conference on Industrial Engineering and Engineering Management, Macao, China, 7–10 December 2010; pp. 1636–1640.

19. Dagoumas, A. Impact of Bilateral Contracts on Wholesale Electricity Markets: In a Case Where a Market Participant Has Dominant Position. *Appl. Sci.* **2019**, *9*, 382. [CrossRef]
20. De, G.; Tan, Z.; Li, M.; Huang, L.; Wang, Q.; Li, H. A Credit Risk Evaluation Based on Intuitionistic Fuzzy Set Theory for the Sustainable Development of Electricity Retailing Companies in China. *Energy Sci. Eng.* **2019**, *7*, 2825–2841. [CrossRef]
21. Pennings, J.M.E.; Heijman, W.J.M. Prospects for an Electricity Futures Market. *Resour. Policy* **1995**, *21*, 283–284. [CrossRef]
22. Deng, S.J.; Oren, S.S. Electricity Derivatives and Risk Management. *Energy* **2006**, *31*, 940–953. [CrossRef]
23. Tussing, A.R.; Hatcher, D.B. Prospects for an Electricity Futures Market Lessons from Petroleum and Natural Gas. *Resour. Policy* **1994**, *20*, 135–141. [CrossRef]
24. Collins, R.A. The Economics of Electricity Hedging and a Proposed Modification for the Futures Contract for Electricity. *IEEE Trans. Power Syst.* **2002**, *17*, 100–107. [CrossRef]
25. Byström, H.N.E. The Hedging Performance of Electricity Futures on the Nordic Power Exchange. *Appl. Econ.* **2003**, *35*, 1–11. [CrossRef]
26. Tanlapco, E.; Lawarrée, J.; Liu, C.C. Hedging with Futures Contracts in a Deregulated Electricity Industry. *IEEE Trans. Power Syst.* **2002**, *17*, 577–582. [CrossRef]
27. Tanrisever, F.; Büke, B.; Jongen, G. Futures Hedging in Electricity Retailing. *Ann. Oper. Res.* **2022**, *330*, 757–785. [CrossRef]
28. Peña, J.I. The Hedging Effectiveness of Electricity Futures in the Spanish Market. *Financ. Res. Lett.* **2023**, *53*, 103507. [CrossRef]
29. Li, J.; Xu, J. Does the Introduction of Market Maker Improve Market Quality? Evidence from China's Sci-Tech Innovation Board. *Financ. Res. Lett.* **2023**, *55*, 103909. [CrossRef]
30. Liu, H.; Wang, Y. Market Making with Asymmetric Information and Inventory Risk. *J. Econ. Theory* **2016**, *163*, 73–109. [CrossRef]
31. Schwartz, R.A.; Peng, L. Market Makers. In *Encyclopedia of Finance*, 3rd ed.; Springer International Publishing: Cham, Switzerland, 2022; pp. 1007–1010. ISBN 9783030912314.
32. Kedia, S.; Zhou, X. Local Market Makers, Liquidity and Market Quality. *J. Financ. Mark.* **2011**, *14*, 540–567. [CrossRef]
33. Rust, J.; Hall, G. Middlemen versus Market Makers: A Theory of Competitive Exchange. *J. Political Econ.* **2003**, *111*, 353–403. [CrossRef]
34. Zhu, M.; Chiarella, C.; He, X.Z.; Wang, D. Does the Market Maker Stabilize the Market? *Phys. A Stat. Mech. Its Appl.* **2009**, *388*, 3164–3180. [CrossRef]
35. Kanamura, T.; Bunn, D.W. Market Making and Electricity Price Formation in Japan. *Energy Econ.* **2022**, *107*, 105765. [CrossRef]
36. Peña, J.I.; Rodríguez, R. Market Makers and Liquidity Premium in Electricity Futures Markets. *Energy J.* **2022**, *43*, 91–109. [CrossRef]
37. Bevin, K.C.; Verma, A. Decentralized Local Electricity Market Model Using Automated Market Maker. *Appl. Energy* **2023**, *334*, 120689. [CrossRef]
38. Lukanima, B.K.; Gómez-Bravo, Y.P.; Sanchez-Barrios, L.J. The Impact of MILA Market-Maker Facility on Volatility of the Colombian Stock Market. *Rev. Contab. Financ.* **2021**, *32*, 345–358. [CrossRef]
39. Energy and Gas Regulation Commission. *Resolution 031-1997*; CREG: Bogotá, Colombia, 1997.
40. Energy and Gas Regulation Commission. *Circular 037-2006*; CREG: Bogotá, Colombia, 2006.

energies

MDPI

Article

Cost of Capital in the Energy Sector, in Emerging Markets, the Case of a Dollarized Economy

Victor Aguilar, Freddy Naula * and Fanny Cabrera

Facultad de Ciencias Económicas y Administrativas, Universidad de Cuenca, Cuenca 010107, Ecuador; victor.aguilar@ucuenca.edu.ec (V.A.); fanny.cabrerab16@ucuenca.edu.ec (F.C.)
* Correspondence: fbenjamin.naulas@ucuenca.edu.ec; Tel.: +593-09-9840-3646

Abstract: This article estimates the weighted average cost of capital (WACC) for the energy sector in Ecuador, a country with a dollarized economy and illiquid stock markets. Thus, reference companies in the region were taken, and at the same time combined with characteristics of national companies, establishing a useful methodology, which makes sense with the acceptable discount rates in the Ecuadorian economy. For the above, four estimation alternatives were used. In method one, the traditional WACC formula was applied using interest rates and risk premiums from the U.S. market, which resulted in an overestimation due to the double penalty of the country risk and the U.S. market premium. Method two adjusted the market risk premium to consider only the Ecuador-specific risk premium, thus avoiding the double penalty. In method three, the credit default swap (CDS) was used to calculate the country risk premium, and the CDS was excluded from the nominal interest rate, avoiding redundancies. Finally, method four combined the U.S. interest rate with the CDS directly to calculate the market risk premium, more accurately reflecting local economic conditions in a dollarized economy. The WACC results range from 12.63% to 29.70%. In addition, a dummy variable was controlled for during the pandemic period. This article highlights the need for methodologies adapted to emerging markets, since traditional approaches would overestimate the WACC.

Keywords: WACC; emerging markets; energy sector; Ecuador

1. Introduction

The energy sector has a strategic role in the economy, being related to economic growth and employment [1], and there is a trend towards renewable energy production [2]. From supporting industrial production to basic household needs [3], it is the core of modern infrastructure. Thus, in the case of Ecuador, this sector is even more critical considering the difficulties in satisfying demand and the recent power outages [4]. Consequently, investment in the electricity sector is paramount. However, it is necessary to have reference indicators of the costs involved, expressed in terms of the rates of return that investors may demand. This paper contributes to this by asking the following: What is the weighted average cost of capital (WACC) of the electricity sector in the case of Ecuador? The answer will allow for not harming either investors or consumers and will mark the way towards a potential private investment, contributing to its sustainability through the respective tariffs, which are expected to be equitable, affordable, and at the same time allow for the recovery of operating and investment costs [5]. In effect, the WACC influences the electricity tariffs set by regulators [6] with a positive relationship.

The above is indispensable, even more so, considering that since the signing of the Paris Agreement in 2015, the world demand for electricity has grown by 2.7% per year, with developing countries being the ones that have grown the most [7]. In the case of Ecuador, this went from a per capita consumption of 1622 KwH in the year 1965 to one of 12,150 KwH by the year 2022 [8]. Incidentally, this trend shows a growth [9], although still insufficient, towards renewable energies [10,11]. This transition adds a new dimension, with implications for both economic growth and environmental sustainability [12].

In the case of Ecuador, significant progress has been made, diversifying towards renewable sources and with efficiency policies [3], expanding the electric grid and building renewable energy plants [13], and improving installed capacity [14]; thus, renewable energy sources represent more than 90% of the country's electricity sources [15]. However, there is still work to be undertaken regarding productivity and efficiency in generation [3]. Energy sovereignty implies facing both technical and financial restrictions, especially considering that the energy sector is capital intensive [16] and especially those from renewable sources [1].

Thus, as mentioned, one of the main factors to consider is the cost of capital (WACC). This is a key evaluation indicator [17,18] for investment decisions [19], reflecting the opportunity cost [6] and the inherent risks, also allowing a valuation [20] if required. In this sense, emerging technologies and markets with higher perceived risks can raise the WACC [17,21,22], while supportive policies and stable regulatory frameworks reduce it [23,24]. Likewise, in the case of Ecuador, oil is an influential aspect. A reduction in its price would have a mixed effect on the electricity WACC. On the one hand, it could reduce operating costs for oil-dependent companies, thus reducing the perceived risk and potentially the WACC. On the other hand, since the economy is strongly linked to oil revenues, a decrease could increase economic uncertainty, which would increase the WACC [25]. Another aspect to consider is the increase in borrowing costs in developing countries, which leads investors to demand higher risk premiums, thus increasing the WACC [26].

In this area, the heterogeneity between regions and nations implies variability in the risk factors [27] and opportunities that companies face, causing differences in WACC rates [6], which can even be influenced by the type of technology used [27] or the quality of future revenues [28]. Thus, for example, Germany, with a WACC of 3.5%, has a relatively low risk perception, while Greece, with a WACC of 12%, has a considerably higher one [21]. Also at the Latin American level, similar patterns of variability are identified, Brazil presents a rate of 11.13% [29], and in contrast, Colombia, according to [19], has a lower WACC of 5.28% for the electricity sector. It can be said, therefore, that the discount rate becomes a vital barometer to measure both the risk and the potential return [30].

Notwithstanding the importance of the WACC, there is a lack in the literature regarding the specific and quantitative analysis of this variable in the Ecuadorian energy sector, despite some attempts [31,32]. The present article provides a solution to this problem, and along the way, faces its own challenges in the calculation methodology, derived from the specificities of Ecuador. For example, the WACC is influenced by the maturity of the financial markets [33], making it unavoidable to consider that the Ecuadorian stock markets are illiquid and not very diversified. Another aspect to consider is the absence of a financial instrument that could be considered risk-free—something indispensable under the most accepted methodology for calculating the cost of equity [34]. Finally, since 2000, the Ecuadorian economy has adopted the dollar as its own currency, discarding the sucre, which adds the nuance of calculating the WACC for a dollarized economy. Advantageously, some outputs have already been established by Maquieira and Espinosa [35], and others have been proposed by the authors; the latter is precisely one of the additional useful contributions to the literature. This is by no means a deviation from the concepts but rather an adaptation to the call to develop useful methodological frameworks for emerging and illiquid markets [36], reinforcing the idea that there are no guiding principles for the estimation of sector WACC [37].

Due to the period of pandemic that the country (and the world) went through, a control variable is introduced, which makes it possible to show its effect on the WACC. The necessary information was gathered both from private suppliers and from the Superintendence of Companies of Ecuador [30], etc. This study contributes significantly to the academic literature in the field of estimating the cost of capital in emerging markets and is established as a methodological reference. It also serves in public policy decision making, helping policy makers to align sector investments and regulations with Ecuador's sustainable and economic development objectives [38].

Based on the above, there are two research questions to be solved:

RQ1. What is the weighted average cost of capital (WACC) for the energy sector in Ecuador?

RQ2. How do the different WACC calculation methodologies affect the estimation of the cost of capital in the Ecuadorian energy sector?

To facilitate the understanding of the process and results of this study, the article has been structured in different sections. In the second section, the materials and methods used are described, clarifying the empirical strategy used. The fourth and fifth sections present the results obtained and the conclusions derived from the research, respectively.

2. Materials and Methods

Descriptive statistics were used to analyze and summarize the main characteristics of the data. These statistics include measures of central tendency and dispersion, such as mean, median, standard deviation and interquartile ranges, which help to understand the distribution and variability of the variables. The python program was used. Table 1 lists the variables used; however, the main ones are described below:

Table 1. Variables used in WACC calculation.

Variable	Description
P	Equity/book value of the company, year 2022
D	Long-term liabilities/book value of the company, year 2022
V	Book value = equity + long-term liabilities, year 2022
K_d	Financial expenses/long-term liabilities, year 2022
T	Average country income tax rate 2018–2022
rf nominal	Nominal risk rate, year 2022
MRP	Market risk premium = equity risk premium (Equity risk premium), year 2022
L	Illiquidity risk premium
π^e	Expected inflation 2022–2027
R_{et}	Variation in foreign company share price, 2018–2022 period
R_{mt}	Variation in share price at the foreign country level, period 2018–2022
Dcov	Takes the value of 1 if the analysis period covers February 2020 to February 2021, otherwise 0
De/Pe	Debt equity ratio = total debt/total equity of the foreign company, average 2018–2022.

Prepared by the authors.

Risk-Free Rate (*rf*): the U.S. Treasury bond rate was used as a proxy due to the lack of an equivalent rate in Ecuador. This rate represents the return on a risk-free investment, essential for calculating the cost of equity and debt. It is a fundamental component of the CAPM model and other financial valuation methodologies.

Market Risk Premium (MRP): The additional premium that investors expect to receive for taking the risk of investing in the stock market rather than opting for a risk-free investment, such as Treasury bonds. The MRP is calculated as the difference between the expected return of the market as a whole and the risk-free rate of return.

Unlevered Beta (β^{sd}): It measures a company's sensitivity to market movements. The unlevered beta allows for comparing the inherent risk of different companies regardless of their financial leverage.

Debt Beta (β_d): It measures the risk associated with the company's debt. In markets where debt is not risk-free, it is important to consider the debt beta to adequately reflect the financial risk in the WACC calculation.

Market Value of Debt (*D*): Market Value of the Company's Debt.. This value is used to weight the cost of debt in the WACC.

Market Value of Equity (P): It is the market value of the company's equity. Similar to the value of debt, this value is used to weigh the cost of equity in the WACC.

Tax Rate (T): It is used to adjust the after-tax cost of debt. Interest on debt is tax deductible, which reduces the effective cost of debt. This adjustment is essential to reflect the tax benefit of leverage.

Cost of Debt (k_d): It is the interest rate the company pays on its debt. It is a direct component of the WACC and reflects the real cost of debt financing.

Cost of Equity Capital (k_p): It is calculated using the capital asset pricing model (CAPM). The cost of equity capital represents the return required by investors to invest in the company's equity.

In this context, the issue of illiquid markets and the difficulty in calculating the relevant betas was solved by using comparable companies. Indeed, in environments where markets are not liquid, as in Ecuador, the use of comparable companies to estimate the betas in the WACC calculation is crucial. Walker [39], with respect to emerging markets, emphasizes the adaptation of methodologies to reflect local conditions, arguing that comparable companies in regions with similar economic and market characteristics provide a more realistic basis for estimating betas, which is in line with Maquieira and Espinosa [35]. In fact, according to Schlegel [40], this practice is fundamental in the financial literature to ensure the relevance and accuracy of discount rates in financial evaluations. Furthermore, Schlegel et al. [41] highlight the importance of properly selecting these companies to capture appropriate market conditions and mitigate the risks associated with WACC estimation in illiquid markets.

Regarding the risk-free rate, the US rate was used; this rate is widely used in the literature [40,42–45]. However, in the case of Ecuador, it is also justified by the following: It does not have a risk-free rate, given its historical default characteristic, which calls into question the fulfillment of its sovereign debt obligations, making it unfeasible to use any government bond or bill from the Ecuadorian treasury or central bank. However, the adoption of the US dollar as the official currency in Ecuador has deepened its economic dependence on US monetary policies [46–48], which has a direct impact on its economy due to the synchronization of economic and financial cycles between the two countries. This relationship allows the use of US risk-free assets, such as Treasury bonds, in Ecuadorian financial models [44]. That is, for the calculation of the weighted average cost of capital (WACC), the risk-free rate can be naturally aligned with US Treasury bond rates due to the dollarization policy.

Evidently, this poses a special situation for neighboring economies such as Colombia, Perú, Chile, etc., which, by having their own currency, even consider the issue of exchange rate risk, or the expectations derived from a currency that is not as stable as the USD.

Considering the above aspects contribute to the correct valuation of the cost of capital in Ecuador in energy sector. This is an essential task for various strategic purposes, including decision making in investment, financing, and business valuation [19,20]. In the case of unlisted companies with debt in their financial structure, the valuation of the firm and the evaluation of the WACC acquire additional complexity [49].

Thus, according to data from the Superintendency of Companies, Ecuadorian companies that are not listed on the stock exchange represent 99.68% of the country's business fabric [50]. These companies often operate under economic and financial dynamics in which the market value of their capital structure is unknown [30]. The lack of available market information adds further complexity to the calculation of the WACC.

The methodology employed in this study is based on the calculation of the equation ex-pressed in (1), which has been used in numerous previous studies [20]. In addition, the comprehensive approach proposed by [35] is adopted to calculate the WACC of unlisted companies. The adaptation of the WACC methodology to this group of companies requires the careful consideration of several factors such as the estimation of the cost of debt, the cost of equity, and the risk premium in Ecuador.

$$WACC_i = k_{pi} \times p_i + k_{di} \times (1 - T) \times d_i \tag{1}$$

Equation (1) is used to calculate the WACC, which represents the weighted average cost of capital of company i. k_p and k_d measure the cost of equity and the cost of debt respectively, T corresponds to the income tax rate in the country, and p_i and d_i represent the capital structure of the company divided between equity and debt ratio, respectively [51].

2.1. Data

The unit of analysis is composed of Ecuadorian companies that operate with some activity in the energy sector. The data comes from the balance sheet corresponding to the year 2022, obtained from the Superintendence of Companies. Initially, information was available for 629 companies in the sector. However, a data cleaning process was carried out in which companies whose net worth was equal to zero were excluded, resulting in a set of 569 companies for the analysis.

In this research, a series of key variables were used for the analysis, and these, together with their respective sources, are detailed in Table 1. This table provides an overview of the key measures and indicators that were used to calculate the WACC of companies in the energy sector in accordance with the methodology described above.

2.2. Calculation of the Cost of Equity

The calculation of the cost of equity for company *i* is performed using Equation (2). In this equation, r_{freal} measures the real risk-free rate for Ecuador, which is calculated by eliminating the effect of expected inflation from the nominal risk-free rate ($r_{fnominal}$) as shown in Equation (3). In turn, the nominal risk-free rate for the country is determined by Equation (4). Following the methodology of Maquieira and Espinosa [35], the U.S. yield (r_{fUSA}) is included along with a penalty for default on the country's debt (credit default swap—CDS)

$$kp_i = rf_{real} + L + MRP \times \beta^d_{pi} \quad (2)$$

where

kp_i : Cost of equity of the company i
rf_{real} : Risk − free rate
L : liquidity risk premium
MRP : Market risk premium
β^d_{pi} : Systematic risk of the company i

$$r_{freal} = \left(\frac{1 + r_{fnominal}}{1 + \pi^e}\right) - 1 \quad (3)$$

where

$rf_{nominal}$: nominal risk − free rate
π^e : Expected inflation rate

$$r_{fnominal} = r_{fUSA} + CDS \quad (4)$$

where

rf_{usa} : U.S.risk − free rate
CDS : penalty for default on the country's debt.

In some markets with low liquidity, the illiquidity risk premium (L) is incorporated in the calculation of the cost of capital to consider the additional risk associated with the difficulty of selling an investment immediately, without incurring losses, as reflected in Equation (2). Finally, the market risk premium (MRP) generally known as the equity risk premium (ERP) is calculated using Equation (5) [30]. This value considers, like the risk-free rate, a part of the US risk premium, in addition to a specific risk premium for the country under analysis (country risk premium—CRP).

$$MRP = ERP_{USA} + CRP \tag{5}$$

where

ERP_{USA} : Equity risk premium
CRP : Country risk premium

Within Equation (2), the component β^{d}_{pi} refers to the leveraged equity beta and evaluates the operational and financial risk of the firm, considering the business risk related to the debt incurred [50]. If $\beta^{d}_{pi} > 1$, it means that the operating and financial risk, considering debt, is higher or more volatile compared to the market in general, while if $\beta^{d}_{pi} < 1$, it implies that the company is less volatile or risky than the market in general. The calculation of β^{d}_{pi} is carried out using [51] which is expressed by Equation (6).

$$\beta^{d}_{pi} = \beta^{sd}_{p}(R)[1 + (1 - T)\times p_i] - (1 - T) \times d_i \times \beta_{di} \tag{6}$$

where

β^{d}_{pi} : Levered equity beta of company i
$\beta^{sd}_{p}(R)$: Unlevered equity beta of company i
T : Corpora tetax rate
d_i : Debt − to − equity ratio
β_{di} : Debt beta

$\beta^{sd}_{p}(R)$ and β_{di} represent the benchmark sector's unlevered equity beta and debt beta, respectively. The former measures the operating risk inherent to the benchmark sector, while the latter assesses the risk associated with the debt.

2.3. Enterprise Operational Risk Benchmarking

To calculate the unlevered equity beta referring to the sector, represented by $\beta^{sd}_{p}(R)$, it is necessary to apply a benchmarking procedure that allows obtaining a specific reference value for the sector. This process involves the use of information relative to companies of the same sector in external foreign economies through the Expression (10).

$$\beta^{sd}_{pe}(R) = \frac{\beta^{d}_{pe}(R) + (1 - T_e)\left(\frac{D_e}{P_e}\right)\beta_{de}}{\left[1 + (1 - T_e)\left(\frac{D_e}{P_e}\right)\right]} \tag{7}$$

In this equation, D_e and P_e represent the value of the foreign firms' debt and equity (e) respectively, and T_e is the income tax rate in the foreign country. In addition, β_{de} corresponds to the debt beta of the foreign firms, and $\beta^{d}_{pe}(R)$ represents the levered equity beta of the benchmark foreign firm.

Prior to estimating Equation (7), it is first required to estimate $\beta^{d}_{pe}(R)$ through β_p which is obtained by estimating Equation (8).

$$R_{et} = \alpha + \beta_p R_{mt} + \gamma \times dcov + \varepsilon_{it} \tag{8}$$

where R_{et} represents the change in the last share price of the benchmark foreign company (e) in period t, while R_{mt} denotes the market return measured through the change in the last price at the benchmark foreign country level in the same period t. In addition, the variable $dcov$ is included to control the estimates during the pandemic period, being a dummy variable that takes the value of one during the pandemic and zero otherwise. The coefficients α, β_p, and γ represent the regression parameters, where β_p measures the effect of country, R_{mt} the foreign firm performance, and γ measures the effect of covid. The parameter of interest is β_p, which represents $\beta^{d}_{pe}(R)$. The estimation of this equation is carried out by applying ordinary least squares with robust standard errors and is calculated n times, where n is the number of foreign firms used.

Once β_p per firm is obtained, it is corrected following the method by Blume [52] to obtain $\beta^d_{pe}(R) = 0.67 + 0.33 * \beta_p$. Subsequently, after estimating (7) and (8), the benchmark unlevered equity beta for the sector is calculated by a weighted average of $\beta^d_{pe}(R)$ of the foreign companies, where the weights are determined based on the book value of each company. With this information, the cost of capital and WACC are calculated for each Ecuadorian company. Finally, the WACC of the sector is obtained as the weighted average of the WACCs of the Ecuadorian companies, using their book values as weights.

2.4. Cost of Debt

The proportion of interest paid on debt in each period is a proxy used to measure the cost of debt. According to Maquieira and Espinosa [35], both the cost of debt (k_d) and the cost of capital or equity (k_p) are calculated using the financial asset pricing model (CAPM). Therefore, the cost of debt is measured through Equation (9).

$$kd_i = r_{freal} + L + MRP \times \beta_{di} \tag{9}$$

The β_{di} component is obtained by solving Equation (10) and is part of the company's debt risk estimate.

$$\beta_{di} = \frac{kd_i - rf_{real} - L}{MRP} \tag{10}$$

2.5. Calculation Strategy

The WACC calculation strategy is broken down into four main phases, outlined in Figure 1. This graphical representation provides a clear overview of the methodology used to determine the WACC. The first phase consists of developing the benchmarking process, for which information from foreign companies listed on the stock exchange in countries that are not in default, such as Chile, Mexico, Brazil, Peru, and Colombia, was used. The data were extracted from the financial statements of each company, covering the period of 2018–2022.

The selection of comparable companies for the cost of capital analysis is based on several key arguments that ensure the relevance and accuracy of the results obtained. First, companies were chosen that operate in Latin American markets with economic and financial characteristics similar to those of Ecuador, such as Chile, Colombia, Brazil, Peru, and Mexico. These countries share comparable market dynamics and economic risks, which allows for a more accurate estimation of the beta and cost of capital applicable to Ecuadorian conditions.

Second, companies belonging to the energy sector were selected. Sectorial representativeness is crucial, since the capital structure and inherent risks are specific to this sector. Choosing companies from the same sector ensures that the betas obtained are directly applicable to energy companies in Ecuador, providing a solid basis for the analysis. The selected companies are listed on stock exchanges, which guarantees the necessary data to perform a robust analysis and obtain meaningful betas. In other words, the selection of comparable companies is based on sector representativeness, availability of reliable data, rigorous statistical criteria, and adjustments to local conditions, thus ensuring the relevance and accuracy of the analysis of the cost of capital in Ecuador's energy sector.

In this process, data was collected from 15 leading companies within the sector. During the calculation of the equity beta of the companies, a linear regression was performed to evaluate their financial performance according to Equation (8). However, not all regressions presented statistically significant coefficients. Therefore, the number of foreign companies used in the analysis was filtered. Following the methodology of Maquieira and Espinosa [35], the results of the regressions that met the following conditions were selected: (1) coefficient of determination greater than 3%; (2) a minimum number of 30 observations; (3) estimated coefficients β_p significant at a 95% confidence level; and (4) estimated coefficients with positive values. After applying these criteria, six of these companies were identified as meeting the above requirements and were therefore considered in the analysis.

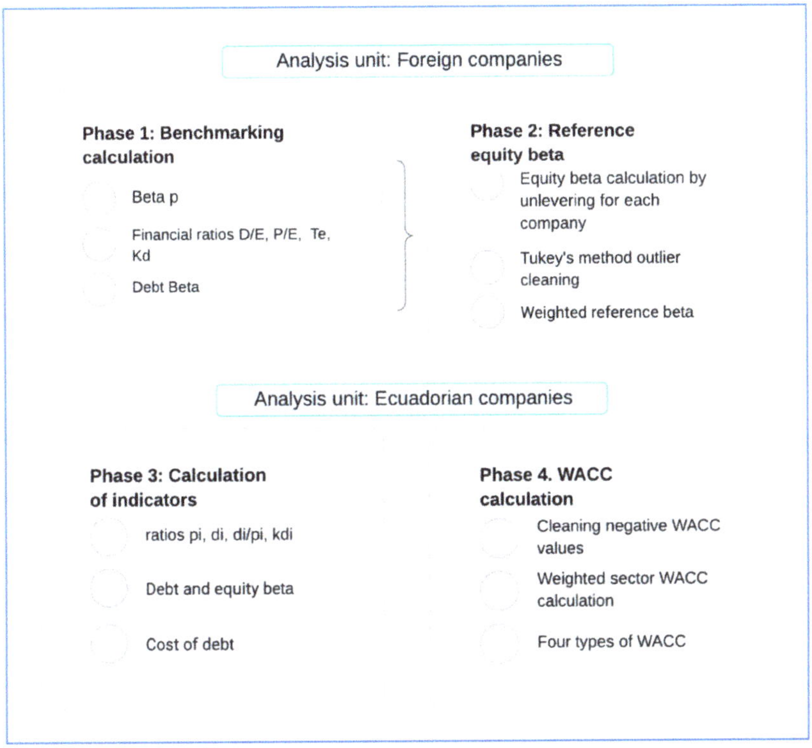

Figure 1. Phases for the calculation of the WACC of the energy sector.

In the second phase, aimed at calculating the benchmark unlevered beta for the sector, refinement processes were conducted to obtain an accurate and representative measure. In this context, the Tukey method was applied to both the cost of debt ratio (K_d) and the unlevered beta. This methodology is based on the elimination of outliers by using the interquartile range. As a result of this process, five foreign companies that met the established criteria were identified and retained.

In the third phase, various financial ratios and indicators are calculated for Ecuadorian companies, using as a basis the reference indicator obtained in the previous phase. During this stage, refinements were applied, which consisted of excluding those companies whose debt beta (B_d) and cost of equity (K_p) resulted in values below zero. This led to a set of 480 companies that met the analysis criteria.

Finally, in the last phase of the process, the WACC was calculated for each individual company. These values were then aggregated to obtain an indicator at the sector level. The aggregation was conducted by applying weights determined since the book value of each company, which ensured an accurate representation of the cost of capital for the sector as a whole.

This analysis incorporates four values of the WACC, and these differ according to the risk-free rate and market risk premium indicators used, as detailed in Table 2. These differences, among the different WACC values are significant and require careful consideration when making financial and strategic decisions.

Table 2. Methods for estimating the WACC.

WACC	Ecuador Risk Rate	Market Risk Premium MRP Ecuador
WACC1	$r_{fnominal} = r_{fUSA} + CDS$	$PRM = ERP_{USA} + CRP$
WACC2	$r_{fnominal} = r_{fUSA} + CDS$	$PRM = CRP$
WACC3	$r_{fnominal} = r_{fUSA}$	$PRM = CRP$
WACC4	$r_{fnominal} = r_{fUSA}$	$PRM = CDS$

Prepared by the authors.

Method one (WACC1) replicates the standard theory for calculating the risk rate and market risk premium by applying Equations (4) and (5). In this method, both the risk rate and the market risk premium are penalized using U.S. rates. However, this approach does not consider that Ecuador has adopted the U.S. dollar as its currency. Therefore, these rates, which may be high, do not reflect the returns that economic agents in Ecuador would be willing to pay.

Method two (WACC2) considers the nominal risk rate described in Equation (4) but avoids the double penalty of the market premium. This method considers only the Ecuador-specific country risk premium (CRP), without reapplying the U.S. risk premium. Since the Ecuadorian economy is dollarized, this approach avoids redundancy in the penalty and provides a more accurate picture of local conditions.

Method three (WACC3) uses the CDS to calculate Ecuador's CRP and adjusts for the relative volatility of emerging markets. However, by using the CDS as the basis for the CRP and considering it in the nominal risk rate (rf nominal), the impact of the CDS would be doubled. To avoid this redundancy, method 3 excludes the CDS in the calculation of the nominal rf for Ecuador.

Method four (WACC4), like method 3, also uses the CDS to calculate the CRP, but introduces a key difference in the market risk premium (MRP). Instead of using the adjusted CRP, the CDS is used directly. This avoids double consideration of the CDS in the nominal rf. This approach is particularly relevant for a dollarized economy such as Ecuador's, as it focuses on recovering investment values internally and more closely reflects local economic conditions.

It is important to note that at the international level, the traditional formula may be applicable, as it reflects the returns that external agents would expect if they were to invest in Ecuador. However, for domestic applications in Ecuador, method four is more viable, since it considers the reality of the dollarized economy and seeks to reflect how local economic agents would be willing to pay as a return within the country.

2.6. Company Segmentation

In order to identify underlying patterns and group companies with similar financial characteristics, unsupervised learning methods, such as clustering techniques, were used on a dataset containing financial information of several companies in the energy sector in Ecuador. These data come from the corporate ranking published by the Superintendence of Companies in the year 2022. The selection of variables for this analysis included critical financial indicators such as acid test, sales turnover, average collection indicator, expense impact indicator, financial burden impact indicator, return on assets (ROA), equity strength as well as the previously calculated WACC. In addition, company characteristics such as number of employees, province, company type, and size classification were added.

To evaluate the quality of the clusters and select the most appropriate method, the Silhouette Score, Calinski–Harabasz Score and Davies–Bouldin Score indicators were used. The method that yielded the highest Silhouette Score and Calinski–Harabasz Score and the lowest Davies–Bouldin Score was chosen in order to obtain groupings that are significant and representative of the financial similarities between the companies in the sector.

The Silhouette Score measures the coherence within clusters and the separation between clusters. Each point has a silhouette value ranging from −1 to 1, where a value close to 1 indicates that the point is well clustered. This method provides a clear interpretation of cluster quality by assessing both cluster compactness and cluster spacing, which is crucial to ensure that the data are well clustered. The Calinski–Harabasz Criterion, also known as the inter-cluster variance index, calculates the ratio of the total dispersion between clusters to the dispersion within clusters. A higher value indicates a better definition of the clusters. This method was chosen because it provides a robust measure of cluster separability and compactness and is especially useful for assessing cluster structure in terms of variance. The Davies–Bouldin Score evaluates the dispersion of clusters and the distance between clusters. A lower value of the coefficient indicates better cluster formation. This method was selected for its ability to assess the relationship between the dispersion within clusters and the proximity between clusters, which helps to identify well-defined and separate clusters.

The combination of these three methods allows a robust validation of the clusters formed, ensuring that the results of the analysis are reliable and useful for decision making. Furthermore, these methods are widely recognized and used in the academic and professional literature, supporting their relevance and effectiveness in the context of this study. This choice is based on their ability to provide a comprehensive and complementary assessment of the clusters, ensuring the consistency and robustness of the analysis presented in this article.

3. Results

The results of the financial analysis of the Ecuadorian energy sector are presented below. This study focuses on the evaluation of several key financial metrics, including capital structure, operating risk, and weighted average cost of capital (WACC) as well as the segmentation of companies in the sector using clustering techniques. These results provide a detailed understanding of the financial dynamics and market conditions in this sector.

3.1. Descriptive Statistics

The descriptive analysis reveals certain significant trends and variabilities to understand the financial dynamics of this sector. In general, there is a high dispersion in the values of the proportion of equity and debt among the companies, indicated by a high standard deviation in both components (see Table 3). This suggests significant diversity in the capital structures among the companies in the sector. A significant proportion of firms (88.91%) are observed to use equity financing without the use of debt.

Table 3. Descriptives of the WACC components.

	Equity	Debt	Kd
Count	478.000000	478.000000	53.000000
Mean	0.951249	0.048751	0.581442
Std	0.175086	0.175086	1.361415
Min	0.021610	0.000000	0.039533
25%	1.000000	0.000000	0.070796
50%	1.000000	0.000000	10.104059
75%	1.000000	0.000000	0.160411
Max	1.000000	0.978390	6.181879
Cv	0.184059	3.591434	2.341444

Prepared by the authors.

The descriptive statistics reveal important implications for their financing needs and credit market conditions. The average equity/asset ratio is high (95.12%), with a low standard deviation, indicating that most firms rely almost exclusively on equity to finance their assets. This preference suggests that companies seek to avoid the risks associated with debt, possibly due to the strict and costly credit conditions in Ecuador. In fact, the average debt/asset ratio is only 4.88%, with most firms having no debt at all, reinforcing the idea of minimal reliance on debt. This situation reflects a generalized aversion to financial risk and a lack of access to favorable borrowing conditions.

The average cost of debt of 58.14% is extremely high and reflects a difficult credit environment for companies in the Ecuadorian energy sector. This high rate could be related to both a perception of high risk on the part of lenders and a lack of control over the financial data reported by the companies. It is possible that companies manipulate the cost of debt figures to reduce their tax burden, which generates a significant disparity in the reported rates. This could also occur at the maximum value of k_d. In both cases, it is a potential manipulation.

In this context, it is important to consider that the use of the lending rate as a reference for calculating the cost of debt (Kd) provides a more realistic and stable view of the cost of financing. The lending rate better reflects market conditions, including factors such as inflation and economic expectations, providing a more reliable basis than potentially manipulated domestic rates. This duality of causes (risk perception and potential data manipulation) justifies the use of the lending rate, avoiding distortions and providing a more accurate assessment of the credit environment faced by companies.

3.2. Operational Risk of the Company

The results obtained by foreign companies in the energy sector, considered in benchmarking, show us that the beta coefficient of equity varies between 0.5 and 0.8, which is significant at 5% (see Appendix A—Table A1). After applying the correction according to Blume [52] and weighting the results, an unlevered equity beta of the sector of 0.8564 was obtained. This indicates significantly lower risk and volatility compared to the overall market.

According to the results, the average leveraged equity beta of the Ecuadorian energy sector is 1.18, which reflects a higher operational and debt risk than the market in general. Once the different risk rates and market risk premiums for Ecuador are applied, different debt beta and cost of capital are obtained. Generally, they are higher the higher the risk rate and the higher the MRP.

3.3. Weighted Average Cost of Capital

The number of companies evaluated varies according to the WACC calculation method, given that in certain cases, those with negative debt beta coefficients or equity cost are excluded, as shown in Table 4. The data indicate that when using the traditional method (WACC 1) to calculate the WACC, a value of 31.77% is obtained. This percentage seems to penalize Ecuador in both the risk rate and the market risk premium. This figure begs the following question: Does this level of WACC reflect an accurate representation of Ecuador's internal financial reality?

Table 4. Nominal WACC and real WACC.

WACC	WACC1	WACC2	WACC3	WACC4
WACC nominal	31.77%	23.41%	17.82%	14.43%
WACC real	29.70%	21.46%	15.96%	12.63%
N. observations				478

Prepared by the authors.

It should be noted that discount rates of such magnitude are rarely used. Instead, the practical approach is to use the opportunity cost of capital for equity, considering the benchmark passive rate, the cost of debt, and the benchmark lending rate. Given that these values vary between 6.48% (passive rate − term one year or more) and 9.54% within the productive business sector (active rate), the resulting discount rate is not even half of the WACC calculated using the traditional method. Therefore, it could be inferred that the traditional WACC calculation tends to overestimate both the expected return and the inherent risk of the Ecuadorian economy.

Likewise, inflation adjustment is crucial in countries with high inflation, such as Colombia, where these adjustments are essential to obtain accurate WACC estimates. The results of several studies [19] show how high inflation in Colombia requires sophisticated methodologies, such as the TD-4 multifactor model, which adjusts the discount rate considering inflation expectations [53–55]. This avoids overestimations of the cost of capital and excessive tariffs for consumers. Mehta [56] also highlight the importance of adjusting discount rates in high inflation environments to adequately reflect risks. Moro [57] stresses the need to mitigate inflation risk in project finance investments in such contexts.

However, this approach is not appropriate for Ecuador due to its dollarized economy and low and stable inflation rates, registering single digit inflation since 2002. Price stability in Ecuador makes it possible to dispense with continuous inflation adjustments in the calculation of the WACC, facilitating more accurate and consistent forecasts. Therefore, alternative methods two, three, and four were explored as viable options for Ecuador, where low inflation makes the complex adjustments used in Colombia and similar countries unnecessary.

It is worth mentioning that method four is presented as a reasonable option, given that it applies an interest rate equivalent to that of the United States, in congruence with that proposed by Damodaran [30] for the calculation of sector betas in other economies. The market risk premium of method four integrates the country's debt default penalty, using the credit default swap (CDS), in line with the methodology proposed by Grabowski [58]. When compared to the traditional method, which already integrates an additional U.S. premium, an overvaluation is evident. Therefore, the use of the CDS value provides a more accurate estimate of the exclusive risk of the Ecuadorian market. Using method four, a weighted nominal WACC of 14.43% and a weighted real WACC of 12.63% is obtained.

This assessment highlights the need to review and adapt the WACC calculation methodologies to economic contexts, such as Ecuador's, to ensure that estimates are consistent with the economic and financial situation of the country in question.

3.4. Financial Segmentation of Companies in the Energy Sector

This study conducted a clustering based on various financial metrics of companies in the energy sector. The objective is to segment the companies into homogeneous groups to better understand the financial trends, behaviors, and challenges within the sector. Table 5 presents descriptive statistics for several key financial variables of energy sector companies in Ecuador, providing a detailed view of their distribution and variability. Since the presence of extreme values can affect the quality and precision of the clustering, we chose to use logarithms for the variables, except for the WACC. The WACC shows a mean of 15.8% with a low standard deviation (0.011), indicating that the cost of capital is relatively consistent across companies in the sector. The acid ratio (Lacid), with a mean of 0.870 and a standard deviation of 1.399, suggests moderate liquidity but with high variability, indicating that some companies have a significantly higher or lower capacity to cover their current liabilities with liquid assets.

The sales ratio (LrotSales) and return on assets (Lroa) have means of 0.410 and 0.087 respectively, with standard deviations of 0.685 and 0.197, reflecting variability in sales and profitability levels between companies. The collection period (Lcollectiom) has a mean of 0.126 and a high standard deviation of 0.845, indicating large differences in collection cycles. Selling and administrative expenses (Lspending), with a mean of 0.149 and a standard deviation of 0.672, and financial burden (Lburden), with a mean of 0.027 and a standard deviation of 0.233, also show significant variability across firms. Finally, equity strength (Lstrength) has a mean of 0.459 and a standard deviation of 0.400, suggesting differences in the financial strength of the companies. These statistics highlight the need for customized approaches to financing and management policies to address the diverse financial conditions within the Ecuadorian energy sector.

Table 5. Descriptive statistics of financial indicators.

Variable	Mean	Std
WACC	0.158	0.011
Lacid	0.870	1.399
LrotSales	0.410	0.685
Lroa	0.087	0.197
Lcollection	0.126	0.845
Lspending	0.149	0.672
Lburden	0.027	0.233
Lstrength	0.459	0.400

WACC—weighted average cost of capital; Lacid—acid test; LrotSales—sales turnover; Lroa—return on assets; Lcollection—collection period; Lspending—impact of the expenditure; Lburden—financial burden; Lstrength—patrimonial strength.

After the application of three different clustering methods, each was evaluated using three different metrics to determine which method is the most appropriate for this analysis. The results of these metrics are presented in Table 6.

Table 6. Clustering Evaluation.

Clustering Method	Silhouette Score	Calinski-Harabasz Score	Davies-Bouldin Score
K-Means	0.4944	1,668,955	0.8432
DBSCAN	0.6412	278,320	10,365
Hierarchical Clustering	0.5581	1,447,916	0.6331

Prepared by the authors.

Although DBSCAN showed the clearest and most defined clustering structure, reflected by the highest Silhouette Score of 0.6412, K-Means proved to be superior in terms of cluster separation and density, with a Calinski–Harabasz Score of 166.8955. However, Hierarchical Clustering had the best Davies–Bouldin Score of 0.6331, indicating greater separation between clusters.

When considering the balance between all metrics, Hierarchical Clustering was selected as the most appropriate method for this analysis, as it provides a balance between the clarity of the clustering structure and the density and the separation of the clusters. Therefore, this study employed Hierarchical Clustering to determine the conglomerates of companies with different financial and operational profiles, reflected in their respective WACCs. The clusters were characterized using the harmonic mean WACC, offering a more robust approach to interpreting variations in this crucial indicator.

According to Figure 2, the identified conglomerates present substantial differences in financial and operating indicators. The intrinsic specificities of the companies in each cluster, including liquidity, profitability, and operating efficiency, together with type or size, and location, play a fundamental role in the definition of the WACC, reflecting variations in the perception of risk and the cost of capital in different business environments.

The results are in line with other studies that highlight the importance of considering the specific conditions of the local market to obtain more accurate estimates of the cost of capital [56,59,60]. The results of the present article are supported by, or are in the same direction as, other studies. For example, Li [18] highlights that traditional methods such as the CAPM may not be appropriate in all contexts, highlighting the need for specific adjustments to better reflect local economic realities [18]. In addition, Coutsiers and Gea [36] found that the WACC in renewable energy projects in Latin America varies significantly between countries due to factors such as country risk, which resonates with our findings on the importance of adjusting methodologies to the Ecuadorian context [36]. Steffen et al. [33] also notes that context-specific adjusted approaches, such as CDS integration, can improve the accuracy of WACC estimates [18]. Finally, these studies underline the need for the continuous evaluation and adjustment of the methodologies used to calculate the cost of capital in different economic and financial environments, reaffirming the validity of the adjusted methods proposed in this study for the Ecuadorian energy sector.

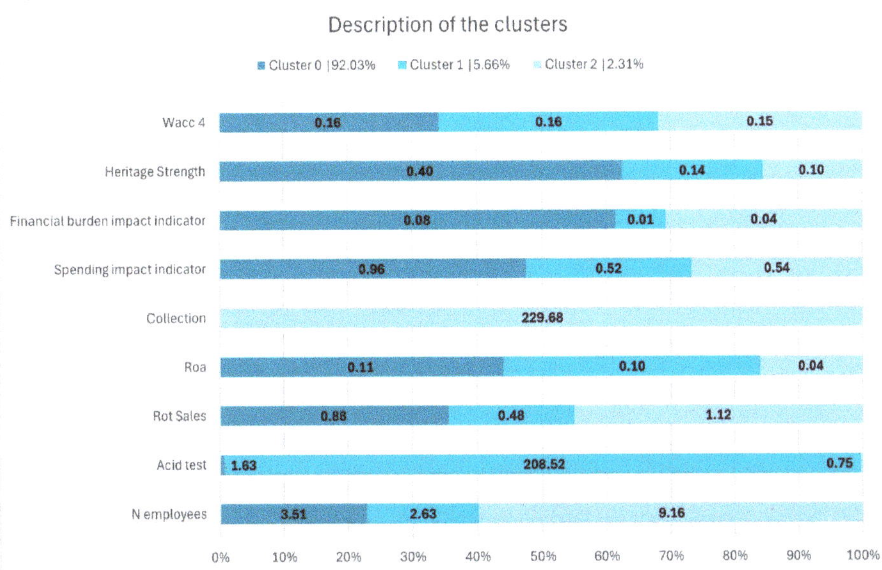

Figure 2. Estimated clusters.

Thus, the hierarchical clustering analysis has revealed the existence of three distinct groups within the sector. Of these, cluster 0 is the most prominent, comprising 92% of the firms in the sector. Cluster 0 is characterized by a harmonic mean WACC of 0.1568. Firms in this group tend to have higher ratios of administrative and selling expenses to revenues. This can be interpreted as a sign that these firms are possibly incurring higher costs in these areas. Similarly, these companies also show a higher financial impact, suggesting that they may be facing higher financial costs in proportion to their sales. A positive feature of this group is their robustness in terms of equity. It indicates that the ratio of equity to total equity is higher compared to other groups. This can be interpreted as a sign of financial soundness and solvency, as it shows that these companies have a stronger capital base.

Finally, cluster 2, with 2.31% of the firms, has a harmonic mean WACC of 0.1465. The firms in this group tend to operate in medium-to-large market segments. This indicates that these firms have considerable presence in their respective markets, either in terms of market share or geographic reach. Although these firms have a long average collection period, which may suggest potential challenges in managing receivables or negotiating terms with customers, this factor does not appear to adversely affect their financial performance. A notable characteristic of cluster 2 is their high level of profitability. This indicates that these firms can generate significant profits relative to their investments and assets. Despite their profitability, the companies in this group show reduced equity strength. This suggests that they have a lower capital base relative to their total equity or that they may have higher levels of debt relative to their equity.

The identified clusters demonstrate that there is no single financial and risk profile that represents the sector. Investors will be interested in investing in those companies that represent the lowest risk, which in this case is represented by the larger companies.

4. Discussion

In line with the present study, it is important to note that project-specific characteristics-such as project risk, capital structure, and the economic and regulatory environment-can lead to significant variations in the WACC calculated for different projects, even within the same industry or country. For example, in KPMG's study [61] on the cost of capital by industry, it was observed that the WACC varies considerably between different sectors due to factors such as regulatory risks and technological changes that impact business models, which is in accordance with [62].

Indeed, the results of this study indicate that the WACC values range between 12.63% and 29.70% depending on the method used. The traditional method presents the highest value, while the combined method offers a more reasonable estimate adjusted to local conditions with a nominal weighted WACC of 14.43% and an actual weighted WACC of 12.63%. These findings also underscore the importance of adapting WACC calculation methodologies to specific economic contexts.

This study aligns with previous research that highlights the need for specific adjustments to traditional WACC calculation methods to better reflect local economic realities. For example, Ref. [27] highlights that the accuracy of WACC estimation can be significantly improved by adapting methodologies to local market conditions. In addition, Refs. [25,33] suggest that factors such as country risk and economic stability have a substantial impact on the cost of capital, which is consistent with the findings of the present article.

In addition, this study covers a key aspect of the Ecuadorian economy: its dollarization. According to Steffen et al. [33], the use of methodologies that accurately incorporate country risk, such as the use of CDS, can provide a more realistic estimate and avoid overvaluation of risk. On the other hand, Pierret [25] highlights the importance of adjusting discount rates to adequately reflect risks in emerging and dollarized economies, supporting the relevance of the combined method used in this study. Also, Noothout [21] emphasize the need for methodologies adapted to illiquid and emerging markets to avoid significant distortions in investment decisions.

In this sense, recent literature suggests that the use of multifactor models can provide a more complete and accurate assessment of the cost of capital in emerging markets. Thus, Bedoya et al. [19] proposed a multifactor model for power transmission system operators in Colombia, showing that additional factors such as regulatory risk and interest rates can better explain variations in returns. Franc [6] also support the incorporation of multiple risk factors, especially in the energy sector, where idiosyncratic risks can be significant. Hashemi et al. [63] emphasize the importance of properly assessing the costs of power outages, as these can significantly increase operating costs and uncertainty for industrial firms in developing economies. Fares and King [64] also underline the relevance of sector-specific risks and the need for tailored methodologies to assess the cost of capital in contexts of high volatility and risk.

5. Conclusions, Implications and Limitations

This study posed two key research questions: What is the weighted average cost of capital (WACC) for the energy sector in Ecuador? How do different WACC calculation methodologies affect the estimation of the cost of capital in the Ecuadorian energy sector?

The answers to these questions were clearly determined. Regarding the first question, it was found that the appropriate WACC for the energy sector in Ecuador, considering the particularities of its economy, is best represented by method four, which combines the U.S. interest rate with the credit default swap (CDS) to accurately reflect the country's debt default risk. This method resulted in a WACC of 12.63% in real terms and 14.43% in nominal terms, in contrast to the traditional method which overestimates the WACC at 31.77%.

Regarding the second question, this study showed that the different WACC calculation methodologies significantly affect the estimation of the cost of capital. While the traditional method overestimates the WACC due to the double penalty of country risk and the U.S. market premium, adjusted methods that consider the specific conditions of the Ecuadorian economy, such as the use of CDS to calculate the market risk premium, provide more accurate and useful estimates. This underscores the importance of adapting WACC calculation methodologies to local economic conditions to obtain realistic and applicable results for strategic and investment decision-making in the Ecuadorian energy sector.

In addition, the financial segmentation analysis revealed the existence of three distinct financial profiles among companies in the energy sector, underscoring the diversity of the sector and the need for customized approaches to financial management and investment. These findings not only effectively answer the research questions posed but also provide a solid foundation for future research and strategic decisions in the sector. Ultimately, this study highlights the importance of adopting financial approaches that consider local economic particularities, allowing companies and investors to make more informed decisions that are strategically aligned with Ecuadorian market conditions.

Likewise, the results of this study have important implications for financial management and strategic decision making in the Ecuadorian energy sector. The adoption of more accurate methodologies, such as the combined use of the U.S. interest rate and the credit default swap (CDS), provides companies and investors with more reliable tools to evaluate the cost of capital. This allows for better alignment of investment decisions with local economic realities, optimizing resource allocation and improving the profitability of energy projects. Furthermore, these findings suggest that traditional models need to be adjusted to specific market conditions, which is crucial for the development of effective regulatory frameworks and financial tools.

However, this study has several limitations. The reliance on historical and projected data from the U.S. market may introduce biases that do not fully reflect the dynamics of the Ecuadorian market. In addition, variability in CDS values and interest rates may affect the accuracy of WACC estimates over time. The methodology, although adjusted, is still a simplification of the complex and multifaceted economic reality. Finally, although the results are applicable to the Ecuadorian energy sector, specific studies in other sectors and regions are needed to validate the applicability of the proposed methodologies in different economic contexts.

Author Contributions: Conceptualization, F.N. and F.C.; methodology, F.C.; software, F.C.; validation, V.A., F.N. and F.C.; formal analysis, V.A.; investigation, F.N.; resources, F.N.; data curation, F.C.; writing—original draft preparation, Víctor Aguilar; writing—review and editing, V.A.; visualization, F.N.; supervision, V.A.; project administration, V.A.; funding acquisition, F.N. All authors have read and agreed to the published version of the manuscript.

Funding: This research was funded by Corporación Ecuatoriana para el Desarrollo de la Investigación y la Academia CEDIA, and Universidad de Cuenca grant number I+D+I-XVII-2022-51 and The APC was funded by Corporación Ecuatoriana para el Desarrollo de la Investigación y la Academia CEDIA.

Data Availability Statement: Data available on request due to restrictions: The databases associated with this research are not public due to rights issues with CEDIA, the institution that funded the research. However, the corresponding author can be contacted if access is required.

Conflicts of Interest: The authors declare no conflict of interest.

Nomenclature

WACC	Weighted Average Cost of Capital
CAMP	Capital Asset Pricing Model
MRP	Market Risk Premium
CRP	Country Risk Premium
CDS	Credit Default Swap
ERP	Equity Risk Premium

Appendix A

Table A1. Foreign companies commonly used during benchmarking.

Country	Name	City/Country	Beta r	p Value	Rsquared	Filter_Beta_p	Beta	Debt Beta	Beta Des	Selection
Chile	AES Andes S.A	Santiago, Chile	0.5914	0.0000	0.1768	1.0000	0.7262	1.8638	1.1201	Yes
Colombia	Celsia	Bogotá, Colombia	0.3068	0.0003	0.1059	1.0000	0.5356	−0.3449		No
Brazil	Centrais Elétricas Brasileiras S.A	Sai Paulo, Brasil	1.2940	0.0000	0.3924	1.0000	1.1970	−0.2523		No
Chile	Colbún	Santiago, Chile	0.8323	0.0000	0.2560	1.0000	0.8877	−20.7753		No
Chile	Enel Chile	Santiago, Chile	0.9420	0.0000	0.3240	1.0000	0.9611	−0.2526		No
Peru	Enel Perú	Lima, Perú	0.5996	0.0000	0.1213	1.0000	0.7317	52.7686	1.9786	No
Brazil	Energias do Brasil	Sau Paulo, Brasil	0.7088	0.0000	0.3931	1.0000	0.8049	2.5731	1.0110	Yes
Brazil	Eneva	Sau Paulo, Brasil	0.7137	0.0000	0.2772	1.0000	0.8082	−2.4494		No
Brazil	Engie Brasil Energia	Sau Paulo, Brasil	0.5242	0.0000	0.3209	1.0000	0.6812	−0.2208		No
Chile	Engie Energía Chile	Santiago, Chile	0.7058	0.0000	0.2044	1.0000	0.8029	2.4954	0.9634	Yes
Peru	Engie Energía Perú	Lima, Perú	0.2619	0.0002	0.0815	1.0000	0.5054	1.8048	0.6579	Yes
Mexico	IEnova	México DF, México	0.8915	0.0000	0.2898	1.0000	0.9273	−1.0644		No
Colombia	Interconexión Eléctrica S.A	Bogotá, Colombia	0.4041	0.0002	0.0800	1.0000	0.6007	1.2035	0.7000	Yes
Peru	Luz del Sur	Lima, Perú	0.2857	0.0120	0.0276	0.0000	0.5214	−0.3597		No
Mexico	Vista Oil & Gas S.A	México DF, México	0.3003	0.3307	0.0199	0.0000	0.5312			No

References

1. Samaniego, J.L.; Galindo, L.M.; Mostacedo, S.J.; Ferrer Carbonell, J.; Alatorre, J.E.; Reyes, O. *El Cambio Climático y El Sector de Energía En América Latina*; Publicación de las Naciones Unidas: Santiago, Chile, 2017.
2. Stoenoiu, C.E.; Birou, I.; Cristea, C.; Serban, F.M. Renewable Energy in European Countries, Retrospective Analysis. *IOP Conf. Ser. Earth Environ. Sci.* **2021**, *664*, 012019. [CrossRef]
3. MERNR. *Energía, Sociedad y Ambiente*; Ministerio de Energía y Minas: Quito, Ecuador, 2020.
4. Español, C. en. Los Cortes de Energía Continuarán en Todo Ecuador, Informa el Gobierno. Available online: https://cnnespanol.cnn.com/2024/04/22/cortes-energia-continuaran-ecuador-orix/ (accessed on 6 January 2024).
5. Dubrovsky, H.; Di Sbroiavacca, N.; Nadal, G.; Lisperguer, R.C. *Rol y Perspectivas Del Sector Eléctrico En La Transformación Energética de América Latina*; Publicación de las Naciones Unidas: Santiago, Chile, 2019.
6. Franc-Dabrowska, J.; Madra-Sawicka, M.; Milewska, A. Energy Sector Risk and Cost of Capital Assessment—Companies and Investors Perspective. *Energies* **2021**, *14*, 1613. [CrossRef]
7. Wiatros, M.; Jones, D.; Broadbent, H.; Fulghum, N.; Bruce, C.; Dizon, R.; Macdonald, P.; Moore, C.; Candlin, A.; Lee, U.; et al. *Global Electriciy Review 2023*; Ember: London, UK, 2023; Volume 5.
8. Ritchie, H.; Rosado, P. Energy. Available online: https://ourworldindata.org/energy (accessed on 5 February 2022).
9. Stoenoiu, C.E.; Balan, M.C.; Serban, F.M.; Cristea, C. Evolution of Renewable Energy Consumption in the European Countries. *IOP Conf. Ser. Earth Environ. Sci.* **2021**, *664*, 012018. [CrossRef]
10. Financial Times. Financing the Energy Transition. Available online: https://white-and-case.ft.com/article/financing-the-energy-transition (accessed on 10 December 2023).
11. IEA. Energy Investment in 2023. Available online: https://www.iea.org/reports/world-energy-investment-2023/introduction (accessed on 19 December 2023).
12. International Energy Agency. *World Energy Outlook*; International Energy Agency: Paris, France, 2023.

13. Barnes, D.F.; Samad, H.; Rivas, S. *Meeting Challenges, Measuring Progress: The Benefits of Sustainable Energy Access in Latin America and the Caribbean*; Inter-American Development Bank: Washington, DC, USA, 2018. [CrossRef]
14. Ministerio de Energía y Minas. *Transformación y Situación Actual Del Sector Eléctrico*; Ministerio de Energía y Minas: Quito, Ecuador, 2020.
15. Ministerio de Energía y Minas. En 2021 el Sector Eléctrico Dinamizó la Economía Nacional con un 93.2 % de Generación Renovable y la Exportación de Más de 500 GWh. Available online: https://www.recursosyenergia.gob.ec/en-2021-el-sector-electrico-dinamizo-la-economia-nacional-con-un-93-2-de-generacion-renovable-y-la-exportacion-de-mas-de-500-gwh/ (accessed on 13 February 2023).
16. Casilda Béjar, R. Energía y Desarrollo Económico En América Latina. *Boletín Económico ICE* **2002**, *2750*, 31–44.
17. Martín, H.; Coronas, S.; Alonso, À.; De La Hoz, J.; Matas, J. Renewable Energy Auction Prices: Near Subsidy-Free? *Energies* **2020**, *13*, 3383. [CrossRef]
18. Li, H. Cost of Capital: Literatures Review about Calculation Methods and Influencing Factors. *J. Serv. Sci. Manag.* **2019**, *12*, 360–370. [CrossRef]
19. Bedoya-Cadavid, J.A.; Lanzas-Duque, Á.M.; Salazar, H. WACC for Electric Power Transmission System Operators: The Case of Colombia. *Energies* **2023**, *16*, 964. [CrossRef]
20. Dobrowolski, Z.; Drozdowski, G.; Panait, M.; Apostu, S.A. The Weighted Average Cost of Capital and Its Universality in Crisis Times: Evidence from the Energy Sector. *Energies* **2022**, *15*, 6655. [CrossRef]
21. Noothout, P.; de Jager, D.; Tesnière, L.; van Rooijen, S.; Karypidis, N.; Brückmann, R.; Jirouš, F.; Breitschopf, B.; Angelopoulos, D.; Doukas, H.; et al. *The Impact of Risks in Renewable Investments and the Role of Smart Policies*; European Commission: Brussels, Belgium, 2016.
22. Đukan, M.; Kitzing, L. A Bigger Bang for the Buck: The Impact of Risk Reduction on Renewable Energy Support Payments in Europe. *Energy Policy* **2023**, *173*, 113395. [CrossRef]
23. DeCotis, P.A. Importance of Energy-Sector Investment in Technology and Infrastructure. *Nat. Gas Electr.* **2020**, *36*, 24–27. [CrossRef]
24. Steffen, B. Estimating the Cost of Capital for Renewable Energy Projects. *Energy Econ.* **2020**, *88*, 104783. [CrossRef]
25. Pierret, D. The Systemic Risk of Energy Markets. *SSRN* **2013**. [CrossRef]
26. Buhr, B.; Murinde, V.; Volz, U.; Pullin, N.; Donovan, C.; King, G.; Lo, Y. *Climate Change and the Cost of Capital in Developing Countries: Assessing the Impact of Climate Risks on Sovereign Borrowing Costs*; Imperial College London: London, UK; SOAS University of London: London, UK; UN Environment: Nairobi, Kenya, 2018; p. 32.
27. Bachner, G.; Mayer, J.; Steininger, K.W. Costs or Benefits? Assessing the Economy-Wide Effects of the Electricity Sector 's Low Carbon Transition—The Role of Capital Costs, Divergent Risk Perceptions and Premiums. *Energy Strateg. Rev.* **2019**, *26*, 100373. [CrossRef]
28. Paper, E.W.; Gohdes, N.; Simshauser, P. *Renewable Entry Costs, Project Finance and the Role of Revenue Quality in Australia's National Electricity Market*; University of Cambridge: Cambridge, UK, 2022.
29. Moreira, L.; Junior, C.; Junior, A.; Castro, R.; Mello, O.; Hugo, V.; Pinheiro, R.B.; Sousa, W.L. Empirical Evidence of the Cost of Capital under Risk Conditions for Thermoelectric Power Plants in Brazil. *Energies* **2022**, *15*, 4313. [CrossRef]
30. Damodaran, A. *Investment Valuation: Tools and Techniques for Determining the Value of Any Asset*, 3rd ed.; Wiley: Hoboken, NJ, USA, 2012.
31. Adriana, G.O.L.; Maritza, T.I.K. *Desarrollo de Una Herramienta de Cálculo para la Determinación del Costo Nivelado de Energía en el Contexto Ecuatoriano*; Universidad Técnica de Cotopaxi: Latacunga, Ecuador, 2022.
32. Masabanda, V. Modelo Económico para la Incorporación de Generación con Fuentes Renovables No Convencionales. Bachelor's Thesis, Universidad Politécnica Salesiana, Cuenca, Ecuador, 2015.
33. Steffen, B.; Waidelich, P. Determinants of Cost of Capital in the Electricity Sector Progress in Energy OPEN ACCESS. *Prog. Energy* **2022**, *4*, 033001. [CrossRef]
34. Ionici, O.; Small, K.; D'Souza, F. Cost of Capital. An Introduction. In *Capital Budgeting Valuation: Analysis for Today's Investment Projects*; Wiley: Hoboken, NJ, USA, 2011; pp. 339–362.
35. Maquieira, C.; Espinosa, C. *Valoración de Empresas*, 1st ed.; LAINU: Santiago, Chile, 2019.
36. Coutsiers, E.; Gea, M.; Rodríguez, R. Estimación de La Tasa de Costo de Capital Para Proyectos de Energía Renovable En Latinoamérica. *Av. En Energías Renov. Y Medio Ambiente AVERMA* **2022**, *26*, 369–379.
37. Lonergan, K.E.; Egli, F.; Osorio, S.; Sansavini, G.; Pahle, M.; Schmidt, T.S.; Steffen, B. Improving the Representation of Cost of Capital in Energy System Models. *Joule* **2023**, *7*, 469–483. [CrossRef]
38. Bank, T.W. RISE—Regulatory Indicators for Sustainable Energy. Available online: https://www.worldbank.org/en/topic/energy/publication/rise---regulatory-indicators-for-sustainable-energy (accessed on 6 January 2024).
39. Walker, E. Cost of Capital in Emerging Markets: Bridging Gaps between Theory and Practice. *Lat. Am. J. Econ.* **2016**, *53*, 111–147.
40. Schlegel, D. Cost-of-Capital in the Finance Literature. In *Contributions to Management Science*; Springer: Berlin/Heidelberg, Germany, 2015; pp. 9–70. [CrossRef]
41. Bruner, R.; Eades, K.; Harris, R.; Higgins, R. "Best Practices" in Estimating the Cost of Capital: An Update. *J. Appl. Financ.* **2013**, *23*, 15.

42. Schlegel, D. A Comparison of Global Empirical Results on Company Cost-of-Capital Practices. *Int. J. Bus. Glob.* **2014**, *12*, 53–62. [CrossRef]
43. Fama, E.F.; French, K.R. Size, Value, and Momentum in International Stock Returns. *J. Financ. Econ.* **2012**, *105*, 457–472. [CrossRef]
44. Yemba, B.P. User Cost of Foreign Monetary Assets under Dollarization. *Financ. Res. Lett.* **2022**, *49*, 103023. [CrossRef]
45. Perold, A. The Capital Asset Pricing Model. *J. Econ. Perspect.* **2017**, *18*, 47–49. [CrossRef]
46. Cohen, B. *America's Interest in Dollarization*; UC Santa Barbara, Global Studies: Santa Barbara, CA, USA, 2004; pp. 5–24.
47. Soto, R. Dollarization, Economic Growth, and Employment. *Econ. Lett.* **2009**, *105*, 42–45. [CrossRef]
48. Castillo-Ponce, R.A.; Truong, B.; De, M.; Rodriguez-Espinosa, L. Dollarization and Economic Interdependence: The Case of Ecuador Dolarizacion E Interdependencia Economica: El Caso De Ecuador. *Rev. Análisis Económico* **2021**, *36*, 85–108. [CrossRef]
49. Maiella, M.; Ramírez, D. Valoración Económica Financiera Con Base En Evidencia de Laboratorios de Producción Farmacéutica. *Actual. Contab. Faces* **2022**, *1*, 34–52. [CrossRef]
50. de Compañias, S. Ranking de Compañias. Superintendencia de Compañías, Valores y Seguros del Ecuador. Available online: https://appscvsmovil.supercias.gob.ec/ranking/reporte.html (accessed on 6 January 2024).
51. Rubinstein, M.E. A mean-variance synthesis of corporate financial theory. *J. Financ.* **1973**, *28*, 167–181.
52. Blume, M. Betas and Their Regression Tendencies. *J. Financ.* **1975**, *30*, 785–795. [CrossRef]
53. Beltrame, F.; Cappelletto, R.; Toniolo, G. *Estimating SMEs Cost of Equity Using a Value at Risk Approach*, 1st ed.; Springer: Berlin/Heidelberg, Germany, 2014.
54. Agustini, A.T. The Effect of Firm Size and Rate of Inflation on Cost of Capital: The Role of IFRS Adoption in the World. *Procedia Soc. Behav. Sci.* **2016**, *219*, 47–54. [CrossRef]
55. The Centre for International Economics. *Inflation and WACC Prepared*; The Centre for International Economics: Canberra, Australia, 2020.
56. Mehta, D.R.; Curley, M.D.; Fung, H.G. Inflation, Budgeting Cost of Capital, and Procedures. *Financ. Manag.* **1984**, *13*, 48–54. [CrossRef]
57. Moro, R. Inflation Risk Management in Project Finance Investments. *Int. J. Financ. Account.* **2012**, *2012*, 198–207.
58. Grabowski, R.J.; Harrington, J.P.; Nunes, C. *International Valuation Handbook-Guide to Cost of Capital*; Wiley: Hoboken, NJ, USA, 2015.
59. Dolbnya, E.A.; Vasilyeva, M.K.; Lyukina, A.Y. Analysis of Methods for Calculating the Weighted Average Cost of Capital of a Company on the Example of an Industrial Enterprise. *Adv. Econ. Bus. Manag. Res.* **2020**, *128*, 2803–2807.
60. Fama, E.F.; French, K.R. The Capital Asset Pricing Model: Theory and Evidence. *J. Econ. Perspect.* **2004**, *18*, 25–46. [CrossRef]
61. KPMG. *Cost of Capital Study 2023*; KPMG: Berlin, Germany, 2023.
62. Damodaran, A. Cost of Equity and Capital (US). Available online: https://pages.stern.nyu.edu/~adamodar/New_Home_Page/datafile/wacc.html (accessed on 29 May 2024).
63. Hashemi, M.; Jenkins, G.P.; Jyoti, R.; Ozbafli, A. Evaluating the Cost to Industry of Electricity Outages. *Energy Sources Part B Econ. Plan. Policy* **2018**, *13*, 340–349. [CrossRef]
64. Fares, R.L.; King, C.W. Trends in Transmission, Distribution, and Administration Costs for U.S. Investor-Owned Electric Utilities. *Energy Policy* **2017**, *105*, 354–362. [CrossRef]

sustainability

MDPI

Article

Analysis of EU's Coupled Carbon and Electricity Market Development Based on Generative Pre-Trained Transformer Large Model and Implications in China

Yao Li [1], Siyuan Ni [1], Xi Tang [2], Sizhe Xie [1,*] and Peng Wang [1,3]

1 School of Electrical and Electronic Engineering, North China Electric Power University, Beijing 102206, China; yaoli@ncepu.edu.cn (Y.L.); nsy@ncepu.edu.cn (S.N.); wangpeng@ncepu.edu.cn (P.W.)
2 Sichuan University—Pittsburgh Institute, Chengdu 610207, China; 2022141520109@stu.scu.edu.cn
3 National Institute of Energy Development Strategy, North China Electric Power University, Beijing 102206, China
* Correspondence: sizhexie@ncepu.edu.cn; Tel.: +86-1311-185-3837

Abstract: With increasing global attention on carbon emission control and sustainable development, the carbon market has become an important tool for promoting environmental sustainability and carbon emission regulation. As an important part of energy trading, the electricity market is closely related to the carbon market and their effective coupling is critical for achieving sustainable energy transitions. Power generation can effectively link carbon prices and electricity prices. Through the promulgation of reasonable policies, we can promote the coupling of the carbon market and the electricity market, and then, through macro-control, promote the steady and joint development of the carbon and electricity markets, improve the construction of the carbon rights market, reduce greenhouse gas emissions, and create a sustainable future for humanity. Given the relative maturity of the EU carbon market and electricity market, this paper identifies key points of market volatility through the coupling coordination model analysis and uses the GPT large model analysis to analyze policy factors that have a greater impact on carbon market and electricity market transactions. The research results show that market-regulating policies and expectation management policies have the greatest impact on the degree of coupling between the carbon and electricity markets. The impact of secondary policies such as international cooperation policies and structural adjustment policies is relatively insignificant. Although the development of China's carbon market faces many challenges, reasonable policy interventions are expected to achieve significant results in the domestic carbon market. Finally, this paper also draws on analogy analysis to draw corresponding implications for China from the EU's carbon–electricity coupling policy promulgation.

Keywords: electricity market; carbon market; coupling analysis; GPT large model

1. Introduction

The current Chinese government is committed to the "3060" plan and has been very effective in building a carbon rights market. On 24 April 2024, the closing price of China's carbon emission trading market exceeded CNY 100 per tonne for the first time, and the green financial attributes of carbon emission rights are being recognized by more and more financial institutions. Meanwhile, China's power generation, distribution, and sales account for a large amount of carbon emissions. Power generation can effectively link carbon prices and electricity prices. By implementing reasonable policies, we can promote the coupling of the carbon market and the electricity market, thereby, through macro-control, pushing for the steady and joint development of the carbon and electricity markets, improving the construction of the carbon rights market, reducing greenhouse gas emissions, and creating a better future for humanity. By the end of 2022, the cumulative trading volume of carbon emission allowances in the power generation industry in China's carbon emission rights trading market reached 230 million tons, with a cumulative turnover of CNY 10.475 billion. The relationship between China's carbon rights market and power market is becoming increasingly close [1].

However, the differences between the electricity market and the carbon market in terms of market elements and trading mechanisms have not yet been well coordinated [2]. The electricity market is a demand-driven market, the trading subject of which is electric energy, and continuous trading is required according to time periods such as years, months, and days. The carbon rights market, on the other hand, is a policy-driven market, the trading subject of which is carbon quotas and their derivatives, which do not have to be continuously traded like the electricity market.

Due to the different characteristics of the markets mentioned above, there are corresponding deficiencies in the connection between the carbon market and the electricity market. For example, the relative independence of the market policy systems has prevented the two markets from establishing close links, and differences in trading methods have prevented the effective transmission of carbon and electricity prices within a short period of time [3,4]. By promoting the coupling of the carbon and electricity markets through effective policies, we can overcome these challenges. Power generation plays a crucial role in linking carbon prices with electricity prices, facilitating the transmission between the two markets. At the same time, China's electricity market is currently in the process of transitioning from planning to the market, which also has a negative impact on the transmission of electricity and carbon prices [5–8]. These problems have greatly constrained the transformation of China's energy system. Therefore, an analysis of the coupling of China's carbon and electricity markets has become an important research task.

Compared with China's relatively underdeveloped carbon electricity market, the EU's carbon electricity market construction has entered a more mature stage [9,10]. Under its highly market-oriented electricity conditions, power companies can directly incorporate the carbon price into the cost of power generation and partially or fully transfer it to consumers, combining the carbon rights market and the electricity market with in-depth price linkage [11]. At the same time, the EU has adopted the approach of no longer allocating free carbon allowances to power companies, forcing power companies to compete in carbon market transactions, which enables the electricity market and the carbon market to develop simultaneously. For China's current carbon electricity market, this approach is advanced and worth learning from.

Published articles have also analyzed the coupling of China's carbon electricity market. Paper [12] analyzed the cause-and-effect relationship between the operation of the electricity market and the carbon market in the Beijing–Tianjin–Hebei region and obtained a dynamic model of the carbon electricity market for simulation. Paper [13] focused on Guangdong Province and studied the impact of the carbon electricity market on the marginal clearing price of Guangdong's electricity trading and the cost of electricity supply. Unlike previous related articles, this article, based on research on China's carbon electricity market, also analyzes the EU carbon electricity market. The carbon electricity markets in the two different regions can be compared, which leads to more targeted opinions. At the same time, this paper combines the GPT large model to analyze relevant policies. The use of AI large semantic models to analyze the impact of relevant policies on the carbon electricity market was rare before now, which is also an innovative aspect of this paper.

Within the overall framework of introducing the EU carbon electricity market for comparative analysis, this article will adopt the following structure: First, an overview of the EU's electricity market and carbon market will be given, introducing the general characteristics of its electricity market and carbon market. Second, the main analysis part of the article will explain in detail the types of EU policies, and based on the GPT model, the corresponding effects of various models will be given. Based on the policy analysis, factors such as the trading volume, unit price, and trading volume of the carbon electricity market will be used as the main variables to establish positive and negative correlation models and give the corresponding functional forms of the coupling degree. On this basis, the validity and rationality of the selected data will be further elaborated, and the results of the carbon electricity market coupling degree based on the established model will be used to visually illustrate the impact of various indicators on the carbon electricity market. Based on the results of the analysis of the factors and coupling degree of the EU market, the article will analyze the corresponding factors of the Chinese carbon electricity market and the actual coupling of the carbon electricity market, so as to more specifically obtain the main deficiencies in the current development of the Chinese carbon electricity market and the types and priority levels of various indicators that need to be improved. After using the analysis results of the EU carbon electricity market to analyze the Chinese carbon electricity market horizontally, the article will summarize all the previous content and draw the final research conclusions.

2. An Overview of Electricity and Carbon Markets in the European Union

Section 2 describes the overview of the EU carbon electricity market separately. The EU market is chosen because of its large carbon electricity market and extremely mature trading mechanism, which facilitates comparison with the Chinese market in Section 4.

2.1. Electricity Market in European Union

In 2023, the EU's total power generation reached 2402 TWh. Of this, renewable power accounted for 44%, with wind power, in particular, accounting for 18% of total power generation, surpassing natural gas for the first time. At the same time, the EU's fossil fuel power generation fell significantly, accounting for less than one-third of EU power. And coal power generation was only 333 TWh, equivalent to 12% of total power generation. This significant change in the energy mix is largely due to the EU's strong market policies for new energy sources, and the proportion of new energy sources in electricity generation is expected to rise further [14].

In addition to the EU's improving electricity energy mix, its relatively complete market trading system and non-uniform pricing system have also brought sufficient vitality to the EU's electricity market [15].

Long-term and short-term electricity trading coexist in the EU. Among them, once a potential spot market is formed, long-term trading will naturally develop without political or regulatory intervention. However, the short-term spot market for electricity is different. Even though the vast majority of participants are private companies, the development of both the day-ahead hourly auction market and the intraday spot market has required political intervention or regulatory support. At the same time, due to the different sizes of the territories of different countries, the sizes of bidding areas in the spot market vary. This complexity has increased market tension, and changes to price areas are difficult to implement due to their political sensitivity. Nevertheless, the policy of combining long-term and short-term electricity trading still ensures the flexibility of the EU electricity market.

In terms of electricity prices, there is no unified transmission and distribution price system in Europe, and European electricity prices also differ greatly in terms of structure and absolute value [16]. Some are based on electricity volume, some on capacity, and some on a combination of the two. At the same time, electricity prices in different regions of the same country may not be the same. Such a system brings more uncertainty to the market, but at the same time, cross-border transactions and competition are also promoted to a certain extent.

The EU electricity market has come a long way since the reforms that began with the gradual liberalization of the monopoly. Before the introduction of competitive markets in the EU, national or regional monopolies covered all public utilities, including electricity production, the power grid, and retail. The EU responded with structural reform measures to promote competition, the cornerstone of which was the separation of competitive and natural monopoly operations: transmission and distribution are natural monopoly operations, but power generation, trading, and the sale of electricity to customers are classified as competitive operations. Since 1999, competition in the market has gradually developed, and the openness of the market has also deepened [17]. The implementation framework of the EU's market opening plan has gradually narrowed from being quite broad at the beginning to the current EU electricity market.

The current EU electricity market is relatively mature and is even able to actively carry out foreign trade while meeting the needs of member states [18]. With the further promotion of carbon peak and carbon neutrality, the EU's power structure is expected to be further improved, and the trading system of the power market is also expected to further innovate and develop, becoming more perfect.

2.2. Carbon Market in European Union

The EU electricity market includes 27 member states and 30 countries in total, including Iceland, Norway, and Liechtenstein. More than 12,000 companies and industrial plants with an energy consumption of more than 20 MW are included in the EU carbon market. At the same time, the EU carbon market has a wide range of business coverage, including steel, cement, glass, ceramics, electricity, shipping, etc. [19]. Among them, high-emission industries account for about 40% of EU carbon emissions.

Such a large scale of carbon emissions requires well-regulated carbon trading rules to ensure compliance. The EU government has adopted a cap-and-trade rule, but it is relatively free. Within the scope of administrative licensing, companies can sell their carbon allowances or purchase additional allowances to ensure that their overall carbon emissions are qualified. Under the government's sampling and supervision, companies commission agencies to conduct annual carbon emission verifications. If a company's carbon emissions exceed the quota, it will be fined at least EUR 100 per unit of allowance [20]. This relatively standardized trading rule has largely ensured the stable operation of the EU carbon market.

In practice, however, the initial penalty specifications were not as high as they are now and were accompanied by a large number of emission allowances. EU carbon trading has been developing since 2005 and has gone through roughly three stages before reaching its current state [21].

In the first phase, from 2005 to 2007, trading only covered the carbon emissions of power generators and energy-intensive industries, and there were substantial subsidies and a relatively low penalty price of EUR 40 per tonne. The second phase ran from 2008 to 2012, when three countries outside the EU joined, subsidies were cut, and the penalty price was raised to its current level. This was followed by the third phase, which ran until 2020, when the different national cap systems were replaced by a standard EU emissions cap and auctioning was introduced as the default method for allocating allowances, with more companies and greenhouse gases included. The period from 2021 to the present is the fourth phase, which has been very successful, with regulated emissions from companies falling by 62% compared to 2005. The new EU emissions trading system 2 (ETS 2) was also introduced [22,23].

The EU carbon rights market today uses the EU Allowance (EUA) as the unit of trade, with one unit of EUA equivalent to one metric ton of carbon dioxide equivalent. It is stored electronically in software. It can be traded on the European Climate Exchange (ECX) or the European Energy Exchange (EEX), both within individual countries and the EU, which greatly improves the flexibility of carbon market transactions [24]. In the future, the free carbon allowances of today may disappear completely, and companies will only be able to obtain carbon allowances through market transactions. At the same time, in order to further accelerate the "carbon reduction" process, the EU may impose additional levies on carbon market transactions as an incentive for companies to make greater contributions to carbon emission reductions and environmental improvements.

3. Coupling Analysis of Carbon and Electricity Markets

Section 3 systematically elaborates on the research content from the following four aspects. First, Section 3.1 introduces the coupled analysis model. This model can calculate and analyze the time series coupling degree of the carbon electricity market, thus providing the coupling degree fluctuation point for the GPT macro model in Section 3.2. Second, Section 3.2 provides an in-depth analysis of the policy factors that cause this fluctuation point based on the GPT macro model. Then, Section 3.3 uses the EU carbon electricity market as an example to conduct a coupling analysis and verify the practical application effect of the proposed algorithm. Finally, Section 3.4 discusses the results of the analysis, summarizes the research findings, and puts forward relevant recommendations.

3.1. Coupling Coordination Model

The coupling coordination model is used to measure the level of interaction and coordinated development between multiple systems. According to the relevant literature [25], the model can quantitatively calculate the degree of coupling coordination between multiple systems.

For a system $x_1, x_2, x_3, \ldots, x_n$, each system has m evaluation indicators. Therefore, the data set of the i-th system is $x_{ij} = \{x_{i1}, x_{i2}, \ldots, x_{im}\}$. The weight vector of each system indicator obtained by the entropy method is w_{ij}.

$$i = 1, 2, 3, \ldots, n. \qquad j = 1, 2, 3, \ldots, m.$$

The data for each system are then standardized to eliminate dimensional effects. The standard value of the j-th indicator for the i-th system is calculated:

$$z_{ij} = [x_{ij} - min(x_{ij})] \div [max(x_{ij}) - min(x_{ij})].$$

Next, the proportion P_{ij} of the value of the j-th indicator for the i-th system to the sum of this indicator across all systems is calculated as follows:

$$P_{ij} = \frac{z_{ij}}{\sum_{i=1}^{n} z_{ij}}$$
$$0 \leq P_{ij} \leq 1$$

The information entropy for the j-th indicator is then calculated as follows:

$$e_j = -\frac{1}{In(n)} \sum_{i=1}^{n} P_{ij} \times InP_{ij}$$
$$0 \leq e_{ij} \leq 1$$

Next, the information entropy redundancy d_j is calculated:

$$d_j = 1 - e_j$$
$$0 \leq e_{ij} \leq 1$$

After that, the evaluation indicator weight w_{ij} is computed as follows:

$$w_j = \frac{d_j}{\sum_{j=1}^{m} d_j}$$
$$w_1 + w_2 + w_3 + \ldots + w_i = 1$$

Finally, the comprehensive evaluation index U_i of each system is calculated. The comprehensive evaluation index is an indicator that measures the overall performance of each system. By multiplying the standardized data with the corresponding weight and summing the terms, a single value reflecting the comprehensive performance of the system can be obtained. This index can help compare the comprehensive performance of different systems.

$$U_i = \sum w_{ij} \times z_{ij}$$

Coupling C measures the strength of interactions and synergies between multiple systems. It reflects the level of interdependence and synergistic development between systems. Coupling is calculated by taking the ratio of the geometric mean of the synthetic evaluation indices of all the systems to their arithmetic mean. The formula for calculating Coupling C is as follows:

$$C = \left(\frac{\prod_{i=1}^{n} U_i}{\left(\frac{1}{n}\sum_{i=1}^{n} U_i\right)^n}\right)^{\frac{1}{n}}$$

U_i is the value for each subsystem, and the standardized result is distributed in the interval $[0,\ 1]$. The coupling degree is also in the interval $[0,\ 1]$. The greater the coupling degree C, the less discrete the subsystems are from each other. Conversely, the greater the degree of discreteness between subsystems, the less the coupling degree is.

The coupling coordination index T is calculated to reflect the strength of the interaction between systems or the degree of interdependence between systems. It is an empirical parameter that is usually determined based on expert opinion, historical data analysis, or model simulation.

$$T = \sum_{i=1}^{n} \alpha_i \times U_i$$

$$\sum_{1}^{n} \alpha_i = 1$$

Here, α_i is the weight of the i-th subsystem, which is generally set to the same weight.

Coordination degree D is based on coupling degree C and takes into account the regulating factor of interaction between systems. By introducing the regulating factor T, the coordinated development level between systems is further refined and adjusted. Therefore, the interaction between systems and the state of coordinated development can be more accurately evaluated. The evaluation criteria for coupling coordination D are shown in Table 1.

$$D = \sqrt{C \times T}$$

Table 1. Coupling coordination evaluation criteria.

Coupling Coordination Degree *D* Value Range	Coordination Level	Degree of Coupling and Coordination
[0, 0.1)	1	extreme imbalance
[0.1, 0.2)	2	severe imbalance
[0.2, 0.3)	3	moderate disorder
[0.3, 0.4)	4	mild disorder
[0.4, 0.5)	5	on the verge of collapse
[0.5, 0.6)	6	barely dysfunctional
[0.6, 0.7)	7	primary coordination
[0.7, 0.8)	8	intermediate coordination
[0.8, 0.9)	9	well coordinated
[0.9, 1]	10	high-quality coordination

3.2. Coupling Analysis Algorithm Based on the GPT Large Model

3.2.1. Policy Classification

To more accurately reflect the role of various policies in market coupling, inspired by the framework proposed by Moslehi and Reddy [26], which emphasizes strategic goals and implementation, the policies promulgated by the Energy Administration for the carbon electricity market have been reclassified. Based on the time frame and implementation purpose of the policies, they are divided into two categories: strategic policies and operational policies. Strategic policies mainly focus on the management of long-term goals and market expectations and usually involve long-term planning and structural adjustments [27–31]. These policies guide the overarching direction of market development and aim to foster sustainable growth, innovation, and systemic transformation. For instance, Hartley et al. [28] discuss the expectations from the European Union in transitioning towards a circular economy, highlighting the importance of strategic policy in achieving long-term sustainability goals. Operational policies mainly focus on short-term market stability and responding to emergencies, and usually involve specific market operations and emergency measures.

Tang and Zhang [32] emphasize the significance of agile and lightweight approaches to emergency management, reflecting the nature of operational policies in addressing immediate challenges. Under these two broad categories, strategic policies are further subdivided into four categories based on the different expected directions of long-term planning and structural change. Operational policies are further subdivided into two categories based on the different approaches to resolving unexpected events that the market faces in the short term. The policy categories and their brief descriptions are shown in Table 2 [26–29].

Table 2. Policy categories and their brief descriptions.

Policy Factor	First-Level Classification	Second-Level Classification	Definition
	strategic policy	market-regulating policy	Intervening directly in the market's supply–demand relationship and price signals, adjusting the market's operating mechanism, and ensuring the market's stability and effectiveness.
		expectation management policy	Formulating long-term strategies and goals, clarifying policy directions, influencing market players' expectations and investment decisions, and guiding the market towards transformation.
		structural adjustment policy	Deep-level reform of market structures and mechanisms to promote the transformation and upgrading of the energy and economic structures and achieve profound changes in the market and industry.
		innovation incentive policy	Policy incentives and financial support promote the development of clean technologies and the use of renewable energy, stimulate technological innovation and industrial upgrading, and promote a green transformation of the economy.
	operational policy	international cooperation policy	Addressing the global challenge of climate change and promoting international action to reduce carbon emissions through international agreements and transnational cooperation.
		emergency adjustment policy	In case of emergency, temporary and targeted short-term measures should be taken to deal with sudden problems and ensure market stability and energy supply.

To help readers better understand the practical applications of these policies, the article provides detailed definitions for each policy type and includes specific examples of their implementation from various countries around the world. By showcasing how different nations have applied these policies in their energy practices, the article demonstrates the wide applicability and effectiveness of these policies in promoting the coupling of carbon and electricity markets. The specific definitions of each policy and their examples are described in detail below.

1. Market-regulating policy: adjusting the market operating mechanism by directly intervening in the supply and demand relationship and price signals in the market to ensure market stability and effectiveness. China: Launch of the national carbon emissions trading market (2021). In July 2021, China officially launched its national carbon emissions trading market. The power generation industry will be included first. Through the quota allocation and trading mechanism, the supply and demand relationship in the carbon market will be directly regulated to achieve a stable carbon price and effective market operation. European Union: Fourth phase of the EU ETS reform (2021). In 2021, the EU will implement the fourth phase of the reform of its emissions trading system (EU ETS). The reform measures include tightening the total number of allowances, increasing the emission reduction target, and introducing a stricter market stability reserve mechanism (MSR) to strengthen the carbon price signal and promote emission reductions by enterprises. Canada: Federal Carbon Pricing Backstop Plan (2019). In 2019, Canada implemented the Federal Carbon Pricing Backstop Plan, which imposes a federal carbon tax on provinces that do

not set their own carbon pricing mechanisms. This policy directly affects the cost of carbon emissions, adjusts market supply and demand, and encourages a low-carbon transition.

2. Anticipatory management policy: formulating long-term strategies and goals, clarifying future policy directions, influencing the expectations and investment decisions of market entities, and guiding the market towards a low-carbon transition. Japan: 2050 carbon neutrality target (2020). In 2020, the Japanese government officially announced the goal of achieving carbon neutrality by 2050 and formulated the "Green Growth Strategy" to guide long-term emission reduction planning for enterprises and society. This goal provides a clear policy signal for market entities and influences their long-term investment decisions. United States: Clean Power Plan 2035 (2021). In 2021, the Biden administration proposed the goal of achieving 100% clean electricity by 2035. This goal has set a direction for long-term investment and development in the energy industry, influenced the expectations and behaviors of market players, and promoted investment in renewable energy.

3. Structural adjustment policy: promoting the transformation and upgrading of the energy structure and economic structure through in-depth reforms of market structures and mechanisms, which involves profound changes in market and industrial structures. Germany: Renewable Energy Sources Act (EEG) amendment (2021). In 2021, Germany amended the Renewable Energy Sources Act (EEG) to further increase the target for the proportion of renewable energy in electricity, accelerate the transformation of the energy structure, promote the withdrawal from fossil fuels, adjust the industrial structure, and achieve low-carbon growth. South Korea: "New Deal for Korea 2.0" (2021). South Korea released "New Deal for Korea 2.0" in 2021, which includes a green transformation plan that invests in renewable energy, hydrogen energy, and other fields. This policy adjusts the industrial structure and aims to achieve low-carbon growth and promote the sustainable development of the economy. UK: Early ban on petrol cars (2020). In 2020, the UK government brought forward the ban on new petrol and diesel cars from 2040 to 2030. This accelerates the structural change in the transport sector and promotes the development of electric vehicles and related infrastructure.

4. Innovative incentive policy: providing policy incentives and financial support to promote the development of clean technologies and the widespread use of renewable energy and promoting technological innovation and industrial upgrading through incentive mechanisms to drive the green transformation of the economy. Australia: Technology Investment Roadmap (2020). In 2020, the Australian government formulated the Technology Investment Roadmap, which identifies key low-emission technology areas and provides funding and policy support to stimulate the development of clean technologies. This policy aims to reduce the cost of clean technologies and improve their market competitiveness. United States: Inflation Reduction Act (2022). In 2022, the United States passed the Inflation Reduction Act, which provides large-scale tax credits and subsidies for clean energy technologies. This policy encourages the research, development, and application of new energy technologies and accelerates the innovation and industrialization of green technologies.

5. International cooperation policy: addressing the global challenge of climate change and promoting international carbon emission reduction actions through participation in international agreements and cross-border cooperation. New Zealand and Switzerland: Carbon trading cooperation agreement (2020). In 2020, New Zealand and Switzerland signed a carbon trading cooperation agreement. The two countries cooperate through the international carbon market mechanism to achieve their respective emission reduction targets, promote cross-border carbon trading, prevent carbon leakage, and improve the flexibility and cost-effectiveness of emission reduction measures. Global: Adoption of the rules for the implementation of Article 6 of the Paris Agreement (2021). At the United Nations Climate Change Conference (COP26) in 2021, countries agreed on the rules for the implementation of Article 6 of the Paris Agreement. The adoption of these rules promotes cooperation and integration of the global carbon market and international cooperation for carbon emission reductions.

6. Contingency adjustment policy: Taking short-term measures in emergencies to deal with sudden problems. They are temporary and targeted to ensure market stability and energy supply. India: Emergency electricity supply measures (2021). In the face of power shortages in 2021, the Indian government urgently adjusted coal supply and power dispatch to ensure power supply during critical periods. By increasing coal production and optimizing power distribution, the pressure on energy supply has been eased. European Union: Measures to address the energy crisis (2022). In 2022, the European Union formulated an emergency response plan in the face of a shortage of natural gas supplies and soaring energy prices. Measures include setting an energy price cap, implementing demand-side management, and accelerating the deployment of renewable energy to stabilize energy markets and ensure the energy security of member states. China: Coal supply and price stabilization policy (2021). In response to the tight power supply and rising coal prices in 2021, the Chinese government took measures to expand coal production capacity, stabilize coal prices, and ensure power supply. Through policy intervention, market stability was maintained, and the energy needs of economic development were met.

The effectiveness of the six-category policy classification method was verified by categorizing the policies promulgated by multiple governments in the past five years that have had a macro impact on the carbon electricity market. These examples not only enrich the specific content of each category but also demonstrate the clarity and applicability of the classification criteria. This classification method can help policy analysts and researchers in China and around the world better understand the dynamic changes in global carbon electricity market policies and provide reference suggestions for future policy formulation and adjustment.

3.2.2. Coupling Analysis Algorithm Process

In order to reveal the coupling relationship between carbon electricity markets, a coupling analysis algorithm was established, and the process is shown in Figure 1.

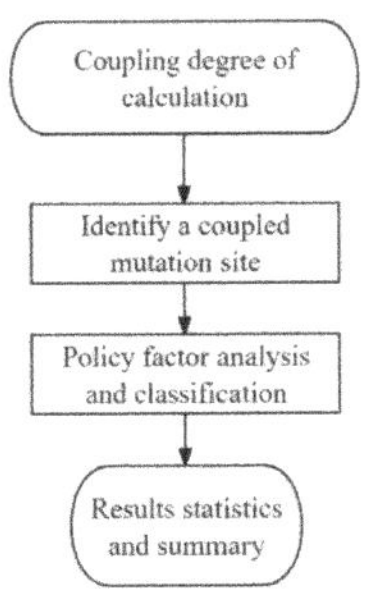

Figure 1. Coupling analysis algorithm process.

1. Calculate the coupling coordination degree D value. Substitute the preprocessed index data of the two systems into the coupling coordination degree model. Use statistical analysis software such as SPSS to obtain the coupling coordination degree D value of the long time series and plot a trend chart of its change over time.

2. Identify coupled mutation points. Take D = 0.4 as the baseline for judgment, analyze the D value trend chart, identify significant isolated peak points and clusters of peak points, and mark the time series numbers and corresponding dates of these peak points.

3. Perform policy factor analysis and classification. Using the GPT model, perform supervised learning and search on policy factors that may affect the coupling degree of the carbon electricity market within one week before the date of each wave peak, and mine and classify policy factors that lead to sudden increases in coupling degree according to the policy classification method proposed earlier.

4. Analyze and summarize statistics. Conduct a statistical analysis of the policy factors identified, summarize the key policy categories that promote increased coupling of the carbon and electricity markets, and summarize their common characteristics and impact mechanisms.

3.3. Data Preprocessing

This section describes the data sources related to this article and the specific methods of data preprocessing.

First, for the coupled objects studied in this paper, there are a total of two market participants, namely the carbon rights trading market and the spot electricity trading market. Therefore, the value of n in the algorithm is set to 2. In addition, each system in this paper has 4 evaluation indicators, namely, daily transaction price, daily transaction volume, daily transaction price volatility, and daily transaction volume volatility. Therefore, the value of m in the algorithm is set to 4. In this paper, the daily transaction price of the EU electricity market is obtained from Energy-Charts. The data on this website are based on the official auction results of electricity markets in various countries and are updated regularly, ensuring the accuracy and timeliness of the data, so they are used in academic research and market analysis.

3.3.1. Electricity Market Data

The electricity market data in this paper focus on the day-ahead market, using the average daily transaction price as the market transaction price. Due to the lack of an authoritative and uniform formula for calculating the size of the electricity transaction and the transaction price, this paper takes the load of each time period as the transaction size. In addition, given that the EU electricity market is conducted on a regional basis, it is more difficult to obtain a uniform price that can represent the entire EU carbon electricity market. Therefore, the transaction data were processed to calculate the weighted average price and transaction size across the EU.

First, the turnover size of the electricity market is calculated. The load of the electricity market consists of four components: cross-border electricity trading, nuclear, non-renewable, and renewable.

The average price of electricity is calculated.

For the k-th day, the average price $\overline{P}_k$ for all regions can be calculated by the following formula:

$$\overline{P}_k = \frac{\sum_{m=1}^{M} P_{km}}{M}$$

where P_{km} is the price of electricity in region m on day k and M is the number of regions involved in the calculation.

In order to more accurately reflect the overall EU electricity market price level, a weighted average price W_k is used and calculated as follows:

$$W_k = \frac{\sum_{m=1}^{N} (\overline{P}_k \times LOAD_k)}{TOTAL_k}$$

Volatility of day k transaction price V_{pk}:

Transaction price volatility and transaction size volatility are calculated based on the daily weighted average price and total load:

$$V_{pk} = \frac{W_k - W_{k-1}}{W_k}$$

Here, $W_k - W_{k-1}$ denotes the weighted average price difference between day k and day $k-1$.

Volatility of day k transaction size V_{lk}:

$$V_{lk} = \frac{LOAD_k - LOAD_{k-1}}{LOAD_k}$$

Through the above data preprocessing, the daily weighted average transaction price, the daily total load, and their respective volatilities of the electricity spot trading market are obtained. These four evaluation indicators will be used as inputs to the first system for coupling analysis. The processed data for the four evaluation indicators are shown in Figure 2.

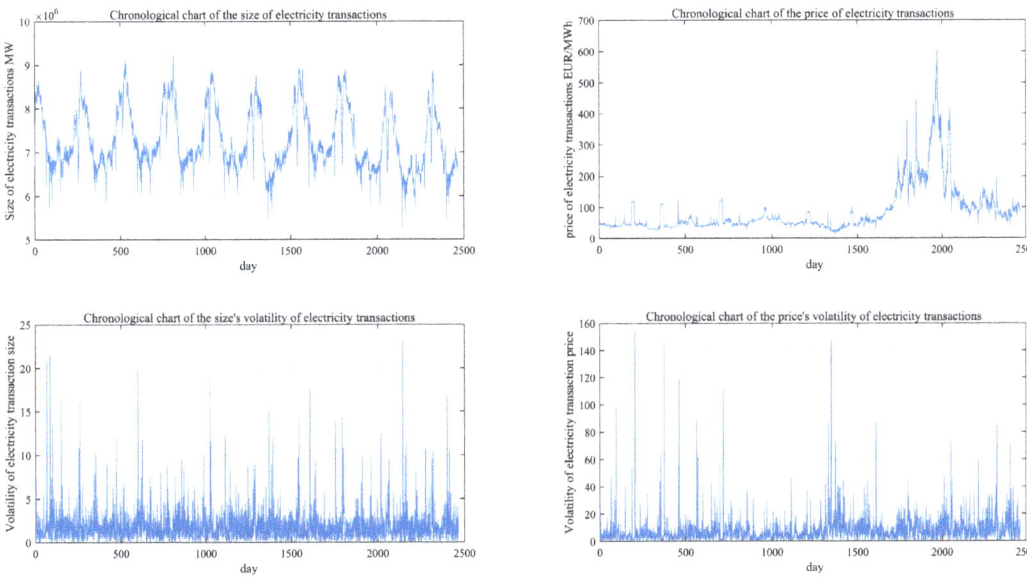

Figure 2. Electricity market timing data.

3.3.2. Carbon Market Data

The data for the carbon emissions trading market come from the official website of the Intercontinental Exchange (ICE). As a world-renowned provider of financial market infrastructure and trading platforms, ICE's data are provided in real time and are accurate, with historical prices and trading data covering a rich time span, supporting time series data analysis. In addition, its market data and trading rules are transparent and suitable for this study. From ICE, you can obtain the daily closing price and trading volume of the carbon emissions trading market. The closing price is used as the clearing price, and the trading volume is used as the transaction size to calculate the price volatility and trading size volatility.

Volatility of carbon rights trading price V_{cpk} on day k:

$$V_{cpk} = \frac{W_{Ck} - W_{Ck-1}}{W_{Ck}}$$

where W_{Ck} is the closing price of carbon emission rights on the kth day.

Day k carbon rights trading size in terms of volatility V_{clk} is as follows:

$$V_{clk} = \frac{LOAD_{ck} - LOAD_{ck-1}}{LOAD_{ck}}$$

where $LOAD_{ck}$ is the trading volume of carbon emission rights on the k-th day.

After data preprocessing, the daily closing price, daily trading volume, and their respective volatilities of the carbon emission trading market were obtained. These four evaluation indicators will be used as the input of the second system for coupling analysis. The time series chart of the four indicators of the carbon market is shown in Figure 3.

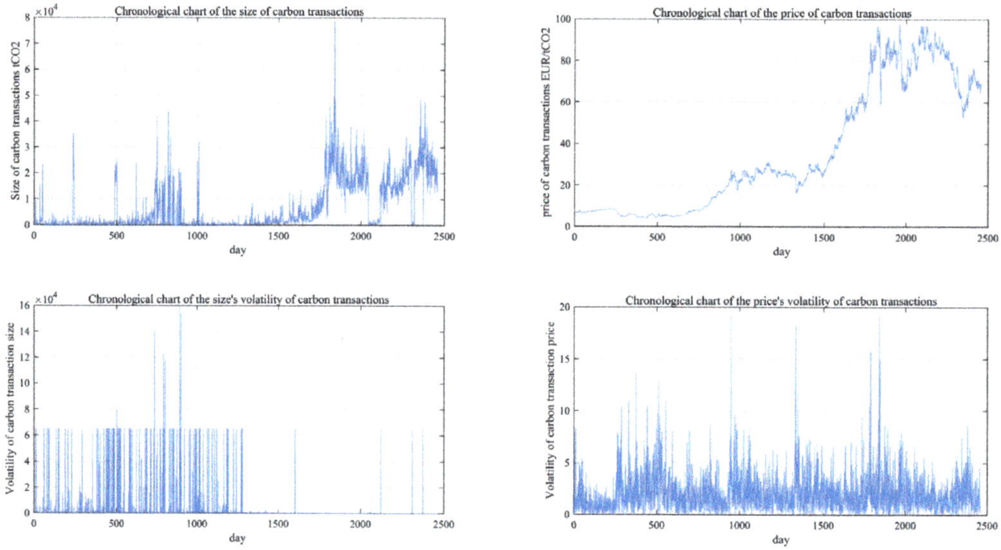

Figure 3. Carbon market timing data.

3.4. Results

The two systems obtained from data preprocessing and their respective four indicators were substituted into the previously mentioned coupling analysis algorithm. First, SPSSAU (Version 24.0) software was used to process and analyze the data, and the change curve of the coupling coordination degree D value of the long time series was obtained, as shown in Figure 4.

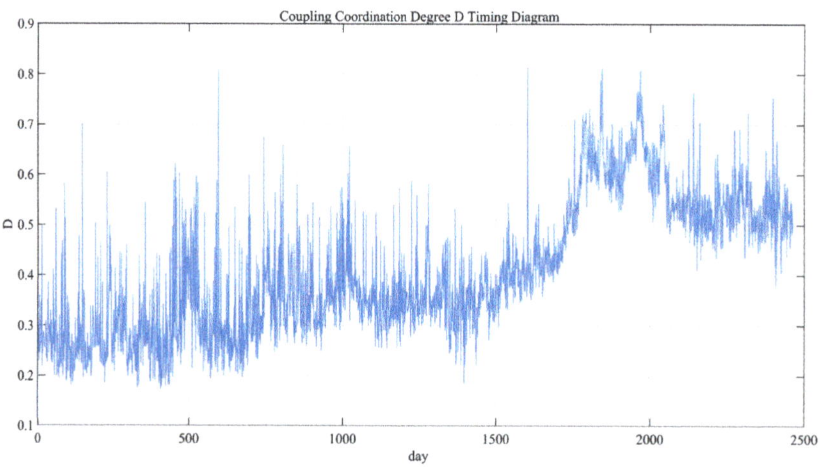

Figure 4. Coupling coordination degree D timing diagram.

Subsequently, the D value curve was analyzed using D = 0.6 as the baseline for judgment, and it was found that there were multiple isolated peaks and a cluster of peaks. The time series positions of these peaks were marked, and the specific dates corresponding to the peaks were determined.

Then, using the GPT large language model, supervised learning and search were performed on policy information within one week before and after the date of each wave peak point, and the relevant policies were classified. The dates of the wave peak points and the corresponding policy factor analysis are shown in Table 3.

Table 3. The dates of the wave peak points and the corresponding policy factor analysis.

Serial Number	Date	$\overline{P}_k$	W_k	$\overline{P}_{Ck}$	W_{Ck}	D	Brief Content of the Policy
1	31 July 2015	↑	↓	↑	↑	0.7	The Market Stabilization Reserve (MSR) was adopted to remove some carbon allowances and regulate the balance between market supply and demand.
2	24 November 2015	↓	↓	↑	↓	0.65	Prepared for the Paris Agreement, proposed reforms to strengthen the carbon market, and anticipated and managed market changes.
3	11 October 2016	↓	↓	↑	↑	0.64	The proposed reform of the EU ETS aims to address the problems of market oversupply and low carbon prices.
4	1 May 2017	↑	↑	↑	↑	0.82	Published the report "Carbon Pricing Status and Trends 2017" to analyze the implementation of carbon pricing mechanisms around the world.
5	19 September 2017	↑	↓	↑	↓	0.67	Published the 2017 Global Carbon Pricing Overview report, which pointed out newly implemented carbon pricing mechanisms.
6	24 November 2017	↑	↓	↑	↓	0.68	An agreement was reached on reforming the EU ETS, with important adjustments to the market mechanism.
7	13 February 2018	↑	↑	↑	↓	0.64	Approved the EU ETS reform plan to enhance market flexibility and adaptability.
8	18 December 2018	↓	↓	↓	↓	0.65	A long-term strategy for EU climate and energy policy was published, emphasizing the synergies of the carbon market and the need for international cooperation.
9	27 December 2018	↑	↓	↑	↓	0.69	Released a draft climate law that sets a target of reducing emissions by at least 55% by 2030 and improved the coverage of the emissions trading system.
10	14 October 2019	↑	↑	↑	↑	0.67	Initial discussions on the European Green Deal to promote the transition to a green economy and climate goals.
11	5 April 2021	↑	↑	↑	↑	0.82	Proposed follow-up reforms to the EU ETS to expand the scope of emissions trading.
12	6 April 2021	↑	↑	↓	↓	0.76	The EU Climate Law was approved, establishing a legal framework for achieving climate neutrality by 2050.
13	1 November 2021	↑	↑	↑	↑	0.66	Signing of the Global Carbon Market Cooperation Statement to discuss the need for carbon market cooperation.
14	2 November 2021	↑	↓	↓	↑	0.73	Initiated capacity-building projects in the carbon market, provided technical assistance and financial support, and helped developing countries participate in the international carbon market.
15	1 April 2022	↓	↑	↓	↑	0.66	Proposals for reform of the carbon market were released, emphasizing market stability and transparency.
16	1 May 2022	↑	↑	↑	↑	0.65	Published annual environmental reports to assess the operation and future prospects of the carbon market.
17	5 May 2022	↓	↓	↓	↑	0.60	The *REPowerEU* initiative was launched to reduce dependence on Russian energy and develop renewable energy sources.
18	20 September 2022	↓	↑	↑	↓	0.60	Proposed urgent energy measures to deal with the energy crisis.
19	1 Dember 2022	↑	↓	↓	↑	0.62	The latest *EU ETS* report was released, highlighting future carbon emission targets and their market impact.
20	3 January 2023	↑	↓	↓	↓	0.61	Published a climate policy work plan for 2023 and committed to future emission reduction measures.
21	13 March 2023	↑	↓	↓	↓	0.63	Discussed the link between green bonds and the carbon market to encourage the development of low-carbon technologies.
22	1 May 2023	↑	↑	↑	↑	0.78	A report on the future development strategy of the carbon market was released, emphasizing the goal of achieving emission neutrality before 2030.
23	18 May 2023	↑	↓	↑	↑	0.65	Discussed enhancing the interoperability of cross-border carbon transactions and promoting market integration.
24	7 August 2023	↑	↓	↑	↑	0.62	Published a carbon market integration report and made recommendations for optimizing the carbon pricing mechanism.
25	23 October 2023	↓	↓	↓	↑	0.63	Encouraged the development of low-carbon technologies through programs that support renewable energy technologies.
26	7 November 2023	↑	↓	↓	↓	0.62	A draft policy for the standardization of cross-border carbon trading was launched to promote market integration.
27	28 November 2023	↑	↑	↑	↓	0.61	Extended emergency energy measures to deal with the impact of the Russia–Ukraine conflict.
28	4 Dember 2023	↑	↑	↓	↓	0.60	Discussed a carbon-neutral policy framework and increased investment in green infrastructure.

Table 3. *Cont.*

Serial Number	Date	$\overline{P}_k$	W_k	$\overline{P}_{Ck}$	W_{Ck}	D	Brief Content of the Policy
29	27 Dember 2023	↑	↓	↓	↑	0.65	Published annual environmental and climate change reports, assessing the performance of the carbon market and recommendations for reform.
30	2 January 2024	↑	↓	↓	↑	0.61	Released the 2024 Climate Policy Framework, which sets out the priorities for carbon market reform.
31	28 March 2024	↓	↓	↑	↓	0.65	Discussed future emission reduction targets and made recommendations to enhance the integration of international carbon markets.
32	1 May 2024	↓	↑	↓	↑	0.78	A report on the future development strategy of the carbon market was released, emphasizing the goal of achieving emission neutrality before 2030.
33	9 May 2024	↑	↑	↑	↓	0.62	Discussed a green bond policy framework to support renewable energy projects.
34	29 May 2024	↓	↑	↓	↑	0.64	Published annual environmental and climate change reports and assessed the operation of the carbon market and reform proposals.

Furthermore, through in-depth analysis, policy factors that lead to the occurrence of serial wave peaks were identified and these factors were classified and organized. Finally, a statistical analysis of the identified policy factors was performed to draw more in-depth conclusions, as shown in Figure 5.

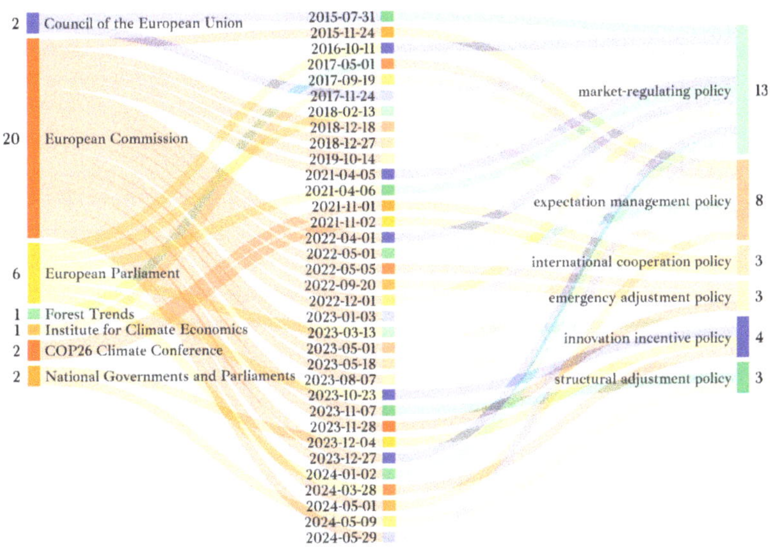

Figure 5. A statistical analysis of the identified policy factors.

The spike at the peak represents a sudden increase in the coupling degree of the carbon electricity market, i.e., the degree of coupling of the carbon electricity market has been significantly improved. Event analysis, case studies, and statistical data were used to identify the policy factors that caused the spike. The key policy factors that can promote the increase in the coupling degree of the carbon electricity market were summarized. These successful policy experiences are of great significance for the Chinese government. China can formulate more effective policy measures based on these policy factors and, combined with the characteristics of its own market, further promote the coupling development of the carbon electricity market and promote the sustainable development of a low-carbon economy.

4. Analogical Analysis of the Chinese Market

Among the relevant electricity market policies, market-regulating policies are the most numerous, issued by the European Council, the European Parliament, the European Commission, and national governments and parliaments. Moreover, these policies were issued earlier and have a longer span. Market-regulating policies have been issued since 2015, and there will be follow-up supplements until July 2024. Next are expectation management policies, which are issued by energy analysis organizations such as the Institute for Energy Economics Research. At the same time, these policies have a time span comparable to market-regulating policies. The other four types of policies are significantly different from the first two in terms of quantity and time span. It can be analyzed that market-regulating policies and market-planning policies play a major role in maintaining the coupling of the carbon and electricity markets. To continue maintaining a good coupling of the carbon and electricity markets, it is essential to continue to promote the release of these two types of policies.

Although China has actively participated in international cooperation activities on green energy, played an important role in important conferences such as COP26, and participated in many international cooperation policies, the starting time for China to issue market regulation policies and market planning policies was much later than that of the EU. In January 2024, the State Council promulgated the "Interim Regulations on the Administration of Carbon Emissions Trading", which came into effect on May 1. This is the first special law in the field of climate change in China. It can be seen that before this, China's market-regulating and market-planning policies for the carbon market were basically lacking, and these are the most important policies for coupling the carbon and electricity markets.

Therefore, improving market-regulating and market-planning policies is currently the most important task in China in terms of policies to promote the construction of carbon and electricity coupling. With sufficient and effective policy adjustments, China's construction of carbon and electricity market coupling is expected to develop further.

5. Conclusions

This paper introduces a coupling coordination model and emphasizes that power generation effectively links carbon prices and electricity prices. By implementing reasonable and sustainable policies, we can promote the coupling of the carbon market and the electricity market. By analyzing various data indicators obtained from the electricity and carbon markets, we can obtain relative results of the degree of coupling between the carbon and electricity markets. Furthermore, the GPT macro model is used innovatively to analyze the role of policies in the carbon and electricity markets by introducing the type of relationship between the mutation points of the analysis results and the corresponding policies on the basis of a preliminary classification of policies. The analysis found that market regulation policies and expectation management policies have the greatest impact on the coupling degree of the carbon and electricity markets. The introduction of favorable policies of these kinds is more likely to promote the coupling construction of the carbon and electricity markets, thereby facilitating the steady and joint development of the carbon and electricity markets, improving the construction of the carbon rights market, reducing greenhouse gas emissions, and creating a sustainable future for humanity. The impact of secondary policies such as international cooperation policies and structural adjustment policies is relatively insignificant.

However, at the same time, this paper does not further analyze the underlying reasons for the impact of carbon market price fluctuations on its trading volume and the impact on the electricity market price. This could be a new direction for follow-up research. But overall, this paper's analysis of the factors influencing the degree of coupling of the carbon and electricity markets is relatively complete.

Author Contributions: Conceptualization, S.X.; methodology, S.X. and X.T.; software, Y.L. and X.T.; validation, S.X. and Y.L.; formal analysis, S.X. and Y.L.; investigation, Y.L.; resources, Y.L.; data curation, Y.L. and S.X.; writing—original draft preparation, S.N., Y.L. and X.T.; writing—review and editing, S.X. and P.W.; visualization, S.X. and Y.L.; supervision, P.W.; project administration, S.X. and P.W.; funding acquisition, Y.L., S.X. and P.W. All authors have read and agreed to the published version of the manuscript.

Funding: This work was partially supported by the Innovation and Entrepreneurship Training Program for College Students of North China Electric Power University (202301019).

Institutional Review Board Statement: Not applicable.

Informed Consent Statement: Not applicable.

Data Availability Statement: The original contributions presented in the study are included in the article, further inquiries can be directed to the corresponding author.

Conflicts of Interest: All authors declare that the research was conducted in the absence of any commercial or financial relationships that could be construed as a potential conflict of interest.

References

1. Cui, J.; Song, F.; Jiang, Z. Efficiency vs. equity as China's national carbon market meets provincial electricity markets. *China Econ. Rev.* **2023**, *78*, 101915. [CrossRef]
2. Liu, X.; Jin, Z. An analysis of the interactions between electricity, fossil fuel, and carbon market prices in Guangdong, China. *Energy Sustain. Dev.* **2020**, *55*, 82–94. [CrossRef]
3. Cheng, Y.; Chung, M.; Tsang, K. Electricity Market Reforms for Energy Transition: Lessons from China. *Energies* **2023**, *16*, 905. [CrossRef]
4. Chi, Y.; Guan, Z.; Zhao, Y. The impact of allocation methods on carbon emission trading under electricity marketization reform in China: A system dynamics analysis. *Energy* **2022**, *259*, 125034. [CrossRef]
5. Guo, H.; Cheng, A.; Zhang, X. Power market reform in China: Motivations, progress, and recommendations. *Energy Policy* **2020**, *145*, 111717. [CrossRef]
6. Cao, J.; Zhang, L.; Xu, Y. When carbon emission trading meets a regulated industry: Evidence from the electricity sector of China. *J. Public Econ.* **2021**, *200*, 104470. [CrossRef]
7. Li, J.; Wang, Y.; Xu, S. China's flexibility challenge in achieving carbon neutrality by 2060. *Renew. Sustain. Energy Rev.* **2022**, *158*, 112112. [CrossRef]
8. Lyu, J.; Sun, Y.; Liu, Y. Price volatility in the carbon market in China. *J. Clean. Prod.* **2020**, *255*, 120171. [CrossRef]
9. Zachmann, G.; Grubb, M.; Newbery, D. *Unity in Power, Power in Unity: Why the EU Needs More Integrated Electricity Markets*; Bruegel Policy Brief No. 03/2024; Bruegel: Brussels, Belgium, 2024.
10. Fleschutz, M.; Fröhlingsdorf, A.; Mattig, B. The effect of price-based demand response on carbon emissions in European electricity markets: The importance of adequate carbon prices. *Appl. Energy* **2021**, *295*, 117040. [CrossRef]
11. Wang, Y.; Chen, M.; Wang, L. Carbon-oriented operational planning in coupled electricity and emission trading markets. *IEEE Trans. Power Syst.* **2020**, *35*, 3145–3157. [CrossRef]
12. Lu, Y.; Liu, W.; Chai, L. Coupling mechanism and synergic development of carbon market and electricity market in the region of Beijing–Tianjin–Hebei. *Energies* **2023**, *16*, 1726. [CrossRef]
13. Yuan, J.; Zhang, H.; Li, R. The impact of electricity-carbon market coupling on system marginal clearing price and power supply cost. *Environ. Sci. Pollut. Res.* **2023**, *30*, 84725–84741. [CrossRef] [PubMed]
14. Potrč, S.; Savić, M.; Mihajlović, B. Sustainable renewable energy supply networks optimization: The gradual transition to a renewable energy system within the European Union by 2050. *Renew. Sustain. Energy Rev.* **2021**, *146*, 111186. [CrossRef]
15. Jamasb, T.; Pollitt, M. Electricity market reform in the European Union: Review of progress toward liberalization and integration. *Energy J.* **2005**, *26*, 11–41. [CrossRef]
16. Ciferri, D.; D'Errico, M.C.; Polinori, P. Integration and convergence in European electricity markets. *Econ. Politica* **2020**, *37*, 463–492. [CrossRef]
17. Newbery, D.; Griffin, J.; Keats, P. Market design for a high-renewables European electricity system. *Renew. Sustain. Energy Rev.* **2018**, *91*, 695–707. [CrossRef]
18. Li, Y.; Liu, X.; Zhang, B. How do the electricity market and carbon market interact and achieve integrated development? A bibliometric-based review. *Energy* **2023**, *265*, 126308.
19. Boutabba, M.A.; Lardic, S. EU emissions trading scheme, competitiveness, and carbon leakage: New evidence from cement and steel industries. *Ann. Oper. Res.* **2017**, *255*, 47–61. [CrossRef]
20. Richstein, J.C.; Chappin, É.J.L.; de Vries, L.J. The market (in-) stability reserve for EU carbon emission trading: Why it might fail and how to improve it. *Util. Policy* **2015**, *35*, 1–18. [CrossRef]

21. Gong, X.; Wang, Y.; Zhang, T. Analyzing spillover effects between carbon and fossil energy markets from a time-varying perspective. *Appl. Energy* **2021**, *285*, 116384. [CrossRef]
22. Bayer, P.; Aklin, M. The European Union emissions trading system reduced CO2 emissions despite low prices. *Proc. Natl. Acad. Sci. USA* **2020**, *117*, 8804–8812. [CrossRef] [PubMed]
23. Braungardt, S.; Bei der Wieden, M.; Kranzl, L. EU emissions trading in the buildings sector: An ex-ante assessment. *Clim. Policy* **2024**, 1–15. [CrossRef]
24. Li, Z.P.; Liu, J.; Zhang, L. Scenario simulation of the EU carbon price and its enlightenment to China. *Sci. Total Environ.* **2020**, *723*, 137982. [CrossRef] [PubMed]
25. Cong, X. Expression and Mathematical Property of Coupling Model, and Its Misuse in Geographical Science. *Econ. Geogr.* **2019**, *39*, 18–25.
26. Moslehi, S.; Reddy, T.A. Sustainable development and engineering practices: Bridging the gap between strategic goals and local implementation. *Sustain. Cities Soc.* **2016**, *26*, 227–239.
27. Wang, M.; Zhang, Q.; Wang, X. Impact of market regulation on economic and environmental performance: A game model of endogenous green technological innovation. *J. Clean. Prod.* **2020**, *277*, 123969. [CrossRef]
28. Hartley, K.; van Santen, R.; Kirchherr, J. Policies for transitioning towards a circular economy: Expectations from the European Union (EU). *Resour. Conserv. Recycl.* **2020**, *155*, 104634. [CrossRef]
29. Wigger, A. The new EU industrial policy: *Authoritarian neoliberal* structural adjustment and the case for alternatives. In *Authoritarian Neoliberalism*; Routledge: London, UK, 2020; pp. 121–137.
30. Gao, X.; Zhang, W. The Role of Innovation Incentive Policies on the Innovation Performance of Knowledge Workers in SOEs. *Sustainability* **2023**, *15*, 2424. [CrossRef]
31. Milner, H.V. *Interests, Institutions, and Information: Domestic Politics and International Relations*; Princeton University Press: Princeton, NJ, USA, 2020.
32. Tang, H.; Zhang, J. An agile and lightweight social computing approach to emergency management. *IEEE Trans. Syst. Man Cybern. Syst.* **2016**, *46*, 1075–1087. [CrossRef]

economies

MDPI

Article

The Importance of Bitcoin and Commodities as Investment Diversifiers in OPEC and Non-OPEC Countries

Angham Ben Brayek *, Hanen Ben Ameur and Farea Mohammed Alharbi

Department of Economic and Finance, Taif University, Taif 21974, Saudi Arabia; hmamer@tu.edu.sa (H.B.A.); fharbi@tu.edu.sa (F.M.A.)
* Correspondence: ambrayek@tu.edu.sa

Abstract: The study aims to critically assess the safe-haven properties of Bitcoin and a diverse set of commodities in mitigating stock market risks during periods of extreme financial turbulence. Specifically, this research seeks to evaluate the effectiveness of these assets as hedging tools or diversifiers in the portfolios of both OPEC and non-OPEC countries, focusing on their behavior during the COVID-19 pandemic. We employ a wavelet coherence approach to analyze the dynamic relationships between the variables. Portfolio optimization is conducted using CVaR to assess the effectiveness of these assets as safe havens, hedges, or diversification tools in mitigating financial risks during periods of heightened market volatility. The diversification benefits of commodities and Bitcoin in OPEC and non-OPEC stock portfolios decrease over time as their co-movement with stock markets increases. During the COVID-19 period, BTC did not act as a safe haven. However, gold served as a hedge for non-OPEC countries. Using CVaR, we found that BTC provides stronger diversification benefits than commodities, followed by gold. We examine the safe-haven role of Bitcoin and various commodities, specifically within the context of both OPEC and non-OPEC countries. Our study offers a more comprehensive analysis of how BTC and commodities function as portfolio assets during financial stress, providing valuable insights for investors and policymakers.

Keywords: Bitcoin; safe haven; OPEC; wavelet; CVaR

1. Introduction

The COVID-19 pandemic has undeniably introduced unprecedented volatility in global financial markets, compelling investors to explore alternative assets as safe havens during economic turbulence. Bitcoin (BTC), often regarded as a digital hedge against traditional market volatility, has garnered significant attention in this context. Several academic studies (e.g., Corbet et al. 2020; Conlon and McGee 2020; Bouri et al. 2020; Agosto and Cafferata 2020; Huber and Sornette 2022; Náñez Alonso et al. 2024) have investigated BTC's behavior under financial duress, particularly during the COVID-19 pandemic, framing it as a potential refuge for investors.

Despite this heightened interest, a critical gap persists in empirical research regarding the optimization of portfolios that include BTC alongside various commodities and traditional stock markets during global crises. The idiosyncratic nature of the COVID-19 pandemic, in contrast to the 2008 Global Financial Crisis (GFC), further amplifies the importance of addressing this gap. Harvey (2020) notes that the COVID-19 crisis has resulted in what he terms the "Great Compression", a phenomenon distinct from the GFC's impact on capital markets. Moreover, Zhang et al. (2020) emphasize that the pandemic's unprecedented stock market volatility requires an updated framework for asset allocation strategies, particularly concerning alternative assets (Náñez Alonso et al. 2024) such as BTC and commodities.

While the allure of BTC as a hedge or safe haven during market stress has been widely speculated, the empirical evidence supporting this narrative is still underdeveloped. Many existing studies tend to generalize BTC's safe-haven role without adequately considering the distinct economic environments and regulatory frameworks of different regions. This is particularly evident in OPEC countries, where BTC markets remain underdeveloped or informal. In countries such as Saudi Arabia and Kuwait, the lack of formalized cryptocurrency markets raises doubts about BTC's viability as an investment tool in these economies. For instance, while BTC is gaining traction as a speculative asset globally, its role as a reliable hedging tool in these oil-dependent economies is questionable. The lack of institutional infrastructure to facilitate secure trading, combined with regulatory ambiguities, limits its accessibility and integration into traditional investment portfolios. Thus, overlooking the role of BTC in portfolio construction for OPEC nations represents a significant blind spot in the existing literature. As financial development and interest in BTC grow within these regions, understanding how BTC performs as a portfolio asset in both OPEC and non-OPEC countries becomes increasingly relevant for investors and policymakers.

This study, therefore, attempts to fill this void by examining the safe-haven characteristics of BTC and a wide range of commodities, including agricultural products, industrial metals, energy, and precious metals.

The goal is to determine whether these assets can mitigate stock market risks during extreme market conditions, particularly in the context of OPEC and non-OPEC countries. Thus, first, we examine the impact of commodities and Bitcoin (BTC) on stock markets, as market participants often believe there is a strong correlation between commodities (or BTC) and stock markets. In the second part, we assess whether commodities or BTC can help diversify OPEC and NON-OPEC stock portfolios by evaluating their potential for risk reduction and determining whether commodities or BTC function as a diversifier, hedge, or safe-haven assets. Specifically, an asset is classified as a diversifier if it is positively (but not perfectly) correlated with another asset or portfolio on average. An asset is considered a hedge if it is uncorrelated or negatively correlated with another asset or portfolio on average, with a strict hedge being strictly negatively correlated on average. An asset is referred to as a safe haven if it is uncorrelated or negatively correlated with another asset or portfolio during periods of market stress or turmoil (Baur and Lucey 2010). By focusing on the three largest oil-exporting countries with significant BTC usage, this research provides a nuanced perspective on how commodities and BTC interact within the portfolios of economies heavily reliant on oil exports. Additionally, we examine the relation between commodities and BTC in the stock market in OPEC and non-OPEC countries to provide a clear analysis of investors' behavior in a turmoil period. OPEC countries are heavily reliant on oil exports, making their economies and stock markets more sensitive to fluctuations in oil prices (Banerjee et al. 2023; Khan et al. 2023). Non-OPEC countries, on the other hand, often have more diversified economies, which may result in different responses to shocks in commodity markets (Ziadat and Maghyereh 2024).

Crucially, the study adopts a sophisticated methodological framework, utilizing the wavelet approach to capture the dynamic dependencies between financial markets, BTC, and commodities. This allows for a more granular understanding of how these assets move in tandem or diverge under varying market conditions. Additionally, the use of Conditional Value at Risk (CVaR) for portfolio optimization is a particularly relevant choice in this context, as it is designed to capture extreme downside risks, which are characteristic of turbulent periods like the COVID-19 pandemic. CVaR's ability to estimate expected losses makes it an invaluable tool for risk-averse investors seeking to minimize exposure to extreme market shocks.

The findings of this research will undoubtedly hold significant value for a wide range of stakeholders, including portfolio managers, institutional investors, and regulatory authorities. For portfolio managers and investors, the insights gained will offer a clearer understanding of how to construct resilient portfolios that incorporate BTC and commodities in a risk-optimized manner. For policymakers, especially in OPEC countries, this study can explain how emerging assets like BTC may play a role in stabilizing financial systems during future crises.

This research contributes to the literature in several unique ways: First, it examines the intersection of Bitcoin (BTC), commodities, and stock markets within the context of global economic instability, a timely and underexplored area. Second, it provides a comparative analysis of BTC, commodities, and stock market behaviors between OPEC and non-OPEC countries, offering insights into regional heterogeneity. Third, the study employs a wavelet approach to capture dynamic dependencies across markets, providing a nuanced understanding of how these assets co-move or diverge under varying conditions. Fourth, by incorporating Conditional Value at Risk (CVaR) for portfolio optimization, the research addresses extreme downside risks, particularly relevant during turbulent periods such as the COVID-19 pandemic. CVaR's focus on estimating expected losses offers significant value for risk-averse investors.

The rest of the paper is structured as follows: Section 2 reviews the relevant literature, Section 3 outlines the methodology, Section 4 presents the results, and the final section provides a comprehensive discussion of the findings.

2. Literature Review

After the 2008 GFC, following the European debt crisis, and, notably, with the emergence of the COVID-19 pandemic, investors and policymakers flew around looking for any safe-haven asset to keep in their reserves. Nicola et al. (2020) argued that COVID-19 will cause a relative economic recession and financial crisis. This might force the investors to continuously manage their portfolios. Accordingly, the safe haven feature of several assets has been the main concern for policymakers and investors. Among these assets, BTC and commodities have been paid considerable attention.

Since it emerged as a solution to the fragile global financial system, BTC has been considered as a leading digital currency and an investment destination, offering investors a novel investment opportunity (Dyhrberg 2016; Bouri et al. 2020). During its first year of creation, BTC was valued at $0 in 2009 and increased to around $1000 at the onset of 2014. In December 2017, the BTC price increased considerably and reached $20,000. As a result, CME Group and the CBOE established futures contracts with BTC as a fundamental asset, making it more legitimized.

This has developed BTC's position to join commodities in futures markets, and it pushed its role to be at the center of the financial world. With the spread of COVID-19, BTC's price rose to over $27,000 at the end of 2020. BTC's role as an investment shelter during stress periods, such as the current health crisis, has been paid considerable attention in academic research. Some studies like (Corbet et al. 2020; Bouri et al. 2020) suggest that BTC can protect investors' portfolios through diversification gains. In the same context, commodities have been considered as significant components of investment portfolios for participants and investors following the susceptibility of stock markets to reduce risk and to make optimal investment choices (Salisu et al. 2020). Different commodities are considered more stable assets, their values reflect pricing in areas, and they provide protection against unexpected increasing prices and recession.

Given its features, both BTC and commodities have attracted investors and academic research to examine its role as a safe haven, especially during turmoil periods. When in—for any reason—times of serious financial and economic disruption, many investors look for alternative instruments (e.g., commodities or BTC) as safe-haven assets. Baur and Lucey (2010) and Shahzad et al. (2020) notice an asset as a safe haven if it is negatively correlated or uncorrelated with another asset during the crisis periods. In this context, studies including Shahzad et al. (2020), Conlon and McGee (2020), Corbet et al. (2020) and Yarovaya et al. (2021) confirm that gold can have the role of a safe-haven asset during periods of crisis. Dutta et al. (2020) and Pho et al. (2021) examine whether gold or BTC is a better portfolio diversifier. Dutta et al. (2020) show that the introduction of both gold and oil can minimize the portfolio risk during the COVID-19 outbreak more than the investment in BTC markets. Similarly, Pho et al. (2021) found that, while the return increases more with BTC than gold, BTC increases the risk more than gold; this indicates that, for risk-averse investors, gold is a better portfolio diversifier than BTC.

However, BTC might be a better alternative for risk-seeking investors. Conlon and McGee (2020) and Corbet et al. (2020), in relation to gold and cryptocurrencies, find consistent evidence that BTC does not offer hedging nor safe-haven properties during the COVID-19 pandemic. Using vine copula to examine the dependence among energy commodities, gold, and BTC returns, Syuhada et al. (2021) find that gold can substantially ameliorate the portfolio, including gold and energy commodities, which indicates the gold safe-haven feature. However, they find an inconsistent role for BTC as a safe haven. However, the study of Mnif et al. (2020) found that BTC became more efficient during the recent pandemic.

Another strand of literature examined the conditional dependencies among commodities and BTC. Bouri et al. (2020) apply the wavelet coherence approach and assess diversification with wavelet VaR to study the dependence of BTC, gold, commodities, and the USA and Chinese stock markets during the period between 2010 and 2018. They reveal that BTC is the least dependent at various time scales, while commodities are the most dependent. This result indicates that BTC dominates both gold and commodities in terms of diversification benefits. Albulescu et al. (2020) find an asymmetric dependence structure between metal, energy, and agriculture price returns during the COVID-19 outbreak. Moreover, the dependence between energy with both metals and agriculture commodities markets at lower tails is higher. Mensi et al. (2020) use the spillover index and wavelet coherence approaches to analyze the co-movements and correlation between precious metals and energy futures markets from 1999 to 2019. They found that dynamic spillovers among markets are intensified during periods of crisis. Similarly, Al-Yahyaee et al. (2019) evaluate the dependence structure among four precious metals using a copula quantile-on-quantile technique. They show that the dependence among markets varies across time and quantiles. Junttila et al. (2018) investigate the correlations between stock and gold and oil futures markets. They find that oil and gold offer both diversification benefits and negative correlations during times of economic turmoil.

Wu (2021) shows that commodities such as crude oil and agriculture commodities behave quite differently during the turmoil periods (e.g., GFC). Therefore, their role as safe-haven assets is worth further exploration, especially with the current COVID-19 pandemic.

Since COVID-19 has brought the global economy into a new crisis period, investor sentiment and market conditions have undergone tremendous changes (Ashraf 2020; Conlon and McGee 2020). Investors' reactions and anticipations differ following the different trends. Therefore, the market dynamics show important variations during this new pandemic that affect all the financial and commodity markets worldwide. Albulescu et al. (2020) discussed that this epidemic leads to a drop in the prices and returns of assets; Mzoughi et al. (2020) demonstrate that the COVID-19 has a stronger impact on the stock market. Goodell (2020) refers to past similar events and points out that COVID-19 could bring a direct global destructive impact, raising the risk of spillovers among different assets. McKee and Stuckler (2020) proposed that there could be either one wave or a series of waves of the pandemic for some countries, which would bring serious financial and economic risks.

Accordingly, several assets show substantial losses at the beginning of 2020 and continue at the same movement along the period of crisis. A spectacular fall in oil price after failed negotiations between Russia and OPEC has worsened the scent further. Two months after the onset of the COVID-19 epidemic in Wuhan city, the per barrel price of the Brent crude slipped to $22.58 in March 2020. At the same time, the US West Texas Intermediate (WTI) price reached less than $20 per barrel. These prices are the lowest in the last decade. Such a drop in oil prices in the midst of the COVID-19 outbreak has induced higher probabilities of tail-risks in the oil-derived assets. Thereafter, the volatility of oil markets has substantially increased, and this caused extreme losses to investments in these markets. The large fluctuations in energy will notably affect the economic growth of OPEC and non-OPEC countries, thus affecting the price of precious metals and other commodities including agricultural products. OPEC countries are heavily reliant on oil exports, making their economies and stock markets more sensitive to fluctuations in oil prices (Banerjee et al. 2023; Khan et al. 2023). Non-OPEC countries, on the other hand, often have more diversified economies, which may result in different responses to shocks in commodity markets (Ziadat and Maghyereh 2024).

Given that this crisis contains several problems, it is of interest to analyze the role of different assets during this period. However, empirical analysis about the optimal portfolio diversification among various types of commodities and BTC in the stock market portfolio is still scarce. This study, therefore, aims to analyze the safe haven, hedge, or diversification property of BTC and different types of commodities in the stock market portfolio in OPEC and non-OPEC countries to identify alternative ways to reduce the risks of exposure to the current shocks and orientate the investment decisions.

To fulfill this task, we use the wavelet approach to analyze the dependency between commodities and BTC in the stock market portfolio. In addition, we examine the optimal portfolio using CVaR. which can show the investor's level of risk aversion through the confidence level associated with each measure.

In fact, this study examines two main hypotheses:

H1. *Commodities and Bitcoin (BTC) significantly influence stock market performance in OPEC and non-OPEC countries, with the magnitude and nature of these effects varying based on the economic structure and dependency on oil exports.*

H2. *Commodities and Bitcoin (BTC) exhibit distinct roles as diversifiers, hedges, or safe havens in OPEC and non-OPEC stock portfolios, with their effectiveness varying under normal conditions and during periods of market turmoil.*

3. Methodology

3.1. Wavelet

The main goal of studying the correlation between commodity and stock markets, as well as between Bitcoin (BTC) and stock markets, is to determine whether commodities or BTC influence stock markets, or vice versa. To address this, we employed the wavelet correlation method, which examines how closely two time series move together, accounting for both time and frequency variations. A coherence value near one indicates strong common behavior between the series, while a value close to zero suggests they do not behave similarly. We also used wavelet phase differences to differentiate between positive and negative correlations.

A key advantage of the wavelet approach is its ability to perform localized analysis of time series, particularly by capturing the movements of index returns and oil prices across two frequency bands. Additionally, this method is well-suited for analyzing non-stationary variables. The wavelet approach provides deeper insight into the spillover effects between global stock, commodity markets, and BTC, highlighting potential spillovers and contagion. As a result, it is a valuable tool for portfolio diversification and risk management.

Wavelet functions are composed of scale parameters, location, and a mother wavelet function ($\psi \in L^2(R)$) defined as

$$\psi_{t,s}(t) = \frac{1}{\sqrt{|s|}} \psi\left(\frac{t-r}{s}\right), s, t \in R, s \neq 0$$

where:

- $\frac{1}{\sqrt{|s|}}$ represents a normalization factor guaranteeing unit variance of the wavelet and $||\psi_{t,s}||^2 = 1$;

- S is a scaling factor that controls the width of the wavelet; scale has an inverse relation to frequency. A higher scale indicates a stretched wavelet that is suitable for detection of a lower frequency;
- τ is a conversion parameter that controls the location of the wavelet.

There are various types of wavelets, but, in this study, we focus on wavelet coherency (WTC), as defined by Torrence and Compo (1998) and Aguiar-Conraria et al. (2008). WTC is the ratio of the cross-spectrum to the product of each series' spectrum and can be interpreted as the local correlation between two time series in the time–frequency domain. According to Torrence and Compo (1998), WTC is defined as follows:

$$R_{xy}^2 = \frac{|SW_{xy}|^2}{S\left(|W_x|^2\right)S\left(|W_y|^2\right)}$$

where S is a sleeking operator in both scale and time. Noticeably, R_{xy}^2 close to one indicates evidence of strong correlation, whereas R_{xy}^2 close to zero provides a weak correlation.

We assess the statistical significance of WTC levels using Monte Carlo methods, as the theoretical distribution for WTC has not been established (Grinsted et al. 2004). Due to the squared nature of WTC, we cannot distinguish between positive and negative correlations. To do so, we use the phase difference tool, which helps identify whether correlations are positive or negative and detect lag–lead relationships between two time series as a function of frequency.

In our study, we interpret the phase difference based on the direction of arrows in the WTC plots. Arrows pointing to the left (or right) indicate that the two time series are out of phase (in phase). Arrows pointing downward or upward represent a causality relationship between the series. Specifically, if arrows point straight down (up), it signifies that the first variable, $y(t)$, is lagging (leading).

3.2. Conditional Value at Risk (CVaR)

Conditional Value at Risk (CVaR), introduced by Uryasev and Rockafellar (1999), is a measure of expected loss that is considered more coherent than Value at Risk (VaR). CVaR estimates the expected loss, given that the loss exceeds the VaR threshold. Unlike VaR, which is not convex, CVaR is convex. This convexity makes it easier to minimize the CVaR function with respect to portfolio weights compared to minimizing a VaR function (Uryasev and Rockafellar 1999). For a given confidence level, CVaR is defined as follows (Uryasev and Rockafellar 1999):

$$CVaR_{\propto} = \frac{1}{1-\propto}\int_{-\infty}^{VaR_{\propto}} xf(x)dx$$

where $f(x)$ represents the marginal probability function of portfolio returns x over the given time period.

4. Results

In Table 1, we examine the relationship between commodities, stocks, and Bitcoin (BTC) from 18 August 2011 to 3 December 2020. Daily prices of Brent and Gasoline are used to represent the energy market, while wheat and sugar are included to represent agricultural products. Gold, platinum, and palladium are chosen to represent precious metals, and aluminum is used for industrial metals. For stock markets, we focus on the S&P3 Saudi Arabia, S&P Kuwait BMI, S&P United Arab Emirates BMI, S&P Russia BMI, NIKKEI225, S&P Mexico BMI, and the S&P index.

In our study, we analyze log-returns, which are calculated as $r_t = ln\ (P_t/P_{t-1})$ from the original price series. Regarding the descriptive statistics, the mean returns of the variables are close to zero, with excess kurtosis and negative skewness, except for Aluminum, Sugar, and Wheat. The series exhibit fat tails, and the Jarque–Bera test rejects the hypothesis of normality. Additionally, the Ljung–Box statistic indicates the presence of serial correlation in all series, except for S&P Russia BMI, Gold, and Sugar.

Table 1. Descriptive Statistics.

	Mean	Maximum	Minimum	Std. Dev.	Skewness	Kurtosis	Jarque-Bera	LM	ARCH
SP500	0.048	8.968	−12.765	1.072	−0.897	22.800	39,955.14 ***	268.54 ***	989.17 ***
MEXICO	0.012	4.733	−6.610	0.929	−0.505	7.960	2589.64 ***	46.109 ***	554.29 ***
RUSSIA	0.022	7.676	−11.152	1.224	−0.901	12.632	9707.21 ***	12.066	213.5 ***
U_A_E_	0.019	10.246	−15.799	1.266	−1.259	25.204	50,477.4 ***	50.366 ***	570.74 ***
SAUDIARABIA	0.013	8.511	−16.897	1.145	−2.281	35.913	11,1607 ***	63.576 ***	161.17 ***
KUWAIT	0.003	6.932	−21.744	0.908	−6.301	149.783	21,9393 ***	116.2 ***	211.71 ***
ALUMINIUM	−0.005	6.395	−7.827	1.163	0.216	5.546	673.823 ***	40.501 ***	225.31 ***
PALLADIUM	0.046	16.961	−15.677	1.869	−0.572	13.702	11,709.6 ***	31.998 ***	420.28 ***
PLATINUM	−0.023	9.341	−14.418	1.362	−0.460	11.194	6873.30 ***	54.422 ***	319.06 ***
SUGAR	−0.029	8.721	−8.418	1.553	0.210	5.1977	505.978 ***	5.9069	77.185 ***
WHEAT	−0.005	23.915	−24.667	2.114	0.227	23.210	41,308.2 ***	45.973 ***	480.76 ***
BRENT	−0.033	57.325	−95.263	3.575	−6.161	247.660	6,066,073 ***	165.83 ***	353.28 ***
GASOLINE	−0.031	27.196	−51.244	2.840	−2.995	65.149	394,065 ***	353.28 ***	348.85 ***
GOLD	0.001	5.432	−10.162	0.982	−0.794	11.562	7665.91 ***	5.4209	72.617 ***
BT	0.307	48.478	−66.395	5.751	−1.127	24.068	45,382.2 ***	41.28 ***	281.06 ***

*** significant at 1%.

4.1. Wavelet Approach

The Supplementary Materials present the wavelet coherence between commodities, BTC, and the return markets of both OPEC and NON-OPEC. The black contour lines indicate the 95% confidence intervals. The horizontal axis represents the study period in days, while the vertical axis shows the frequency. The color scale ranges from blue to yellow, with blue indicating low coherence and yellow indicating high coherence. The lighter black line marks the boundary of regions with high power and the "cone of influence", where edge effects become significant. The direction of the arrows provides information about the phase lag–lead relationship between commodities, BTC, and the return stock markets.

Arrows pointing to the right signify that the variables are in phase, while those pointing to the left indicate that the variables are out of phase. Additionally, arrows pointing left–up or right–down suggest that commodities or BTC lead the stock markets, whereas arrows pointing left–down or right–up suggest that commodities or BTC lag behind the stock markets. Areas where variables are in phase suggest a cyclical interaction between markets, while out-of-phase areas indicate an anti-cyclical effect. Regions with stronger interdependence in the time-frequency domain suggest that commodities or BTC have a lower potential as safe havens or hedges for stock markets, and, thus, offer reduced benefits when included in stock portfolios.

For stock markets, The Supplementary Materials indicates that the Brent–stock market pairs exhibit a strong in-phase co-movement at long-term frequency scales (256–1024 days) during the COVID-19 period, as evidenced by the concentration of yellow regions and arrows pointing to the right. The high correlation between OPEC and NON-OPEC economies with Brent suggests that higher Brent prices are associated with increased stock market revenues, as higher Brent prices tend to lead to higher stock market prices. Conversely, at shorter time frames (0 to 32 days), the co-movement between Brent and the stock market is generally low, with WTC values below 0.3. At medium-term horizons (32 to 128 days), the contour plots reveal some evidence of significant co-movement, particularly around the stock market crashes during the European sovereign debt crisis in 2012 and COVID-19 in 2020.

The direction of the arrows in regions of high co-movement indicates that energy commodities demonstrate a time-varying lag–lead relationship with the stock market in the time–frequency domain. At frequencies beyond 256 days and at lower frequencies, we observe alternating periods of right–down arrows, which indicate that energy commodities lag behind the stock market, and right–up arrows, which show that crude oil leads the stock market. However, the leading position of energy commodities is more common than their lagging position.

The Supplementary Materials highlights a significant out-of-phase co-movement at the long-term frequency band (256–512 days). The yellow region at the bottom indicates a strong co-movement between energy commodity prices and stock markets at high frequencies. The arrows pointing to the right suggest that the co-movements of energy commodities and stock markets for both OPEC and NON-OPEC countries were in phase, indicating a positive relationship between energy commodity prices and stock markets. The figure shows that this interdependence is stronger over long-term scales compared to short-term scales. For OPEC and NON-OPEC countries, the connection between stock markets and oil prices is weak in the short term (less than 128 days) but becomes more pronounced in the long-term and medium-term frequencies. The results are similar for agricultural, industrial, and other metal commodities, except for gold, which exhibits a hedging role. This finding aligns with the results of Bouri et al. (2020).

The variation in interdependence between OPEC and NON-OPEC countries suggests that deviations in different types of commodities significantly influence stock markets in these regions. Based on these results, we conclude that, from a time-domain perspective, there was a strong yet heterogeneous relationship during the COVID-19 period across all countries.

Our findings on the co-movements between oil price returns and stock returns align with those of Mensi et al. (2021), who observed that such co-movements predominantly occur over the long term. Similarly, we corroborate the observations of Younis et al. (2025) regarding stronger co-movements in GCC countries, particularly Kuwait, Saudi Arabia, and the UAE. Our study, however, advances this understanding by identifying specific lead–lag dynamics and heterogeneities between OPEC and non-OPEC markets, which have been less emphasized in prior research. In contrast, our results diverge from those of Buyuksahin et al. (2008) and Büyükşahin and Robe (2014), likely due to variations in macroeconomic factors, financial market conditions, and increased commodity speculation during our study period. Additionally, our findings are consistent with Xu and Kinkyo (2023), who demonstrated Bitcoin's effectiveness as a short-term risk hedge compared to gold in G7 stock markets during the COVID-19 pandemic. By extending these insights to OPEC and non-OPEC markets, we highlight Bitcoin's superior diversification benefits, adding a novel perspective to the existing literature.

4.2. Results of Conditional Value at Risk (CVaR)

Modern portfolio theory suggests that investors seek to diversify their portfolios to minimize the market risk. Previous studies have indicated that commodities and BTC can offer substantial diversification benefits due to their low correlations with stocks. In essence, modern portfolio theory is an investment framework focused on constructing and selecting portfolios based on the principles of hedging and diversification. This involves carefully choosing a mix of investment assets that collectively exhibit lower risk compared to investing in a single asset class.

The descriptive statistics reveal that the data exhibit fat tails and excess kurtosis. To determine the optimal portfolios that balance maximizing returns with minimizing risk, we will use Conditional Value at Risk (CVaR) as a downside risk measure. CVaR can capture the impact of heavy tails and allows us to reflect the investor's risk aversion through the confidence level associated with each measure. The optimal portfolio is identified by minimizing risk while targeting a specific expected return.

We will divide our study period to assess whether the role of commodities or BTC changes across different time frames. Specifically, we will examine the optimal portfolios before and after COVID-19. The CVaR results will be compared across these periods to evaluate how risk levels have shifted.

4.2.1. Results Before COVID-19

Specifically, an investor aiming to minimize risk for OPEC countries should focus on a portfolio that includes BT, Palladium, and stock markets of the UAE, Kuwait, and

Saudi Arabia. This strategy will be advantageous if BT or Palladium increases, as there is a positive correlation between these assets and the stock market indices.

For non-OPEC countries, the optimal risk-minimizing portfolio should include BT, Gold, and stock markets of the USA and Mexico. This portfolio allows the investor to benefit from increases in BT due to its positive correlation with stock market indices, while also gaining from decreases in Gold, as it has a negative correlation with the stock markets.

4.2.2. Results During COVID-19

For OPEC countries, there is a positive correlation between BT and the stock market, meaning that an increase in BT will enhance portfolio performance. Similarly, there is a positive correlation between Palladium and the stock market, as well as between Platinum and the stock market.

For non-OPEC countries, the correlation between Gold and the stock markets is negative. Therefore, investors can benefit from a decline in Gold. Overall, the results indicate that, during the COVID period, including BT and Gold in the portfolio helps minimize risk.

The findings can be summarized as follows: First, for both OPEC and non-OPEC countries, the relationship between stock markets and oil prices is relatively weak in the short term (less than 128 days) but strengthens over medium- and long-term time horizons. A similar pattern is observed for agricultural, industrial, and other metal commodities, with the exception of gold, which serves as an effective hedge. Second, a CVaR analysis reveals that Bitcoin (BTC) offers greater diversification benefits than commodities, with gold ranking second. Our results indicate that incorporating BTC into investment portfolios can help reduce risk, even for OPEC countries.

5. Conclusions

We have examined the benefits of including commodities and Bitcoin (BTC) in stock portfolios for both OPEC and NON-OPEC countries, using daily data from 2011 to 2020. Our primary contribution is assessing BTC's role as a safe haven, hedge, or diversifier against stock markets in these countries—a topic not previously explored, especially in regions where BTC trading is not formally regulated. Additionally, we identify the optimal portfolio configurations before and during the COVID-19 crisis using Conditional Value at Risk (CVaR).

Our methodology involves two main steps. First, we use the wavelet approach to explore the relationships between BTC and stock markets, as well as between commodities and stock markets in both OPEC and non-OPEC countries. Second, we evaluate the optimal portfolio using CVaR.

Our findings reveal a reduction in the diversification benefits of commodities and BTC for stock portfolios in both OPEC and non-OPEC countries over the long term, as the co-movement between commodities, BTC, and stock markets increases from low to high frequencies. During COVID-19, the high synchronization among these assets undermines BTC's potential as a safe haven. Moreover, the varying co-movement across frequencies suggests that a constant hedging coefficient and fixed asset allocation between BTC and stocks are unsuitable for portfolio management. The wavelet analysis provides valuable insights into the frequency-domain relationships among commodities, BTC, and stock markets.

We also find that, for non-OPEC countries, gold serves as a hedge for stock markets. This means that holding gold can compensate for losses during both stable and turbulent periods due to its positive relationship with BTC, despite its negative correlation with stock markets.

Given the strong correlations between BTC (and gold) and stock markets in both OPEC and non-OPEC countries, constructing a multi-asset portfolio to mitigate risk through diversification is essential. Traditional risk measures, such as equilibrium analysis and standard deviations, are insufficient for capturing diverse and transient risk behaviors.

Therefore, we use CVaR to address the limitations of conventional models. Our CVaR analysis demonstrates that BTC provides superior diversification benefits compared to commodities, followed by gold. These findings align with Bouri et al. (2020), which suggest that BTC acts as a unique risk minimizer in portfolios. BTC's price has surged notably, remaining virtually uncorrelated with stock markets, indicating its potential as a new form of "virtual gold." While stock market inflation is partially due to quantitative easing, this does not apply to Bitcoin, as most new money has not been invested in it due to various regulatory and institutional issues. Our analysis shows that including BTC in portfolios can reduce risk even for OPEC countries.

These results offer valuable insights for investors and traders, providing empirical evidence that Bitcoin shares some of the benefits of commodities in protecting against extreme downturns in global stock markets for both OPEC and non-OPEC countries.

Supplementary Materials: The following supporting information can be downloaded at: https://www.mdpi.com/article/10.3390/economies12120351/s1.

Author Contributions: Conceptualization, A.B.B., H.B.A. and F.M.A.; methodology, A.B.B.; software, A.B.B.; validation, H.B.A. and F.M.A.; formal analysis, A.B.B.; investigation, A.B.B.; resources, H.B.A. and F.M.A.; data curation; writing—original draft preparation, A.B.B., H.B.A. and F.M.A.; writing—review and editing, A.B.B., H.B.A. and F.M.A.; visualization, A.B.B., H.B.A. and F.M.A.; supervision, A.B.B. and H.B.A.; project administration, A.B.B., H.B.A. and F.M.A.; funding acquisition, A.B.B., H.B.A. and F.M.A. All authors have read and agreed to the published version of the manuscript.

Funding: This research received no external funding.

Data Availability Statement: The data presented in this study are available on request from the corresponding author.

Conflicts of Interest: The authors declare no conflicts of interest.

References

Agosto, A., and A. Cafferata. 2020. Financial bubbles: A study of co-explosivity in the cryptocurrency market. *Risks* 8: 34. [CrossRef]

Aguiar-Conraria, L., N. Azevedo, and M. J. Soares. 2008. Using wavelets to decompose the time–frequency effects of monetary policy. *Physica A: Statistical Mechanics and Its Applications* 387: 2863–78. [CrossRef]

Albulescu, C. T., A. K. Tiwari, and Q. Ji. 2020. Copula-based local dependence among energy, agriculture and metal commodities markets. *Energy* 202: 117762. [CrossRef]

Al-Yahyaee, K. H., W. Mensi, D. Maitra, and I. M. W. Al-Jarrah. 2019. Portfolio management and dependencies among precious metal markets: Evidence from a Copula quantile-on-quantile approach. *Resources Policy* 64: 101529. [CrossRef]

Ashraf, B. N. 2020. Stock markets' reaction to COVID-19: Cases or fatalities? *Research in International Business and Finance* 54: 101249. [CrossRef]

Banerjee, R., S. Majumdar, and Z. Mohammed. 2023. Oil price changes and stock market performance in UAE: Evidence of cointegration persists in economic diversification era. *International Journal of Energy Economics and Policy* 13: 552–61. [CrossRef]

Baur, D. G., and B. M. Lucey. 2010. Is gold a hedge or a safe haven? An analysis of stocks, bonds and gold. *Financial Review* 45: 217–29. [CrossRef]

Bouri, E., S. J. H. Shahzad, D. Roubaud, L. Kristoufek, and B. Lucey. 2020. Bitcoin, gold, and commodities as safe havens for stocks: New insight through wavelet analysis. *The Quarterly Review of Economics and Finance* 77: 156–64. [CrossRef]

Büyükşahin, B., and M. A. Robe. 2014. Speculators, commodities and cross-market linkages. *Journal of International Money and Finance* 42: 38–70. [CrossRef]

Buyuksahin, B., M. S. Haigh, and M. A. Robe. 2008. Commodities and Equities: 'A Market of One'? *SSRN Electronic Journal*, 1069862. [CrossRef]

Conlon, T., and R. McGee. 2020. Safe haven or risky hazard? Bitcoin during the COVID-19 bear market. *Finance Research Letters* 35: 101607. [CrossRef] [PubMed]

Corbet, S., C. Larkin, and B. Lucey. 2020. The contagion effects of the COVID-19 pandemic: Evidence from gold and cryptocurrencies. *Finance Research Letters* 35: 101554. [CrossRef] [PubMed]

Dutta, A., D. Das, R. K. Jana, and X. V. Vo. 2020. COVID-19 and oil market crash: Revisiting the safe haven property of gold and Bitcoin. *Resources Policy* 69: 101816. [CrossRef] [PubMed]

Dyhrberg, A. H. 2016. Bitcoin, gold and the dollar—A GARCH volatility analysis. *Finance Research Letters* 16: 85–92. [CrossRef]

Goodell, J. W. 2020. COVID-19 and finance: Agendas for future research. *Finance Research Letters* 35: 101512. [CrossRef]

Grinsted, A., J. C. Moore, and S. Jevrejeva. 2004. Application of the cross wavelet transform and wavelet coherence to geophysical time series. *Nonlinear Processes in Geophysics* 11: 561–66. [CrossRef]
Harvey, C. 2020. The Economic and Financial Implications of the COVID-19 Pandemic. Available online: https://www.darden.virginia.edu/sites/default/files/inline-files/COVID-19%20Presentation_Cambell%20Harvey.pdf (accessed on 6 October 2024).
Huber, T. A., and D. Sornette. 2022. Boom, bust, and bitcoin: Bitcoin-bubbles as innovation accelerators. *Journal of Economic Issues* 56: 113–36. [CrossRef]
Junttila, J., J. Pesonen, and J. Raatikainen. 2018. Commodity market based hedging against stock market risk in times of financial crisis: The case of crude oil and gold. *Journal of International Financial Markets, Institutions and Money* 56: 255–80. [CrossRef]
Khan, M. H., J. Ahmed, M. Mughal, and I. H. Khan. 2023. Oil price volatility and stock returns: Evidence from three oil-price wars. *International Journal of Finance and Economics* 28: 3162–82. [CrossRef]
McKee, M., and D. Stuckler. 2020. If the world fails to protect the economy, COVID-19 will damage health not just now but also in the future. *Nature Medicine* 26: 640–42. [CrossRef] [PubMed]
Mensi, W., M. U. Rehman, and X. V. Vo. 2020. Spillovers and co-movements between precious metals and energy markets: Implications on portfolio management. *Resources Policy* 69: 101836. [CrossRef]
Mensi, W., M. U. Rehman, D. Maitra, K. H. Al-Yahyaee, and X. V. Vo. 2021. Oil, natural gas and BRICS stock markets: Evidence of systemic risks and co-movements in the time-frequency domain. *Resources Policy* 72: 102062. [CrossRef]
Mnif, E., A. Jarboui, and K. Mouakhar. 2020. How the cryptocurrency market has performed during COVID 19? A multifractal analysis. *Finance Research Letters* 36: 101647. [CrossRef] [PubMed]
Mzoughi, H., C. Urom, G. S. Uddin, and K. Guesmi. 2020. The Effects of COVID-19 Pandemic on Oil Prices, CO_2 Emissions and the Stock Market: Evidence from a VAR Model. *SSRN Electronic Journal*, 3587906. [CrossRef]
Náñez Alonso, S. L., J. Jorge-Vázquez, M. Á. Echarte Fernández, and D. Sanz-Bas. 2024. Bitcoin's bubbly behaviors: Does it resemble other financial bubbles of the past? *Humanities and Social Sciences Communications* 11: 715. [CrossRef]
Nicola, M., Z. Alsafi, C. Sohrabi, A. Kerwan, A. Al-Jabir, C. Iosifidis, M. Agha, and R. Agha. 2020. The socio-economic implications of the coronavirus pandemic (COVID-19): A review. *International Journal of Surgery* 78: 185–93. [CrossRef]
Pho, K. H., S. Ly, R. Lu, T. H. Van Hoang, and W.-K. Wong. 2021. Is Bitcoin a better portfolio diversifier than gold? A copula and sectoral analysis for China. *International Review of Financial Analysis* 74: 101674. [CrossRef]
Salisu, A. A., L. Akanni, and I. Raheem. 2020. The COVID-19 global fear index and the predictability of commodity price returns. *Journal of Behavioral and Experimental Finance* 27: 100383. [CrossRef] [PubMed]
Shahzad, S. J. H., E. Bouri, D. Roubaud, and L. Kristoufek. 2020. Safe haven, hedge and diversification for G7 stock markets: Gold versus bitcoin. *Economic Modelling* 87: 212–24. [CrossRef]
Syuhada, K., D. Suprijanto, and A. Hakim. 2021. Comparing gold's and Bitcoin's safe-haven roles against energy commodities during the COVID-19 outbreak: A vine copula approach. *Finance Research Letters* 46: 102471. [CrossRef]
Torrence, C., and G. P. Compo. 1998. A practical guide to wavelet analysis. *Bulletin of the American Meteorological Society* 79: 61–78. [CrossRef]
Uryasev, S., and R. T. Rockafellar. 1999. *Optimization of Conditional Value-at-Risk*. Gainesville: Department of Industrial and Systems Engineering, University of Florida.
Wu, B.-B. 2021. The dynamics of oil on China's commodity sectors: What can we learn from a quantile perspective? *Journal of Commodity Markets* 23: 100158. [CrossRef]
Xu, L., and T. Kinkyo. 2023. Hedging effectiveness of bitcoin and gold: Evidence from G7 stock markets. *Journal of International Financial Markets, Institutions and Money* 85: 101764. [CrossRef]
Yarovaya, L., R. Matkovskyy, and A. Jalan. 2021. The effects of a "black swan" event (COVID-19) on herding behavior in cryptocurrency markets. *Journal of International Financial Markets, Institutions and Money* 75: 101321. [CrossRef]
Younis, I., M. A. Naeem, W. U. Shah, and X. Tang. 2025. Inter-and intra-connectedness between energy, gold, Bitcoin, and Gulf cooperation council stock markets: New evidence from various financial crises. *Research in International Business and Finance* 73: 102548. [CrossRef]
Zhang, D., M. Hu, and Q. Ji. 2020. Financial markets under the global pandemic of COVID-19. *Finance Research Letters* 36: 101528. [CrossRef] [PubMed]
Ziadat, S. A., and A. Maghyereh. 2024. Energy profile and oil shocks: A dynamic analysis of their impact on stock markets. *Eurasian Economic Review* 14: 757–80. [CrossRef]

MDPI AG
Grosspeteranlage 5
4052 Basel
Switzerland
Tel.: +41 61 683 77 34

MDPI Books Editorial Office
E-mail: books@mdpi.com
www.mdpi.com/books

www.ingramcontent.com/pod-product-compliance
Lightning Source LLC
Chambersburg PA
CBHW061623210926
51850CB00009B/2414
9783725874187